Choreographing Copyright

Choreographing Copyright

*Race, Gender, and Intellectual Property Rights in
American Dance*

ANTHEA KRAUT

OXFORD
UNIVERSITY PRESS

Oxford University Press is a department of the University of
Oxford. It furthers the University's objective of excellence in research,
scholarship, and education by publishing worldwide.

Oxford   New York
Auckland   Cape Town   Dar es Salaam   Hong Kong   Karachi
Kuala Lumpur   Madrid   Melbourne   Mexico City   Nairobi
New Delhi   Shanghai   Taipei   Toronto

With offices in
Argentina   Austria   Brazil   Chile   Czech Republic   France   Greece
Guatemala   Hungary   Italy   Japan   Poland   Portugal   Singapore
South Korea   Switzerland   Thailand   Turkey   Ukraine   Vietnam

Oxford is a registered trademark of Oxford University Press
in the UK and certain other countries.

Published in the United States of America by
Oxford University Press
198 Madison Avenue, New York, NY 10016

Library of Congress Cataloging-in-Publication Data
Kraut, Anthea, author.
Choreographing copyright : race, gender, and intellectual property rights in
American dance / Anthea Kraut.
pages cm
Includes bibliographical references and index.
ISBN 978–0–19–936036–9 (hardback : acid-free paper) —
ISBN 978–0–19–936037–6 (pbk. : acid-free paper)
1. Copyright—Choreography—United States.   2. Dance—Law and legislation—United States.
3. Dance—Social aspects—United States.   I. Title.
KF3054.C56K73 2015
346.7304'82—dc23
2015010794

Printed in Canada
3 5 7 9 8 6 4 2

For Avie and Luna

CONTENTS

PREFACE

It started with a bit of typed text on a sheet of paper at the Institute of Jazz Studies at Rutgers University. I was doing a little digging for an earlier project in the papers of Marshall Stearns, author of the indispensable *Jazz Dance: The Story of American Vernacular Dance*. Curious what Stearns had to say about the Black Bottom, a popular African American vernacular dance from the 1920s, which appeared in a theatrical concert I was researching, I checked out his notes on the dance, and there it was: "Alberta Hunter, the first woman to present the dance, had it copyrighted."[1] Sourced to Abel Green and Joe Laurie Jr.'s 1951 edition of *Show Biz*, the claim never made it into the published version of *Jazz Dance*, but it continued to gnaw at me as I completed my first book. Although, as I discuss in Chapter 3, the claim proved impossible to corroborate, more likely rumor than verifiable fact, there was something defiant about it that was equally impossible to ignore. A copyright by an African American blues woman on the kind of dance that is generally considered "authorless"? The Black Bottom was one in a long string of social dances, like the Charleston, the Lindy hop, and the twist, that originated in African American communities, were disseminated on vaudeville, nightclub, and musical theater stages, as well as on screen, and became national "crazes" when Euro-Americans began performing them. The claim that Hunter "had it copyrighted" thus struck me as a powerful refusal of the entrenched racialized logic that generally assigns authorship and ownership of discrete acts of creative expression to individual white artists while "invisibilizing" the creative labor of individual and

[1] The Marshall Winslow Stearns Collection, Institute of Jazz Studies, Rutgers University Libraries.

collective artists of color.[2] Was Hunter's alleged copyright an effort to thwart just this kind of invisibilization? At a time when copyright appears increasingly like a tool for the already rich and powerful to become even more so, the suggestion that a black woman in the 1920s asserted intellectual property rights to a popular dance sparked my desire to look more closely at the history and uses of choreographic copyright in American culture.

That the tidbit about Hunter's copyright on the Black Bottom resonated so strongly with me owed much to my work on Zora Neale Hurston's staging of black folk dance in the 1930s and the raced and gendered politics that engulfed her theatrical venture.[3] Recovering Hurston's contributions to American dance and trying to identify the causes of her erasure from the official dance record exposed the ways in which the mis-recognition of black choreographic labor enabled white modern dancers to construct themselves as innovative artists—in effect, as choreographers—working with black "raw material." At the same time, discovering how plagued Hurston's concerts were by contests for control over the folk material they contained and how intensely Hurston was supervised by a white female patron and black male adviser gave explanatory force to Hurston's own investment in authorship.

Choreographing Copyright extends my first book's critical examination of authorship—its hazards and its values—by interrogating the raced and gendered politics of ownership in dance in the United States from the late nineteenth century to the early twenty-first.[4] Because copyright is not only a discursive concept but also a material, legal structure with specific, if historically contingent, requirements and ramifications, a study of choreographic copyright both magnifies and makes more complex the power dynamics inherent to choreographic authorship. Taking a longer view of these dynamics

---

[2] On the "invisibilization" of African diasporic influences on American culture, see Brenda Dixon Gottschild, *Digging the Africanist Presence in American Performance: Dance and Other Contexts* (Westport, CT: Greenwood Press, 1996).

[3] See Anthea Kraut, *Choreographing the Folk: The Dance Stagings of Zora Neale Hurston* (Minneapolis: University of Minnesota Press, 2008).

[4] Authorship and ownership, of course, are closely intertwined and interdependent terms. Scholars of copyright have written that the "distinguishing characteristic of the modern author … is proprietorship" and that copyright law is designed to "encourage the enterprise of authorship." Mark Rose, *Authors and Owners: The Invention of Copyright* (Cambridge, MA: Harvard University Press, 1993), 1; Jessica Litman, "The Public Domain," *Emory Law Journal* 39.4 (Fall 1990): 970. Yet the two terms are not interchangeable: property rights are by definition alienable (more about this later), meaning that the copyright holder of a work may or may not be its author. Within dance studies, an examination of copyright complements recent work that historicizes and problematizes the terms "choreography" and "choreographer." See especially Susan Leigh Foster's chapter, "Choreography," in *Choreographing Empathy: Kinesthesia in Performance* (London: Routledge, 2011), 15–72.

makes it possible to connect them to the propertization of bodies in chattel slavery and to track how they have and have not changed from the advent of early modern dance, through the heyday and ostensible decline of tap dance, through the institutionalization of modern dance and the "Golden Age" of Broadway, through the death of some of the giants of twentieth-century concert dance, and into the digital age.

As became evident when I turned my fuller attention to copyright for choreography, the contention that Hunter copyrighted the Black Bottom defied legal as well as racial logic. In the United States, federal copyright law excluded choreography until the 1976 Copyright Act added "choreographic works" to the list of protectable categories, and even then, social dances were considered outside the scope of copyrightable subject matter.[5] The story that is most often told about this late (relative to other countries')[6] legal recognition of choreography is one of the courts', Congress's, and the US Copyright Office's stubbornly slow recognition of the legitimacy of concert dance and of dance's slow overcoming of the problem of conforming to Copyright Law's requirement

---

[5] Although statutory (that is, official, written) legal protection was not extended to choreographic works until 1978, when the 1976 Copyright Act took effect, there is another area of copyright law—common law—which could in theory protect choreography that has not been "published" or "fixed," both prior to and since 1978. To my knowledge, there have been only two cases alleging common law copyright in choreography that have gone to trial, and in both cases, the copyright claims were rejected. But in a 1974 article, Jeffrey Roth maintains that there is no reason that common law copyright could not successfully be applied to choreography. See Jeffrey I. Roth, "Common Law Protection of Choreographic Works," *Performing Arts Review* 5.1–2 (1974): 75–89. Unlike statutory copyright law, common law copyright exists the moment a work is "created." I discuss the two cases involving common law copyright for choreography—*Savage v. Hoffman* (1908) and *Dane v. M & H Company* (1963)—in Chapter 4.

[6] The Berne Convention for the Protection of Literary and Artistic Works, an international agreement forged initially between primarily European countries, specified protection for choreographic works as far back as 1908. The United States did not become a signatory to the Berne Convention until 1988. A 1959 report to Congress recommending revision to US Copyright Law reviewed the protection for choreographic works afforded by international conventions and foreign laws. See Borge Varmer, "Copyright in Choreographic Works," Study No. 28, *Studies Prepared for the Subcommittee on Patents, Trademarks, and Copyrights of the Committee on the Judiciary*, United States Senate, 86th Cong., 2d Sess. (Washington, DC: US Government Printing Office, 1961): 98–99. For a general history of international copyright law in the nineteenth century, see Catherine Seville, *The Internationalisation of Copyright Law: Books, Buccaneers and the Black Flag in the Nineteenth Century* (Cambridge: Cambridge University Press, 2006). While copyright laws are specific to nation-states, choreography has never been contained by geographic boundaries. See Laurent Carrière's "Choreography and Copyright: Some Comments on Choreographic Works as Newly Defined in the Canadian *Copyright Act*" (1995–2003) for a summary of Canadian copyright law as it pertains to choreography and for a useful survey of pertinent case law in the United States and a number of European countries. Available at www. robic.ca/admin/pdf/279/105-LC.pdf. Accessed February 4, 2015.

that works be "fixed" in a tangible medium of expression. Nearly all tellings of choreographic copyright's evolution trace a progress narrative that moves from failure to triumph and that centers on several key players and events: Loïe Fuller, one of the white "foremothers" of modern dance, whose 1892 copyright infringement suit against the chorus girl Minnie Bemis was denied on the grounds that Fuller's dancing told no story and therefore did not qualify as a "dramatic composition"; the German emigré Hanya Holm, whose successful 1952 copyright registration of her choreography for the Broadway musical *Kiss Me, Kate* (1948), documented in Labanotation, signaled the Copyright Office's growing appreciation of modern dance and growing acknowledgment that dance could indeed be "fixed" in a tangible form; and the white ballet artist Agnes de Mille, who lobbied hard for copyright reform in the 1950s and '60s after she received only a trivial share of royalties from the smash hit *Oklahoma!* (1943), whose dances she choreographed. In this narrative, the 1976 Copyright Act represents an outright accomplishment for American ballet and modern dance, an overdue victory following decades of disrespect.[7]

This book sets out to tell a different story. To begin with, I expand the cast of characters involved in the formation of intellectual property rights for choreography to include dancers of color and dancers devoted to genres other than modern and ballet. Fuller, Holm, and de Mille do figure prominently in *Choreographing Copyright*, as do arguably the two most celebrated white choreographers of the twentieth century: George Balanchine and Martha Graham, whose copyright lawsuits are the only major cases to have gone to trial since the passage of the 1976 Copyright Act. But I also demonstrate that dancers' interest in ownership rights pre-1976 was not limited to white choreographers who worked on the high art stage. In addition to Hunter's rumored copyright, the case studies in *Choreographing Copyright* cover the South Asian dancer Mohammed Ismail, who sued the white modern dancer Ruth St. Denis in 1909 for failing to compensate him as the source of one of her choreographic works; the African American performer Johnny Hudgins, who secured a copyright for

---

[7] For a sample of accounts that trace this progress narrative, see Barbara L. Meyer, "The Copyright Question: Some Words to the Wise," *Dance Magazine*, April 1961, 44–45, 60–61; Joan E. Fitzgerald, "Copyright and Choreography," *CORD News*, vol. 2 (July 1973): 25–42; Heather Doughty, "The Choreographer in the Courtroom: Loie Fuller and Léonide Massine," *SDHS Proceedings*, Fifth Annual Conference, Harvard University, February 13–15, 1982, 35–39; Nicholas Arcomano, "Choreography and Copyright, part one" *Dance Magazine*, April 1980, 58–59; Adaline J. Hilgard, "Can Choreography and Copyright Waltz Together in the Wake of *Horgan v. Macmillan, Inc.*?" *U.C. Davis Law Review* 27 (Spring 1994): 757–89; Barbara A. Singer, "In Search of Adequate Protection for Choreographic Works: Legislative and Judicial Alternatives vs. the Custom of the Dance Community," *University of Miami Law Review* 38 (1984): 287–319.

his blackface pantomime routines in London in the 1920s; African American tap dancers at the Hoofers Club, who developed informal methods of protecting their steps in the 1920s and '30s; and Faith Dane, a white-appearing burlesque dancer who claimed common law copyright protection in a number she originated for *Gypsy* (1959) and tried to collect royalties from the musical's producers.

Choreographing Copyright also attempts to do more than recover the efforts of unheralded dancers to claim possession of their choreographic output. With the benefit of insights from critical race and gender theory and from other cultural studies of copyright, the failures as well as the victories in the development of intellectual property rights for choreography, the major cases as well as the minor incidents, take on a different hue. Accordingly, this book offers what might be considered a counter-history of choreographic copyright in the United States. In place of a progress narrative, my counter-history advances two interrelated arguments. First, although race and gender rarely surfaced as explicit factors in dancers' pursuit of copyright protection or in the law's uneven bestowal of that protection, choreographic copyright has served to consolidate and to contest racial and gendered power. Whether dancers' copyright claims shored up or unsettled existing power structures—or, equally likely, did both simultaneously—depended on the dancers' positions in a raced, gendered, and classed hierarchy, and on the historical conditions in which they made, and made claims on, their dances. So, for example, I maintain that Fuller's, Holm's, de Mille's, and Dane's campaigns for copyright protection were as much attempts to harness the privileges of whiteness as efforts to challenge the patriarchal conditions of the theatrical stage; that Ismail's, Hudgins's, and Hunter's property claims were attempts to check white power; that the legal recognition afforded choreography at mid-century was as much about the elevation of the white choreographer as it was about the acceptance of Labanotation as a system for recording choreography; and that the divergent outcomes of copyright cases involving the estates of Balanchine and Graham had the effect of reinforcing white male choreographic authority and undermining white female choreographic authority.

The second main argument I make is that much of copyright's value for choreographers lay in the way it enabled them to position themselves as possessive individuals and rights-bearing subjects rather than as commodities and objects of exchange. On the most basic level, choreographic copyright legally sanctions dance-makers to control and curb the copying of their creative works. As such, it has been a response to, and sometimes an anticipation of, a perceived crisis: not the crisis posed by dance's disappearance (as an influential strand of dance and performance studies theory posits) but the peril of its reproduction. Because choreographic works are corporeal in nature, they carry strong ties to the bodies that generate them; dance-makers' bodies are deeply implicated in the circulation of their choreography. The threat of dance's circulation, therefore, is that it can enact a kind of bodily commodi-fication, turning producers into products, subjects into things. This threat carries a particular charge in a country haunted by the legacy of slavery—the propertization of black persons—and in a field in which the female perform-ing body has so often been objectified. For white female dancers like Fuller, Holm, and de Mille, securing ownership rights in their choreography was a means of distancing themselves from the sexualized and racialized bodies that were seen as interchangeable commodities in the theatrical marketplace. For dancers of color like Ismail, Hudgins, and Hunter, copyright was a means of eschewing a status as objects of property—in defiance of a history of forced commodification and of ongoing perceptions of black and brown bodies' inter-changeability. Even for revered choreographers who were deceased at the time their copyright claims were adjudicated, as were Graham and Balanchine, copyright represented protection for the subject at risk of dispersal.

Choreographic copyright, in other words, has been a key site for all kinds of dancers' negotiation of subjecthood, including and especially their status as raced and gendered subjects (always cross-cut by class).[8] Yet, as I also propose, choreographic copyright is an intrinsically fraught construct that can never completely deliver on its promise of averting objectification. The nature of dance as embodied expression means that the lines between the dance-maker as possessive subject and the dance as possessed object are frequently muddy. Claims of intellectual property rights in dance are thus uniquely suited to highlight the contradictions of subjecthood and the instabilities of power.

Begun by the accidental discovery of Alberta Hunter's rumored copyright, *Choreographing Copyright* tells a story, or rather a series of stories, about raced and gendered subjects struggling with these contradictions as they sought to control the circulation of their embodied output in different economies of

---

[8] Scholars in critical race and ethnic studies have argued that thinking of subjecthood in terms of property has profound limitations and may even reinscribe the terms of settler colonialism. As Alexander Weheliye writes, the "idiom of personhood-as-ownership" is a "restricted one" that "maintains the world of Man and its attendant racializing assemblages, which means in essence that the entry fee for legal recognition is the acceptance of categories based on white supremacy and colonialism, as well as normative genders and sexualities." Alexander G. Weheliye, *Habeas Viscus: Racializing Assemblages, Biopolitics, and Black Feminist Theories of the Human* (Durham, NC: Duke University Press, 2014), 4, 77. I agree that the idea of "self-ownership" does little if anything to undo the problematic logic of possessive individualism. But I cannot easily discard how powerful "self-ownership" has been for dancers whose bodies are caught up in capitalist exchange, nor can I set aside how much value the dancers in this study have placed on occupying the position of "subject of property."

reproduction. The Introduction that follows outlines the theoretical and disci-
plinary stakes of the book, placing notions of choreography and copyright in
dialogue with one another and locating the project at the intersection of dance
studies, critical race and gender studies, and cultural studies of copyright.
Chapter 1, "White Womanhood and Early Campaigns for Choreographic
Copyright," recounts white modern dancer Loïe Fuller's pursuit of intellectual property rights in the late nineteenth century. Focusing on the 1892 case
Fuller v. Bemis, the conditions that gave rise to it, and its repercussions, I argue
that Fuller's lawsuit against the chorus girl Bemis must be viewed as part of
a gendered struggle to attain proprietary rights in whiteness. To make this
argument, I situate Fuller's practice in the context of the patriarchal economy
that governed the late nineteenth-century theater and examine the lineage
of Fuller's *Serpentine Dance*, including the oft-neglected Asian Indian dance
sources to which it was indebted. I then show how the "theft" of her *Serpentine
Dance* occasioned a crisis of subjecthood for Fuller, and how her assertion
of property rights in the dance was an attempt to (re)establish herself as a
property-holding subject. The chapter ends by considering the copyright bids
of two dancers who followed in Fuller's wake: one of her imitators, Ida Fuller,
and Ruth St. Denis, another "mother" of modern dance in the United States,
as well as the counter-claims of Mohammed Ismail, one of St. Denis's South
Asian dancers.

Chapter 2, "The Black Body as Object and Subject of Property," examines
the flip side of the historical affinity between whiteness and property rights by
looking at the legacy of slavery as it bore on the case of Johnny Hudgins. Famous
in his time but virtually forgotten today, Hudgins was an African American
blackface comic pantomimist, best known for his signature "Mwa, Mwa" act,
in which he opened and closed his mouth in imitation of an accompanying
trumpet. In 1924, the white producer of the all-black musical *The Chocolate
Dandies* sued Hudgins for breach of contract. *Whitney v. Hudgins* alleged that
Hudgins was "unique and irreplaceable," reportedly the first time such a claim
had been made about an African American performer. In his ultimately successful defense, Hudgins disavowed any originality, maintaining that he was
an entirely ordinary and expendable commodity. Several years later, Hudgins
took a very different stance when he obtained a copyright in London on his
repertoire of pantomime acts. Reading the lawsuit and the copyright claim
together, and reading both alongside Hudgins's blackface routine, I argue that
Hudgins's copyright was his attempt to counter a history of commodification
by asserting himself as a subject rather than object of property, an assertion
that is no less significant for being fraught.

Chapter 3, "'Stealing Steps' and Signature Moves: Alternative Systems
of Copyright," looks beyond the official archive of copyright records and

legal actions to ask what and how notions of property infused the practices of African American vernacular dancers in the 1930s and '40s. A number of scholars have persuasively argued that Western ideas of singular authorship and fixity embedded in US copyright law are ill suited to collective black expressive forms like the blues and jazz. Certainly, the custom of trading steps among African American tap dancers suggests that these artists honed their craft in something more closely resembling a gift economy than a capitalist, proprietary one. Yet published oral histories of tap and jazz dancers reveal that many of them worked to protect dance steps they considered their property via extra-legal means, corporeal and otherwise. The chapter analyzes these alternative methods, from the spreading of rumors about Hunter's alleged copyright on the Black Bottom; to the vigilant surveillance and public shaming of copycats who appeared at Harlem's Lincoln Theater; to the "trademarking" of "signature" moves, like Bill "Bojangles" Robinson's stair dance and Josephine Baker's eye-crossing. Because these methods of protection among black vernacular dancers bear directly on questions of dance's (non)reproducibility and seeming ephemerality, unpacking them re-animates debates about the ontological status of performance.

Chapter 4, "'High-brow' Meets 'Low-Down': Copyright on Broadway," investigates the campaign for choreographic copyright in the commercial arena of Broadway in the middle of the twentieth century. In the 1940s and '50s, Euro-American modern dance and ballet increasingly infiltrated the musical and, in the process, displaced African American jazz and tap dance, which had dominated the Broadway stage in the first part of the twentieth century. During this transitional period, the German-born modern dancer Hanya Holm secured a copyright "victory" by successfully registering the notated choreographic score for *Kiss Me, Kate*. Also during this time, Euro-American ballet dancer and choreographer of the smash hit *Oklahoma!* Agnes de Mille waged an outspoken battle for choreographers' property rights. Exploring how these women's choreography for the Broadway stage relied on and concealed a set of racialized power relations, I argue that Holm's and de Mille's foray into the racially tinged, middle-brow domain of Broadway elevated the figure of the white female choreographer such that their advocacy for choreographic copyright, including their testimony for a 1961 congressional report, helped clear a path for the Copyright Act of 1976. Yet the status afforded Holm and de Mille did not extend to all white female dancers on Broadway. The chapter concludes by looking at the case of the white burlesque dancer Faith Dane, who sued the producers of the Broadway musical *Gypsy* in 1962, claiming that the military striptease number she devised during her audition was protected under common law. The court's ruling, which rejected her claim on the grounds that her performance was immoral, indicates the continued sexual and class divisions structuring female bodies' access to the racialized privilege of property rights.

Chapter 5, "Copyright and the Death/Life of the Choreographer," assesses the two major choreographic copyright cases that have gone to trial since the passage of the 1976 Copyright Act, both of which involved highly esteemed, deceased choreographers. In the 1986 case *Horgan v. Macmillan, Inc.*, the executor of the estate of ballet choreographer George Balanchine sued the publishers of a book of photographs of Balanchine's *Nutcracker* ballet. An appeals court judge ruled that the photographs were "substantially similar" enough to Balanchine's choreography to warrant an injunction against the book's publication. In the 2002 case *Martha Graham School and Dance Foundation, Inc., and Ronald Protas v. Martha Graham Center of Contemporary Dance, Inc.*, a judge ruled that modern dance legend Martha Graham was a "worker-for-hire" for the non-profit corporation that housed her company and therefore not in a position to transfer the rights to her choreography to her heir. The ruling set off shock waves among the contemporary dance community: how could the most towering figure in American modern dance *not* own her own choreography? This chapter queries the discrepant decisions in these two cases, asking whether and how gender continues to inflect formulations of choreographic copyright. Together, the cases force us to consider the implications of the literal "death of the author," famously theorized by poststructuralists, for the field of dance, where the separation of the dancer from the dance is so vexed.

Read separately, each chapter offers an in-depth look at the contingencies of power that drove some dance-makers to assert intellectual property rights in their embodied output and the contingent responses to those assertions. Read together, the chapters paint a picture not of steady progress but of change as well as stubborn continuity across a knot of recurrent issues: raced and gendered hierarchies in the theatrical marketplace; white women's complicated relationship to property rights; legacies of ownership of black bodies and appropriation of non-white labor; copyright as a discourse of domination and of resistance; the contradictions of self-ownership; and the tension between dance's ephemerality and its reproducibility.

Of course, I am not arguing that racial and gender progress have not been made. Just as (high art) choreography gained legitimacy in the eyes of the law over the course of the twentieth century, so too has the US dance landscape shifted to expand the opportunities for women and dancers of color. In the Coda to the book, I attend to the controversy surrounding African American pop music star Beyoncé's 2011 music video "Countdown," portions of which borrowed choreography from the Belgian avant-garde artist Anne Teresa De Keersmaeker. Looked at from one angle, Beyoncé's unauthorized reproduction of the white avant-garde suggests that, in the age of YouTube, a leveling of racialized hierarchies between protectable works of authorship and the unrestricted public domain has taken place. Yet I also caution against reading this apparent leveling as a sign of the undoing of white privilege. The response to Beyoncé's use of De Keersmaeker's work indicates the extent to which racially tinged anxieties about the reproduction of choreography in the global marketplace and the directions in which it is allowed to flow have yet to subside.[9]

Indeed, as I worked on this book during the summers of 2013 and 2014, US law's protection of the rights of its citizens seemed anything but level. The Supreme Court's overturning of a key provision of the 1965 Voting Rights Act in *Shelby v. Holder*; the acquittal of neighborhood watchman George Zimmerman for the shooting death of the unarmed African American teen Trayvon Martin; the police shooting death of Michael Brown, another unarmed African American teen, whose body was left lying in the middle of the street for hours after his killing, and who, like Martin, was demonized in the grand jury non-indictment of his case: these events give the lie to post-racial views of US history. Disputes over intellectual property rights in dance may seem a far cry from these tragic events and far-reaching court decisions. But, as I argue in the following pages, choreographic copyright emerged out of the same racialized logic of property that has persistently treated some bodies as fungible commodities and others as possessive individuals. Just as the election of Barack Obama as president did not signal the end of racial inequality in the United States, neither does Beyoncé's appropriation of the white avant-garde signal the end of a property interest in whiteness, always already sanctioned by law but perpetually seeking fortification.

---

[9] On the tenacity of racial "sightlines" and acts of racial violence that resist standard narratives of change over time, see Matthew Pratt Guterl, *Seeing Race in Modern America* (Chapel Hill: University of North Carolina Press, 2013), and Harvey Young, *Embodying Black Experience: Stillness, Critical Memory, and the Black Body* (Ann Arbor: University of Michigan Press, 2010).

ACKNOWLEDGMENTS

In a book that is so fundamentally about the allocation of credit, it is only fitting to start by acknowledging the numerous people who helped give it life. The support of two different Susan's has been profoundly important to me. Susan Leigh Foster nurtured my preliminary investigation into choreographic copyright when she convened the "neworldances" roundtable and shepherded the *Worlding Dance* volume into existence. My sincere thanks to her and to all of the members of that roundtable: Yutian Wong, Jacqueline Shea Murphy, Ananya Chatterjea, Anna Beatrice Scott, Lena Hammergren, and Marta Elena Savigliano, and especially Priya Srinivasan, who, as sounding board and accomplice, helped shape some of my earliest thinking about this project. The other Susan to whom I owe an immeasurable debt is Susan Manning, who has given so much to me personally through her ongoing mentorship and friendship, and so much to the field of dance studies at large. Her feedback on a penultimate draft of this manuscript helped make the book tighter and clearer.

So many individuals helped with the research for this project. As a legal novice, I had a lot of questions about copyright law and am lucky to know some very obliging lawyers, including Frank Menetrez, Menesh Patel, Harry Surden, and my uncle Jon Hyman, all of whom helped me track down sources or pointed me in the right direction. For their archival help, I am grateful to Elizabeth Aldrich at the Library of Congress, Teresa Conaway at the La Verne Law School library, Lizbeth Lanston at the UC Riverside library, Christopher O. Magee at the National Archives at Kansas City, Joe VanNostrand at the County Clerk Archives in New York City, Mei-Chen Lu and Mira Kim at the Dance Notation Bureau, Charles Perrier and Arlene Yu at the New York Public Library for the Performing Arts, and Libby Smigel at the Dance Heritage Coalition. I was fortunate to have a host of research assistants at various stages during the long gestation of this project. For their able sleuthing and transcribing, my thanks to Ariel Osterweis, Asheley Smith, Natalie Zervou, Meghan Quinlan, Leah Weinryb Grohsgal, Nixon Ky Ma, Neghin Kheverdi, and Sarah Lindblom. Daniela Blei was an enormous help in the laborious process of tracking down photographic reproductions and permissions and in compiling the book's index. The munificence of Brian Harker and the late Jean-Claude Baker made possible my research on Johnny Hudgins, and K. J. Greene generously shared his work on African American music and intellectual property law. My thanks as well to Jonathan Prude for granting me permission to consult and cite from the Agnes de Mille Papers at the New York Public Library for the Performing Arts, and to Karen Holm Trautlein for granting me permission to reproduce an excerpt of Hanya Holm's Labanotated *Kiss Me, Kate* score.

Funds from UC Riverside's Committee on Research and Academic Senate helped make this research possible. A fellowship from the American Council of Learned Societies gave me the invaluable gift of time to complete the manuscript. Nor could I have completed this book without fantastic child care. My thanks especially to the wonderful staff at the Early Childhood Center and The Children's School in Claremont, California, who gave me the peace of mind to write.

Early on in this project, I had the immense pleasure of being part of a Resident Faculty Fellowship group at UC Riverside's Center for Ideas and Society. My sincere thanks to the Center and to the members of that group—Jayna Brown, Tiffany Lopez, and Deborah Wong—for supporting and inspiring me. I am also grateful to others who read and offered feedback on portions of this work over the course of its development, including Cindy Garcia, Brian Herrera, Rebekah Kowal, Marta Savigliano, Priya Srinivasan, Susan Manning, Derek Miller, Kate Elswit, and Harvey Young. I benefited as well from the suggestions of several anonymous reviewers along the way. Norm Hirschy is without question the most responsive, encouraging editor anyone could hope for. My thanks to Norm for championing this project from the get-go and for guiding it so expertly toward publication.

I am particularly fortunate to call the Dance Department at UC Riverside my academic home. It is a gift to be in a place where I am surrounded by brilliant dance scholars and artists, by stimulating graduate and undergraduate students, and by passionate dancing. My gratitude especially to my past and present faculty colleagues: Jens Giersdorf, Neil Greenberg, Imani Kai Johnson, Taisha Paggett, Jose Reynoso, Wendy Rogers, Susan Rose, Marta Savigliano, Anna Beatrice Scott, Jacqueline Shea Murphy, Joel Smith, Priya Srinivasan, and Linda Tomko.

While authorship is never singular, I do take full ownership of any and all of the book's shortcomings.

None of this would be as meaningful without the love of my incredible family. My parents, Richard and Susan (the other monumentally important Susan in my life), my sister Naomi, and my brother Jonah are all amazing role models for me. My sister offered support in the form of phone conversations almost daily; I would be so lost without her. My heartfelt thanks to my husband Dave, a partner in every sense of the word, who keeps me grounded and makes me laugh and think. Finally, this book is dedicated to my daughters, Avie and Luna, who came into this world while I worked on this project and have given me so much more than I could ever articulate or repay.

Choreographing Copyright

Introduction

Dance Plus Copyright

This book focuses on attempts by dance-makers based in the United States to control the circulation of their choreography. There has, I argue, been much at stake for dancers when their compositions were reproduced without their authorization: not only economic and artistic capital but also status in a raced and gendered hierarchy. Dance-makers have accordingly employed a range of strategies—legal, rhetorical, corporeal—to assert themselves as owners of what their bodies produce. Prime among these has been copyright, the branch of intellectual property law that grants authors exclusive rights to their creations for limited times. Although US federal copyright law did not officially recognize choreographic works as a protectable class until 1976, dancers' attempts to secure intellectual property rights for themselves began at least eight decades earlier.[1] *Choreographing Copyright* is a historical, cultural, and political analysis of those efforts.

Even as this book insists on the importance of such efforts, let me say from the outset that I view copyright for choreography as inherently fraught. There is even a slight absurdity to it, perhaps best encapsulated in tap dancer Eddie Rector's remark, "Shuck, if you could copyright a step ... nobody could lift a foot."[2] Although proponents of choreographic copyright never sought to protect discrete steps, only the arrangements of steps (much as literary works

---

[1] I alternately refer to the subjects of this book as dancers, dance-makers, and choreographers. This is not to imply that these terms are interchangeable: not all of the artists I write about were primarily dancers (George Balanchine, for example); nor were all of the dancers I write about considered choreographers (a term whose racial politics I have explored elsewhere, and which receives continued scrutiny in this book). See Anthea Kraut, *Choreographing the Folk: The Dance Stagings of Zora Neale Hurston* (Minneapolis: University of Minnesota Press, 2008), 53–89. Nonetheless, in switching between these terms, I do want to call attention to the fluidity between them and to suggest how often dancing bodies, even when they did not wear the mantle "choreographer," produced dances that could become the objects of intellectual property claims.

[2] Marshall and Jean Stearns, *Jazz Dance: The Story of American Vernacular Dance* (New York: Schirmer Books, 1968), 338. I return to Rector's comment in Chapter 3.

1

but not words themselves can be copyrighted), Rector's observation captures how readily one person's proprietary rights in bodily movement can impinge on another's mobility. How could anyone possess exclusive rights to a way of moving?[3] Not only is the circulation of dance across bodies integral to its transmission and therefore its existence, but dance movement is also difficult to contain. Often figured as "contagious,"[4] dance is prone to going "viral."[5]

The more farcical dimensions of choreographic copyright were evident in 2007, when a man named Richard Silver launched accusations of copyright infringement against a number of performers of the popular 1970s line dance known as the Electric Slide. Claiming to have invented the dance in 1976, Silver registered a video of it with the Copyright Office in 2004. Under the Digital Millennium Copyright Act of 1998, which regulates the circulation of copyrighted material on the Internet, Silver began issuing takedown notices for online videos featuring the Electric Slide. His concern, he maintained, was that people were performing the dance incorrectly, but he demanded monetary compensation from the *Ellen DeGeneres Show*, which ran a segment in which the Electric Slide was enacted. It is worth noting that Silver's copyright registration likely only applied to the video documentation of the dance he submitted to the Copyright Office rather than to the Electric Slide itself. As I discuss later in this book, while there is no agreed-on legal definition of "choreographic work," "social dances and simple routines" are exempt from copyright protection.[6] Still, Silver's invocation of intellectual property rights in the dance raised the prospect that performing the Electric Slide at a wedding could result in getting "charged with illegal motion."[7]

---

[3] As W. T. Lhamon Jr. has written, gestures could be "saleable but never exclusive property." *Raising Cain: Blackface Performance from Jim Crow to Hip Hop* (Cambridge, MA: Harvard University Press, 1998), 15.

[4] Barbara Browning, *Infectious Rhythm: Metaphors of Contagion and the Spread of African Culture* (New York: Routledge, 1998), 6.

[5] See Harmony Bench, "Screendance 2.0: Social Dance-Media," *Participations: Journal of Audience & Reception Studies* 7.2 (November 2010), http://www.participations.org/Volume%207/Issue%202/special/bench.htm. Accessed November 7, 2013.

[6] The most recent *Compendium of U.S. Copyright Practices*, a 1,200-page document that lays out the administrative practices of the US Copyright Office, a public draft of which was released in August 2014, goes to great lengths to explain the uncopyrightability of "social dances" and "simple routines." See *Compendium of U.S. Copyright Practices*, Third Edition, US Copyright Office, Public Draft, August 19, 2014, Chapter 800, section 805, 70–84, http://copyright.gov/comp3/. Accessed September 15, 2014.

[7] Renee Montagne, "Creator Seeks to Preserve 'Electric Slide,'" *Morning Edition*, February 20, 2007, http://www.npr.org/templates/story/story.php?storyId=7492263. Accessed September 24, 2013. When the Electronic Frontier Foundation sued Silver in 2007 on behalf of a San Francisco-based engineer who had posted a video on YouTube of people performing the Electric Slide at a convention, Silver settled and agreed to stop demanding the removal of

Dance "piracy" in the digital age was also the impetus behind the 2009 work *Punk Yankees* by the Chicago-based dance theater ensemble Lucky Plush Productions and the website they created in conjunction with the work, stealthisdance.com. As the site explains,

> The proliferation of highly networked systems of exchange for moving images (such as You Tube and related sites), obscure[s] the relationship between intellectual property and dance making. Lucky Plush is interested in provoking the paradoxes inherent in this topic: how "theft" in the dance field is both embedded in a long history of appropriation and a completely new phenomenon taking place on the internet, and how "stealing" choreography can be both irresponsible and transformative.[8]

The evening-length *Punk Yankees* samples a host of choreographic works—from George Balanchine's *Apollo* and Ohad Naharin's *Minus 16* to Michael Jackson's "Thriller" and Beyoncé's "Single Ladies (Put a Ring on It)" (which itself samples

---

videos depicting the dance. See http://news.cnet.com/The-copyright-buzz-from-the-Electric-Slide/2008-1026_3-6188297.html; http://news.cnet.com/Electric-Slide-on-slippery-DMCA-slope/2100-1030_3-6156021.html?tag=mncol; http://ric06379.tripod.com/id6.html. Accessed November 10, 2009. See also Silver's website: http://ric06379.tripod.com/id6.html. Accessed September 24, 2013. According to Elizabeth Aldrich, the curator of dance in the Music Division of the Librarian of Congress, in late 2008 or early 2009, Silver's lawyers came back to the Copyright Office in the hopes of obtaining a copyright on the actual choreography. Reluctant to extend Silver the registration, Copyright Office representatives sought assistance from Aldrich and others in arriving at a definition of choreography that would exclude the Electric Slide—an undertaking in which no one was eager to become involved. Personal conversation with Elizabeth Aldrich, June 1, 2009. In fact, the recently released draft of the latest edition of the *Compendium of Copyright Practices* seems to have Silver's case explicitly in mind when it gives the following example of uncopyrightable subject matter:

> Seymour Winkler created a line dance for a song titled "The Slip," which was featured in a famous music video. The dance consists of a few steps, a turn, a hop, and a snap, which is then repeated in different directions. "The Slip" is often performed at weddings and other social occasions, and members of the general public often perform Seymour's line dance when the song is played. The U.S. Copyright Office would refuse to register this line dance, because it is a social dance that is commonly performed by members of the public as a participatory social activity (rather than a theatrical performance for the enjoyment of an audience).

Compendium of U.S. Copyright Practices, Third Edition, Public Draft, Chapter 800, section 805, 79. There are, it should be noted, parallels between Richard Silver's attempt to copyright social dance choreography and the claim that Alberta Hunter copyrighted the Black Bottom (mentioned in the Preface and discussed at length in Chapter 3). The discrepancies in their respective relationships to a white power structure, however, give their claims a different resonance.

[8] http://stealthisdance.com/wordpress/?page_id=820. Accessed September 26, 2013.

Bob Fosse)—and, through the use of video and text, exposes the sources of the performed movement. The piece also explores the dance lineages of the eight dancers in the company.[9] Stealthisdance.com, meanwhile, the title a nod to Abbie Hoffman's 1971 *Steal This Book*, presents itself as a place where you can "steal/buy/share" dance. With sections that feature company members sampling from video and from their own embodied memories, another in which they fuse different movement styles, and still another devoted to a "moves boutique," in which users are encouraged to purchase dance moves, the site is both a thoughtful exploration of various modes of appropriating and valuing dance and a satire of the very idea of owning movement.[10]

However intelligent its work, what Lucky Plush does not address, and what hovers over Richard Silver's Electric Slide infringement claims, are the racial dynamics of appropriation and ownership in dance. Sampling does not take place in a vacuum, and the exchange of dance almost never occurs on an equal playing field. As recent dance scholarship has shown, the history of dance in the United States is also the history of white "borrowing" from racially subjugated communities, almost always without credit or compensation.[11] While stealthisdance.com is silent on this issue, Silver's claim to have invented and hold ownership rights to the Electric Slide, sometimes referred to as a black wedding dance, reproduces the dominant pattern of racialized appropriation in US culture. Silver, who is white, may well have devised an Electric Slide dance, though his allegations on his website to be the choreographer behind African American dance styles such as popping, locking, and breakdancing seem tenuous at best.[12] Their veracity aside, in light of the cyclical nature of

---

[9] I should note that I have not seen the full work, only video excerpts available on YouTube. See, for example, https://www.youtube.com/watch?v=PdGWF6-Hetk. Accessed September 26, 2013.

[10] In a similar vein, Sally Banes cites two postmodern choreographers—Daniel McCusker and Nina Martin—who parodied the idea of intellectual property in dance in the early 1980s. See "Homage, Plagiarism, Allusion, Comment, Quotation: Negotiating Choreographic Appropriation," in *Before, Between, and Beyond: Three Decades of Dance Writing*, ed. Andrea Harris (Madison: University of Wisconsin Press, 2007), 207, 214n27.

[11] Influential scholarship in this vein includes Brenda Dixon Gottschild, *Digging the Africanist Presence in American Performance: Dance and Other Contexts* (Westport, CT: Greenwood Press, 1996); Susan Manning, *Modern Dance, Negro Dance: Race in Motion* (Minneapolis: University of Minnesota Press, 2004); Jacqueline Shea Murphy, *"The People Have Never Stopped Dancing": Native American Modern Dance Histories* (Minneapolis: University of Minnesota Press, 2007); Priya Srinivasan, *Sweating Saris: Indian Dance as Transnational Labor* (Philadelphia, PA: Temple University Press, 2011); Yutian Wong, *Choreographing Asian America* (Middletown, CT: Wesleyan University Press, 2010).

[12] http://ric06379.tripod.com/id6.html. Accessed October 4, 2013. For a sense of the outrage generated by Silver's claims on the Electric Slide, see

white appropriation of dances developed by black and brown bodies, the light-heartedness of *Punk Yankees* and stealthisdance.com feels somewhat ahistorical (despite their nod to a "long history of appropriation"), and Silver's attempt to police the Electric Slide feels like history repeating itself.

One of the premises of this book is that discussions of ownership in dance must take into account histories of white "love and theft."[13] Questions of who possesses the rights to which movement, of who is authorized to borrow from whom, and of who profits from the circulation of dance are all entangled in legacies of racial injustice. For those familiar with scholarship in critical dance studies, including my own earlier publications, this is hardly a radical premise. But because, as I discuss further below, property itself is a raced, gendered, and classed construct, attention to dancers' efforts to assert intellectual property rights in their compositions can cast new light on how the inequities that have structured the US dance landscape took shape. That is, the struggle to win copyright protection for choreography did not just play out within a context of raced, classed, and gendered hierarchies; it was a vital site for the formation of those hierarchies, as well as for resistance to them.

Rather than setting out to provide an exhaustive history of intellectual property rights for dance, *Choreographing Copyright* moves through a series of case studies that showcase how copyright for choreography in the United States has intersected with axes of race and gender, always in relationship to class. Each chapter focuses on a dancer or group of dancers who sought to exert rights over their choreography at a different historical moment: from the early white modern dancer Loïe Fuller at the end of the nineteenth century (Chapter 1); to the African American pantomimist Johnny Hudgins and other black tap and jazz dancers in the early decades of the twentieth century (Chapters 2 and 3); to the white artists Hanya Holm and Agnes de Mille, and the lesser known Faith Dane, who made dances for Broadway at mid-century (Chapter 4); to the legendary white choreographers George Balanchine and Martha Graham, whose respective copyright cases went to trial at the end of the twentieth century and the start of the twenty-first (Chapter 5). *Choreographing Copyright* collects these examples not to advocate for or against copyright protection for choreography, nor for or against reform of current copyright law. Instead, it argues that copyright and choreography productively illuminate one another and the workings of race and gender in American dance. In the remainder of this introduction, I further address some of the problems that plague copyright as

http://mokellyreport.blogspot.com/2007/10/electric-slide-white-owned-and-operated. html. Accessed October 4, 2013.

[13] Eric Lott, *Love and Theft: Blackface Minstrelsy and the American Working Class* (New York: Oxford University Press, 1993).

a legal institution, theorize the overlap and tension between choreography and copyright, establish the racial and gendered dimensions of property rights, and articulate how I see this book contributing to recent scholarship in dance studies and cultural studies of copyright.

Against Copyright?

For all the zeal with which some dancers campaigned to win legal protection for choreography, and for all the meaning this book assigns to those campaigns, copyright is hardly a universal preoccupation among dance-makers. The number of choreographers who have gone to the trouble of registering their works with the Copyright Office in the wake of the 1976 Copyright Act is strikingly small,[14] and only two major legal cases involving choreographic property have gone to trial since the passage of the act. According to legal scholar Barbara Singer, who conducted interviews with about a dozen (predominantly white) contemporary choreographers in the early 1980s, dance-makers reject the legal mechanism of copyright out of "a belief that the customs of their own community offer equal, if not superior, protection for choreographic works."[15] Relying on licensing agreements to regulate the reproduction of their works and on a "close-knit, protective community" to police any breaches of contract, contemporary choreographers, Singer concludes, rarely have cause to turn to the costly legal arena to enforce their rights.[16] Dance scholar Sally Banes echoes Singer's assessment, adding that the concert dance field's "almost feudal"-like dependence on oral transmission and apprenticeship breeds an antipathy to formal, legal institutions.[17] Writing about a potential case of copyright infringement among the hip-hop dance community, meanwhile, blogger

[14] In 1980, only 63 out of a total of 464,742 total registrations were choreographic works or pantomimes. US Copyright Office, Report of the Register of Copyrights, 1980, at 27; quoted in Singer, "In Search of Adequate Protection," 290 fn11. In 2009, 545 out of 424,427 registered works were classified as "Dramatic Works, Choreographic Works, and Pantomimes," although it does not appear possible to separate out choreographic works from the other two categories. Quoted in Eriq Gardner, "Why an Allegation that Beyoncé Plagiarized Dance Moves Is Truly Unique (Analysis)," *The Hollywood Reporter* online, October 13, 2011, http://www.hollywood-reporter.com/thr-esq/why-an-allegation-beyonc-plagiarized-248208. Accessed December 9, 2013.

[15] Singer, "In Search of Adequate Protection," 290.

[16] Ibid., 296.

[17] Banes, "Homage, Plagiarism, Allusion, Comment, Quotation," 205. Interestingly, Banes attributes some of this disinclination toward the law to the fact that the "American dance world is dominated by women who in the past have preferred to negotiate within informal networks" (205–6). This is a notable counterpoint to the gendered analysis I offer in this book.

Merlyne Jean-Louis speculates that choreographers are unlikely to pursue legal action because they "are honored and feel respected when others perform their pieces."[18]

Instead of filling a book with stories of choreographic copyright, then, why not write a study of the ways in which dance operates outside of and perhaps even in opposition to the legal regime of intellectual property rights? Why not approach the circulation of dance in terms of a gift economy? (This was a suggestion I occasionally received when I described the current project.) Mark Franko, via Jacques Derrida, Marcel Mauss, and Gregory Bateson, has written provocatively about the transmission of dances as gift,[19] and certainly, Lewis Hyde's formulation of the gift as "property that perishes" would seem to accord with theorizations of dance's ephemerality and resistance to commodification.[20] Although dance may participate simultaneously in gift and capitalist economies, thinking dance through copyright is important precisely because it forces us to confront dance's collusion with liberal and neoliberal ideologies.

Aversion to copyright also stems from the fact that it is an undeniably "Euro-modernist" institution.[21] Rooted in Western Enlightenment notions of the individual as the bearer of rights, copyright law in the United States descends directly from British law. The first US Copyright Act, passed in 1790, was modeled after Britain's 1710 Statute of Anne, which sought to regulate the book trade by assigning to authors a fourteen-year copyright term, with the possibility of a fourteen-year renewal.[22] As I discuss further in Chapter 3, copyright law's fixity

[18] Merlyne Jean-Louis, "Dancing Around the Issue of Copyright of Choreographic Works," The Entertainment, Arts and Sports Law Blog, http://nysbar.com/blogs/EASL/2011/07/dancing_around_the_issue_of_co.html. Accessed September 17, 2013. The blog post was written in response to a controversy in which an Atlanta hip-hip dance duo known as D*Day performed a sequence from a routine by a French hip-hop pair named Les Twins in an audition episode of the popular dance competition television show *So You Think You Can Dance*. Although fans of Les Twins were angered by the theft, Les Twins forgave the Atlanta pair and wished them luck in the TV competition.

[19] Mark Franko, "Given Movement: Dance and the Event," in *Of the Presence of the Body: Essays on Dance and Performance Theory*, ed. André Lepecki (Middletown: Wesleyan University Press, 2004): 113–23. On dance's status as or relationship to the gift, see also Harmony Bench, "Dancing in Digital Archives," in *Transmission in Motion*, ed. Maaike Bleeker (forthcoming); and Anurima Banerji, "Dance and the Distributed Body: Odissi, Ritual Practice, and Mahari Performance," *About Performance* 11 (2012): 7–39.

[20] Lewis Hyde, *The Gift: Creativity and the Artist in the Modern World* (New York: Vintage Books, 2007 [1979]), 10. See especially Peggy Phelan, *Unmarked: The Politics of Performance* (London: Routledge, 1993) for a view of performance as ontologically resistant to capitalist reproduction, discussed further below.

[21] John L. and Jean Comaroff, *Ethnicity, Inc.* (Chicago: University of Chicago Press, 2009), 33.

[22] On the history of copyright law in the United States, see Siva Vaidhyanathan, *Copyrights and Copywrongs: The Rise of Intellectual Property and How It Threatens Creativity* (New York: New York University Press, 2001), 37–55. On copyright law as it existed in nearly all of the colonies prior

and originality requirements, as well as its emphasis on individual rather than communal creativity, privilege a Western approach to art-making. Copyright is unmistakably one of the master's tools, and as such, following Audre Lorde, cannot dismantle the master's house.[23]

Equally problematic, copyright law increasingly benefits large corporations at the expense of both artists and the public. The steady expansion of copyright terms (from fourteen years in 1790 to the author's life plus seventy years as of 1998) and the growing enforcement of intellectual property rights by multinational corporations have had all sorts of deleterious effects that scholars like Rosemary Coombe, Lawrence Lessig, James Boyle, Siva Vaidhyanathan, Kembrew McLeod, and Joanna Demers have documented:[24] from the suppressing of free speech;[25] to the shrinking of the public domain, the zone of never or no longer privatized cultural material from which artists draw to create new works; to the "freezing [of] the connotations of signs and symbols and fencing off [of] fields of cultural meaning with 'No Trespassing' signs";[26] to the advantaging of well-known artists over and above lesser-known, emerging artists.[27] Copyright law can even shut down performance completely. Vaidhyanathan's book *Copyrights and Copywrongs* concludes with an epilogue titled "The Summer without Martha Graham," a reference to the hiatus imposed on the Graham Company while a legal dispute between parties claiming the rights to Graham's choreography was pending (addressed in Chapter 5). For Vaidhyanathan, the cessation of dancing is

to the 1790 Act, see Francine Crawford, "Pre-constitutional Copyright Statutes," *Bulletin of the Copyright Society of the U.S.A.* 23 (1975): 11–37. My thanks to Derek Miller for calling my attention to the existence of pre-federal copyright law and to Crawford's work.

[23] Audre Lorde, "The Master's Tools Will Never Dismantle the Master's House," in *Sister Outsider: Essays & Speeches by Audre Lorde*, ed. Audre Lorde (Freedom, CA: Crossing Press, 1984), 110–14.

[24] Rosemary J. Coombe, *The Cultural Life of Intellectual Properties: Authorship, Appropriation, and the Law* (Durham, NC: Duke University Press, 1998); Lawrence Lessig, *Free Culture: The Nature and Future of Creativity* (New York: Penguin Books, 2004); James D. A. Boyle, *Shamans, Software, and Spleens: Law and the Construction of the Information Society* (Cambridge, MA: Harvard University Press, 1996); Vaidhyanathan, *Copyrights and Copywrongs*; Kembrew McLeod, *Owning Culture: Authorship, Ownership, and Intellectual Property Law* (New York: Peter Lang, 2001); Joanna Demers, *Steal This Music: How Intellectual Property Law Affects Musical Creativity* (Athens: University of Georgia Press, 2006).

[25] Vaidhyanathan, *Copyrights and Copywrongs*, 187–88.

[26] Coombe, *The Cultural Life of Intellectual Properties*, 69.

[27] Oliver Gerland's article, "From Playhouse to P2P Network: The History and Theory of Performance under Copyright Law in the United States" (*Theatre Journal* 59.1 [2007] 75–95), offers a useful analysis of how a legal theory of performance that regards each transmission of a recorded performance as a discrete performance enabled the "growth of vertically integrated megamedia companies during the 1990s" (88).

evidence that the current copyright system is "squelching beauty, impeding exposure, stifling creativity."[28]

Growing concerns about the perceived "tyranny" of copyright law have given rise to an alliance of lawyers, legal scholars, authors, artists, and activists who support an alternative method of protection, known as "Copy Left." Borrowing an expression originally used by software programmers, this group is not opposed to copyright per se; rather, its diverse members "see themselves as fighting for a traditional understanding of intellectual property in the face of a radical effort to turn copyright law into a tool for hoarding ideas."[29] At the heart of the "Copy Left" or "free culture" lobby is the belief that an abundance of expressive material in the public domain is essential to a healthy society. One outgrowth of this movement is the Creative Commons, an organization founded in 2001 that embraces the idea of "some rights reserved" and provides tools by which authors can give others "the right to share, use, and even build upon" their work.[30]

The Dance Heritage Coalition (DHC), a national non-profit organization founded in 1992 to support the institutional documentation of dance, shares much of the philosophy of the Commons. In a publication titled "Statement of Best Practices in Fair Use of Dance-Related Materials," the DHC encourages dance collections to invoke "fair use," a doctrine codified in the 1976 Copyright Act that grants exceptions to the exclusivity of copyright. Written from the point of view of the researcher and teacher rather than the dance creator, the DHC's position, which has been endorsed by the leading US-based dance scholarly organizations, paints copyright law as a barrier to access to dance records, and therefore to the nation's dance "heritage."[31]

In view of the current backlash against copyright law and of its inherent shortcomings, there is a certain contrariness to this book's focus on efforts to expand rather than restrict or circumvent copyright protection for choreography. For the most part, the dancers I consider in these pages believed strongly in the efficacy of copyright as a tool to protect their compositions; the injustice they were passionate about correcting was the law's failure to recognize choreography as a copyrightable art form. The campaign for choreographic copyright in the United States was also a campaign against deep-rooted tendencies

---

[28] Vaidhyanathan, *Copyrights and Copywrongs*, 185.

[29] Robert S. Boynton, "The Tyranny of Copyright?" *New York Times Magazine*, January 25, 2004, http://www.nytimes.com/2004/01/25/magazine/the-tyranny-of-copyright.html?pagewanted=all&src=pm. Accessed September 19, 2013.

[30] http://creativecommons.org/about. Accessed September 19, 2013.

[31] "Statement of Best Practices in Fair Use of Dance-Related Materials," Washington, DC: Dance Heritage Coalition, 2009.

to see dance as immoral and sexualized, feminized and racialized, and devoid of meaning. Copyright represented a means of putting dance on equal footing with more "respectable" forms, like music, drama, and literature. However statistically small the number of dancers who actually took legal action, the idea of intellectual property rights in dance has mattered immensely to dance-makers from a range of backgrounds. Ultimately, it is because of and not despite its manifold problems—political, sociological, ontological—that choreographic copyright is worthy of analysis. Approached as a site where power is both consolidated and contested, choreographic copyright offers a window onto and distills all kinds of struggles: between dancers and legal officials, between patriarchy and its challengers, between white supremacy and those seeking to overturn it, between capital and labor, between dance genres vying for status and recognition, between choreography's disappearance and its ongoingness.

Theorizing Choreographic Copyright

Copyright is one branch of intellectual property law in the United States, situated alongside patent and trademark law. Where patent law protects inventions and trademark law protects names or symbols identified with goods or services, copyright law protects the expression of ideas. Unlike an invention, which must be deemed "novel"—defined as unknown to the public—to qualify for patent protection, copyright law's protection for "original works of authorship" ostensibly requires only that a work originate with its author rather than be copied from another source.[32] A copyright actually grants an owner a bundle of rights: the right to reproduce, perform, display, and distribute the work, and to create derivative works of the original.[33]

Copyright "is not a transcendent moral idea" but "a specifically modern institution, the creature of the printing press, the individualization of authorship in the late Middle Ages and early Renaissance, and the development of the advanced marketplace societies in the seventeenth and eighteenth centuries."[34] In *Authors and Owners: The Invention of Copyright*, Mark Rose traces

[32] NOLO's Plain English Law Dictionary explains that novelty means that "all material elements of an invention cannot have been disclosed in any previous technology or publication (prior art)," http://www.nolo.com/dictionary/novelty-term.html. Accessed December 12, 2013. On copyright's originality requirement, see "Copyright Basics," United States Copyright Office, available at http://copyright.gov/. Accessed November 8, 2013; and Paul K. Saint-Amour, *The Copywrights: Intellectual Property and the Literary Imagination* (Ithaca, NY: Cornell University Press, 2003), 7.

[33] "Copyright Basics."

[34] Rose, *Authors and Owners*, 142, 3.

the development of copyright in eighteenth-century Britain, demonstrating how the Statute of Queen Anne, generally recognized as the world's first copyright law, endorsed the concept of author's rights in order to end a single company's monopoly over the book printing trade. The refinement of copyright laws in subsequent years resulted from a battle between booksellers. Out of these battles grew an idea of the author as proprietor, as well as an idea of literary property, itself a complicated construction that mixed ideas of originality and personality, landed property and immaterial thought, paternity and propriety.[35]

US copyright law's rootedness in print culture is evident in Article 1, Section 8, of the Constitution, known as the Copyright Clause, which authorizes Congress to grant "Authors and Inventors the exclusive Right to their respective Writings and Discoveries" in order "To promote the Progress of Science and useful Arts."[36] The original provision submitted to the framers of the Constitution was designed "to secure to literary authors their copyrights for a limited time," and the first copyright law enacted in the United States protected only books, maps, and charts.[37] In 1831, printed music was added to the list of protectable categories, and in 1856, dramatic works became a protected class. Over the years, the list has steadily expanded: photographs gained protection in 1865, motion pictures in 1912, sound recordings in 1972, choreographic works and pantomimes in 1976, and architectural works in 1990.

Given its literary antecedents, it is hardly surprising that copyright has proven an awkward fit with choreography. One case in point is US copyright law's idea/expression dichotomy, which reserves protection for the expression of ideas, not ideas themselves. Pointing out how problematic this binary is for music, Joanna Demers asks, "When does music cease to be an idea and start to become an expression?"[38] The same could well be posed of choreography. Is choreography "expressed" only when it is embodied in the

---

[35] See also Martha Woodmansee, *The Author, Art, and the Market: Rereading the History of Aesthetics* (New York: Columbia University Press, 1994). Ronan Deazley's *On the Origin of the Right to Copy: Charting the Movement of Copyright Law in Eighteenth Century Britain (1695–1775)* (Portland, OR: Hart Publishing, 2004) argues that the emergence of copyright in Britain was more complex than the narrative presented by scholars like Rose. Lionel Bentley's, Uma Suthersanan's, and Paul Torreman's edited volume *Global Copyright: Three Hundred Years since the Statute of Anne, from 1709 to Cyberspace* (Cheltenham, UK: Edward Elgar, 2010), meanwhile, complicates the view that the Statute of Anne was the origin of all subsequent copyright laws. My thanks to Derek Miller for calling these latter works to my attention.

[36] http://www.copyright.gov/title17/92preface.html. Accessed October 5, 2013.

[37] http://www.copyright.gov/circs/circ1a.html. Accessed October 5, 2013.

[38] Demers, *Steal This Music*, 32–33.

moment of performance? To put it another way, "If a dance isn't danced, does it really exist?"[39] Such questions bear directly on the issue of dance's ontology. Copyright law's prerequisite that a work be "fixed in any tangible medium of expression" before it can be eligible for protection, however, insists on something other than embodiment;[40] only a transcribed version of choreography, temporally and spatially removed from the time/space of embodied performance, meets the criteria of expression under the law. The fixation requirement has indisputably been a hurdle for choreography (although qualifying as a "useful art" and demonstrating dramatic content have at times proven greater obstacles).[41] As this book documents, dance-makers have turned to various methods—textual description, notation, video—to meet this requirement. But the discrepancies between the medium of creation and the medium of fixity generate ambiguity about what exactly is being protected. Does a copyright on a choreographic score grant exclusive rights to performances of the choreography or only to publications of the score (see Chapter 4)? Do photographs of a protected choreographic work constitute reproductions of the choreography or are they separate works? (This latter question came before the court in *Horgan v. Macmillan*, covered in Chapter 5.) Such problems exist more acutely for choreography than they do for art forms that are (more or less) fixed and tangible in the first instance.[42]

Notwithstanding copyright's debt to print culture, there are some interesting and perhaps surprising ontological parallels between copyright and choreography. From a certain angle, "choreographic copyright" is little more

[39] Richard Daniels, quoted in Jennifer Dunning, "Warning: Ephemeral but Private Property; Notions of Ownership Tie Up Dance Legacies," *New York Times*, July 26, 2000, http://www.nytimes.com/2000/07/26/arts/warning-ephemeral-but-private-property-notions-ownership-tie-up-dance-legacies.html?pagewanted=all&src=pm. Accessed November 8, 2013.

[40] U.S. Code, Title 17, Section 102. Available at http://www.law.cornell.edu/uscode/text/17/102. Accessed November 8, 2013.

[41] As recently as 2014, a federal judge denied protection for a dance routine on the grounds that the performance had not been fixed in a tangible medium of protection. The case, *Catherine Conrad v. AM Community Credit Union et al.*, U.S. Court of Appeals, Seventh Circuit, No. 13–2899, April 14, 2014, arose when Conrad, known as the "Banana Lady," sued the organizers of a credit union trade association event for failing to prevent audience members from uploading pictures and videos of her routine onto the Internet. See https://www.techdirt.com/articles/20140414/18072826914/judge-richard-posners-ruling-wacky-banana-lady-case-highlights-just-how-wrong-judge-kozinski-was-about-copyright.shtml. Accessed November 3, 2014.

[42] For more on fixation as a problem for choreography, see Julie Van Camp, "Copyright of Choreographic Works," in *1994–95 Entertainment, Publishing and the Arts Handbook*, ed. Stephen F. Breimer, Robert Thorne, and John David Viera (New York: Clark, Boardman, and Callaghan, 1994), 59–92. Also available at http://www.csulb.edu/~jvancamp/copyrigh.html. Accessed September 5, 2013.

than choreography writ large. In a recent essay, Gerald Siegmund draws on Giorgio Agamaben's analysis of the 1679 *Habeas Corpus* act, which codified rights of self-ownership and legal personhood, to read William Forsythe's 2005 work *Human Writes*. Choreography, Siegmund proposes, serves as the bridge between the body and the law, whose relationship is always one of friction. Even choreography that varies with each performance functions as a "quasi-legal agreement," a set of "rules" and "limitations" that governs how dancers interact with one another and with audience members and that creates a "communal togetherness" for the duration of a performance.[43] If choreography is like the law, the composite term "choreographic copyright" is overdetermined from the start. Yet, however much choreography may be *like* the law, a history of choreographic copyright makes clear how uneasy the relationship between the two has been.

Conceptually speaking, "choreographic copyright" is perhaps more productively viewed as a meeting place between theories of intellectual property on the one hand and theories of the body, dance, and choreography on the other. Placed side by side, the two terms illustrate points of commonality as well as points of conflict between one another. The following sections flesh out these convergences and divergences, focusing specifically on issues of in/tangibility, dis/embodiment, and in/alienability.

The Material of Dance

Although the term "property" colloquially implies a physical possession, copyright law is designed to protect something "wholly immaterial":[44] the fruits of intellectual labor. Definitions of intellectual property law vary, but their protection of "*intangible* cultural goods" is a constant.[45] Intellectual property law might even be thought of as doubly intangible: not only does it cover "creations of the mind," but also, as the prominent property scholar C. B. Macpherson has emphasized, property is "not things but *rights*."[46] Both intellectual property law's content and its form are thus intangible. Again, we tend to think

---

[43] Gerald Siegmund, "Negotiating Choreography, Letter, and Law in William Forsythe," in *New German Dance Studies*, ed. Susan Manning and Lucia Ruprecht (Urbana: University of Illinois Press), 206, 211, 213.

[44] Rose, *Authors and Owners*, 73.

[45] Boatema Boateng, *The Copyright Thing Doesn't Work Here: Adinkra and Kente Cloth and Intellectual Property in Ghana* (Minneapolis: University of Minnesota Press, 2011), 7, emphasis in original.

[46] http://www.wipo.int/about-ip/en/index.html. Accessed October 7, 2013; C. B. Macpherson, ed., *Property: Mainstream and Critical Positions* (Toronto: University of Toronto Press, 1978), 2, emphasis in original.

through copyright in tangible terms: the landed estate is a recurrent trope in the discourse of intellectual property rights, and spatial metaphors—such as the idea of the "enclosure" of the commons, or the idea of trespassing—are particularly prevalent in discussions of copyright.[47] Nevertheless, "intellectual property's lack of 'thingness,'" to quote legal scholar Jessica Litman, makes it "difficult to fit intellectual property within the real property rubric."[48] The lack of physical boundaries surrounding intellectual property is in fact what gave rise to the fixity and tangibility requirements of copyright law.[49]

Dance, too, is (in)famous for its lack of "thingness." Within dance theory, the very idea of a "choreographic work" imposes on dance a concreteness and discreteness that arguably go against its materiality—the fact that it is always fluid, never final. Actually, one of the central paradoxes for dance studies is that dance and the body can be figured as tangible and intangible, material and immaterial. Consider the following descriptions of the body from two foundational texts in dance studies, published within a year of one another:

> Illusive, always on the move, the body is at best *like* something, but it never is that something. Thus, the metaphors, enunciated in speech or in movement that allude to it are what give the body the most tangible substance it has.[50]

And

> *Corporealities* seeks to vivify the study of bodies through a consideration of bodily reality, not as natural or absolute given but as a tangible and substantial category of cultural experience.[51]

Taken together, the body becomes both airy and solid, the product of discourse and the thing that grounds discursive experience. By a similar token, references to dance's materiality can denote either the concrete physicality of the body or the transience of performance. In André Lepecki's volume *Of the Presence of the Body*, Ramsay Burt describes the "materiality of the body"

[47] Wendy Gordon, "An Inquiry into the Merits of Copyright: The Challenges of Consistency, Consent and Encouragement Theory," *Stanford Law Review* 41 (1989): 1346–47.

[48] Litman, "The Public Domain," 971.

[49] Gordon, "An Inquiry," 1380.

[50] Susan Leigh Foster, "Introduction," in *Choreographing History*, ed. Susan Leigh Foster (Bloomington: Indiana University Press, 1995), 4, emphasis in original.

[51] Susan Leigh Foster, "Introduction," *Corporealities: Dancing Knowledge, Culture and Power*, ed. Susan Leigh Foster (London: Routledge, 1996), xi.

as that which "troubles and disturbs" disembodied ideas about what constitutes choreography, while Lepecki equates dance's materiality with its alleged ephemerality, a problem that documentation systems seek to "correct."[52]

Writing about "the materiality of performance" more broadly, Erika Lin helpfully outlines the various meanings that "materialist" has taken on within academic discourse, ranging from studies of everyday objects, to Marxist analysis of the social relations of production, to Judith Butler's influential theory of reiterative citation, to Foucaultian "baseline assumptions and expectations," or "that which need never be spoken but which tacitly structures modes of comprehension."[53] For her part, Lin approaches performance

> both as an object of study, located in the interstices between the tangible and the intangible, and as an epistemology, a way of knowing that bears within it transformative force. Its immateriality as the former is essential to its materiality as the latter: it is only because performance is *not* fixed that it can take one thing and turn it into something else.[54]

I find Lin's location of performance "in the interstices" between tangibility and intangibility a useful place to situate the body, dance, and choreography. Because the body—incontrovertibly physical but always in the process of becoming and always slowly disintegrating[55]—confounds oppositions

---

[52] Ramsay Burt, "Genealogy and Dance History: Foucault, Rainer, Bausch and de Keersmaeker," in *Of the Presence of the Body: Essays on Dance and Performance Theory*, ed. André Lepecki (Middletown, CT: Wesleyan University Press), 30; Lepecki, "Inscribing Dance," in *Of the Presence of the Body*, 130. Likewise, in Susan Leigh Foster's most recent book, *Choreographing Empathy: Kinesthesia in Performance* (London: Routledge, 2011), it is notation that imparts to dance the (masculine) materiality that positions it on an equal playing field with other art forms, like music (38, 42–43). In another important dance studies volume, Amy Koritz critiques the ways in which, in the work of some cultural studies and feminist studies scholars in the early 1990s, "attention to the body is supposed to authorize intellectual work by guaranteeing its relevance to the material 'real world.'" Koritz, "Re/Moving Boundaries: From Dance History to Cultural Studies," in *Moving Words: Re-writing Dance*, ed. Gay Morris (London: Routledge, 1996), 91. Standing in for material reality, that is, the body is supposed to do the work of grounding discourse. See Andrew Hewitt, *Social Choreography: Ideology as Performance in Dance and Everyday Movement* (Durham, NC: Duke University Press, 2005) on the contested nature of materiality in aesthetic discourse in the nineteenth century.

[53] Erika T. Lin, *Shakespeare and the Materiality of Performance* (New York: Palgrave Macmillan, 2012), 8.

[54] Ibid., 7.

[55] See Foucault, "Nietzsche, History, Genealogy," in *Language, Counter-Memory, Practice: Selected Essays and Interviews by Michel Foucault*, ed. Donald F. Bouchard (Ithaca, NY: Cornell University Press, 1977) on the body as "a volume in perpetual disintegration" (148).

between tangibility and intangibility, dance and choreography too are caught betwixt and between these poles.

Rather than seeing choreography and copyright in terms of conflicting materialities, then, we might more productively see them in terms of overlapping and equally volatile im/materialities. Relative to the literary work that copyright law was originally designed to protect, choreography may seem the opposite of tangible; relative to the defined boundaries of real estate, intellectual property likewise dissolves into intangibility, so much so that it has been described, like dance and performance, as "intrinsically evanescent."[56] This is important to bear in mind given how frequently dancers' pursuit of intellectual property rights for choreography has been framed as a quest for the status of materiality (see especially Chapter 4). Understanding that quest as inexorably fraught, we can approach choreographic copyright as a provocative problem rather than a solution. As well, understanding the constant pull between materiality and immateriality within copyright can provide a useful model for conceptualizing dance's ontological status.

Personhood and Dis/Embodiment

Another node of intersection between choreography and copyright can be found in the notions of personhood that reside within each. To shine light on this intersection, it is worth rehearsing some of the theories of property that underpin US copyright law. The idea of property itself "has a complex legacy that has filtered through the ideas of key political thinkers from John Locke to Karl Marx and beyond."[57] In the United States, copyright law is particularly indebted to a tradition of liberalism in which the autonomous individual and self-ownership reign supreme. A consensus holds that a Lockean labor theory of value, also known as natural rights theory, heavily influenced the view of property embedded in the Constitution.[58] Cited in nearly every study

[56] Comaroffs, *Ethnicity, Inc.*, 34. As Alan Hyde writes in his study of discursive constructions of the body in American legal discourse, "the body is material only in a world that has already constructed a great deal else as nonmaterial." *Bodies of Law* (Princeton, NJ: Princeton University Press, 1997), 9.

[57] Laura Brace, *The Politics of Property: Labour, Freedom and Belonging* (New York: Palgrave Macmillan, 2004), 1.

[58] See, for example, Macpherson, *Property*, 13; Justin Hughes, "The Philosophy of Intellectual Property," *Georgetown Law Journal* 77 (1988): 288. There are exceptions to this consensus, however. B. Zorina Khan, for example, argues that the US intellectual property system differed dramatically from Europe's in its pragmatic pursuit of economic development over and above the embrace of an individual's "natural" rights. Khan sees the US Constitution's codification of intellectual property as epitomizing the country's democratic ideals. B. Zorina Khan,

of intellectual property rights, John Locke's 1690 *Two Treatises of Government* states:

> Though the Earth, and all the inferior Creatures be common to all Men, yet every Man has a *Property* in his own *Person*. This no Body has any Right to but himself. The *Labour* of his Body, and the *Work* of his Hands, we may say, are properly his. Whatsoever then he removes out of the State that Nature hath provided, and left it in, he hath mixed his *Labour* with, and joined to it something that is his own, and thereby makes it his *Property*.[59]

The key innovation of Locke's theory was his assertion of property as a "natural" right of the individual, independent of any civil society or government.[60] According to C. B. Macpherson, Locke's notion of property in one's person helped give rise to the powerful doctrine of "possessive individualism," which unified "English political thought from the seventeenth to the nineteenth centuries," became one of the cornerstones of liberal democracy, and remains a central feature of modern Western culture.[61] It also underpins the idea that authors are entitled to the products of their intellectual labor. Of course, as I discuss below, Locke's individual is decidedly gendered as well as raced, giving the lie to the universality of his "natural rights."

The other principal way of justifying intellectual property rights is through what is known as the personality theory. Associated with the German philosopher Georg Wilhelm Friedrich Hegel and advanced by the legal scholar Margaret Radin, the "personhood perspective" defends copyright on the grounds that "an idea belongs to its creator because the idea is a manifestation of the creator's personality or self."[62] In general, this perspective is more closely aligned with the moral rights doctrines of Continental copyright systems, which are more expansive and more concerned with the "integrity" of the author than is US copyright

---

The Democratization of Invention: Patents and Copyrights in American Economic Development, 1790–1920 (New York: Cambridge University Press, 2005), esp. 15, 8.

[59] John Locke, *Two Treatises of Government*, ed. Peter Laslett (London: Cambridge University Press, 1967 [1690]), 305–6, emphasis in original.

[60] C. B. Macpherson, *The Political Theory of Possessive Individualism: Hobbes to Locke* (London: Oxford University Press, 1962), 198.

[61] Ibid., vii; Richard Handler, "Who Owns the Past? History, Cultural Property, and the Logic of Possessive Individualism," in *The Politics of Culture*, ed. Brett Williams (Washington: Smithsonian Institution Press, 1991), 63–74.

[62] Hughes, "The Philosophy of Intellectual Property," 330; Margaret Jane Radin, "Property and Personhood," *Stanford Law Review* 34.5 (1982): 957–1015.

law.[63] But the ties between personality and property are by no means absent from the history of copyright in this country.[64] Personality emerged explicitly in the 1903 Supreme Court case *Bleistein v. Donaldson Lithographing Co.*, which concerned the copyright of circus posters. Weighing whether commercial advertisements designed by the plaintiff qualified for copyright protection, Justice Oliver Wendell Holmes concluded that

> The copy [here, the chromolithographed poster] is the personal reaction of an individual upon nature. Personality always contains something unique. It expresses its singularity even in handwriting, and a very modest grade of art has in it something irreducible, which is one man's alone. That something he may copyright.[65]

Writing about the decision, theater scholar Julia Walker notes that Holmes's thinking drew on the contemporaneous expressive culture movement, "where 'personality' meant that which was wholly unique and unreproducible within the individual."[66]

Both the Lockean and the personality theories, then, root property in the uniqueness and sanctity of the individual.[67] Precisely because of his uniqueness—and it is safe to say that neither Locke nor Holmes used "men" in an ecumenical sense—each individual is conceived of as the rightful proprietor of that which issues from his body, his labor, and his personality. Although Holmes does not mention the body explicitly, his reference to handwriting lodges personality in the distinctness of the (moving, signing) body. In Locke and Holmes, in other words, both labor and personality are embodied; the

[63] As intellectual property scholar Peter Jaszi explains, authors' moral rights include "the right to control the circumstances in which the work will be released to the public ..., the right to withdraw the work from circulation, the right to claim of attribution ..., and the right to object to the distortion or mutilation of the work." See Peter Jaszi, "Toward a Theory of Copyright: The Metamorphoses of 'Authorship," *Duke Law Journal* 40.2 (1991): 496.

[64] Radin argues that personhood is "often implicit in the connections that courts and commentators find between property and privacy or between property and liberty" ("Property and Personhood," 957).

[65] *Bleistein v. Donaldson Lithographing Co.*, 188 U.S. 239 (1903) at 250.

[66] Julia A. Walker, *Expressionism and Modernism in the American Theatre: Bodies, Voices, Words* (Cambridge: Cambridge University Press, 2005), 85.

[67] Mark Rose's study of the origins of copyright asserts that concerns about an author's reputation and persona were as much at stake in early concepts of literary property as economic issues. He writes, "The attempt to anchor the notion of literary property in personality suggests the need to find a transcendent signifier, a category beyond the economic to warrant and ground the circulation of literary commodities." *Authors and Owners: The Invention of Copyright* (Cambridge, MA: Harvard University Press, 1993), 128.

body is the source of and the mechanism through which labor and personality express themselves. Embodiment thus provides the link between property and personhood.

Following this logic, it is not hard to see why some dance-makers have argued so ardently for intellectual property rights in choreography. The notion that each dancer possesses a unique way of moving, and that something of her personality manifests itself in her movement style, runs deep. Dance has its own version of handwriting—the "signature step"—which, I propose in Chapter 3, is an embodied way of claiming possession of movement. Ballet choreographer Agnes de Mille, a vociferous crusader for choreographic copyright (and one of the chief subjects of Chapter 4), explained that, as an artist, she was compelled to respond to stimuli "through [her] instinctive gestures" that reflect "a personality habit." "There is further personal identification in choreography," she added, "because most choreographers compose on their own bodies. Certain recurring steps can be explained simply by the fact that the choreographer performs these steps well and has a tendency to use them when demonstrating."[68] By way of example, she cited Martha Graham's penchant for choreographing split kicks on the left leg, but we could also point to Bob Fosse's "signature" pigeon-toed stance and slouching posture. He attributed his style to his "own limitations as a dancer," which "forced [him] into a certain economy of movement."[69]

The development of modern dance, moreover, is bound up with theories of the expressivity and individuality of the body. Sharing artistic modernism's emphasis on the autonomous individual and heavily influenced by the movement principles of Francois Delsarte, who approached movement as an expression of one's emotional interiority, US modern dance in the first decades of the twentieth century rested on and advanced the notion that original movement proceeded "from the core of the individual"; in early modern dance, bodies externalized what was internal and proper to the self.[70]

---

[68] Agnes de Mille, *And Promenade Home* (Boston: Little, Brown, 1958), 185–86.

[69] Kevin Boyd Grubb, *Razzle Dazzle: The Life and Work of Bob Fosse* (New York: St. Martin's Press, 1989), 25.

[70] See Julia Foulkes, *Modern Bodies: Dance and American Modernism from Martha Graham to Alvin Ailey* (Chapel Hill: University of North Carolina Press, 2002), 34; Shea Murphy, *The People Have Never Stopped Dancing*, 55; Foster, *Choreographing Empathy*, 178; Mark Franko, *Dancing Modernism/Performing Politics* (Bloomington: Indiana University Press, 1995), especially x, 8. For more on the influence of Delsarte on American modern dance, see Nancy Chalfa Ruyter, *Reformers and Visionaries: The Americanization of the Art of Dance* (New York: Dance Horizons, 1979), and Ted Shawn, *Every Little Movement* (Pittsfield: Eagle Printing and Binding, 1954). Recent dance scholarship has pointed to the raced and gendered implications inherent in the idea of modern dance as expressive of an interiority. Susan Manning observes that, in the early decades of the twentieth century, white bodies were perceived as "intentionally expressive," while black

As we will see, however, the legal arena has not always been receptive to the idea that female dancing bodies are expressive of anything. Much more common was the view of women dancers as vacuous spectacles. If the concept of an embodied self has helped justify intellectual property rights in certain kinds of works, embodiment in practice has had a much more problematic relationship to legal and political subjecthood. The "body" that emerged in legal discourse in the nineteenth century, Alan Hyde explains, referred to an individuated person who lived inside a body and who controlled that body but was "not identical to it."[71] By the same token, "To be a subject in the bourgeois public sphere required identification with a disembodied public subject."[72] Achieving the status of personhood has thus depended equally on ownership of one's body and the ability to abstract or transcend that body. This privilege, as I review below, has historically been reserved for white, property-owning males. The bodiliness of dance has unquestionably complicated dance-makers' legal claims to possessive individualism, which simultaneously hinges on and disavows the subject's corporeality. Yet, what choreographic copyright offered dancers, the case studies in this book suggest, was precisely the prospect of abstracting the body from choreography. Like choreography itself, and like legal personhood, choreographic copyright "simultaneously include[es] and exclude[es] the body."[73] In fixing and boosting one version of a dance to the status of a legally protected "work," choreographic copyright has held out the paradoxical promise that it could materialize (make matter, as in solidify and render important) and de-materialize (detach from the purely corporeal) the dancing bodies of those seeking its protection.

bodies were seen as "naturally rhythmic and expressive" (*Modern Dance, Negro Dance*, 4). In the same period, Susan Leigh Foster notes, "oriental dances" were conceived as "concentric and compressive" in contrast to "occidental dances," which were "eccentric and emotionally expressive" (*Choreographing Empathy*, 58). Julia Foulkes, meanwhile, argues that the "newer emphasis on the expressive and internal forms of self allowed for more female participation in the arts, partly because women had been identified with sentiment and feeling over intellect, and also because the process of internalization that these beliefs inspired required little public forum" (*Modern Bodies*, 34).

[71] Hyde, *Bodies of Law*, 9.

[72] Coombe, *The Cultural Life of Intellectual Properties*, 171. For more on subjecthood and the public sphere, see Michael Warner, "The Mass Public and the Mass Subject," in *Habermas and the Public Sphere*, ed. Craig Calhoun (Cambridge, MA: MIT Press, 1991), 377–401; and Nancy Fraser, "Rethinking the Public Sphere: A Contribution to the Critique of Actually Existing Democracy," *Social Text* 25/26 (1990): 56–80.

[73] Siegmund, "Negotiating Choreography," 204.

Commodification and In/Alienability

If copyright and choreography jointly grapple with issues of in/tangibility and dis/embodiment, their relationship to commodification—and attendant issues of reproducibility and alienability—is more lopsided. As a rule, intellectual property closely "follows the lines of commodity production."[74] Commodification, in turn, would not be possible without ownership. David Harvey writes that "Commodification presumes the existence of property rights over processes, things, and social relations, that a price can be put on them, and that they can be traded subject to legal contract."[75] Conversely, copyright transforms expression into commodified "works" with exchange value in a capitalist marketplace. Authorizing certain copies and prohibiting others, copyright is essentially about the "double movement of circulation and restriction" of these works within an economy of reproduction.[76] Dance, however, has a vexed relationship to the commodity form, and its circulation is not identical to that of a physical object like a novel or playscript. Addressing the conversion of choreography into property, therefore, requires asking how the reproduction of dance does and does not follow the lines of commodity production.

It is tempting to see dance as resistant to commodification. In his discussion of the historical difficulties facing those who have tried to assess what a dancer produces and how to assign market value to it, Mark Franko describes dance as "the artwork least suggestive of itself as a stable object or product."[77] Acclaimed choreographer Bill T. Jones has likewise pointed to dance's lack of a product as responsible for its relatively low value in contemporary culture.[78] Much of the appeal of defining dance as ephemeral surely lies in how unconducive it makes dance seem to commodification. In her famous alignment of performance with disappearance, Peggy Phelan asserts that "Performance clogs the smooth machinery of reproductive representation necessary to the circulation of capital."[79] The existence of choreographic copyright intrudes on this arguably romanticized view, forcing us to recognize dance's complicity with a capitalist reproductive economy.[80]

[74] Jane M. Gaines, *Contested Culture: The Image, the Voice, and the Law* (Chapel Hill: University of North Carolina Press, 1991), 192.

[75] David Harvey, *A Brief History of Neoliberalism* (New York: Oxford University Press, 2005), 165.

[76] Gaines, *Contested Culture*, 9.

[77] Mark Franko, *The Work of Dance: Labor, Movement, and Identity in the 1930s* (Middletown, CT: Wesleyan University Press, 2002), 2.

[78] Quoted in Rachel Aviv, "The Imperial Presidency," *The New Yorker*, September 9, 2013, 64.

[79] Phelan, *Unmarked*, 148.

[80] Of course, Phelan's argument about performance's ontology has been contested from multiple angles by scholars working in dance, theater, and performance studies. Perhaps most pointedly, thinking about black performance in the United States requires us to confront the

To that end, it is helpful to think of commodities in broader terms than mass-produced articles of commerce. Arjun Appadurai's recommendation that we view a commodity as *"any thing intended for exchange"* and that we look "at the commodity potential of all things rather than searching fruitlessly for the magic distinction between commodities and other sorts of things" is a useful starting place for figuring dance's relationship to commodification.[81] Like other forms of cultural production, dance can "move in *and* out of the commodity state."[82] Intellectual property is one such example of a commodity state, a condition that choreography moves through as dance-makers make ownership claims on embodied activity and as those claims are tested by the judicial system.

Still, we should not entirely dismiss dance's ability to create disruptions in the machinery of commodification. As Thomas DeFrantz points out with respect to black social dance, even as it circulates readily in global markets under the neoliberal sign of freedom, its "protean abilities ... render it less available as a whole to methodologies that could create easily owned materials of commodity."[83] In addition to its mutability, dance has a problematic relationship to alienability. A term with many meanings, "alienation" typically refers to some form of estrangement. For Marx, alienation was a "characteristic feature of modern capitalism," a result of the privatization of property and the worker's lack of ownership over the means of production; under Marxist

circulation of capital *as* the circulation of performing bodies, a view I explore in Chapter 2, where I draw on the challenge to Phelan developed by Fred Moten in *In the Break: The Aesthetics of the Black Radical Tradition* (Minneapolis: University of Minnesota Press, 2003). My invocation of Phelan here is not meant to re-hash the debate about performance's ontology but to suggest how a focus on copyright may problematize the very terms of the debate. In the argument this book advances, choreographic copyright represents dance's simultaneous complicity with and attempted resistance to commodification. More recently, the growing importance of "immaterial" or "affective" labor to the global economy has prompted reconsiderations of performance's kinship with—rather than opposition to—the structures of late capitalism. For example, as Nicholas Ridout and Rebecca Schneider suggest in their introduction to a journal issue on "Precarity and Performance": "At one time, claims for resistance to commodity capitalism were addressed through the idea that performance does not offer an object for sale. What of the performing body in an economy where the laboring body, and its production of affect, is the new commodity du jour?" "Precarity and Performance: An Introduction," *TDR: The Drama Review* 56.4 (Winter 2012): 6.

[81] Arjun Appadurai, "Introduction: Commodities and the Politics of Value," in *The Social Life of Things: Commodities in Cultural Perspective*, ed. Arjun Appadurai (Cambridge: Cambridge University Press, 1986), 9, 13, emphasis in original.

[82] Ibid., 13.

[83] Thomas DeFrantz, "Unchecked Popularity: Neoliberal Circulations of Black Social Dance," in *Neoliberalism and Global Theatres: Performance Permutations*, ed. Lara Nielsen and Patricia Ybarra (New York: Palgrave Macmillan, 2012), 135.

theory, "alienated labor ... and private property ... stand in a reciprocal relationship."[84] Alienation is critical to property law, under which the term simply means "the action of transferring legal ownership of something."[85] Copyright itself has a twofold relationship to alienability. First, like all forms of property, intellectual property is legally transferrable from one person to another. And second, in its conversion of the expression of ideas into property, copyright executes a separation between the author and her work, between her ideas and the expression of those ideas. This is implicit in the very term "copyright," literally the right to copy: the severability of copies from an original is a basic precondition of copyright. Alienability is also one of the primary distinctions between Anglo-American copyright law and the Continental legal system of "author's rights," which are generally considered inalienable.[86]

It is here, within copyright's alienability, that dance poses complications. As the Yeats line goes, "How can we know the dancer from the dance?" Especially when the author is also the performer (as was the case in the early examples I examine in this book), is it possible to detach the choreographic work from the choreographer, the dancing body from the choreography? Priya Srinivasan has written that "In the labor of dance, the dancing body as a commodity cannot be separated from its means of production."[87] In other words, if we define commodities "as goods and services that are, or could be, bought and sold at some point," choreography presents itself as simultaneously good and service: to exist as a good, it requires the service of dancing.[88] Or, to state it yet another way, "dance requires an enactment, an embodied practice and labor of performance, in order to be."[89] If a complete separation between labor and product, author and work, is not always possible in dance, we might say there is something inalienable about choreography. As a result, though dance is by no means immune to commodification, it may remain

---

[84] "Alienation," in David Macey, *The Penguin Dictionary of Critical Theory* (London: Penguin Books, 2000), 7; Jane Gaines, *Contested Culture*, 195.

[85] "Alienation," OED, http://www.oed.com/view/Entry/4999?redirectedFrom=alienation#eid. Accessed November 13, 2013.

[86] See Jaszi, "Toward a Theory of Copyright," 478n.87; Saint-Amour, *The Copywrights*, 235n.1. The one exception to the alienability of US copyright law is in the realm of visual arts. Under the Visual Artists Rights Act of 1990, non-commercial painters, illustrators, sculptors, and photographers retain rights of attribution and integrity regardless of who owns the work itself. Jaszi, "Toward a Theory of Copyright," 499.

[87] Srinivasan, *Sweating Saris*, 144.

[88] Martha M. Ertman and Joan C. Williams, "Preface: Freedom, Equality, and the Many Futures of Commodification," in *Rethinking Commodification: Cases and Readings in Law and Culture*, ed. Martha Ertman and Joan Williams (New York: New York University Press, 2005), 3.

[89] Marta Savigliano, "Worlding Dance and Dancing Out There in the World," in *Worlding Dance*, ed. Susan Leigh Foster (London: Palgrave Macmillan, 2009), 165.

"incompletely commodified—neither fully commodified nor fully removed from the market."[90]

Which parts of dance are commodified when choreography becomes intellectual property, and which parts remain uncommodified? If the impracticality of removing dancers from choreography suggests that the body is the portion that evades complete commodification, it is also true that the body is always implicated in the commodification of dance. This is what is precisely so unsettling in thinking about dance as commodity: it can mean the "reduction of the person (subject) to a thing (object)."[91] Because it is an embodied form, the commodification of dance can feel unseemly, not so far afield from practices like prostitution, surrogacy, and the sale of human organs, which have generated much debate among scholars over what kinds of limits we should place on commodification.[92] Yet, as I suggested above and as I will argue throughout this book, dancers who turned to copyright did so to counter the commodification of their bodies; claiming copyright was an assertion of propertied subjecthood against the forces of objectification. This is one of the principal paradoxes of choreographic copyright: it is simultaneously an acknowledgment of dance's susceptibility to commodification and a means of resisting that commodification. It simultaneously renders the dancing body owner and thing owned.

Racing and Gendering Property

Property, personhood, possessive individualism, in/alienability: these concepts are part of the legacy of the Enlightenment's emphasis on the autonomous

[90] Margaret Jane Radin, "Market-Inalienability," *Harvard Law Review* 100.8 (June 1987): 1855. Radin develops the concept of "market-inalienability" to consider whether some things should be non-salable: "market-inalienability does not render something inseparable from the person, but rather specifies that market trading may not be used as a social mechanism of separation" (1854). My interest here, by contrast, is in a kind of inalienability that does render a product inseparable from a person. Radin cites the regulation of labor as an example of what she calls "the social aspect of incomplete commodification": "collective bargaining, minimum wage requirements, maximum hour limitations, health and safety requirements, unemployment insurance, retirement benefits, prohibition of child labor, and antidiscrimination requirements" are regulations that attempt to "take into account workers'... personhood, to recognize and foster the nonmarket significance of their work" (1919–20).

[91] Margaret Jane Radin and Madhavi Sunder, "Introduction: The Subject and Object of Commodification," in *Rethinking Commodification*, 8.

[92] See generally Ertman and Williams, *Rethinking Commodification*. Carol Wolkowitz's *Bodies at Work* (London: Sage, 2006) offers a useful survey of various conceptualizations of the body in scholarship on prostitution/sex work. See also Kate Elswit's chapter on the commodification of female bodies in *Watching Weimar Dance* (New York: Oxford University Press, 2014), 60–94.

individual. Far from universal, such constructs have been key instruments of exclusion and domination along more than one axis. That property ownership has functioned to "crystalli[z]e" and "reinforce" class difference is rather self-evident, given the ties between land ownership, status, and wealth.[93] Perhaps less obvious but no less consequential is the imbrication of property with race and gender.

Feminist scholars have written persuasively about the patriarchal foundations of property as both idea and material reality. For Carole Pateman, the very notion of "the 'individual' as owner" provides "the fulcrum on which modern patriarchy turns," because only "masculine beings are endowed with the attributes and capacities necessary to enter into contracts."[94] For Margaret Davies, histories of objectifying, commodifying, and literally owning women render property "deeply gendered" and inflect the category of gender "with the thought of property."[95] Davies also points to the structural parallels between the owner/owned and male/female dyads. Within this equation, "the concrete, bodily aspect of property (the thing owned) is female, while the conceptual, abstract, sovereign dimension is male. *Being* property characterizes the female condition, while *having* it denotes self-owning masculinity."[96] Melissa Homestead's work on the intersections in the nineteenth-century United States between copyright law and coverture, a common law doctrine that prevented married women from owning property, provides a powerful example of the real-world implications of this logic. Despite achieving literary and commercial success, the (mostly white, middle-class) women authors on whom Homestead focuses were confined to a legal status as "nonproprietary subjects."[97] Coverture laws were no longer in place at the end of the nineteenth century when the examples in this book begin. But the ramifications of the gendering of property-ownership seem especially profound when we are

[93] Brace, *The Politics of Property*, 41.

[94] Carole Pateman, *The Sexual Contract* (Cambridge, UK: Blackwell, 1988), 14, 5–6.

[95] Margaret Davies, "Queer Property, Queer Persons: Self-Ownership and Beyond," *Social Legal Studies* 8 (1999): 329, 330. Davies's brilliant essay proposes that "queering" property may be a way of challenging its binaristic logic.

[96] Ibid., 340, emphasis in original. See also Ngaire Naffine, "The Legal Structure of Self-Ownership: Or the Self-Possessed Man and the Woman Possessed," *Journal of Law and Society* 25.2 (June 1998): 193–212; and Ann Bartow, "Fair Use and the Fairer Sex: Gender, Feminism, and Copyright Law," *Journal of Gender, Social Policy, and the Law* 14.2 (2006): 551–84. Laura J. Rosenthal's gendered analysis of plagiarism, *Playwrights and Plagiarists in Early Modern England* (Ithaca, NY: Cornell University Press, 1996), similarly argues that "the position of owner emerges as ... tenuous for most people and sometimes explicitly unavailable to women and to men outside of dominant masculinity or elite status" (4).

[97] Melissa J. Homestead, *American Women Authors and Literary Property, 1822–1869* (New York: Cambridge University Press, 2005), 10.

talking about an already feminized medium like dance, and when the property in question possesses not only a "bodily aspect" but is itself bodily. For female choreographers, following this thinking, copyrighting dance becomes an act of both reinscribing and subverting gender norms: further feminizing the dance (as property) while masculinizing the choreographer (as property owner). Although *Choreographing Copyright* focuses more on the material than the figurative dimensions of intellectual property rights, the women examined here inarguably sought to take on the male prerogative of possessive individualism, with mixed success.

Scholars have offered equally forceful insights about property's racial entanglements. The institution of slavery, some have observed, was the "precondition" to the Lockean principle of property in one's person.[98] Locke's self-owning individual, that is, emerged "not merely in contrast to but to a certain extent on the backs of non-white subpersons."[99] Certainly, in the antebellum United States, slaves had no access to Locke's "natural right" and no access to legal personhood. Further still, Saidiya Hartman has proposed that "as property, the dispossessed body of the enslaved is the surrogate for the master's body since it guarantees his disembodied universality and acts as the sign of his power and dominion."[100] The thingness of the slave served to secure the personhood of the white slave owner.

Critical race theory, often abbreviated as CRT, has been particularly influential on my own thinking about intellectual property. Spearheaded by Kimberlé Williams Crenshaw in the late 1980s, CRT is not a homogenous legal doctrine but is united by a commitment to examining "the unconscious ways that race shapes legal thinking."[101] Broadly speaking, Richard Delgado and Jean Stefancic explain, CRT "sets out not only to ascertain how society organizes itself along racial lines and hierarchies, but to transform it for the better."[102] The pioneering work of K. J. Greene has extended this approach to the arena

[98] Gaines, *Contested Culture*, 19.

[99] Charles W. Mills, *Blackness Visible: Essays on Philosophy and Race* (Ithaca, NY: Cornell University Press, 1998), 128.

[100] Saidiya V. Hartman, *Scenes of Subjection: Terror, Slavery, and Self-Making in Nineteenth-Century America* (New York: Oxford University Press, 1997), 21.

[101] Lovalerie King and Richard Schur, "Introduction: 'Justice Unveiled,'" in *African American Culture and Legal Discourse*, ed. Lovalerie King and Richard Schur (New York: Palgrave Macmillan, 2009), 6. Key scholars in the CRT movement also include Richard Delgado, Neil Gotanda, Mari Matsuda, Stephanie Phillips, Kendall Thomas, Derrick Bell, and Patricia Williams. On the relationship between the critical legal studies movement and the critical race theory movement, see Richard L. Schur, *Parodies of Ownership: Hip-Hop Aesthetics and Intellectual Property Law* (Ann Arbor: University of Michigan Press, 2009), 25–27.

[102] Richard Delgado and Jean Stefancic, *Critical Race Theory: An Introduction* (New York: New York University Press, 2001), 7.

of intellectual property law. As Greene writes, "An underlying assumption of race-neutrality pervades copyright scholarship. However, not all creators of intellectual property are similarly situated in a race-stratified society and culture." Focusing on the systematic appropriation and exploitation of African Americans in the music industry, Greene exposes "the significant inequality of protection in the 'race-neutral' copyright regime."[103] He also suggests reparations as a possible remedy to the large-scale deprivation of black musicians "of credit, compensation and control."[104]

I share CRT's rejection of the idea that legal formations like copyright are neutral, apolitical structures, as well as its premise that the law has historically been weighted toward dominant white interests. Without question, the situation for African American dancers vis-à-vis copyright mirrors that outlined by Greene. Like their musician counterparts, black dancers in the United States have faced institutional discrimination, entrenched patterns of appropriation, and insidious stereotypes that refuse to recognize them as artists or authors, all of which have contributed to an unequal allocation of intellectual property rights. This book highlights those inequities by documenting the repeated treatment of non-white dance forms as part of the public domain and of black and brown dancing bodies as interchangeable commodities. At the same time, I am as interested in unearthing the ways in which whiteness and property rights have bolstered one another, especially in the lead-up to the 1976 Copyright Act that first extended protection to choreographic works, as on exposing the antagonism between intellectual property law and African American dancers.

Accordingly, this book is indebted at its core to another key work of critical race theory: Cheryl Harris's "Whiteness as Property." In this groundbreaking 1993 article, Harris argues that "rights in property are contingent on, intertwined with, and conflated with race," that whiteness is not only an identity but a legally protected status, and that it has functioned like a property right in the United States.[105] Harris locates the origins of whiteness's property-like functions in twin systems of oppression: the institution of chattel slavery, which

---

[103] K. J. Greene, "Copyright, Culture & Black Music: A Legacy of Unequal Protection," *Hastings Communication & Entertainment Law Journal* 21.2 (Winter 1999): 343. Other important work on racial inequality in intellectual property law includes Olufunmilayo B. Arewa, "Copyright on Catfish Row: Musical Borrowing, Porgy and Bess, and Unfair Use," *Rutgers Law Journal* 37.2 (2006): 277–353; and Keith Aoki, "Distributive and Syncretic Motives in Intellectual Property Law (with Special Reference to Coercion, Agency, and Development)," *UC-Davis Law Review* 40 (2007): 717–801.

[104] K. J. Greene, "'Copynorms,' Black Cultural Production, and the Debate over African-American Reparations," *Cardoza Arts & Entertainment Law Journal* 25.3 (2008): 1182.

[105] Cheryl I. Harris, "Whiteness as Property," *Harvard Law Review* 106.8 (1993): 1714.

exploited African American labor by rendering black people "objects of property," and the systematic "seizure and appropriation" of Native American land by whites.[106] After the abolition of slavery, Harris shows, American law continued to protect a racialized privilege in whiteness, first by sanctioning whites' right to exclude, as evident in the Supreme Court case *Plessy v. Ferguson* (1896), which ratified segregation, and then more subtly, in cases like *Brown v. Board of Education* (1954), which established "substantial inequality as a neutral base line" even as it overturned de jure segregation.[107] In the present day, the safeguarding of a property interest in whiteness is achieved "by embracing the norm of colorblindness," evident in recent affirmative action cases taken up by the Supreme Court.[108] Applying Harris's "racialized conception of property" to the realm of choreographic copyright underscores how central concerns about status were, and how pivotal the right to exclude was, to dance-makers' pursuit of legal protection.[109] Seen through the lens of CRT, that pursuit was alternately a fight to extend, defend, and challenge whiteness as property.

None of this is to say that I see race and gender as the primary factors in dancers' decisions to pursue copyright protection for their choreography or in determining the outcomes of their pursuits. Nor do I believe that race and gender are the only productive lenses that could be applied to the formation of choreographic copyright in the United States. What I do maintain is that because property rights in general have functioned as such a fundamental site of privilege and difference, we cannot ignore the ways in which copyright has operated similarly in the field of dance.

For Dance Studies

Bringing the insights of critical race and gender theory to bear on the history of copyright for choreography, *Choreographing Copyright* seeks to

[106] Ibid., 1716, 1715.

[107] Ibid., 1753.

[108] Ibid., 1768. In a related vein, George Lipsitz's 1998 book *The Possessive Investment in Whiteness* argues that "whiteness is invested in, like property, but it is also a means of accumulating property and keeping it from others." Discriminatory home lending practices, unequal educational opportunities, and intergenerational transfers of wealth, Lipsitz demonstrates, have all worked to sustain racial hierarchies and protect the "cash value" of whiteness. *The Possessive Investment in Whiteness* (Philadelphia: Temple University Press, 1998), vii–viii. For more on the property-like features of whiteness, see Derrick Bell, "White Superiority in America: Its Legal Legacy, Its Economic Costs," in *Black on White: Black Writers on What It Means to Be White*, ed. David R. Roediger (New York: Schocken Books, 1998), 138–50.

[109] Harris, "Whiteness as Property," 1715.

advance the conversation about how racial and gender difference matter in US dance.[110] The highly visible role of white women like Fuller, Holm, and de Mille in the fight to win copyright protection makes it impossible to overlook the importance of gender to the formation of choreographic copyright. In arguing that these women's pursuits of intellectual property rights were always in part an effort to challenge the patriarchal conditions of the theatrical marketplace, I continue the work of dance scholars who have so productively applied feminist theory to dance studies.[111] At the same time, my case studies confirm what other dance scholars have established: that gender never functions in isolation from other axes of difference and that the workings of gender cannot be divorced from the workings of race.[112]

Indeed, one of my foremost goals in this book is to contribute to discussions about the racialization of dancing bodies in the United States. In the last few decades, critical dance studies scholars have fruitfully critiqued the taken-for-granted privilege of white modern dance and the racial stratification that has governed the American dance landscape. Long overdue scholarship on African American, Native American, Asian American, and Latina/o American dance production, often in relation to Euro-American dance production, has theorized racial difference in dance as a matter of performance practices (i.e., aesthetic preferences, ways of moving, and representational conventions) and material structures (i.e., systems of patronage and federal

---

[110] My subsection title here is a nod to Randy Martin's chapter, "For Dance Studies," in *Critical Moves: Dance Studies and Theory and Politics* (Durham, NC: Duke University Press, 1998), 181–218. Randy Martin's gifts to the field of dance studies were vast and deep. He will be sorely missed for years to come.

[111] See, for example, Susan A. Manning, *Ecstasy and the Demon: Feminism and Nationalism in the Dances of Mary Wigman* (Berkeley: University of California Press, 1993); Ann Daly, *Done into Dance: Isadora Duncan in America* (Bloomington: Indiana University Press, 1995); Susan Leigh Foster, *Choreography and Narrative: Ballet's Staging of Story and Desire* (Bloomington: Indiana University Press, 1996); Ann Cooper Albright, *Choreographing Difference: The Body and Identity in Contemporary Dance* (Hanover, NH: Wesleyan University Press, 1997); Sally Banes, *Dancing Women: Female Bodies on Stage* (New York: Routledge, 1998); and Linda J. Tomko, *Dancing Class: Gender, Ethnicity, and Social Divides in American Dance, 1890–1920* (Bloomington: Indiana University Press, 1999).

[112] See, for example, Nadine George-Graves, *The Royalty of Negro Vaudeville: The Whitman Sisters and the Negotiation of Race, Gender, and Class in African-American Theater, 1900–1940* (New York: St. Martin's Press, 2000); Manning, *Modern Dance, Negro Dance*; Wong, *Choreographing Asian America*; Srinivasan, *Sweating Saris*; Ramón H. Rivera-Servera, *Performing Queer Latinidad: Dance, Sexuality, Politics* (Ann Arbor: University of Michigan Press, 2012); Cindy Garcia, *Salsa Crossings: Dancing Latinidad in Los Angeles* (Durham, NC: Duke University Press, 2013); and Rebecca Rossen, *Jewish Identity in American Modern and Postmodern Dance* (New York: Oxford University Press, 2014).

policies like immigration and citizenship laws).[113] Because my driving interest is in the formation of property rights in dance rather than performance analysis, *Choreographing Copyright* emphasizes the material conditions of race. As I explain below, I hope to push beyond notions of race as a strictly visual operation (perceptions of one's skin color and phenotype) or a cultural tradition (movement style) to show how it is equally a contest for rights over what dancers produce.

In particular, running through this book is an attempt to racialize whiteness—to treat whiteness not as the absence of race but, rather, as a powerful and historically contingent racial formation. As such, *Choreographing Copyright* places dance studies into dialogue with the field of whiteness studies. Cohering around a view of race as a social construction, whiteness studies emerged as an interdisciplinary academic field in the 1980s and 1990s, spurred by influential works like Peggy McIntosh's "White Privilege: Unpacking the Invisible Knapsack" (1989), David Roediger's *The Wages of Whiteness* (1991), Toni Morrison's *Playing in the Dark* (1992), Ruth Frankenberg's *White Women, Race Matters* (1993), and Richard Dyer's *White* (1997).[114] The roots of the project, though, extend back to W. E. B. Du Bois's 1935 work *Black Reconstruction in America 1860–1880*, which first offered the insight that white workers were more likely to identify along racial lines with other whites than along class lines with recently freed slaves because whiteness yielded a "public and psychological wage."[115] Collectively, literature on whiteness asks "how the taken-for-granted and invisible character of whiteness reinforces systems of advantage and disadvantage and how the construction of whiteness supports the hegemony of white power and the class structure."[116]

---

[113] See especially Gottschild, *Digging the Africanist Presence*; Manning, *Modern Dance, Negro Dance*; Thomas DeFrantz, ed., *Dancing Many Drums: Excavations in African-American Dance* (Madison: University of Wisconsin Press, 2001); Wong, *Choreographing Asian America*; Shea Murphy, *The People Have Never Stopped Dancing*; Srinivasan, *Sweating Saris*; Rivera-Servera, *Performing Queer Latinidad*; SanSan Kwan, *Kinesthetic City: Dance and Movement in Chinese Urban Spaces* (New York: Oxford University Press, 2013); Garcia, *Salsa Crossings*.

[114] Peggy McIntosh, "White Privilege: Unpacking the Invisible Knapsack," *Independent School* 49.2 (1990): 31–36; David Roediger, *The Wages of Whiteness* (New York: Verso, 1991); Toni Morrison, *Playing in the Dark: Whiteness in the Literary Imagination* (Cambridge, MA: Harvard University Press, 1992); Ruth Frankenberg, *White Women, Race Matters: The Social Construction of Whiteness* (Minneapolis: University of Minnesota Press, 1993); Richard Dyer, *White* (London: Routledge, 1997). For a discussion of three "waves" of whiteness studies, see France Winddance Twine and Charles A. Gallagher, "Introduction: The Future of Whiteness: A Map of the 'Third Wave,'" in *ReTheorizing Race and Whiteness in the 21st Century: Changes and Challenges*, ed. Charles Gallagher and France Twine (New York: Routledge, 2012), 1–20.

[115] W.E.B. Du Bois, *Black Reconstruction in America 1860–1880* (New York: Harcourt, Brace, 1935).

[116] Margaret L. Anderson, "Whitewashing Race: A Critical Perspective on Whiteness," in *White Out: The Continuing Significance of Racism*, ed. Ashley W. Doane and Eduardo Bonilla-Silva (New York: Routledge, 2003), 22.

Notwithstanding its commitment to anti-racism and to making visible invisible power structures, whiteness studies has come in for some incisive criticism. Focusing attention on whiteness necessarily runs the risk of reifying it "as a concept, as an experience, as an identity."[117] To the extent that it "provides a new academic opportunity for white people," moreover, whiteness studies seems to instate "a new form of white privilege."[118] Even efforts to de-universalize whiteness can be dubious. As Robyn Wiegman points out, one of the foundational moves of the field is to locate the history of whiteness in a "prewhite ethnic" past, the racialization of the Irish (often referred to as "black Irish") in the nineteenth century being the example par excellence. In this narrative, history functions to "rescue ... contemporary whiteness from the transcendent universalism that has been understood as its mode of productive power by providing prewhite particularity, which gets reproduced as prewhite injury and minoritization."[119] In Wiegman's trenchant analysis, attempts to shift the locus of white identity claims toward a "minoritized whiteness" that could serve as the basis for an anti-racist project actually do little to divest whiteness of its attachment to universalism, for "the white subject's claim to nonwhite particularity can be asserted only from the position of the universal." It is "in the space of the universal," that is, "and never the particular, that the theoretical mobility of political identification by definition takes place." We are left with "no theoretical, historical, or methodological escape from the impossibility of the antiracist white subject, partly because the very focus on the subject has far too much of the universal at stake."[120]

Critiquing whiteness studies from another angle, Eva Cherniavsky highlights what she sees as the narrow equation between white privilege and "colorlessness/unmarking."[121] The problem of approaching race "as a differentiating mark," with non-whiteness as the marked category and whiteness as the unmarked, is that it limits us to thinking about race as merely "a bodily inscription" in which "race makes a difference to the figuration of the body, exclusively, not to the fundamental condition of embodiment itself."[122] The marked/unmarked dyad, in other words, assumes that all bodies share a priori "a discrete organic form"—that bodies are conceptualized and lived identically across racial lines. Cherniavsky proposes that we replace a model of racial

[117] Ibid., 28.

[118] Ibid., 33.

[119] Robyn Wiegman, "Whiteness Studies and the Paradox of Particularity," *boundary 2* 26.3 (Fall 1999):137.

[120] Ibid., 147, 139, 147.

[121] Eva Cherniavsky, *Incorporations: Race, Nation, and the Body Politics of Capital* (Minneapolis: University of Minnesota Press, 2006).

[122] Ibid., xiii, xiv.

inscription with one of racial performativity. "The premise of performative identity," she explains,

> is that no body precedes its cultural determinations or offers an already constituted surface for inscription. Instead, this analysis seeks to account for the cultural production of bodies and bodily surfaces—how bodies take shape, in the first place, through activating and deactivating specific bodily zones, affects, and receptivities. The investigation of performative race therefore holds open the possibility that not all bodies may adhere to the same compositional logic of organic (good) form.[123]

Cherniavsky proceeds by developing a concept of "incorporated embodiment," defined as "a specific idea of the body as the proper (interior) place of the subject." Her argument is that one of the main privileges of whiteness lies in the perceived "boundedness" of white bodies. In contradistinction to the "raced subject," which is "characterized by a missing or attenuated hold on interior personhood," the white body serves as the container of an inalienable core self that is protected from the incursions of capitalist commodification.[124] That Cherniavsky's theorization of race returns us to questions of personhood and in/alienability is no accident, for she too draws on studies of possessive individualism and on Cheryl Harris's work on whiteness as property.[125]

What are the implications of Cherniavsky's critique of whiteness as unmarkedness for dance studies? Her recommendation that we view racial identity as performative rather than inscriptive would seem to be wholly in keeping with dance studies' approach to the body's agentive potential. ("A body … is a bodily writing," as Susan Leigh Foster influentially wrote.)[126] To the extent that dance scholars have theorized whiteness, however, it has been primarily through the lens of the marked/unmarked binary. Joann Kealiinohomoku's pathbreaking essay "An Anthropologist Looks at Ballet as a Form of Ethnic Dance," originally published in 1969–1970, is a cogent critique of dance conventions that regard only non-Western dance forms as ethnically specific and only Western forms like classical ballet as universal.[127] Although her essay doesn't use

[123] Ibid., xiv.

[124] Ibid., xv, xxii, xx

[125] Cherniavsky also cites Hortense Spillers as a principal influence on her approach to racial embodiment. See Spillers, "Mama's Baby, Papa's Maybe: An American Grammar Book," *diacritics* 17.2 (1987): 65–81.

[126] Foster, "Introduction," *Choreographing History*, 3.

[127] "An Anthropologist Looks at Ballet as a Form of Ethnic Dance," in *Moving History/ Dancing Cultures: A Dance History Reader*, ed. Ann Cooper Albright and Ann Dils (Middletown, CT: Wesleyan University Press, 2001), 33–43.

the terms "marked" and "unmarked" and doesn't invoke race explicitly, her work diagnosed the insidious effects of this binary: hierarchies of dance that reproduce legacies of racism and colonialism.

If "marked" and "unmarked" function as ways of categorizing dance in Kealiinohomoku's account, they become "perceptual constructs"—"ways for linking physical bodies and theatrical meanings"—in Susan Manning's *Modern Dance, Negro Dance: Race in Motion* (2004), which traces the interdependent formation of white modern dance and African American concert dance in the United States from the 1930s to the 1960s. In what is arguably the most rigorous theorization of whiteness in American dance, Manning defines "whiteness" as "the social and artistic privilege that adheres to dancing bodies that can be read as racially unmarked, the legitimating norm against which bodies of color take their meanings." "Blackness," meanwhile, denotes "the social and artistic meanings that adhere to dancing bodies that can be read as marked by the culture and history of Africans in the New World."[128] Emphasizing that these categories did not necessarily reduce to skin tone, Manning shows how they manifested in "casting conventions and representational conventions" that shaped what choreographers staged and what spectators saw when they ascribed meaning to bodies in motion.[129] Crucially, unmarkedness emerges as a historically contingent status in Manning's account, a product of the growing authority garnered by African American choreographers in the 1940s. Reformulating whiteness in response, Euro-American choreographers established a convention that Manning calls "mythic abstraction": the privilege of representing "universal subjects without the mediation of bodies marked as culturally other."[130]

For Manning, marked and unmarked are perhaps simultaneously inscriptive and performative, imprinting meaning upon bodies even as they "illuminate the sociohistorical process whereby physical bodies accrue social meanings."[131] Nevertheless, as Cherniavsky might say, the limitation of this approach is that it doesn't get at how dancers—as bodies and subjects—were conceptualized apart from the meanings they acquired via theatrical representations. Neither is *Choreographing Copyright* about racial (or gendered or classed) embodiment as such. It does, however, query how bodies manage their circulation

---

[128] Manning, *Modern Dance, Negro Dance*, xv.

[129] Ibid., 180.

[130] Ibid., 118. Other valuable work on whiteness in dance studies includes Danielle Robinson, "Performing American: Ragtime Dancing as Participatory Minstrelsy," *Dance Chronicle* 32.1ʹ (2009): 89–126; Hannah Schwadron, "White Nose, (Post) Bawdy Bodies, and the Un/ Dancing Sexy Jewess," Ph.D. Dissertation, University of California, Riverside, 2013; and Sarah W. Holmes, "The Pilates Pelvis: Racial Implications of the Immobile Hips," *Dance Research Journal* 46.2 (August 2014): 57–72.

[131] Manning, *Modern Dance, Negro Dance*, xix.

in reproductive economies and examine what kinds of rights they assert over their embodied activity. Foregrounding the issue of property allows us to press on our thinking about how race structures the field of dance: not only in terms of representational and spectatorial conventions but also in terms of how bodies make claims to legal subjecthood and how they negotiate their relationship to capital and labor. More than mark identity visually on the body, race—as it intersects with class, gender, and sexuality—mediates dancers' relationships to what their bodies produce.[132]

For Cultural Studies of Copyright

As much as *Choreographing Copyright* is written with a dance studies audience in mind (in case the appearance of the word "choreographing" in the title left any doubt),[133] I also draw on and aim to contribute to other cultural studies of copyright. This interdisciplinary subfield owes much to a movement known as critical legal studies, which, beginning in the 1970s, trained attention to the constructedness and ideological effects of legal concepts.

[132] Even as I try to push beyond approaching dance artists as either raced or unraced, marked or unmarked, I am hardly immune to some of the problems that plague whiteness studies. In arguing for a correlation between whiteness and the formation of choreographic copyright, I too run the risk of reinforcing whiteness's power. While I have tried to write an integrated history of intellectual property rights in dance, the bulk of the evidence that I have uncovered, and therefore the bulk of my case studies, concern white artists. My chapters, moreover, are largely segregated by race, with Chapters 1, 4, and 5 focusing predominantly on white artists, and Chapters 2 and 3 focusing on African American artists. Thus, despite the outsize influence of Orientalism on the development of modern dance, and aside from the cameo appearance by a South Asian dancer in Chapter 1, the book largely reproduces a black/white binary that remains a shortcoming of much dance scholarship. I am also conscious of the status of this book *as* intellectual property and of the capital that I, a white academic, stand to accrue from its publication and circulation. Still, my hope is that the book's commitment to racializing whiteness can advance the conversation about how race matters in and to dance.

[133] Here I am referencing the cluster of books by dance scholars with the term "choreographing" in their title, among them, Susan Leigh Foster's *Choreographing History*; Albright's *Choreographing Difference*; Anthony Shay's *Choreographing Identities: Folk Dance, Ethnicity and Festival in the United States and Canada* (Jefferson, NC: McFarland, 2006); Yutian Wong's *Choreographing Asian America*; my own *Choreographing the Folk*; and Foster's *Choreographing Empathy*. Of course, as I am grateful to Kate Elswit for pointing out, terms like "choreographing" and "dancing" are often used figuratively by non-dance scholars in ways that have little if anything to do with dance. I am cognizant that my own title employs "choreographing" in a metaphorical sense; no one in this book literally choreographed copyright. Still, I want to hold on to the term's ability to signify in multiple directions—to suggest the structuring of various kinds of movement, the theorization of identity, and political mobilization, all the while serving as a site of privilege and exclusion (see Foster, *Choreographing Empathy*, especially 2–6).

Where the law itself "cannot question its own categories (authorship, private property, right), since it depends upon them for its perpetuation," scholars in critical legal studies, sometimes depicted as a merging of cultural studies and legal studies, have scrutinized "the workings of power and the effects of subjection and subjugation that pervade even the most facially neutral areas of legal doctrine."[134] Two particular works in this vein, Jane Gaines's *Contested Culture: The Image, The Voice, and the Law* (1991) and Rosemary Coombe's *The Cultural Life of Intellectual Properties: Authorship, Appropriation, and the Law* (1998), have been instrumental to my approach to choreographic copyright as an ideological construction embedded in shifting cultural politics. More generally, critical legal studies serves as a reminder that not only bodies but also the institutions that appear to govern them, like the law, are mired in fields of power.

Poststructuralist challenges to the stability of the "author" and "the work" (which I rehearse in Chapter 5) likewise helped turn scholars' focus toward the history of intellectual property law. As Coombe noted in a 1994 review of Mark Rose's *Authors and Owners* (1993), Martha Woodmansee's *The Author, Art, and the Market* (1994), and David Saunders's *Authorship and Copyright* (1992), the "resurgence of historical interest in intellectual property law" emphasized the contingency and cultural specificity of copyright's emergence.[135] In the years since, such investigations have continued apace, giving rise to a lively and steadily expanding body of scholarship that historicizes and critiques copyright.[136] Literary scholars have been particularly active in this trend,[137] but scholars working in the fields of music and media studies have also produced important studies on intellectual property law and the culture

---

[134] Gaines, *Contested Culture*, 15; Coombe, *The Cultural Life of Intellectual Properties*, 7.

[135] Rosemary J. Coombe, "Challenging Paternity: Histories of Copyright," *Yale Journal of Law and the Humanities* 6.2 (1994): 397.

[136] See, for example, Vaidhyanathan, *Copyrights and Copywrongs*; Brad Sherman and Lionel Bentley, *The Making of Modern Intellectual Property: The British Experience, 1760–1911* (Cambridge: Cambridge University Press, 1999); McLeod, *Owning Culture*; Lessig, *Free Culture*; Catherine Seville, *The Internationalisation of Copyright Law: Books, Buccaneers and the Black Flag in the Nineteenth Century* (Cambridge: Cambridge University Press, 2006); Deazley, *On the Origin of the Right to Copy*; Isabella Alexander, *Copyright Law and the Public Interest in the Nineteenth Century* (Portland, OR: Hart, 2010); and Ronan Deazley, Martin Kretschmer, and Lionel Bentley, eds., *Privilege and Property: Essays on the History of Copyright* (Cambridge: Open Book, 2010).

[137] For a small sample, see Rose, *Authors and Owners*; Martha Woodmansee and Peter Jaszi, ed., *The Construction of Authorship: Textual Appropriation in Law and Literature* (Durham, NC: Duke University Press, 1994); Woodmansee, *The Author, Art, and the Market*; Rosenthal, *Playwrights and Plagiarists in Early Modern England*; Saint-Amour, *The Copywrights*; and Homestead, *American Women Authors and Literary Property*.

industries.[138] In the field of theater and performance studies, Philip Auslander, Oliver Gerland, and Derek Miller have each written thoughtfully about the rich intersections of live performance and copyright.[139] Where Auslander and Gerland have explored how US copyright law theorizes performance, Miller has examined the nineteenth-century phenomenon of "copyright performances"—a theatrical staging whose sole purpose was to establish a playwright's British performing rights in his dramatic work—as evidence of the commodification of performance.

Dance has registered minimally if at all in this resurgence.[140] In Paul St. Amour's interdisciplinary volume *Modernism and Copyright* (2010), for example, which argues for the significance of copyright in shaping the "composition, publication, reception, and institutionalization of modernisms in a range of media," Loïe Fuller's copyright efforts warrant only a single paragraph.[141] Nor have dance scholars devoted much thought to intellectual property rights.[142] This is somewhat surprising given the renown of so many of the artists

[138] See, for example, Simon Frith and Lee Marshall, ed., *Music and Copyright* (New York: Routledge, 2004); Demers, *Steal This Music;* and Peter Decherney, *Hollywood's Copyright Wars: From Edison to the Internet* (New York: Columbia University Press, 2012).

[139] Philip Auslander, *Liveness: Performance in a Mediatized Culture* (London: Routledge, 1999), 131–53; Gerland, "From Playhouse to P2P Network"; Derek Miller, "Performative Performances: A History and Theory of the 'Copyright Performance,'" *Theatre Journal* 64.2 (2012): 161–77. A larger sample of scholarship on copyright for theater and drama includes Lisa Surwillo, *The Stages of Property: Copyrighting Theatre in Spain* (Toronto: University of Toronto Press, 2007); Robert D. Hume, "Theatre as Property in Eighteenth-Century London," *Journal for Eighteenth-Century Studies* 31.1 (2008): 17–46; James J. Marino, *Owning William Shakespeare: The King's Men and Their Intellectual Property* (Philadelphia: University of Pennsylvania Press, 2010); Jessica Litman, "The Invention of Common Law Play Right," *Berkeley Technology Law Journal* 25 (2010): 1381–426. Available at http://works.bepress.com/jessica_litman/15; and Isabella Alexander, "'Neither Bolt nor Chain, Iron Safe nor Private Watchman, Can Prevent the Theft of Words': The Birth of the Performing Right in Britain," in Deazley, Kretschmer, and Bently, *Privilege and Property*, 321–46.

[140] Auslander devotes a page to *Horgan v. Macmillan*, the case concerning the copyrights to Balanchine's choreography, focusing on the role that spectatorial memory played in that decision. At time of his writing, *Horgan* was the only choreographic copyright to have seen trial post-1976. See *Liveness*, 152.

[141] Paul K. Saint-Amour, ed., *Modernism and Copyright* (New York: Oxford University Press, 2011), 5. Fuller is discussed in Peter Decherney's essay, "Gag Orders: Comedy, Chaplin, and Copyright," 137–38.

[142] Two important exceptions are Heather Doughty's 1982 presentation at the Fifth Annual Society of Dance History Scholars Conference, titled, "The Choreographer in the Courtroom: Loïe Fuller and Léonide Massine;" and Sally Banes's 1998 presentation at the American Society for Theatre Research conference, titled "Homage, Plagiarism, Allusion, Comment, Quotation," a published version of which appears in *Before, Between, and Beyond.* Doughty's paper summarizes the facts of *Fuller v. Bemis* (1892) and *Massine v. de Basil* (1937), the latter of which was tried in English Chancery Court and arose out of a dispute between Colonel W. de Basil, who ran the Ballet Russe de Monte Carlo, and choreographer Massine. According

who publicly pushed for choreographic copyright. By way of contrast, there are numerous law review articles advocating different solutions to the conundrums that dance and copyright law pose for one another.[143]

Two legal scholars, Julie Van Camp and Caroline Joan S. Picart, have attempted to create a bridge between dance studies and legal scholarship on copyright. In a trio of articles, one published in an arts and entertainment handbook, one in an arts management and law journal, and one in the dance history journal *Dance Chronicle*, Van Camp helpfully delineates the repercussions of judicial rulings in the copyright lawsuits brought by the Balanchine and Graham estates and explores notions of artistic creation through the lens of copyright law.[144] More recently, in 2013, Picart published *Critical Race Theory and Copyright in American Dance: Whiteness as Status Property*.[145] Written from the position of a legal scholar immersed in critical race theory, Picart's book

to Doughty, the judge in that case ruled that the employer de Basil owned the rights to a number of Massine's ballets, an affirmation of the copyrightability of ballet (in England). Banes's paper outlines the protection US copyright law affords to choreographers, addresses the reasons for ballet and modern dancers' hesitancy to embrace that law, and raises questions about how well the law serves choreographers. Sadly, although Banes states that her paper is "preliminary to a larger work-in-progress," the massive stroke she suffered in 2002 intervened (199).

[143] As Sally Banes notes, citing a *New York Times* piece, "the number of law review articles on choreography and copyright by far exceeds the number of court cases." "Homage, Plagiarism, Allusion, Comment, Quotation," 198. Banes cites Laura Mansnerus, "The Dance Is Made and Danced: Now, Whose Property Is It?" *New York Times*, May 14, 1990, C13. These law review articles include Melanie Cook, "Moving to a New Beat: Copyright Protection for Choreographic Works," *UCLA Law Review* 24 (1977): 1287–312; Martha M. Traylor, "Choreography, Pantomime and the Copyright Revision Act of 1976," *New England Law Review* 16 (1980): 227–55; Adaline J. Hilgard, "Can Choreography and Copyright Waltz Together in the Wake of *Horgan v. Macmillan, Inc.*?" *U.C. Davis Law Review* 27 (Spring 1994): 757–89; Leslie Erin Wallis, "The Different Art: Choreography and Copyright," *UCLA Law Review* 33 (1986): 1442–71; Patricia Solan Gennerich, "One Moment in Time: The Second Circuit Ponders Choreographic Photography as a Copyright Infringement: *Horgan v. Macmillan, Inc.*," *Brooklyn Law Review* 53 (spring 1987): 379–407; Kathleen Abitabile and Jeannette Picerno, "Dance and the Choreographer's Dilemma: A Legal and Cultural Perspective on Copyright Protection for Choreographic Works," *Campbell Law Review* 27 (Fall 2004): 39–62; Joi Michelle Lakes, "A Pas de Deux for Choreography and Copyright," *New York University Law Review* 80 (2005): 1829–61. Another legal scholar working at the intersection of law and dance is Francis Yeoh, who completed a dissertation titled "Copyright Law Does Not Adequately Accommodate the Art Form of Dance" at Birkbeck Law School, University of London, and has published several articles in legal venues on choreographic copyright. See, for example, "Choreographers' Moral Right of Integrity," *Journal of Intellectual Property and Practice* 8.1 (2013): 43–58; and "Choreographer's Copyright Dilemma," *Entertainment Law Review* 7 (2012): 201–8.

[144] See Van Camp, "Copyright of Choreographic Works"; Van Camp, "Creating Works of Art from Works of Art: The Problem of Derivative Works," *Journal of Arts Management, Law & Society* 24.3 (Fall 1994): 209–22; Van Camp, "Martha Graham's Legal Legacy," *Dance Chronicle* 30.1 (January 2007): 67–99.

[145] Caroline Joan S. Picart, *Critical Race Theory and Copyright in American Dance: Whiteness as Status Property* (New York: Palgrave Macmillan, 2013).

complements my own in its investigation of "the lacunae connecting whiteness, copyright protection, and choreography" and in its attention to the ways gender and class structured access to white privilege in dance.[146] Not surprisingly, given how few choreographic copyright cases have gone to trial, there is considerable overlap in the artists and cases that Picart and I examine: Fuller, Graham, and Balanchine figure prominently in both our books.[147] While Picart and I draw some of the same conclusions about the raced and gendered underpinnings of copyright for choreography in the United States, Picart's dance research relies heavily on secondary sources, and there are some holes in her historical analysis.[148] Still, her book indicates the value of placing dance, feminist and critical race theories, and intellectual property law in conversation with one another.

Written from a critical dance studies perspective that foregrounds race and gender rather than from a legal studies vantage point, *Choreographing Copyright* nonetheless aims to be instructive for interdisciplinary scholarship on copyright more broadly. As have other historical and cultural studies of the development of copyright, I challenge the naturalness and coherence of terms like "author" and "originality," unearth the complicated power struggles that accompanied the legal sanctioning of an intellectual property right, and question whom that right has favored and whom it has not. But the story of intellectual property rights in dance also departs in some significant ways from that of other copyrightable forms of expression. While the dominant scholarly trend is to lament the increasing reach of copyright law, *Choreographing Copyright* offers a reminder of why copyright has held such allure for those excluded from its jurisdiction and how those on the margins of power have sought refuge in the protection it seemed to promise. And, because it took so long for choreography to earn copyright protection, the book is able to cast light on the close relationship between shifting hierarchies of race, class, and gender and shifts in intellectual property law. To be sure, the book (most explicitly in Chapter 4) makes the case that the emergence of choreographic copyright is properly understood as the product of those shifting hierarchies.

---

[146] Ibid., 10.

[147] Picart's study also covers Josephine Baker, Katherine Dunham, Merce Cunningham, and Alvin Ailey, although copyright is not the explicit focus in her discussion of them.

[148] For example, Picart's statement that "it is with Balanchine that choreography first gained copyright protection" completely overlooks Holm's successful copyright registration (though classified as a "dramatic composition"), and she neglects to mention Balanchine's failed efforts to copyright his choreography in the early 1950s (addressed here in Chapter 4). Picart, *Critical Race Theory and Copyright*, 87. In addition, while she claims to incorporate a dance studies approach and does cite some of Brenda Dixon Gottschild's scholarship, Picart does not consider how Gottschild's important excavation of the Africanist elements of Balanchine's ballet choreography might problematize her own contentions about his "hyper-whitened aesthetic." See Gottschild, *Digging the Africanist Presence*.

The potential for dance to contribute to cultural studies of intellectual property rights, and to critical race studies, does not end there. Dance studies proves particularly fertile ground for probing the stakes and complications of claiming rights in one's body, especially as a means of negotiating one's status in a capitalist marketplace. As I suggested above, dance-makers' bodies are not wholly extractable from the choreographic work that is rendered property under copyright law. If, following Cherniavsky, one of the key protections afforded by whiteness is "incorporation," or the boundedness of the body, how is such boundedness tenable within the economy of choreographic copyright? How could a white dance-maker copyright the product of her embodied labor without enacting the very bodily objectification from which white privilege was supposed to shield her? How could a non-white dance-maker find relief from objectification within the regime of copyright? This book proposes that in the case of choreography, because the body is implicated in both the person of the author and the substance of the work, property rights in the body prove an insecure site of privilege.

Bearing in mind that one of the chief ideological rationales for copyright is a Lockean notion of property in one's person, the instabilities of choreographic copyright might even be seen as a magnification of problems inherent to all forms of copyright and possessive individualism. Differently stated, dance is well positioned to illuminate the contradictions within any claims of "self-possession." As legal scholar Patricia Williams points out, such claims have been absolutely central to ideas of justice. And yet, she observes, "ownership of the self" is an equivocal concept, referring equally to a "person as transactor" of her "body as commodity" and to an "inalienable corporeal integrity."[149] *Choreographic Copyright* throws this duality and ambiguity into focus by exploring how US dance-makers from the late nineteenth to the early twenty-first century embraced intellectual property rights in the pursuit of self-ownership.

A Note on the Copyright Archive

Despite its temporal sweep, this book makes no claims to comprehensiveness.[150] While I have documented as many of the efforts to copyright choreography in the years leading up to the 1976 Copyright Act as possible (see

---

[149] Patricia J. Williams, *The Rooster's Egg* (Cambridge, MA: Harvard University Press, 1995), 230.

[150] One important issue that this book does not explore (although I consider it briefly in the Coda) is the tension between the transnational flow of dance and dance-makers and the nation-state specificity of copyright law. Loïe Fuller's criss-crossing of the Atlantic and exposure to Indian dance sources in London, African American dancer Johnny Hudgins's pursuit of a copyright on his pantomimed choreography in London, and Beyoncé's turn to the European

the Appendix for a timeline), the inevitable limits of the archive make it near-certain that some such attempts have slipped beneath my radar. In many ways, the US Copyright Office is synonymous with the official archive, which undeniably favors the powerful. Choreography was not explicitly recognized by federal copyright law before 1976, and there is no way to conduct a systematic search for choreographic works that were registered under other categories, as literary or musical or dramatic works, for example. This meant that my research was built on a foundation of better-known cases—in particular, Loïe Fuller's failed infringement lawsuit against Minnie Bemis in 1892 and Hanya Holm's successful copyright registration in 1952—that received a good deal of attention in the press.[151] I then had to rely on the rather arbitrary (if not unproductive) method of "stumbling upon" additional tidbits of information about dancers who made copyright (or copyright-like) claims on their material. Practically speaking, this entailed a lot of time combing through dancers' published biographies, autobiographies, and oral histories and a lot of time conducting digital searches of various databases with different configurations of terms like "copyright," "plagiarism," "infringement," "property," "dance," and "choreography." These search methods led me not only to copyright registrations, court documents, and employment contracts but also to newspaper reports, programs, clippings files, correspondence, photographs, and film recordings.

My archive, in other words, is a combination of traditional performance sources and traditional legal sources. And, as much as my research confirms

avant-garde for inspiration (all taken up by this book) place pressure on the US parameters of this study. Looked at in a global context, the cultural politics of intellectual property rights for dance necessarily become more complex. Two works that address the propertization of dance through the framework of UNESCO's "intangible heritage" program are Rachmi Diyah Larasati, *The Dance That Makes You Vanish: Cultural Reconstruction in Post-Genocide Indonesia* (Minneapolis: University of Minnesota Press, 2013), and Elizabeth Kurien, "*Kutiyattam*: Intangible Heritage and Transnationalism," Ph.D. Dissertation, University of California, Riverside, 2013. Although not about dance, Boatema Boateng's *The Copyright Thing Doesn't Work Here* is an astute analysis of intellectual property rights in a Ghanaian context. Ariana Hernández-Reguant's article "Copyrighting Che: Art and Authorship under Cuban Late Socialism" (*Public Culture* 16.1[Winter 2004]: 1–29), meanwhile, is an illuminating examination of the "encounter between socialist structures and neoliberal forms of value in the cultural arena" in Cuba (19). My thanks to Elizabeth Schwall for calling this article to my attention.

[151] Julie Van Camp's "Copyright of Choreographic Works" was an indispensable starting point for me. An analysis of the 1986 *Horgan v. Macmillan* decision, which assessed the scope of copyrights held by the George Balanchine estate, Van Camp's article also provides, via footnote, a summary of efforts to secure copyright protection for choreography prior to the 1976 Copyright Act. Although Van Camp mistakenly identifies *Gypsy* rather than *Kiss Me, Kate* as the Broadway musical whose choreographic score Hanya Holm copyrighted in 1952, her discussion of extant sources on the history of choreographic copyright was a crucial steppingstone for my own research.

that the copyright archive reflects and reproduces larger power structures, it also demonstrates the value of legal proceedings as a site for dance and performance historiography. Dancers and dance-makers did not spend their entire lives in rehearsal and performance, and legal institutions were among the many formations they "rubbed up against or moved alongside," leaving behind partial records as they did so.[152] Sometimes, as in the case of African American pantomimist Johnny Hudgins, the focus of Chapter 2, who was embroiled in a breach of contract lawsuit in the 1920s, court records can provide critical insight into a forgotten performer's career and into the racialized structures of the theatrical marketplace. Legal documents can be particularly useful in reconstructing the material and ideological frameworks that mediated dancers' relationships to their cultural production and in calling attention to the labor that surrounded, supported, and sometimes impeded the work of dance.

The next five chapters are best approached as case studies—a series of discrete but related examinations of how dance-makers with various degrees of privilege, working in the genres of modern dance, ballet, tap, and jazz at various historical moments, engaged with the discourse and legal apparatus of intellectual property law. The examples to which I attend lend themselves to analysis because they left sufficient archival traces for me to recover and, equally important, because they illuminate the ways dancers both participate in and resist the commodification of their embodied work, the stakes involved in that participation and resistance, and the effects of race and gender on both.

Case studies inevitably raise questions about how much we can extrapolate from the evidence at hand. What should we make, for instance, of the fact that the copyright registration Hudgins received in Britain for his pantomimed dance routine in the 1920s is the only one I was able to discover by an African American dancer pre-1976? Should we read this as proof of the friction between copyright law and African American dance practices or as a symptom of the challenges of recovering marginalized subjects from the archive? Surely the answer is a combination of both, but the partialness of the evidence prevents us from drawing definitive conclusions. Likewise, what should we make of the fact that the only two choreographic copyright cases that have gone to trial since the passage of the 1976 Copyright Act, the focus of Chapter 5, upheld the intellectual property rights of George Balanchine but rescinded those of Martha Graham? To what extent can we read this discrepancy as evidence of a gender

---

[152] Susan Leigh Foster, "Choreographing History," in *Choreographing History*, ed. Susan Leigh Foster (Bloomington: Indiana University Press, 1995), 5.

politics at work in allocations of intellectual property rights? As much as the answer may well depend on who is asking, and as much as case studies may prevent us from generalizing on a grand scale, their promise as a research method is that they enable and require a close reading practice that attends to the richness and suggestiveness of detail and that demonstrates the rewards of choosing to find meaning in the dispersed fragments that comprise dance history.

White Womanhood and Early Campaigns for Choreographic Copyright

In 1892, Loïe Fuller, often figured as one of the "mothers" of modern dance, brought an infringement suit in New York against a chorus girl named Minnie Renwood Bemis in an attempt to enjoin her from performing a version of the *Serpentine Dance*, which Fuller claimed to have invented. The dance, distinctive for its use of yards of illuminated silk fabric, made the American-born Fuller famous in Europe and spawned a host of imitators on both sides of the Atlantic. Intent on staking her proprietary claim on the dance, Fuller submitted a written description of it to the United States Copyright Office. Ultimately, however, a US Circuit Court judge denied Fuller's request for an injunction on the grounds that the *Serpentine Dance* told no story and was therefore not eligible for copyright protection.[1] Although Fuller clearly regarded her expressive output as intellectual property, dance at the time merited protection only if it qualified as a "dramatic" or "dramatico-musical composition."[2]

The precedent set by *Fuller v. Bemis* remained in place in the United States until the 1976 Federal Copyright Law explicitly extended protection to choreographic works. The case therefore looms large in historical accounts of copyright for choreography in this country. For dance historians, the court's finding that the *Serpentine Dance*, with its manipulations of fabric and light, was too abstract to count as dramatic is taken as evidence of Fuller's pioneering modernism.[3] Conventional wisdom holds that it was not until "abstract" modern

---

[1] *Fuller v. Bemis*, 50 F. 926 (C.C.S.D.N.Y. 1892).

[2] While an earlier case, *Daly v. Palmer* (6 F.Cas. 1132 [C.C.S.D.N.Y.1868] [No. 3,552]), determined that pantomime did meet the bar for protection, the judge in *Fuller v. Bemis*, as I detail below, refused to find any narrative content in Fuller's choreographic composition.

[3] In a Society of Dance History Scholars paper, for example, Jody Sperling dubbed the *Serpentine Dance* "America's first modern dance." Sperling, "Loïe Fuller's Serpentine Dance: A Discussion of Its Origins in Skirt Dancing and a Creative Reconstruction," in *Proceedings of the Twenty-Second*

dance won wider legitimacy in the mid-twentieth century that Congress saw the need to classify choreography as a copyrightable work, relieving it from the "dramatic" requirement.[4]

Yet *Fuller v. Bemis* is consequential for reasons beyond its insistence that dance tell a story. Approached as an originary moment in the story of dance's interface with copyright law, the case introduces a number of issues that are central to the history of intellectual property rights for choreography: the circulation of dance in an economy of reproduction, the tensions between "originators" and imitators, the patriarchal structure of the theatrical marketplace, the commodification of female bodies, white women's status as possessive individuals, the racial underside of choreographic "innovations," and the ways embodiment and the law operate in tandem and in tension with one another. Close scrutiny of *Fuller v. Bemis*, the conditions that gave rise to it, and the repercussions it had illuminates undercurrents that would remain key to the pursuit of choreographic copyright for the next hundred years.

Exploring all of these issues, this chapter's central argument is that Fuller's lawsuit against Bemis, as well as subsequent attempts by white female dancers to establish themselves as property-holding subjects, must be viewed as part of a gendered struggle to attain proprietary rights in whiteness. While attention to Fuller has surged in recent years, including from biographers, dance scholars, queer theorists (she lived openly as a lesbian), and performing artists who have reconstructed her most well-known dance works, the raced and gendered dynamics of her pursuit of property rights deserve careful examining.[5]

Annual Society of Dance History Scholars Conference (Stoughton, WI: Society of Dance History Scholars, 1999), 53. As Rhonda Garelick summarizes, critics tend to regard Fuller "as the earliest manifestation of a vast array of modernist developments including performing recital dance with no balletic technique, discarding constricting costumes and elaborate stage sets, using classical music for cabaret dance, downplaying narrative, working with light and shadow onstage in proto-cinematic fashion, and incorporating electricity and technology into her onstage work." Rhonda K. Garelick, *Electric Salome: Loie Fuller's Performance of Modernism* (Princeton, NJ: Princeton University Press, 2007), 9.

[4] See Nicholas Arcomano, "Choreography and Copyright, Part One," *Dance Magazine* 54.4 (April 1980): 58–59.

[5] See especially Ann Cooper Albright, *Traces of Light: Absence and Presence in the Work of Loïe Fuller* (Middletown, CT: Wesleyan University Press, 2007); Garelick, *Electric Salome*; Sally R. Sommer, "Loïe Fuller," *Drama Review* 19.1 (1975): 53–675; Elizabeth Coffman, "Women in Motion: Loïe Fuller and the 'Interpenetration' of Art and Science," *Camera Obscura* 17.1 (2002): 73–105; Julie Townsend, "Alchemic Visions and Technological Advances: Sexual Morphology in Loïe Fuller's Dance," in *Dancing Desires: Choreographing Sexualities on and off the Stage*, ed. Jane C. Desmond (Madison: University of Wisconsin Press, 2001), 73–96; Tirza True Latimer, "Loïe Fuller: Butch Femme Fatale," in *Proceedings of the Twenty-Second Annual Society of Dance History Scholars Conference* (Stoughton, WI: Society of Dance History Scholars, 1999), 83–88; Felicia McCarren, "Stéphane Mallarmé, Loïe Fuller, and the Theater of Femininity," in

Doing so opens up a new vantage point on Fuller's significance to the development of modern dance, casting fresh light on the ways in which race and gender mattered to its formation. As dance scholars have demonstrated in the past two decades, white female dancers like Isadora Duncan, Ruth St. Denis, and Martha Graham (considered the other "mothers" of modern dance) overturned gender hierarchies to claim leadership positions as choreographers on the public stage, even as they actively reinforced racial hierarchies.[6] On the one hand, these white women "projected a kinesthetic power that challenged male viewers to see the female dancer as an expressive subject rather than as an erotic object."[7] On the other hand, they relied on essentialized racial distinctions between their own "universal" artistry and the putatively "primitive" dance practices of non-white subjects, often while claiming the right to represent those subjects in their choreography. Actually, to state it in these terms—to imply that the gendered and raced dimensions of early modern dance were parallel rather than inextricably linked operations—misses the point. Differentiating themselves from racialized, sexualized dancing bodies is precisely what *enabled* these white women to gain legitimacy for themselves as artists (not objects) on the theatrical stage. This was equally Loïe Fuller's goal. Yet her embrace of copyright suggests that race and gender influenced more than the representational conventions and discursive strategies of early white modern dancers; these same axes of difference also critically shaped dancers' efforts to position themselves as propertied subjects, entitled not only to wear the mantle of artist but also to own the products of their intellectual and bodily labor. The assertion of property rights, that is to say, was another—and, for some, a crucial—avenue through which white female dancers negotiated their status.

Bodies of the Text: Dance as Theory, Literature as Dance, ed. Ellen W. Goellner and Jacqueline Shea Murphy (New Brunswick, NJ: Rutgers University Press, 1995), 217–30. This chapter draws on these valuable secondary sources as well as on Fuller's 1913 autobiography, court records, and contemporaneous accounts, homing in on the ways in which race, gender, and political economic considerations underlay and propelled Fuller's pursuit of intellectual property rights for dance.

[6] See, among others, Jane Desmond, "Dancing Out the Difference: Cultural Imperialism and Ruth St. Denis's 'Radha' of 1906," *Signs: Journal of Women in Culture and Society* 17.1 (1991): 28–49; Ann Daly, *Done into Dance: Isadora Duncan in America* (Bloomington: Indiana University Press, 1995); Yutian Wong, "Towards a New Asian American Dance Theory: Locating the Dancing Asian American Body," *Discourses in Dance* 1.1 (2002): 69–90; Susan Manning, *Modern Dance, Negro Dance: Race in Motion*. Minneapolis: University of Minnesota Press, 2004; and Priya Srinivasan, *Sweating Saris: Indian Dance as Transnational Labor* (Philadelphia, PA: Temple University Press, 2011).

[7] Susan Manning, "The Female Dancer and the Male Gaze: Feminist Critiques of Early Modern Dance," in *Meaning in Motion: New Cultural Studies of Dance*, ed. Jane Desmond (Durham, NC: Duke University Press, 1997), 163.

To lay the ground for this argument, I re-visit theories of whiteness and/as self-possession (rehearsed in the Introduction), with special attention to how they apply to white women. I then situate Fuller's practice in the context of the gendered economic relations of production that governed the late nineteenth-century theater and examine the lineage of Fuller's *Serpentine Dance*, including the oft-neglected Indian dance sources to which it was indebted. Next, I turn to Fuller's reaction to the "theft" of her choreography and the claims she made in her infringement suit against Minnie Bemis. A discussion follows presenting the outcome and effects of the legal decision in this and other lawsuits in which Fuller was involved. Finally, I consider the pursuit of intellectual property rights by two dancers who came in Fuller's wake: one of her imitators, Ida Fuller, and Ruth St. Denis, another "pioneer" of modern dance in the United States. Together, these early attempts to use the legal system to secure ownership of a choreographic work have much to tell us about how assiduous and contradiction-filled female dancers' fight for the entitlements of whiteness could be.

White Womanhood and Property Rights

My argument about Fuller builds on the work of American studies scholar Eva Cherniavsky, who herself builds on legal scholar Cheryl Harris's insights about the property interests in whiteness.[8] Cherniavsky's proposition, as discussed in this book's Introduction, is that one of the key protections afforded to whites—during slavery but also, arguably, in its wake—is an "inalienable property in the body."[9] That is to say, whereas racialized and colonized persons are characteristically rendered "fully open to capital" and "susceptible to abstraction and exchange" as commodifiable objects, white persons are granted the rights of "possessive individualism."[10] For Cherniavsky, the "status of the body (the difference between selling one's bodily labor and becoming a salable body in which others may traffic)" has been a key site of racial division, one with enormous implications.[11] In the formulation of modern liberal-democratic theory, with its roots in seventeenth-century conceptions

[8] Cheryl I. Harris, "Whiteness as Property," *Harvard Law Review* 106.8 (1993): 1707-1793

[9] Eva Cherniavsky, *Incorporations: Race, Nation, and the Body Politics of Capital* (Minneapolis: University of Minnesota Press, 2006), 84.

[10] Ibid., 89.

[11] Ibid., 85.

of the individual as the "proprietor of his own person or capacities," whiteness equals property ownership equals proper subjecthood.[12]

Whiteness, however, is far from monolithic, and gender as well as class have complicated the equation between whiteness and propertied personhood. Possessive individualism has been an institution not only of whiteness, as scholar Grace Hong has observed, but also of masculinity, "subtended by bourgeois domesticity."[13] Cherniavsky likewise notes that "White women's juridical and social self-possession is ... historically belated and decidedly tenuous when measured against the legal and conventional protections extended to white men."[14] Relegated to the private sphere, stripped of legal rights independent from those of their husbands under nineteenth-century coverture laws, denied the franchise until 1920 in the United States, middle-class white women were long considered objects rather than subjects of property and have long been exchanged *as* property by men.[15]

Nonetheless, as Cheryl Harris stresses in "Finding Sojourner's Truth," the patriarchal system that emerged out of slavery was a thoroughly racialized one, with white women's oppression by no means identical to that of African Americans. Even when excluded from the public sphere, white women were still considered "within the polity" and were afforded a "derivative relationship" to white male power that was denied others.[16] Historian Louise Newman has shown that white women activists in the late nineteenth-century United States measured their rights not only against those of white men but also against the rights of men and women of color, especially former slaves and immigrants. In their fight for equal political rights, white women "thought of themselves as widely different from white men in sexual terms," yet as "fundamentally similar to white men in racial-cultural terms."[17] Accordingly, parsing

[12] C. B. Macpherson, *The Political Theory of Possessive Individualism: Hobbes to Locke* (London: Oxford University Press, 1962), 3. See also Eric O Clarke, "The Citizen's Sexual Shadow," *boundary* 26.2 (1999): 163–91.

[13] Grace Kyungwon Hong, *The Ruptures of American Capital: Women of Color Feminism and the Culture of Immigrant Labor* (Minneapolis: University of Minnesota Press, 2006), 5, emphasis added.

[14] Cherniavsky, *Incorporations*, xxv.

[15] Laura Brace, *The Politics of Property: Labour, Freedom and Belonging* (New York: Palgrave Macmillan, 2004), 189–99; Gayle Rubin, "The Traffic in Women: Notes on the 'Political Economy' of Sex," in *Feminist Anthropology: A Reader*, ed. Ellen Lewin (Malden, MA: Blackwell, 2006), 87–106.

[16] Cheryl Harris, "Finding Sojourner's Truth: Race, Gender, and the Institution of Property," *Cardoza Law Review* 18.2 (1996): 321, 322.

[17] Louise Michele Newman, *White Women's Rights: The Racial Origins of Feminism in the United States* (New York: Oxford University Press, 1999), 10.

white women's relationship to property rights requires factoring their shifting positionality vis-à-vis both white men and non-white men and women.

Cherniavsky's treatment of racialized gender focuses on how technological mediations that transformed white women into "commodity-images" threatened to undermine the expectation of white self-possession. She argues that the mechanical reproduction of cinema, allegedly "the first medium in which whiteness ... circulates independently of white persons," jeopardized the privileged status of white bodies, chiefly those of white female stars, who constitute "the primary commodity-image of Hollywood cinema."[18] In a 2009 article, Eden Osucha also explores the crisis produced by the circulation of white women's image via visual technology—in this case, photography. Reading Samuel Warren and Louis Brandeis's influential 1890 legal article "The Right to Privacy," in which the two jurists fretted over the "invasive" and "corrosive effects" that the rise of photography and the media industry were having on bourgeois codes of propriety and the domestic sphere, alongside a 1902 case, *Roberson v. Rochester Folding Box Company*, in which a young white woman's photographic image was used without her consent to advertise a flour mix, Osucha shows how "spectacles of white women in peril saturate the early discourses of media privacy."[19] Crucially, Osucha also places the legal treatise and court case in the context of American commodity racism and the consumer marketplace's permeation with images of blackface stereotypes, such as the figure of Aunt Jemima, used to sell pancake mix. When these are viewed in conjunction, it becomes clear that "the cultural anxieties that held unwanted media publicity to be an experience of proprietary dispossession reflect the understanding that to be subject to media publicity is to be, in effect, racialized."[20]

Following Cherniasky's and Osucha's lead, I approach Loïe Fuller's attempt to regulate the circulation of her *Serpentine Dance* as an effort to protect herself from mass commodification, replete with racialized implications, and to claim for herself the right of self-possession, which, because of the public nature of her livelihood, was always under threat. Although photography and film were not the primary media through which Fuller's body circulated, both visual technologies were important to her career. The *Serpentine Dance*, performed by Fuller and her imitators, was captured on film, including by Thomas Edison.[21]

---

[18] Cherniavsky, *Incorporations*, 127–28, 101.

[19] Eden Osucha, "The Whiteness of Privacy: Race, Media, Law," *Camera Obscura* 24.1 (2009): 67, 73.

[20] Ibid., 73.

[21] Ann Cooper Albright, *Traces of Light: Absence and Presence in the Work of* Loïe *Fuller* (Middletown, CT: Wesleyan University Press, 2007), 188. Several of these imitation *Serpentine Dances* are available on YouTube. See, for example, https://www.youtube.com/

More generally, as Rhonda Garelick writes, Fuller "exploited the era's fascination with the alchemy inherent in the union of human and machine."[22] Fully imbricated in a culture of visual technology, Fuller developed a skill at commodifying her image that qualifies her as "a direct forerunner of today's modern media celebrities."[23]

Yet the divergences between Fuller and the examples raised by Cherniavsky and Osucha are equally significant. It was not merely visual iconography that was at issue for Fuller; it was the circulation of her live dancing body. Her case thus raises questions about what bearing liveness had on white women's relationship to commodification on the one hand and possessive individualism on the other. Unlike a mechanically reproduced commodity like a photograph or film, the property in question in Fuller's case—the *Serpentine Dance*—was disseminated both independently of the "originating" body (as when the dance was reproduced by performers other than Fuller) and via that body (as when Fuller herself was caught up in the transactional flows of the commercial theater). Fuller's image—the representation conveyed by the *Serpentine Dance*—was thus an embodied one but also capable of being dis-embodied (or re-embodied by another). This duality raised the stakes and amplified the complexities of trying to control the traffic in her image, and thus protect her status, by controlling the circulation of her choreography.

"Singular Migrations of Personality": (Re)Producing Loïe Fuller's Dancing Body

Born Mary Louise in Fullersburg, Illinois, in 1862, Loïe Fuller's early years were spent in Chicago where her father ran a tavern. Although the details of her upbringing are not well documented, Fuller's family appears to have been neither prosperous nor poor. Like other middle-class white women at the turn of the twentieth century, Fuller had access to some of the "racial-cultural" privileges of whiteness without full access to propertied subjecthood. In contrast to

---

watch?v=O8soP3ry9y0. Accessed June 12, 2014. Felicia McCarren reports that this version of the *Serpentine Dance* by filmmaker Louis Lumière does not actually feature Fuller. *Dancing Machines: Choreographies of the Age of Mechanical Production* (Stanford, CA: Stanford University Press, 2003), 234n24. McCarren describes Fuller's choreography of moving images as among the forms of entertainment "that anticipated cinema, staging elements that the cinematograph would bring together," such as "stereoscopic photography producing a theatrical three-dimensional effect" and "magic lantern projections" (63, 50).

[22] Garelick, *Electric Salome*, 6.

[23] Ibid.

the wave of European immigration to the United States in the late nineteenth century, Fuller's roots on both her paternal and maternal side stretched back to the Revolutionary War, which, as biographers Richard and Marcia Current point out, entitled Fuller to join the Daughters of the American Revolution, though she never did.[24] Contrary to the cultural norm of domesticity for middle-class white women, Fuller entered show business at an early age and developed a multifaceted and prolific stage career. Before she began performing the solo dances that would make her famous, she worked as a temperance lecturer, a playwright, and an actress, touring the United States and London with various theater comedies in soubrette and cross-dressing roles. In 1892, she debuted in Paris, where she was quickly embraced by the emerging Art Nouveau and Symbolist movements and became an inspiration for such artists as Stéphane Mallarmé, Auguste Rodin, and Henri de Toulouse-Lautrec. She later opened her own dance school, experimented with film, and became an impresario for Japanese theater companies and for Isadora Duncan, who, with Fuller, is figured as a "mother" of modern dance. Fuller died in 1928.

When Fuller toured United States and London vaudeville, burlesque, and music hall circuits in the 1880s and 1890s, stage dancing was hardly a respectable art form. With "feminized spectacle" in ascendancy, theatrical dancing on both sides of the pond was seen primarily as "a form of female erotic display performed by women of questionable moral status"; even "ballet girls" were morally suspect.[25] If Fuller's choice of career made her vulnerable to the sexualized gaze, she took explicit measures to counteract the eroticization of her body, as dance scholars writing about Fuller almost uniformly underscore. Explaining the appeal of her work as a temperance lecturer, for example, Linda Tomko observes that "The temperance identification offered Fuller something that employment in a stock play or burlesque could not—control over presentation of her self."[26] Scholars also point to Fuller's choreographic techniques, from the veiling of her body, to her emphasis on fluid motion rather than static poses, to her use of projection to render her body a "desexualized screen," as evidence of her success at resisting the erotic gaze.[27]

[24] Richard Nelson Current and Marcia Ewing Current, *Loie Fuller: Goddess of Light* (Boston: Northeastern University Press, 1997), 6.

[25] Robert Clyde Allen, *Horrible Prettiness: Burlesque and American Culture* (Chapel Hill: University of North Carolina Press, 1991), 96; Amy Koritz, *Gendering Bodies/Performing Art: Dance and Literature in Early-Twentieth-Century British Culture* (Ann Arbor: University of Michigan Press, 1995), 2.

[26] Linda J. Tomko, *Dancing Class: Gender, Ethnicity, and Social Divides in American Dance, 1890–1920* (Bloomington: Indiana University Press, 1999), 45.

[27] Albright, *Traces of Light*, 32; Sally Banes, *Dancing Women: Female Bodies on Stage* (New York: Routledge, 1998), 71.

As notable as these strategies were, there were limits to Fuller's ability to counter dance's low art status. One chief constraint was the structural position dance held within a theatrical economy, which determined how dancing bodies circulated at the end of the nineteenth century. Accompanying its low repute, dance also lacked autonomy as a medium: rather than stand on its own, it appeared in mixed theatrical revues alongside musical and dramatic routines.[28] Bearing little if any relationship to the content of surrounding acts, individual dance numbers could be and were inserted into a variety of stage productions. This lack of self-sufficiency actually facilitated dance's circulation, for a given dance specialty could appear on multiple programs and, if necessary, be replaced without disrupting the overall coherence of a show. In other words, dance functioned something like an exchangeable commodity within a larger theatrical framework.

This was precisely the situation with the *Serpentine Dance*. Fuller initially developed the dance in the context of an 1891 play called *Quack, M.D.*, in which she played a widow who underwent hypnosis. As Rhonda Garelick writes, "The part was so small that Fuller's name did not appear in the program, she had to provide her own costume, and she was left to devise her own brief dance number."[29] When the play closed some weeks later, Fuller "was left with her new routine and nowhere to perform it."[30] She proceeded to audition the dance for Rudolph Aronson, the theatrical manager of New York's Casino Theatre, and was soon performing it between the acts of a musical comedy called *Uncle Celestin*. Departing that production after a conflict with Aronson (to be discussed below), Fuller found work performing the *Serpentine Dance* as an entr'acte number in the musical *A Trip to Chinatown*.[31]

Because dance occupied such an "incidental" position in theatrical productions, performers seeking to maximize profits could arrange to perform the same dance in between the acts of concurrently running shows. For example, as the *New York Times* reported, in one week in 1893, Fuller was slated to appear "with apparent simultaneousness, at three different theatres, to wit: between

---

[28] Koritz, *Gendering Bodies*, 16.

[29] Garelick, *Electric Salome*, 28.

[30] Current and Current, *Loie Fuller*, 32.

[31] Sally R. Sommer, "Loïe Fuller," in *International Encyclopedia of Dance*, ed. Selma Jeanne Cohen (New York: Oxford University Press, 1998), 91–92. Opening in 1890 and running for a record-setting 650 performances, Charles Hoyt's musical comedy *A Trip to Chinatown* was a white-oriented show set in San Francisco. Chinatown signified an exotic ethnic locale in the musical but was apparently never actually depicted. See Sabine Haenni, "Filming 'Chinatown': Fake Visions, Bodily Transformations," in *Screening Asian Americans*, ed. Peter X. Feng (Rutgers, NJ: Rutgers University Press, 2002), 49n40. Fuller's *Serpentine Dance* bore no relation to the musical's plot.

the acts of 'Fanny' at the Standard Theatre, between the acts of 'Panjadrum' at the Broadway Theatre, and, finally, between the acts of a play unknown at a theatre hitherto unidentified, in Boston."[32] While the reporter marveled at how Fuller's "small if lively body" was capable of such "singular migrations of personality," Fuller had a matter-of-fact explanation for how she could appear at three different theaters on the same day. "At each house," she stated, "I shall have awaiting me a separate and distinct set of costumes, accessories, properties, gasmen, stereopticons, and other necessary articles. So that the same identical dance, under the same identical conditions, will be repeated in each theatre." Even as the reporter voices skepticism about the reproducibility of dance, given its dependence on live(ly) bodies, Fuller assures him that with the right planning and resources, stage dances are as portable as the dancers who execute them. For Fuller, "migrations of personality"—the circulation of her dancing self through the sale of her bodily labor—were a means to increase her exposure and her revenue.

The problem, as Fuller also indicated to the *Times* reporter, was that her migrations were dependent on the male managers and producers who presided over dancers' contracts. Describing her scheduled engagements, Fuller refers not to the names of productions but to the theatrical management of each venue: "On Monday next I intend to perform at a theatre to be hereafter decided upon by, and under the management of, Mr. McDonald and Mr. Drohan; at the Columbia Theatre, in Brooklyn, under the management of Mr. Charles Frohman, and at the Broadway Theatre, in this city, under the management of Mr. Benjamin Franklin Stevens." When asked why she was not planning to appear at the Standard Theatre under the management of J. M. Hill, who had also advertised her performance, Fuller explained that her own manager, Robert Grau, had leased her to Colonel Hill without her approval or signature, and that she therefore did not intend to honor the contract. (A follow-up article reported that she had changed her mind and would be appearing at the Standard after differences over the contract had been "amicably adjusted.")[33] This threat to ignore her contract—a simultaneous flouting of the law and upholding of its letter (quite literally) through her insistence on the presence of her signature—is a testament to Fuller's frustration with the terms of her participation in the labor market as well as to her resourcefulness in using whatever capital she possessed to try to re-negotiate those terms.

Even after she had become a major attraction as "La Loïe," Fuller thus felt herself constrained by the (white) men who monopolized the means of

[32] "La Loie Interprets Law," *New York Times*, September 3, 1893, p. 9.
[33] "Loie Has Changed Her Mind," *New York Times*, September 4, 1893, p. 5.

production of commercial theater and controlled the traffic in female perform-ers.[34] Early in her career, Fuller attempted to assume the position of producer herself and mount plays on her own, but without adequate financial backing, she had to resort to contracting her labor to male theatrical managers.[35] As the above incident suggests, she frequently butted heads with those managers. Her autobiography is full of similar conflicts and confrontations over the stipula-tions of her employment contracts.[36] These contracts were essential to the allo-cation of both economic and cultural capital, for their provisos not only set a performer's salary but also determined what kind of billing she received. And lacking sufficient bargaining power, Fuller often found it difficult to receive artistic credit for her choreographic work.[37]

Her dispute with Aronson over the terms of her engagement in *Uncle Celestin*, in fact, centered around the issue of credit, and a closer look at the lawsuit she filed against the New York Concert Company, Ltd., the company that operated the Casino Theatre, where she performed in *Uncle Celestin*, and which was run by the producer Rudolph Aronson, sheds light on the nature of her grievances. Filed in New York's Court of Common Pleas in March 1892, but not tried until June, *Loie Fuller v. New York Concert Company, Limited* was a clash over contracts, publicity, and attribution.

In January of 1892, according to Fuller's testimony, Aronson engaged her to "perform and execute a certain dance known as the Serpentine dance" for the New York Concert Company in the play *Uncle Celestin*. (Fuller did not make her appearance in the show until February 15.) Fuller evidently agreed to accept a weekly salary of $50, on the condition that the plaintiff "advertise and feature her by special announcement of such engagement and by the distribution of pictures of the plaintiff representing her in the dress in which such dance was to be performed, such pictures to bear the plaintiff's name together with the announcement of such dance." A week after her debut, having received rave reviews, Fuller complained to Aronson that the Company "had broken its con-tract with her in having failed specially to feature and advertise her and have her name printed upon the lithographs of herself which had been generally

---

[34] These constraints may have been heightened by the capitalist transformations occurring in stage entertainment in the late nineteenth century. As Bruce McConachie writes, in the 1890s, "group creation gave way to individual production, the 'individual' being either a capitalist or a corporation, the legal extension and enhancement of individual power under capitalism." "Historicizing the Relations of Theatrical Production," in *Critical Theory and Performance*, ed. Janelle G. Reinelt and Joseph R. Roach (Ann Arbor: University of Michigan Press, 1992), 171.

[35] Current and Current, *Loie Fuller*, 26, 30–32.

[36] Loie Fuller, *Fifteen Years of a Dancer's Life* (Boston: Small, Maynard, 1913).

[37] Albright, *Traces of Light*, 27.

distributed throughout the City of New York and on exhibition in the windows of stores and other conspicuous places." In other words, the publicity placards for *Uncle Celestin* depicted Fuller's dancing body along with the words "The Serpentine Dance," but failed to mention her by name. Claiming breach of contract, Fuller refused to remain on in the production without an increase in salary. According to her deposition, when the defendant professed to accept Fuller's demands, which included recalling the circulating lithographs to have her name printed on them, she went on performing in the production, giving two performances on February 22, at which point she was notified that "her terms would not be considered." She promptly left, taking her *Serpentine Dance* to the Madison Square Theatre, where it was inserted between the acts of *A Trip to Chinatown*. But the continued use of the lithographs bearing her image to advertise *Uncle Celestin*, Fuller charged, was "perpetrating a fraud upon the public" and depriving her of "the benefit of the attendance of such of the public as may desire to see her dance, but are led by such advertisement to believe that she is still performing at the Casino." Fuller sought damages in the amount of $1,000.[38]

The nuances of Fuller's complaints in this suit reveal how complicated the relationship between commodity-image and live dancing body was. Her initial objection—that she was not explicitly credited in the publicity lithographs—indicates that it was not the circulation of her likeness that was problematic for her; it was, rather, the detachment of her name from the image. How could she capitalize on her circulating likeness if that likeness remained anonymous? Yet once she terminated her engagement in the production being advertised, the likeness of her posed a problem for precisely the opposite reason: it was *too* identified with her and therefore misled theatergoers about where she was actually performing. The "damage" that Fuller claimed was caused by the publicity from the lithographs was thus a result of both the distance and the proximity between the mechanically reproduced representation of her and her embodied identity. For Fuller, the lack of power to control the circulation of her commodity-image stripped her ability to derive value from it.

The counterargument of the defense, which moved to dismiss Fuller's complaint, was entirely devoid of nuance. While Aronson's lawyers maintained that Fuller had "violated her contract in leaving the Casino," Fuller's lawyer evidently erred in suing the New York Concert Company rather than Aronson himself, for the defense claimed that in its capacity as a corporation,

---

[38] Current and Current, *Loie Fuller*, 41; Fuller, *Fifteen Years*, 38–40; *Fuller v. New York Concert Company, Limited*, Court of Common Pleas, New York City, 1892, Municipal Archives, N.Y.C. Department of Records and Information Services, 31 Chambers Street, New York City.

the Company was not responsible for Fuller's dealings. More specifically, they denied "each and every allegation" made by Fuller, including that they had hired her for the express purpose of performing the *Serpentine Dance*, that they had ever "made or entered into any contract or agreement of any kind with the plaintiff," and that they ever agreed to advertise her dance performance in any specific way. Three months after Fuller filed her complaint, Judge L. A. Giegerich granted the motion to dismiss and ordered Fuller to pay $44.32 in costs to the defendant.[39]

Meanwhile, Fuller had endured a further violation. In a chain of events that suggests a connection between the circulation of commodity-images and the circulation of live bodies, Fuller's dispute with Aronson and subsequent departure from *Uncle Celestin* led Aronson to hire the chorus girl Minnie Bemis as Fuller's replacement in the *Serpentine Dance*.[40] If Fuller felt a sense of injury from the unchecked circulation of her commodity-image, being summarily exchanged for another white female body only heightened this sense. Though she was fully prepared to orchestrate her own "migrations," her relative powerlessness to control the conditions and contractual relations under which her dancing body was (re)produced is key to understanding the appeal that the legal discourse of self-possession held for her.

"A Bit of the Nautch Dance": Serpentine Sources

A thorough appraisal of Fuller's proprietary claims must also attend to the ambiguous racial sources of her dance. To tease out these sources, it is helpful to look more closely at Fuller's choreography for the *Serpentine Dance*, this time turning to the textual description she recorded and submitted for copyright registration.[41] (That this description reads like instructions for re-creating the solo dance, complete with directions for stage lighting, indicates the paradoxes of copyright; the very act of protecting the work could also be a vehicle for its reproduction.) Fuller's version of the solo dance was comprised of three

---

[39] Current and Current, *Loie Fuller*, 42; *Fuller v. New York Concert Company*.

[40] Fuller's unannounced absence from the production evidently caused quite a commotion: when Fuller and her *Serpentine Dance* failed to appear in the third act of *Uncle Celestin*, a spectator drew a pistol and demanded his money back. A "stampede for the box office" followed. Bemis was promptly hired to take Fuller's place. "A Pistol Drawn at the Casino," *New York Sun*, February 25, 1892, p. 8. The failure to announce Fuller's withdrawal was "due to the fact that Manager Aronson did not believe Miss Fuller would enforce her demands."

[41] The description of the dance that Fuller submitted as part of her copyright registration was included as an exhibit in *Fuller v. Bemis*. It was also re-printed in "Copyright—'Dramatic Composition'—Stage Dance," *Albany Law Journal*, August 27, 1892, 165–66.

tableaus, each commencing with a dark stage, building to a "graceful climax," and ending with the dancer executing an eye-catching pose. In between, the dancer moved (at times with waltz-like steps) up- and downstage and performed a series of turns, all the while manipulating the ample material of her dress, such that, when combined with the effects of colored lighting, her body seemed to appear and disappear as images of flowers, butterflies, and waves materialized and faded away. For example, in Tableau 1, the soloist "dances down center to footlights, followed by several whirls or turns which bring dancer back to center. (All this time the dress is held up above the head....) She makes two turns, dropping dress, which the two whirls or turns bring into place. She takes dress up at each side, turns body from side to side, swinging dress from one side low in front to high at back, forming a half-umbrella shape over the head." Later, the dancer "gives a rounding, swerving movement that causes dress to assume the shape of a large flower, the petals being the dress in motion."

As other Fuller scholars have noted, though Fuller claimed the dance was a completely original creation, her use of fabric owed much to skirt dancing, a dance genre popular on music hall and vaudeville stages in the late nineteenth and early twentieth centuries. First introduced around 1876 at London's Gaiety Theater by the ballet dancer Kate Vaughan and later made famous by Letty Lind, the skirt dance was a solo form in which a female performer used a flowing skirt to accentuate her turns and kicks.[42] While Vaughan and Lind's skirt dancing won them celebrity status, economic success, and praise for their embodiment of feminine grace, as the dance spread, it developed an association with the erotic spectacle of burlesque, and it is clear that Fuller sought to distance herself from the run-of-the-mill skirt dancer.[43] Fuller had, however, performed as an actress and dancer at the Gaiety Theater in 1889, giving her plenty of opportunity to absorb Lind's style. She may even have replaced Lind for a time in the musical *Carmen-up-to-Data*.[44] The prototype for the *Serpentine Dance* that Fuller performed in *Quack, M.D.* on the heels of her London engagement was "essentially a modified skirt dance."[45] Eventually, scholar and Fuller reconstructor Jodi Sperling observes, "By adding substantially more fabric to the width of the skirt and introducing novel lighting effects, Fuller shifted the skirt dancer's emphasis from displays of pretty refinement or leg-revealing

[42] Martie Fellom, "Skirt Dance," in *International Encyclopedia of Dance*, 605.

[43] See Catherine Hindson, *Female Performance Practice on the Fin-de-Siecle Popular Stages of London and Paris: Experiment and Advertisement* (Manchester: Manchester University Press, 2007) for more on the gender ideology of the skirt dancer.

[44] Sommer, "Loïe Fuller" 1975, 55–56; Current and Current, *Loie Fuller*, 30–31.

[45] Sperling, "Loïe Fuller's Serpentine Dance," 54.

Figure 1.1 Image of skirt dancer named Silvia Grey. Photo by Otto Sarony. Jerome Robbins Dance Division, The New York Public Library for the Performing Arts, Astor, Lenox, and Tilden Foundations.

suggestion ... [to the creation of] abstract visual imagery."[46] Dance scholars are correct to point out the ways in which the *Serpentine Dance* evolved out of and departed from the skirt dance. Yet their insistence on Fuller's aesthetic elevation of the popular dance makes them complicit in the project of dissociating her from the exchangeable sexualized bodies of the variety stage.

Furthermore, in placing so much emphasis on the skirt dance as predecessor, scholars have largely neglected the debt Fuller's choreography owed to Nautch dancing, the generic, colonialist term for Indian dance in the

[46] Ibid., 53.

nineteenth and early twentieth centuries.[47] Reports of how Fuller fortuitously "discovered" the possibilities inherent in skirt manipulation vary widely, but they are marked by a recurrent Indian motif. Testifying for the defense in the 1892 infringement suit against Bemis, the manager of Madison Square Garden, James Morrissey, cited an interview with Fuller that ran in the *World* on February 21, 1892, in which she purportedly explained the evolution of the *Serpentine Dance* as follows:

> When I was in Paris, I saw ever and ever so much dancing. I had a teacher there, and studied a lot of difficult steps and funny skewjiggered things, because I had a notion always that I would like to dance, and I went to see every new thing in Paris in the dancing line. What interested me most was the dancing of the Nautch girls at the Exposition. I went there day after day, but in the meantime the teacher was drilling me in a lot of Parisian dances. It seemed to me that with the Nautch dance as a basis, a good thing might be built up. . . . I thought the skirt was the main point in the effectiveness of the whole business.[48]

Fuller's reference to the Exposition makes it likely that she was in Paris in 1889, and her mention of a sustained encounter with Nautch performers is significant in the direct contact it establishes between Fuller and Indian dancing bodies. But it was also an anomaly, for other narratives of the derivation of the *Serpentine Dance* bypassed Indian bodies to focus on the skirt material. For example, one of Fuller's later imitators claimed that she and Loïe had both modeled the fabric that became the basis for the *Serpentine Dance* off the costumes used for a musical revue called *The Nautch Girl* at the Gaiety Theater in London. In subsequent interviews with journalists, Fuller adamantly denied this account and offered up her own origin stories. First she maintained that

---

[47] See Srinivasan, *Sweating Saris,* and Uttara Asha Coorlawala, "Ruth St. Denis and India's Dance Renaissance," *Dance Chronicle* 15 (1992): 123–52. Jody Sperling is one scholar who does take notice of the influence of Nautch dancing on the development of Fuller's *Serpentine Dance.* Sperling, "Skirting the Image: The Origins of Loïe Fuller's Serpentine Dance," 2001, www.timelapsedance.com/files/skirting_the_image.pdf. Accessed May 1, 2012. Sally Sommer also notes that the "filmy transparent costume" used in a Nautch number in *The Arabian Nights* (1887), in which Fuller also appeared, was "not unsimilar to the one used later by Fuller." Sommer, "Loïe Fuller," 1975, 55.

[48] *Fuller v. Bemis.* This account bears striking similarities to Ruth St. Denis's encounter with "Nautch" girls at Coney Island in 1904, to be discussed below. The timing of Fuller's study in Paris is a bit unclear, but she may have traveled there while stationed in London in 1889, which would have coincided with the Paris Exposition of 1889.

Figure 1.2 Loïe Fuller in the *Serpentine Dance* in *Uncle Celestin* (1892). Jerome Robbins Dance Division, The New York Public Library for the Performing Arts, Astor, Lenox, and Tilden Foundations.

her skirt was "an old Hindoo costume" presented to her by a British officer stationed in India. She subsequently claimed that it was a leftover Oriental costume used in a production at London's Savoy Theatre, and shortly thereafter, that it was "a Nautch girl's dress" from Calcutta sent to her by a friend.[49] In her 1913 autobiography, she described the fabric as a "Hindu skirt ... sent me by my two young officers."[50] Eventually, she dropped the Indian references altogether, asserting that the skirt material was "yards and yards of cheese-cloth" rummaged up in an old trunk in a London hotel garret.[51]

[49] Current and Current, *Loie Fuller*, 59–60.
[50] Fuller, *Fifteen Years*, 28.
[51] Current and Current, *Loie Fuller*, 60–61.

Figure 1.3 "Nautch" girl dancing with accompanying musicians, Calcutta, India, circa 1900. Library of Congress Prints and Photographs Division.

The accuracy of any of these accounts aside, there are documentable links between Fuller's *Serpentine Dance* and the traffic in Orientalia that characterized high and low culture alike in turn-of-the-century Britain and America. Fuller herself "partook heavily of her era's Orientalism," performing in Orientalist fare in the United States and Europe.[52] In New York in 1887, she assumed the title role in *Aladdin's Wonderful Lamp*, a pantomime adaptation of *The Thousand and One Nights*. Among the show's fourteen dance numbers were an Indian "nautch" dance and a "Veil of Vapor Dance," in which Fuller performed "behind a translucent 'curtain' of steam over which colored lights were projected."[53] Spectators duly detected the influences on the *Serpentine Dance*: describing Fuller's 1892 performance in *Uncle Celestin*, a reviewer for the *New York Blade* wrote, "in the limelight it seemed as though the great skirt had a million folds and every one a yard.... When she came back ... she twirled the skirt on both arms—she wound it up and her figure showed out clear through the white. *That was a bit of the Nautch dance.*"[54]

[52] Garelick, *Electric Salome*, 17.
[53] Ibid., 25–26.
[54] Quoted in Sommer, "Loïe Fuller" 1975, 57, emphasis added.

This critic's framing of Fuller's performance reveals that above and beyond her use of "Hindoo" fabric, the *Serpentine Dance* bore the "kinesthetic traces" of Nautch dancing.[55] As Priya Srinivasan argues, Indian dancers who traveled to and performed in North America under the name Nautch beginning in 1880 left their mark on American modern dance, one that most historical accounts have failed to acknowledge. Srinivasan's work focuses on the encounter between the white modern dance "pioneer" Ruth St. Denis and a group of Nautch dancers who performed at Coney Island in 1904, but her statement that "The labour of Nautch dancing women … haunts American dance histories through the very basic dance principles of movement[:] spiral turns and whirls" could apply equally to Fuller.[56] The exposure of her figure through the translucent silk; the whirls and turns detailed in her copyright registration: these are among the core elements of Fuller's "signature" dance.[57] Circulated through the bodies of touring Indian dancers and adapted for Orientalist-themed Western stage productions, Nautch dancing, as much as skirt dancing, must be recognized as an important source from which Fuller drew to create her *Serpentine Dance*.

This Eastern influence is hardly surprising given the role Orientalism played in the emergence of white modern dance. As revisionist dance historians like Srinivasan, Yutian Wong, Jane Desmond, and Amy Koritz, building on the work of Edward Said, have pointed out, early modern dancers such as Ruth St. Denis and Maud Allan, whose choreography took on Oriental subjects, simultaneously enacted and distanced themselves from the East and thereby carved out a space for themselves as white female performers on the public stage.[58] By adopting Eastern themes, these women displayed their mastery of the Oriental Other; by emphasizing the aesthetic and spiritual dimensions of their danced "innovations," they displaced any suspect eroticism onto the racialized East. In doing so, early modern white female dancers buttressed white supremacy and legitimized their artistic practice.

Here we see how the property functions of whiteness facilitate the dynamics of appropriation. In a discussion of "the property of enjoyment" that

[55] Srinivasan, *Sweating Saris*, 23, 68, 72.

[56] Priya Srinivasan, "The Bodies beneath the Smoke or What's Behind the Cigarette Poster: Unearthing Kinesthetic Connections in American Dance History," *Discourses in Dance* 4.1 (2007): 8.

[57] See Albright, *Traces of Light*, for a discussion of the *Serpentine Dance* as Fuller's signature.

[58] Srinivasan, *Sweating Saris*; Yutian Wong, *Choreographing Asian America* (Middletown, CT: Wesleyan University Press, 2010); Desmond, "Dancing Out the Difference"; Amy Koritz, "Dancing the Orient for England: Maud Allan's *The Vision of Salome*," in *Meaning in Motion: New Cultural Studies of Dance*, ed. Jane C. Desmond (Durham, NC: Duke University Press, 1997), 133–52.

complements Cheryl Harris's, Saidiya Hartman explains how the right to use and enjoy became an "inheritance of chattel slavery" for whites.[59] Citing *Black's Law Dictionary's* definition of the term "enjoy" as "to have, possess, and use with satisfaction; to occupy or have the benefit of," Hartman demonstrates how the property expectations of whites under slavery also presumed ownership of African American cultural displays. This same logic underwrote the institution of blackface minstrelsy, in which white men appropriated and stereotyped their own racist versions of black music, song, and dance—a tradition that continued for many years after the abolition of slavery.[60] Likewise, when early white modern dancers took on Eastern themes, they were exercising their right "to take delight in, to use, and to possess" non-white expressive practices. The complement of the right to enjoy was the right to exclude: only those who were excluded from full white subjecthood, and thus rendered objects, were capable of being possessed and "enjoyed" as property. As Srinivasan demonstrates, the right to exclude was literalized in the United States through increasingly restrictive anti-immigration laws that targeted Asians in the early twentieth century.[61] Once barred from US shores, Indian dancers were prevented from contesting the use of their dance material by white women. In this way, the property-like rights of whiteness directly affected how Nautch dancing circulated, with white Western bodies becoming the privileged consumers and interpreters of Oriental dance.

Yet for white female dancers, the act of seizing "representational control" of the East was not without risk. As Amy Koritz writes, in order for a white woman to "retain the privileges of her ethnicity, she cannot be too closely identified with the Orientalized subject."[62] Thus, early modern dancers adopted methods like extracting select Eastern movement motifs (recall Fuller's "bit" of the Nautch dance), abstracting and aestheticizing them, and/or combining them with Western "expressive" styles, all the while wrapping their resulting choreography in the discourse of the modern and the artistic.[63] The task of preserving a safe distance from their non-white subjects, however, could be difficult when

---

[59] Saidiya V. Hartman, *Scenes of Subjection: Terror, Slavery, and Self-Making in Nineteenth-Century America* (New York: Oxford University Press, 1997), 23–24.

[60] On blackface minstrelsy and its persistence into the twentieth century, see Eric Lott, *Love and Theft: Blackface Minstrelsy and the American Working Class* (New York: Oxford University Press, 1993) and Michael Rogin, *Blackface, White Noise: Jewish Immigrants in the Hollywood Melting Pot* (Berkeley: University of California Press, 1996). I address the relationship between black slavery and blackface minstrelsy further in Chapter 2.

[61] Srinivasan, *Sweating Saris*.

[62] Koritz, "Dancing the Orient," 144.

[63] For example, early modern dancers like St. Denis drew on the "expressive" principles of the American Delsarte system of movement. See Desmond, "Dancing Out the Difference," 33–35.

white women were not in command of the (re)production of their choreography. Even as they claimed ownership of Eastern "raw materials" through their choreographic practice, these women's dancing bodies became products subject to alienation and exchange by men. As much as Fuller's white skin gave her the privilege to control what she embodied on stage, she had much less control over how her bodily representations circulated in the theatrical marketplace. As discussed above, the traffic in her choreography, just as for Nautch and skirt dancers, was regulated by contracts and dependent on the investments and inclinations of male managers and producers. How, then, could a white female dancer trying to situate herself as a proper(tied) artist ensure that the capitalist market would differentiate between her position as a possessive individual and that of racialized and/or sexualized subjects who were so susceptible to commodification? For Fuller, I want to suggest, the proliferation of the *Serpentine Dance* threatened to obscure the distinctions between her "legitimate" choreography and commercial versions of Nautch and skirt dancing. The unchecked circulation of Fuller's dance and image alongside these commodities called into question the extent of her hold on white property rights.

"They Had Stolen My Dance": Theft, Personhood, and Proprietorship

Fuller's alarm over the replication of her choreography is evident in her description of the events leading up to her lawsuit against Minnie Bemis. In her autobiography, she describes eagerly awaiting the debut of advertising placards for her appearance as a specialty act in *Uncle Celestin*. On February 16, 1892, the day after the show opened in New York following a six-week tour, Fuller woke up to find

> the whole city ... plastered with lithographs, reproduced from one of my photographs, representing me larger than life, with letters a foot high announcing: 'The Serpentine Dance! The Serpentine Dance!' But there was one circumstance came near giving me heart failure. My name was nowhere mentioned.

Furious over the lack of attribution, as recounted above, Fuller resigned (or was fired) from *Uncle Celestin* and secured a new contract with a manager at the Madison Square Theatre. In no time, she learned that Aronson, her former manager at the Casino Theatre, had employed the chorus girl Minnie Bemis to continue performing the *Serpentine Dance* in her stead. Her reaction to the news is telling:

They had stolen my dance.

I felt myself overcome, dead—more dead, as it seemed to me, than I shall be at the moment when my last hour comes. My very life depended on this success, and now others were going to reap the benefit. I cannot describe my despair. I was incapable of words, of gestures. I was dumb and paralyzed.

Fuller came in for a similar shock several months later when she arrived at the Folies-Bergère in Paris in hopes of securing an engagement. "Imagine my astonishment," she writes, "when, in getting out of the carriage in front of the Folies, I found myself face to face with a 'serpentine dancer' reproduced in violent tones on some huge placards. This dancer was not Loie Fuller. Here was the cataclysm, my utter annihilation."[64]

What strikes me about these passages, however hyped for dramatic effect, is the way Fuller portrays the theft of her choreography as the dispossession of her very personhood. For her, the dissemination of her image without her control, and the inability to "reap the benefit[s]" of what she considered her artistic "discovery," amounted to a kind of obliteration of the self. Robbed of the power to capitalize on her dance or contain its reproduction, Fuller senses herself transformed from subject to object. Her description of this loss of control over her bodily labor resonates with Eva Cherniavsky's claim that under the logic of possessive individualism, being rendered "open to capital" amounts to "a missing or attenuated hold on interior personhood."[65] The inability to contain the circulation of her bodily image—her "migrations of personality"—left Fuller feeling deprived of a core, inalienable self and signified her vulnerability to the "invasive forces of capital" from which white (masculine) subjects have generally been protected.[66]

Suing Bemis, who, after replacing Fuller in *Uncle Celestin*, went on to perform the *Serpentine Dance* at the Madison Square Roof Garden, was in part Fuller's answer to this attenuation of subjecthood. Originally filed in May 1892, and argued before Judge E. Henry Lacombe in the US Circuit Court in New York on June 18 of that year, Fuller's copyright infringement case is worth examining in detail, for it touches on issues ranging from authorship, originality, and reputation to the suitability of dance to copyright law.

---

[64] Fuller, *Fifteen Years*, 41–42.

[65] Cherniavsky, *Incorporations*, xx. Eden Osucha similarly notes that "if one's self-possession implies the possession of one's image, then the unbidden circulation of that image can constitute a kind of theft" ("The Whiteness of Privacy," 77).

[66] Cherniavsky, *Incorporations*, 89.

Officially listed as *Marie Louise Fuller versus Minnie Renwood Bemis*, Fuller's case depended on four overarching and interrelated claims. The first was that the *Serpentine Dance* was an original work of authorship. More specifically, as spelled out in the official Bill of Complaint against Bemis, Fuller's lawyer maintained that she, the orator, was

> the author, inventor, designer and proprietor of a dramatic composition know as the Serpentine Dance. That said dramatic composition and each and all of the incidents, scenes and tableaus therein are the original conception and invention of your orator and said composition in character, incidents, situations and dramatic and theatrical effect are wholly original with your orator and designed and suited for public representation.

The fact that novelty was not necessary to prove originality under copyright law did not stop Fuller's lawyer from contending that the *Serpentine Dance* was "entirely novel and unlike any dramatic incident, scene or tableau known to have been heretofore represented on any stage, or invented by any author, before [she] invented and composed" it. Crucially, this disavowal of antecedents positioned Fuller in a class apart from the skirt and Nautch dancers who functioned as exchangeable commodities on the commercial stage, despite her indebtedness to them. Touted as "one of the most novel, attractive, and graceful and unique and beautiful incidents and productions ever represented on the public stage," the *Serpentine Dance*, the lawsuit implied, was the work of a creative genius.[67]

To make her case against Bemis, that is, Fuller claimed the status of the white Romantic artist. Reaching its apotheosis in the late eighteenth and early nineteenth centuries (although I would argue it still holds sway in modern and much post-modern and contemporary dance), the Romantic notion of originary authorship constructs the artist as a singular visionary whose work is by definition new and unique rather than imitative or derivative.[68] Scholars like Martha Woodmansee have shown how this modern conception of the artist as genius emerged when shifts in production, distribution, and consumption in the late eighteenth century created a need to "'rescue ...' art from determination by the market"; the idea that creative inspiration emanated from the interiority of a solitary self insulated authors from the mass public on whom

[67] *Fuller v. Bemis.*

[68] Martha Woodmansee and Peter Jaszi, "Introduction," in *The Construction of Authorship: Textual Appropriation in Law and Literature*, ed Martha Woodmansee and Peter Jaszi (Durham, NC: Duke University Press, 1994), 3.

their economic survival was increasingly dependent.[69] Just so, Fuller's insistence on limning her choreography as "novel" and "unique" was meant to signal her distance from the chorus girls, skirt dancers, and Nautch dancers of the commercial stage.

The second claim Fuller's lawsuit made was that she possessed a valid copyright on the *Serpentine Dance*. Here, the classification of the dance as a dramatic composition was essential since choreography was not protectable in its own right. Citing the precedent of *Daly v. Palmer* (1868), which defined a drama as "a composition in which the action is not narrated or described, but represented" and held that "movement, gesture and facial expression ... are as much a part of the dramatic composition as is the spoken language," Fuller's lawyer maintained that her creation, too, was a dramatic composition under the meaning of the law.[70] Bolstering this assertion, Fuller herself testified that

> This composition is called a dance for want of a more appropriate term. It is in reality a series of gyrations of the body and manipulation of the dress for the purpose of producing pleasing effects upon and graceful postures to the eye, and is dramatic and theatrical in effect in that it portrays ... and depicts in fanciful and poetic ways certain effects and incidents, such as the appearance of an umbrella, the shape of various flowers, waves or breakers as of the surf, butterfly and other postures.

The emphasis, then, was not on the movements of the Serpentine Dance per se but on the "effects" that its "incidents, scenes and tableaux" had on spectators. The affidavits of several Fuller supporters echoed this assessment. For example, Therese Lee, identified as the wife of the well-known actor Henry Lee, affirmed that the *Serpentine Dance*

> is very dramatic in that it portrays and represents ideas, it appeals to the eye and judging from the applause with which it is received, is a source of great entertainment and satisfaction to the spectators. Each situation and tableau[,] each motion and turn gives rise to new ideas in the mind of the spectator.

---

[69] Martha Woodmansee, *The Author, Art, and the Market: Rereading the History of Aesthetics* (New York: Columbia University Press, 1994), 33.

[70] *Daly v. Palmer*; "Copyright—'Dramatic Composition'—Stage Dance."

Suggesting some coaching on the part of Fuller's attorneys, the affidavits of two actors, O'Kane Hillis and Flora Clitherow, contained the following identical statements about the Serpentine Dance: "There are different incidents therein expressed and portrayed and each movement raises and represents a different idea and appeals to the higher emotions." The standardized language suggests how critical proving dramatic content was to Fuller's case, how insistent her lawyers were that the *Serpentine Dance* signified something for and did something to spectators.

In addition to emphasizing the dramatic nature of her composition, Fuller's lawyers were careful to document the legal steps Fuller had taken to secure her copyright registration. In May 1892 she mailed two printed copies of her composition to the Librarian of Congress, together with the fifty-cent registration fee, and on the title page of each published version of her composition she had printed the words, "Copyright, 1892, by MARIE LOUISE FULLER, New York."[71] Fuller's lawyers submitted a copy of this publication as an exhibit in their suit.

Having asserted her authorship and copyright of the *Serpentine Dance*, Fuller then claimed the corresponding entitlements: the exclusive rights of ownership. As Mark Rose has argued, "the distinguishing characteristic of the modern author ... is proprietorship; the author is conceived as the originator and therefore owner of a special kind of commodity, the work."[72] Just so, Fuller's lawsuit hinged on the contention that her copyright granted her not only "the sole and exclusive right and liberty to print and publish such dramatic composition," but also "the sole and exclusive right to act, perform and represent the said dramatic composition and cause it to be acted, performed and represented on any stage or public place during the whole period for which the said copyright was obtained." The assertion of the latter, the exclusive right to publicly perform the *Serpentine Dance*, was in keeping with the 1856 Copyright Act, which added performance rights to the list of entitlements for authors of dramatic compositions.[73]

---

[71] *Fuller v. Bemis.* Prior to the 1909 Copyright Act, registration was a prerequisite for copyright protection. The 1909 act made publication with notice (i.e., the affixation of a copyright symbol) the means of establishing copyright. See David Rabinowitz, "Everything You Ever Wanted to Know about the Copyright Act before 1909," *Journal of the Copyright Society of the U.S.A.* 49 (Winter 2001): 650–61.

[72] Mark Rose, *Authors and Owners: The Invention of Copyright* (Cambridge, MA: Harvard University Press, 1993), 1.

[73] Copyright Act of Aug. 18, 1856, 34th Congress, 1st Session, *U.S. Statutes at Large,* 11:138.

Finally, on these grounds, Fuller asserted that Minnie Bemis was infringing upon her property rights and should be enjoined from performing the
Serpentine Dance. In legal language, Fuller's lawyer stated that Bemis,

> without the knowledge, privity or consent of your orator has produced
> upon the public stage and is about to continue to produce upon the
> public stage in theatres throughout the United States, said dramatic
> composition of your orator in a manner which was and is intended to
> differ from it only slightly so as colorably to be a different work when
> it substantially retained and retains the attractive features of your ora-
> tor's composition, and that she has advertised and caused to be adver-
> tised her said dance as "the Serpentine Dance."

That Bemis's version of the dance departed from Fuller's only "colorably"
was critical to Fuller's case, and she recruited several witnesses to provide evidence to this effect. While an actor named John Bauer testified that "the imitation by the defendant of the complainant's dance was as close a one as it could
be," another, O'Kane Hillis, concluded that "to the ordinary observer ... there
would be no difference whatever between the dances of the complainant and
defendant." Another witness, George R. Hall, was apparently recruited for the
sole purpose of combing newspaper articles that commented on the relationship between Bemis's and Fuller's acts. In his deposition, he cited references
to Bemis as an "exact counterfeit of Miss Fuller," "a perfect duplication," and
"an observant understudy" who had "succeeded in reproducing every pose and
gesture of the original."[74] To prove infringement, Fuller thus characterized
Bemis as the unauthorized copy to her original.

Unabated performances of this counterfeit *Serpentine Dance*, Fuller further
alleged, were doing her acute harm. "The continuance of [Bemis] at a rival theatre," Fuller testified, "will cause and tend to cause me irreparable injury in that
it has deprived me and will continue to deprive me of the applause and credit
of such performance and in that it tends to give to another the reputation and

---

[74] Interestingly, the discussion around copying took on a pointed gendered cast. Among the
reports cited was one from the *New York Recorder* of February 28, 1892, which read: "The Casino
people are jubilant over the huge success of Miss Fuller's successor in the Serpentine dance. The
imitativeness possessed by the majority of women is certainly marvelous. Like man's original
ancestor—according to Darwin—they can imitate almost anything in a surprisingly short space
of time and with comparatively little effort. Before Miss Fuller had introduced this dance no one
had over seen it, yet she had been dancing for less than a week when an observant understudy succeeded in reproducing every pose and gesture of the original." Fuller's claims of originality thus
disrupted the perception that female cultural production was only ever reproductive, even as her
accusations against Bemis sustained it. *Fuller v. Bemis.*

profit of the performer of said composition which rightfully belongs to me." Bemis was thus not only robbing Fuller of economic capital but also of her "rightful" reputation. Here Cheryl Harris's discussion of "status property" is helpful, for, as she argues, one of the ideas that ensued from the Lockean notion of "self-ownership" was "that reputation, as an aspect of identity earned through effort," was like property, and that "the loss of reputation was capable of being valued in the market."[75] Made at a time when American women were not yet enfranchised citizens, Fuller's injury claims implicitly align her with the capital of the white, male propertied subject.

Each and every one of Fuller's claims was vehemently contested by the opposing counsel in *Fuller v. Bemis*. The chief point of contention was the originality of the *Serpentine Dance*. In answer to Fuller's list of complaints, Bemis's lawyers, led by Allan McCulloh, asserted that it was "not true that the complainant is the author, inventor, designer and proprietor" of the *Serpentine Dance*, nor that "all or any of the incidents, scenes and tableaux therein, were the original conception and invention of the complainant, or that the said alleged composition in character, incidents, situations and dramatic and theatrical effect, or any of them, is or are wholly or partly original with the complainant." As the star witness for the defense, Minnie Bemis testified at length about the ordinariness of the dance that, in her account, she had been performing for about three years. Maintaining that the "movements, steps and gyrations" that comprised her act were "common in fancy, character and ballet dances," Bemis argued that "the only features [*sic*] of said dance, as now produced by me, which is not in very common use, is the use at times of a long skirt, instead of the usual short ballet skirt." The skirt, Bemis claimed, was "wholly designed by myself." She further alleged

> That there is nothing novel in said dance, and that the same may be performed by any graceful professional dancer. That I have many times seen the same movements of the body, arms and limbs which are used by complainant also used by other professional dancers upon the public stage for upwards of eight or ten years.
>
> That I have seen the complainant herein perform what she terms her serpentine dance, and that the movements and gyrations by the complainant in said dance are not novel or original, but have been performed for many years, in connection with other movements, by ballet and other professional dancers upon the public stage.

[75] Harris, "Whiteness as Property," 1734–35.

> That the complainant in performing her said dance, does not, as
> understood in the profession, use any dance steps other than perhaps
> a waltz step, which is in no way novel.

Even while disputing the novelty of Fuller's movements, Bemis cast doubt on the possibility of duplicating them precisely. Acknowledging that she and Fuller were performing at the Casino Theatre at the same time, she nonetheless maintained that she "did not at that time have opportunity to see the whole of any performance by the complainant herein, and have never previously seen her dance." She went on:

> From my knowledge and experience in the matter of public dancing,
> I believe it to be entirely impossible for any dancers to imitate strictly
> or in a colorable manner any dance possessing the novelty and origi-
> nality alleged by the complainant to be possessed by her alleged dra-
> matic composition or dance, except after repeated, close and careful
> attending and study of the same, and of the whole thereof.

Using Fuller's own logic against her, Bemis asserts that truly innovative dancing is not replicable without sustained scrutiny. Finally, Bemis challenged the originality of Fuller's use of calcium lights, which Bemis claimed to have "many times seen upon the public stage in the City of New York, and elsewhere."

Deponent after deponent, including the manager of Madison Square Garden and a host of dance teachers, testified to the same effect, insisting that there was "nothing novel" about Fuller's dancing. Rather, they alleged, Fuller's *Serpentine Dance* was "in every respect a skirt dance in the well known sense of the term," save for its length, and that "hundreds of dancers" were currently performing similar "poses, steps and glides" on the public stage. Citing a number of antecedents, they compared Fuller's dancing to that of the British skirt dancer Letty Lind (whom Bemis likewise named as an influence), a Viennese ballet dancer named Bertha Linde, who also used a long skirt, and the actress Maggie Mitchell, who had apparently performed a "Shadow Dance" using lights in a manner similar to Fuller's use some two decades earlier. (Fuller responded by testifying that while she had worked in the same company with Letty Lind for a year, Lind "never wore a skirt such as I wear in the Serpentine Dance or performed a dance similar thereto.") Interestingly, the only reference to Nautch dancing among the many affidavits came when one witness quoted a newspaper interview with Fuller, in which, as cited above, Fuller described seeing "Nautch girls" at the Paris Exposition. Like dance scholars generations later, Fuller's contemporaries identified her principally with the tradition of

skirt dancing, exhibiting a blindness to the non-Western sources of her movement. Unlike present-day scholars, dance teachers in Fuller's time (if only
those recruited to testify on Bemis's behalf) found her performance entirely
lacking in creativity.

Furthermore, where Bemis commented on the difficulty of replicating
another's dance movements if they were truly original, most of the dance
teachers asserted that originality itself was a virtual impossibility in dance. For
example, Edward Collyer submitted that "it is not possible ... for any one now
alive to lay claim to the authorship or invention of one single step, pose, posture, movement or glide in any manner, shape or form," for "every movement
or pose or step taken by any dancer on the public stage at this present date is
merely one of a series of movements taught in the regular course of instruction." Augusta Sohlke added that "the movements of arms and limbs and body
of complainant and defendant in their respective dances are old and are such as
have been used from time immemorial in conjunction with other movements
of limbs and gyrations of the body on the ballet and variety stages." From the
perspective of these dance teachers, whose profession, after all,. depended
on passing down "movements, gestures, and steps" that they themselves had
learned, dances were not inventions so much as re-arrangements of existing
moves that were transmitted from one body to another. By this logic, dance
hardly seemed an appropriate candidate for copyright protection.

The defense countered the legitimacy of Fuller's copyright in other ways
as well. Undermining Fuller's classification of the *Serpentine Dance* as a dramatic composition, Bemis described it as "a mere spectacle," lacking "any
literary or dramatic character[,] ... any verbal accompaniment or dialogue,"
and any "attempt to portray any narrative." More prosaically, the defense challenged Fuller's contention that she had obtained a copyright certificate for
the *Serpentine Dance*. Among the affidavits submitted on Bemis's behalf was
one from an attorney named Aldis Browne, evidently recruited for the express
purpose of investigating the status of Fuller's copyright application. He maintained that the Librarian of Congress had unequivocally refused Fuller's copyright because there was "no authority in the Copyright Law by which a dance
could be copyrighted nor the directions for such a dance be construed as a
literary composition of any nature entitled to such copyright." In support of
these assertions, Browne attached a letter received from A. R. Spofford, the
Librarian of Congress, dated May 27. It stated that

> the entry of Copyright on "a Serpentine Dance," by Marie L. Fuller,
> was not made—for the reason that it does not come within the des-
> ignation of any of the articles which are lawful subjects of Copyright.
> The two copies purporting to be this "Dramatic Composition" are

nothing but written directions for dances, tableaux, poses, etc. without a word of dialogue or literary composition of any kind.

Unwilling to let these assertions stand, lawyers for Fuller responded by
entering into evidence their own correspondence with Spofford. Apparently,
Spofford had initially returned Fuller's registration fee and refused to
enter her description of the *Serpentine Dance* as a dramatic composition. In
reply, Lewinson and Falk wrote an angry letter to Spofford, dated May 28,
re-submitting the registration fee and making three arguments: first, that as
the Librarian of Congress, Spofford was "not a judicial officer" who possessed
the authority to decide "whether writings are compositions or not"; second,
that they had submitted the typewritten copies of the *Serpentine Dance* not as a
dramatic composition but as "a description of the dramatic composition" and
only asked that Spofford enter into his records the title of the *Serpentine Dance*;
and third, that "Although you are not a judicial officer and cannot construe the
law, it may interest you to know that a dramatic composition does not necessarily consist of 'dialogue or literary compositions of any kind.' "[76] On June 13,
Isaac Falk testified that Spofford had yet to take any subsequent action, leaving no "intimation ... whether he would issue the certificate applied for or not
although he has received the fees for such certificates and has had the same in
his possession now for two weeks since last sent to him."

So, it would seem, the status of Fuller's copyright claim remained uncertain up to and through her infringement trial. The fact that Fuller's lawyers
contended, on one hand, that the *Serpentine Dance* did qualify as a dramatic
composition based on precedent and, on the other, that her copyright was only
intended to cover the description of the dance is a fitting indicator of the ambiguity that has surrounded the question of dance's copyrightability. Indeed, the
issues debated by lawyers for Fuller and Bemis—about whether a dance could
qualify as a dramatic composition, and about how to construe the relationship
between a "fixed" transcription of a dance and the actual movement—would
remain unsettled for virtually the next eight decades.

Exploiting equally the doubt around the copyrightability of the *Serpentine
Dance* and Fuller's status as a Romantic artist, Bemis's defense effectively
argued that Fuller's proprietary claims on the *Serpentine Dance* had no legal
standing. To the extent that Fuller's case rested on shoring up her difference
from other female dancing bodies who circulated as interchangeable commodities in the theatrical marketplace, the defense's case rested on eviscerat-
ing that difference. If there was nothing original about the *Serpentine Dance*, if

[76] Lewinson and Falk cited *Palmer v. Daly*, 6 Blatch, 256.

it was not a dramatic composition, if the Copyright Office had denied Fuller's registration request, and if dance in general consisted only of recycled steps, then Fuller could enjoy no more entitlement to perform the *Serpentine Dance* than Bemis, and Fuller's claims of injury were devoid of merit.

"Merely Mechanical Movements": Legal Judgments

The arguments of the defense ultimately won the day. On June 10, 1892, Judge E. Henry Lacombe announced his ruling in the case. Declaring that the matter had been "fully argued" and that the court was "fully advised in the premises," the judge decided "after due deliberation … that the complainant is not entitled to a preliminary injunction."[77] In his judgment, which was reported in several newspapers, he rejected the use of *Daly v. Palmer* as a relevant precedent, declaring that it was "not authority for the proposition that complainant's performance is a dramatic composition within the meaning of the Copyright Act." He went on to explain his criteria for meeting the dramatic requirement:

> It is essential to such a composition that it should tell some story. The plot may be simple. It may be but the narrative or representation of a single transaction: but it must repeat or mimic some action, speech, emotion, passion or character, real or imaginary. And when it does, it is the ideas thus expressed which become subject of copyright.
>
> An examination of the description of complainant's dance, as filed for copyright, shows that the end sought for and accomplished was solely the devising of a series of graceful movements, combined with an attractive arrangement of drapery, lights and shadows, telling no story, portraying no character, depicting no emotion. The merely mechanical movements by which effects are produced on the stage are not subjects of copyright where they convey no ideas whose arrangement makes up a dramatic composition. Surely those described and practiced here convey, and were devised to convey, to the spectator, no other idea than that a comely woman is illustrating the poetry of motion in a singularly graceful fashion. Such an idea may be pleasing, but it can hardly be called dramatic.[78]

---

[77] *Fuller v. Bemis.*
[78] "Copyright—'Dramatic Composition'—Stage Dance."

Ignoring witnesses for Fuller who testified that the *Serpentine Dance* did, in fact, depict images that appealed to spectators' emotions, Judge Lacombe chose to construe the kinesthetic components of Fuller's performance as "merely mechanical movements," thus evacuating the *Serpentine Dance* of any meaning. As such, the decision crops up frequently in literature about choreographic copyright, where it is held up as evidence of the considerable hurdles dancers faced in their bids for copyright protection prior to the 1976 Copyright Act, and in scholarship on Fuller, where it is seen as proof of her pioneering artistic status. Fuller's failure to meet the judge's expectation that dancing must relay a story to contain ideas, that is, signals the radical modernism of her choreographic practice. As Rhonda Garelick has written, "The judge's remarks offer a neat explanation of the difference between nineteenth-century narrative or character-based dance and its twentieth-century abstract, modern descendant."[79] In a slightly different vein, Ann Cooper Albright reads the ruling in terms of Fuller's non-conformity with the "expressive paradigm" that other dance scholars like Mark Franko have limned as the "foundational narrative of modern dance, where the (feminine) body translates interior and transcendent 'ideas' into physical forms."[80] In other words, Albright finds that Fuller "refused the 'natural' interiority of a feminine body" that Judge Lacombe expected, inaugurating instead a different kind of kinesthetic expressivity that "required a new way of seeing."[81]

The gendered implications of the judge's decision certainly deserve attention. The opposition he sets up between narrative, representation, and ideas, on one side, and gracefulness, comeliness, and visual pleasure, on the other, pointedly absents the female dancing body from the realm of legal consequence. Like Albright, I read Judge Lacombe's language as a gender-coded finding that Fuller's moving body lacked interiority. But rather than seeing this lack in aesthetic terms, as Fuller's rejection of a certain kind of expressivity, I see this missing interiority as a blunt rejection of her possessive individualism. Deemed no more than a "comely woman," Fuller is reduced to a feminized object and deprived of the "incorporated embodiment" that would enable her to claim anything as proper to her subject.[82] In denying that Fuller's choreography constituted the expression of meaningful ideas, Judge Lacombe concomitantly denied her status as an authorial subject entitled to ownership rights in her bodily labor. In short order, his decision demoted Fuller from Romantic artist to a body that is "all surfaces" and "fully open to capital."[83]

---

[79] Garelick, *Electric Salome*, 30.
[80] Albright, *Traces of Light*, 28.
[81] Ibid.
[82] Cherniavsky, *Incorporations*, xv.
[83] Ibid., xvii.

Just how open is made clear by the other lawsuits that Fuller lost in the immediate aftermath of Judge Lacombe's ruling. Just four days later, on June 14, 1892, came the dismissal of Fuller's complaint against Aronson and the New York Concert Company, which, as described above, Fuller originally filed in March. Two days after that, Fuller lost a third suit, this one filed against her by Hoyt & Thomas, the management company of Madison Square Theatre. Heard in New York City's Superior Court, *Hoyt et al. v. Fuller* was, like *Fuller v. New York Concert Company, Limited*, a case about contract violations, but this time, Fuller was on the receiving end of breach accusations. Evidently, Fuller, described by the court as "an actress and *danseuse*," had agreed to perform the *Serpentine Dance* in *A Trip to Chinatown* for the length of its run at the Madison Square Theatre, and then during a road tour, until August 1, 1892. The point of contention was whether, though the contract apparently did not explicitly state as much, Fuller had granted Hoyt "the exclusive right to her services" and whether she had thus violated the contract by performing the *Serpentine Dance* at Amberg's Theatre during the run of *A Trip to Chinatown*.[84] While Fuller had "expressly refused to sign a contract with a clause to the effect that she was to appear with Hoyt & Thomas exclusively," claiming "the privilege of appearing ... at other places, as her time is not wholly occupied at the plaintiffs,'" the plaintiffs alleged that exclusivity was part of the spirit and intent of the employment contract.[85] Seeking an injunction against Fuller, Hoyt asserted that he had engaged Fuller "as a special feature to induce people to come to witness her performance, who would not otherwise attend his theater, and her appearance at other theaters would result in pecuniary injury to him." On June 16, Judge J. McAdam issued a ruling in favor of the plaintiffs, granting the injunction against Fuller until August 1, "unless the plaintiffs sooner elect to terminate the contract, according to the option therein contained."[86]

The decision in this case is striking insofar as it renders Fuller open to capital—with her male managers given full and exclusive access to her—even while it grants her a kind of power that verdicts in earlier lawsuits denied her. For, in order to recognize Hoyt & Thomas's injury claims, Judge McAdam had to find that Fuller's performance of the *Serpentine Dance* was utterly original. In an ironic twist, the judge, pointing to Fuller's infringement suit against Bemis, used her legal claims of uniqueness against her. Quoting Fuller's own characterization of the "originality and extraordinary novel nature" of the *Serpentine Dance* in *Fuller v. Bemis*, Judge McAdam concluded, "If this graphic

---

[84] *Hoyt v. Fuller*, 19 N.Y. 962.
[85] *New York Clipper*, June 25, 1892, 247; *Hoyt v. Fuller*.
[86] *Hoyt v. Fuller*.

description be correct, it is evident that no one can be procured as a substitute for the defendant. She is the original and only artistic serpentine dancer, while her would-be rivals are but poor imitators." Rather than affirming Fuller's rights, however, this designation of originality enhanced those of her managers, who deserved to profit fully from her uniqueness. Here, recognition of Fuller's value only reinforced her status as a commodity, as "an attractive feature" and "a drawing card" for consumers.

Taken together, the logic of the verdicts in the three lawsuits in which Fuller was involved in close proximity is both contradictory and consistent. Although two of the cases were concerned with contract violation and one with copyright infringement, all three were essentially about the extent to which Fuller's image—either as static visual representation or as live dancing body—should be allowed to circulate in the theatrical marketplace, and who possessed the rights to profit from that circulation. On the former question, the legal decisions seem to be at odds. While the judge in *Fuller v. New York Concert Company* allowed lithographic images of the *Serpentine Dance* to circulate with impunity, the judge in *Hoyt v. Fuller* restricted the dance's circulation by confining Fuller to a single theater. While the judge in *Fuller v. Bemis* gave no heed to Fuller's claims of uniqueness and thus sanctioned other performers' imitations of the dance, the judge in *Hoyt v. Fuller* used these same claims to justify strict limits on the dance's reproduction. Yet, on the latter question—who had the right to regulate and profit from the circulation of the *Serpentine Dance*—the legal findings were in agreement: not Fuller. All three of the cases thus underscore and reinforce Fuller's lack of ownership over her choreographic labor. Without the rights of the possessive individual, her efforts to control the terms under which her dancing body circulated were ineffectual, rendering her "susceptible to abstraction and exchange" in the male-dominated marketplace.

In this context, it is worth returning to Judge Lacombe's use of the term "mechanical" to describe Fuller's choreography. Calling her movements "merely mechanical" likens them to a mass-produced commodity; they convey no more ideas than a "pleasing" lithographic representation of her and require no greater thought to reproduce. Yet collectively, the three legal cases draw conflicting conclusions about the difference between the commodity image and the live dancing body. When Fuller is the plaintiff, she is granted no more entitlement to limit live enactments of her dance than mass-produced images of it. But when she is sued by male managers with a financial stake in her performance, the "uniqueness" and "exclusivity" of her live body suddenly become paramount, justifying restrictions on the *Serpentine Dance*. It would seem, then, that the legal system's answer to the question of how exchangeable Fuller's dancing body was and should be was a gendered one that depended heavily on who was asking and who stood to gain.

To a great extent, though, the inconsistencies surrounding the reproducibility of Fuller's choreography and image were inherent to her position as a commoditized dancing body. Her refusal to assign exclusive performing rights to the Hoyt & Thomas management company is a reminder that Fuller was invested in her own circulation—she only sought to control its terms herself. And her copyright registration of the *Serpentine Dance* was as much an acknowledgment of as a response to the dance's ability to be replicated. Arguably, it was the very act of making her white female body available for public consumption that rendered her susceptible to the "invasive forces of capital" and threatened her self-possession. By this logic, it is possible to see her copyright claim and associated legal actions as belated attempts to restore a proprietary white subjecthood that had already been compromised (or never fully instated).[87] Likewise, we might view the judicial rulings against Fuller as denying her inalienable property rights to an embodied self that was already alienated. But if these decisions lent legal authority to and compounded a condition that was engendered by the circulation of her live dancing body, that same body provided Fuller with a partial solution that the law refused her.

"Sure of My Own Superiority": Corporeal Judgments

On the heels of the *Fuller v. Bemis* decision and the denial of copyright protection for choreography, imitations of the *Serpentine Dance* continued to proliferate. During the summers of 1892 and 1893, the dance became a regular feature of variety shows staged on the roof garden theaters of New York.[88] As suggested above, one imitator, named Mabelle Stuart, was already performing the dance at the Folies-Bergère in Paris when Fuller arrived there.[89] Copycats on both sides of the Atlantic were so numerous that, as biographers Richard and Marcia Current write, "'Serpentine' [became] both a specific and a generic term: it referred to a particular dance of Loie's but also to her style of dancing in general."[90]

[87] I am indebted to an anonymous reviewer of an earlier incarnation of this work for suggesting this possibility.

[88] Stephen Burge Johnson, *The Roof Gardens of Broadway Theatres, 1883–1942*, Theater and Dramatic Studies no. 31 (Ann Arbor, MI: UMI Research Press, 1985), 28.

[89] On June 28, 1892, Fuller secured an immediate release from her contract with Hoyt & Thomas and sailed to Germany and then Paris. Current and Current, *Loie Fuller*, 44.

[90] Ibid., 51. The most famous of these imitators was Ada Fuller, who claimed to be Loïe's sister-in-law. Current and Current, *Loie Fuller*, 58. In his biography of Fuller, Giovanni Lista describes her as simultaneously "inimitable" and "imitated everywhere" and proceeds to list over thirty Fuller imitators. Lista, *Loïe Fuller: Danseuse de la Belle Epoque* (Paris: Stock-Éditions D'Art Somogy, 1994), 28–30.

Figure 1.4 Loïe Fuller imitator, between 1890 and 1909. Photo by Theodore C. Marceau. Jerome Robbins Dance Division, The New York Public Library for the Performing Arts, Astor, Lenox, and Tilden Foundations.

Despite the diffusion of her signature dance, Fuller soon learned that imitators did not necessarily diminish the value inherent in her own dancing body. In her autobiography, she recounts her experience as witness to Stuart's performance at the Folies-Bergère:

> It would be hard to describe what I saw that evening. I awaited the "serpentine dancer," my rival, my robber—for she was a robber, was she not, she who was stealing not only my dances but all my beautiful dreams?

Finally she came out. I trembled all over. Cold perspiration appeared on my temples. I shut my eyes. When I reopened them I saw there on the stage one of my contemporaries who, some time before, in the United States, having borrowed money from me had neglected to repay it. She had kept right on borrowing, that was all. But this time I had made up my mind to force her to give back what she had taken from me. Presently I ceased to want to do anything of the sort. Instead of further upsetting me the sight of her soothed me. The longer she danced the calmer I became. And when she had finished her "turn," I began to applaud sincerely and with great joy.

It was not admiration that elicited my applause but an entirely opposite feeling. My imitator was so ordinary that, sure of my own superiority, I no longer dreaded her. In fact I could gladly have kissed her for the pleasure that her revelation of inefficiency gave me.[91]

Cold sweat giving way to calm joy, Fuller undergoes a reversal of the "annihilation" of self that the original "theft" of her dance occasioned. Stuart's "revelation of inefficiency" is, for Fuller, a revelation that while her choreography and image could be expropriated, her particular corporeality could not. Confident of the "superiority" of her dancing skill—of the singular way she performs the *Serpentine Dance*—Fuller's sense of abjection dissolves, replaced by a renewed sense of possessive individualism and subjecthood. Her confidence was borne out when her audition for the Folies-Bergère manager resulted in an offer to replace Stuart immediately. This time, it was Fuller who appeared under her imitator's name until the publicity materials could be changed. Fuller was so well received, she proudly reports, that she "was obliged to repeat *her* [Stuart's] dance four or five times."[92] In performance, if not in the law, Fuller found it possible to reap the benefits of "originality" by outshining the imitators who gave only a "feeble copy" of the *Serpentine Dance*.[93] Accordingly, Fuller began billing herself as "La Loïe Fuller," the "La" signifying her status as "the genuine article."[94]

However much Fuller touted her ability to capitalize on shoddy imitations, she did not abandon her efforts to contain the circulation of her choreographic work. In January 1893, some six months after the US Circuit Court rejected her copyright claim, Fuller publicly announced her intention to take legal action against anyone who copied her dances on the Parisian stage. Advised by

---

[91] Fuller, *Fifteen Years*, 53–54.
[92] Ibid., 57, emphasis added.
[93] Ibid., 56.
[94] Current and Current, *Loie Fuller*, 51.

a French jurisconsult of the unlikelihood of winning such cases, Fuller turned to patent law to protect the stage devices she used in her productions. On April 8, 1893, Fuller secured a French patent on a "garment for dancers"—a skirt and bodice with wands attached to the skirt that enabled the dancer to manipulate the material. So began a string of patents that Fuller obtained, not only in France but in the United States and Germany as well, on effects such as a mirrored room and a mechanism that illuminated a dancer's figure from below the stage.[95]

This switch in strategy—pursuing property rights in her scientific inventions rather than in her artistic work—adds another wrinkle to Fuller's vexed relationship to propertied subjecthood. Thwarted in her legal attempts to own choreography itself, Fuller settled for ownership rights over the trappings of production that surrounded and mediated her dancing body. In doing so, she established her status as the subject of property without having to alienate herself from her choreography, as copyright required. But these patents did little to secure for her the property rights *in the body* that were, at least theoretically, a prerequisite of self-possession and yet proved so elusive from a legal standpoint. Little wonder, then, that Fuller continued to sue others for infringement of her choreography as well as her inventions. In 1894 she threatened an injunction against two producers in New York for "the use of mirrors for scenic effect in dancing," and by 1910, Fuller's sense of proprietorship was evidently expansive enough that she sought an injunction against the producers of a "barefoot dance" at New York's Plaza Music Hall.[96]

Clearly, the pursuit of intellectual property rights, in scientific "discoveries" and in the body, was an ongoing project for Fuller, a means of negotiating and attempting to elevate her station in a crowded theatrical marketplace. The fact that the dancers and producers whom Fuller accused of theft were white, as she was, should not detract from the not only gendered but also racialized nature of her predicament or her claims. Her concern about who controlled the commodification of her bodily labor and her turn to legal institutions to curb the traffic in her choreography cannot be divorced from her status as a white woman. While emphasizing the tacit correlation between whiteness and property rights surely does not exhaust the range of possible interpretations of

[95] Margaret Haile Harris, *Loïe Fuller, Magician of Light: A Loan Exhibition at the Virginia Museum, March 12–April 22, 1979* (Richmond: The Museum, 1979), 18–19; Current and Current, *Loie Fuller*, 61–62. In addition, Fuller imposed a policy of strict secrecy on her assistants, refusing to discuss the details of her costumes or lighting effects. Harris, *Loïe Fuller*, 20; Current and Current, *Loie Fuller*, 60.

[96] "Theatrical Gossip," *New York Times*, February 15, 1894, p. 8; "Reserve Decision on 'Barefoot Dance,'" *New York Times*, March 10, 1910, p. 9.

Fuller's actions, it does lend critical insight into a defining aspect of her career. Seeking a way to navigate the patriarchal organization of the mixed-race commercial stage, Fuller strove to position herself as a propertied subject and thereby take hold of racial prerogatives typically reserved for white men. To the extent that Loïe Fuller helped inaugurate the modernist movement in dance, she did so as much for her efforts to claim the rights of possessive individualism as for her embrace of "barefoot" dancing.

In Fuller's Legal Footsteps

Ida Fuller

Fuller's influence following her infringement suit against Minnie Bemis was evident in both the theatrical and legal arenas, as subsequent white female dancers took up the pursuit of intellectual property rights in their creations. One of these was a Fuller imitator, Ida Fuller, who adopted Loïe's surname and claimed to be either her sister or sister-in-law. In the late 1890s, Ida Fuller began performing a *Fire Dance* in Europe. This was a version of *Le Danse Feu* that Loïe had first presented in 1896, and which became, along with the *Serpentine Dance,* one of her best-known works. Where Loïe's *Fire Dance* employed underlighting and played with the relationship between light and shadow, Ida developed a theatrical device that used silken ribbons, a fan, and red lights to give the appearance of an onstage fire, and in 1899, she applied for a patent for it. Three years later, Ida sought to enjoin the producers of a melodrama called *The Ninety and Nine,* which played at the Academy of Music, from using an appliance in a fire scene that, she alleged, infringed on her patent. As she explained to the court, she had traveled to the United States from France for the purpose of performing her *Fire Dance* on the vaudeville circuit but found herself unable to obtain engagements "due to the usurpation of her device by the defendants."[97]

Fuller v. Gilmore et al. was tried in the United States Circuit Court before the same Judge Lacombe who had rejected Loïe's infringement claim ten years earlier. This time, Lacombe looked more favorably on the dancer's petition, suggesting again that patent law was a more hospitable province for dancers' assertions of possessive individualism than was copyright law. While lawyers for the defendants argued that Ida Fuller's patent had yet to be adjudicated and validated, the judge held that the patent "appeared to be novel, useful,

---

[97] "'Ninety and Nine' Fire Enjoined," *New York Daily Tribune,* December 24, 1902, p. 7; *Fuller v. Gilmore et al.,* Circuit Court 121 F. 129; 1902 U.S. App. LEXIS 5326; "Cuts Dancer's Award," *New York Times,* April 26, 1907.

and ingenious" and thus found the injunction warranted. Interestingly, Judge Lacombe referred back to Loïe Fuller in his ruling:

> In the device employed by an earlier "fire dancer," which was before this court in *Fuller v. Bemis, 50 Fed. 926*, the waving draperies of the performer, agitated solely by her own movements, were illumined, as in the device in suit, by colored lights cast up from beneath the stage; but there was no air-blast, the aperture for light being covered with a plate of glass.

The distinction the judge draws between the two "fire dancers" is worth noting: whereas Loïe used "solely ... her own movements" to create the movement of fabric, Ida uses the "air-blast" of a fan. Perhaps not surprising in a case centering on a patent, the implication is that an actual machine is more deserving of protection than a body's so-called mechanical movements. However subtly, Judge Lacombe's language and his divergent rulings in the two cases reinforce a hierarchy between a scientific invention and an embodied work of authorship.[98]

Yet like her predecessor, Ida Fuller's success with patent law did not stop her from claiming more expansive intellectual property rights in her dancing, as explained in a 1907 report in *Variety*, titled "Has Act Protected":

> Through her attorneys this week Ida Fuller, the "fire dancer" at the New York Theatre, notified the United Booking Offices that Rialto, a dancer playing at the Union Square this week, was infringing upon her dance and the management would be held accountable if continued. The case of Miss Fuller against Gilmore & Tompkins and Frank McKee, the managers who allowed an infringement in the Academy of Music in 1902, was cited to the United as a further warning, Miss Fuller having received a verdict against the managers in that action.[99]

Although it is not clear whether Fuller did actually attempt to register her act with the Copyright Office, she quite plainly sought to leverage her earlier legal victory to protect herself from—or at least scare off—other fire dancers.

---

[98] Although damages are not discussed in *Fuller v. Gilmore*, Ida Fuller was subsequently awarded the remarkable sum of $22,000 as compensation for the sixteen weeks in which the producers of *The Ninety and the Nine* used the fire-simulating device that was deemed an infringement on her patent. In 1907, a judge reduced that figure to $3,200. "Cuts Dancers's Award."

[99] "Has Act Protected," *Variety*, September 21, 1907, p. 6.

The irony in this chain of imitations and copyright claims should not be lost. Where Loïe Fuller sued Minnie Bemis for copyright infringement of an act modeled on skirt and Nautch dancing, Ida Fuller, who took not only her more famous counterpart's *Fire Dance* but also her name, threatened to sue another dancer for infringement of her act. If Loïe Fuller's copyright defeat made it more possible for her impersonators to carry on, it does not appear to have had a dampening effect on white female dancers' interest in positioning themselves as propertied subjects.

Ruth St. Denis

A more prominent successor to Loïe Fuller in the pursuit of copyright protection was Ruth St. Denis (1879–1968), considered another "pioneer" of American modern dance. In 1905, St. Denis registered two of her choreographic works, *Egypta* and *Radha*, as dramatic compositions with the Copyright Office. Unlike Fuller's *Serpentine Dance*, copies of Ruth Dennis's (as she was known before she adopted the name "St. Denis") compositions survive in the Library of Congress, possibly suggesting less resistance to her registration. This may have been because both choreographic works are cataloged as playscripts: *Egypta* is labeled "An Egyptian play in one act," and *Radha* is "A Hindoo Play in One Act Without Words."[100] The texts lay out the cast of characters, the scene settings, and the general actions that comprise each "play," but they are short on specific movement descriptions. For example, the "mystic dance" at the center of *Radha* is transcribed as follows:

> The dance is comprised of three figures, the first being performed in five circles one within the other, each circle representing one of the five senses. The second figure is danced on a square, representing, according to Buddhist theology, the four-fold miseries of life, and is done with writhings and twistings of the body to portray the dispair [*sic*] of unfulfillment. At the end of this figure Radha sinks to the ground in darkness. After a short interval a faint light discloses her in an attitude of prayer and meditation. This light coming from a hanging lamp designed from the lotus, is first concentrated upon her figure, then diffused with increasing power over the whole stage. Radha now rises from a kneeling posture with her face illumined by the light of joy within, and holding a lotus flower, now begins the third figure of the dance, which follows the lines of an open lotus, the steps of which lead from the center of the flower to the point of each

---

[100] Ruth Dennis, *Egypta*; Ruth Dennis, *Radha*, Copyright Office, Library of Congress.

petal. This figure is danced on the balls of the feet, and typifies the
ecstasy and joy which follow the renunciation of the senses, and the
freedom from their illusion. The close of this figure which finishes the
message, Radha dances slowly backward toward the shrine holding
aloft the lotus flower and followed by the priests, the curtain slowly
descending. When the curtain rises the image of Radha is seen once
more seated in the shrine, (her spirit having merged into Logos). The
worship is over, the lights are out, the priests are gone, leaving the idol
alone once more to the shadows and silence of the temple.

St. Denis deposited this copy of *Radha*, as well as her copy of *Egypta*, before
she had premiered either work.[101] In other words, in contrast to Fuller, who
submitted the *Serpentine Dance* for copyright registration only after she felt
the sting of Minnie Bemis's imitations, St. Denis preemptively established her
proprietary rights over the dance works that would make her famous before
they had actually done so. As St. Denis biographer Suzanne Shelton writes, the
copyright deposits were a reflection of her confidence in the ideas behind the
works, which she believed she could market "to the novelty-hungry producers
in vaudeville."[102]

As with Fuller, St. Denis's interest in property rights must be understood as
an attempt to navigate a confluence of overlapping economic, artistic, racial,
and gender factors. St. Denis, as other dance scholars have noted, began her
career in the commercial realm of show business but aspired to "art" dance
status.[103] Having played a range of bit parts and chorus girl roles in standard
theatrical fare, St. Denis was eager to establish herself as a solo dance artist,
for which she needed both financial resources and cultural legitimacy. Linda
Tomko has pointed to the indispensable role that elite club and society women
played in providing both kinds of capital for St. Denis.[104] Her pursuit of copyright protection, I would argue, was similarly a bid to secure and protect both
economic and artistic capital. Convinced of the market value of *Radha* and
Egypta, St. Denis saw these works as both commercially viable and the basis for

---

[101] Biographer Suzanne Shelton records 1905 as the date for the initial copyright for *Egypta*.
Suzanne Shelton, *Divine Dancer: A Biography of Ruth St. Denis* (New York: Doubleday, 1981), 299.
My own research at the Copyright Office of the Library of Congress yielded a copy of *Radha* from
1905 and a copy of *Egypta* from 1910. Nevertheless, although *Egypta* did not premiere until 1910,
it was conceived in 1904, making it entirely plausible that St. Denis registered it at the same time
as *Radha*. Ted Shawn, *Ruth St. Denis: Pioneer and Prophet; Being a History of Her Cycle of Oriental
Dances* (San Francisco: Printed for J. Howell by J. H. Nash, 1920), 4, 48.

[102] Shelton, *Divine Dancer*, 49, 50.

[103] Tomko, *Dancing Class*, 48.

[104] Ibid., 47–58.

building a solo career. But there were also inherent risks for St. Denis in trying to exploit the commercial appeal of her dancing in order to elevate herself as an artist, and copyright served as a safeguard against at least some of these risks. For one, it would theoretically prevent others from capitalizing on her ideas. And too, it signaled her status as a possessive individual rather than a racialized, sexualized commodity.

The latter was particularly important for St. Denis given the unconcealed racial dynamics of her performances. If Fuller's *Serpentine Dance* contained "a bit" of Indian Nautch dancing that was overshadowed by most spectators' focus on skirt dancing antecedents, St. Denis's compositions, as the titles and descriptions indicate, were firmly entrenched in Orientalia, even advertised as "Hindoo dances."[105] While St. Denis also worked as a skirt dancer early in her career and "employed the tools of the skirt dancer, a smattering of sentimentalized ballet tippy-toe turns and waltz steps, simple *attitudes* and *degagés*" to create her choreography, her performances were blatantly indebted to "Oriental" sources.[106] As scholarship by Priya Srinivasan has shown, contrary to standard narratives, the stimulus for St. Denis's *Radha* came not merely from a cigarette poster of an Egyptian diety, nor solely from library research on India. Rather, St. Denis was inspired by her kinesthetic encounters with a troupe of Nautch dancers whom she observed at Coney Island in 1904. St. Denis herself wrote about this encounter in her autobiography:

> My whole attention was not captured until I came to an East Indian village which had been brought over in its entirety by the owners of the Hippodrome. Here, for the first time, I saw snake charmers and holy men and Nautch dancers, and something of the remarkable fascination of India caught hold of me.

She then became "determined to create one or two Nautch dances, in imitation of these whirling skirted damsels."[107] Yet, while St. Denis absorbed some of the basic elements of the Nautch dancing she witnessed, in replacing brown bodies with her own white body in works like *Radha*, she effectively effaced the labor of the female Indian dancers whose practices she imitated.[108]

St. Denis's copyright registrations, submitted a year after her encounter with Nautch dancers at Coney Island, were the legal supplement to the kinesthetic action of "seiz[ing] representational and discursive control" of racially

---

[105] "What the Week Promises in the Theatres," *New York Times*, November 14, 1909.

[106] Tomko, *Dancing Class*, 47; Shelton, *Divine Dancer*, 62.

[107] Ruth St. Denis, *An Unfinished Life* (New York: Harper & Brothers, 1939), 55.

[108] Srinivasan, *Sweating Saris*, 82.

marked bodily practices.[109] Declaring herself the sole author of compositions based on imitation, St. Denis claimed exclusive ownership rights and marked her distinction from the Nautch dancers who remained unnamed and unentitled.

Yet, as Fuller well knew, the act of submitting a composition to the Copyright Office was no guarantee of exclusive control over the work. In an episode that bears a striking resemblance to Fuller's experience at the Folies-Bergère some fourteen years earlier, St. Denis arrived in Paris in 1906 with an engagement to perform *Radha*, only to discover posters plastered everywhere advertising a "Radha, danseuse hindique" at another theater.[110] As biographer Shelton recounts, St. Denis reacted to this "horrendous betrayal" by hiring a lawyer to serve an injunction against the rival dancer.[111] She also pleaded her case in a letter to the editor of the Paris edition of the New York *Herald*. "As an American girl, and feeling I have been imposed on in a foreign country," St. Denis began the letter, titled "The Only 'Radha,'" "I naturally turn to the HERALD and would be very glad if you would afford me the strong protection of publicity in the columns of your popular paper." She continued:

> I am the originator of a series of Hindoo dances, which I produced in New York and London, dancing under the name of "Radha," and on July 20 had the honor to dance before His Majesty the King of England at the house of the Duke of Manchester, under the patronage of the duchess. While at London I was approached by several theatrical managers for engagement here. One of the managers, representing the "Olympia," offered me a price below what it cost me to produce the dances, and I, of course, declined, but afterwards entered into a contract with the Marigny Theatre, where my performances will begin September 1.
>
> Meantime, I find greatly to my surprise, that the "Olympia" has brought out another dancer under the name of "Radha." They have imitated me at least in name, in the goddess wife of Krishna, also the Cobra, or Snake-Charmer, and in the matter of scenery and properties, but have been unable to do so in the execution of the dance itself. I will be very grateful if the HERALD will kindly take the matter up for me through its columns, so that both the French and American people may know that mine is the real and only "Radha," and that I deserve to reap the fruits of my creation.[112]

[109] Ibid., 69.
[110] Shelton, *Divine Dancer*, 73.
[111] Ibid.
[112] Ruth St. Denis, "The Only 'Radha,'" Letter to the Editor, New York *Herald*, August 20, 1906, p. 8.

While the rival apparently soon disappeared from view, there was, as Shelton observes, a certain irony to St. Denis's accusations, given the tradition of imitation in vaudeville. "St. Denis herself," Shelton writes, "might have been considered an imitator by some Parisians, for the previous summer [the Dutch exotic dancer] Mata Hari had appeared in Paris in bare feet and gold chains and 'worked herself into a frenzy of worship' in a Brahman dance."[113] Certainly, St. Denis was hardly alone in capitalizing on the Orientalist vogue on both sides of the Atlantic. But it was precisely the ease with which dances that were part of this vogue circulated across different bodies—both brown and white—that made assertions of possessing the "real and only" *Radha* (backed up, of course, by the US copyright registration) so meaningful. Even while St. Denis prides herself, like Loïe Fuller, on the uniqueness of her performance, assuring readers that imitation was not possible "in the execution of the dance itself," she appeals to the print media to enforce the distinction between her choreography and that of her competitors.

Three years later, St. Denis's exclusive claims on her dances received another challenge. This time, the threat came not from a rival female dancer but from a member of her own company. Although St. Denis never shared the stage with Indian female dancers, she did perform alongside a company of Indian male dancers. As scholars Yutian Wong and Priya Srinivasan have pointed out, St. Denis's early "solo" performance of *Radha* was not truly a solo, for an entourage of Indian men surrounded her as she danced, playing supporting roles as priests. St. Denis recruited this group of men, which included both Muslims and Hindus of various caste backgrounds, from Coney Island, local stores, and Columbia University, and they toured with her for a number of years.[114] In November 1909, one of them, Mohammed Ismail, sued St. Denis in New York City Court, alleging that he had originated and taught her the material for *Radha* and that she owed him $1,250 ($2,000 in another account) for services rendered. According to the report in the New York *Sun*, Ismail "says that Miss St. Denis engaged him in 1905 to train her for an Oriental act which she is now playing under the name 'Radha.' He says he taught her to do the act and played the high priest for a time."[115] St. Denis entered a denial in the suit, countering that "she first met Ismail after he came [to New York] from the St. Louis exposition" and that "she had made a study of Hindu worship long before she saw him." In early May 1910, the case went to trial. As the *New York Times* reported,

---

[113] Shelton, *Divine Dancer*, 73.

[114] Ibid., 51–52; Srinivasan, *Sweating Saris*, 87; Wong, *Choreographing Asian America*, 48.

[115] "Must Push St. Denis Suit," New York *Sun*, November 27, 1909, p. 5.

Ismail, accompanied by some of his be-turbaned fellow country-men, made a picturesque spectacle in Part IV of the City Court. But after he had undergone a searching cross-examination about his past as a cook, waiter, and house servant, and had heard Miss St. Denis and various other witnesses testify that she had danced her Oriental dances long before she ever saw him, Ismail asked to be allowed to withdraw his action, and Judge Lynch dismissed the jury.[116]

Legal records of the court case have been lost to history, leaving three short newspaper articles all that remain of the incident. But the information in these accounts speaks volumes. That fact that Ismail filed a complaint against St. Denis in the US legal system at all is as significant as its swift dismissal. It is not known how or how much St. Denis remunerated her male performers, but Ismail clearly believed it was insufficient compensation for his contributions to *Radha*, which, by 1909, had made St. Denis quite famous. The question of what he contributed, of course, was the crux of the legal contest. While St. Denis admitted only that Ismail had "played the part of the high priest for a time,"[117] Ismail asserted that his services were much more extensive, including, as the initial *Times* report put it, having "originated an Oriental Dance ... and taught [St. Denis] the steps." In other words, Ismail's allegations directly challenged St. Denis's authorial status and undermined her copyright claim. Reversing the hierarchy of the two dancers' roles, Ismail positioned himself as the choreographer/teacher and St. Denis as the student/performer.

Yet this reversal could not hold up under the weight of an early twentieth-century racial schema. As the second account in the *Times* suggests, the spectacle of race and the power of racial stereotyping overwhelmed Ismail's claims. Already visually othered by the "picturesque" backdrop of his "be-turbaned fellow country-men," Ismail's work history as a "cook, waiter, and house servant" located him on a lower rung on the racial/class order. Writing about the lawsuit in her book *Sweating Saris: Indian Dance as Transnational Labor*, Srinivasan observes that the emphasis on Ismail's past employment, surely a strategic move on the part of St. Denis's lawyers, "pigeonholed [him] into the stereotype of Asians and Indians as manual or day laborers" and thereby undercut "his authority as a dancer, dance teacher, and choreographer."[118] Despite Ismail's contention that he first worked with St.

---

[116] "Hindu Didn't Teach Her," *New York Times*, May 3, 1910, p. 3. His first name alternately spelled "Mahomed" and "Mahomet" in newspaper reports, Ismail, Srinivasan clarifies, was not Hindu, as he was identified, but Muslim. *Sweating Saris*, 90.

[117] "Must Push St. Denis Suit," 5.

[118] Srinivasan, *Sweating Saris*, 90.

Figure 1.5 Ruth St. Denis with "native Hindus" in *Radha*, 1906. It is possible that one of the seated male dancers is Mohammed Ismail. Jerome Robbins Dance Division, The New York Public Library for the Performing Arts, Astor, Lenox, and Tilden Foundations.

Denis in 1905, the year before she premiered *Radha*, her claim that she "had danced her Oriental dances long before she ever saw him" trumped whatever facts were on his side.

Still, it would be misguided to view this legal skirmish in simple, binaristic terms, as a straightforward victory for St. Denis and an unqualified loss for Ismail. Rather, Ismail's legal action is better understood, as Srinivasan proposes, as a "performative gesture" that serves to "highlight the labor that otherwise remains unacknowledged by St. Denis."[119] Seen as an act of resistance against St. Denis's ability to capitalize on East Indian sources while those sources remained largely invisible (even when in plain sight), Ismail's charge of an unpaid debt was also a protest against the entitlements that whiteness conferred to "use and enjoy" non-white cultural material with minimal credit or compensation. The fact that his performative gesture took place in the courts, where it garnered enough attention to leave a record in the press, indicates that, at least initially, he saw legal adjudication as a promising means for contesting white domination. Just as St. Denis turned to copyright law to position herself

[119] Ibid., 84.

as a possessive individual, Ismail turned to the law to rectify a dispossession of his individual rights.

Although made on the basis of uncompensated services rather than copyright infringement, Ismail's complaint is another example of the instability and contestability of copyright for dance around the turn of the twentieth century, even when it was registered under the category of dramatic composition. Like Loïe Fuller's before her, Ruth St. Denis's claim of ownership over a dance, or, more precisely, the claim that she alone originated *Radha*, did not go unchecked. The fact that St. Denis's claim was challenged by a non-white dancer under her employment rather than by legal authorities (from below rather than from above) is a reminder of white female dancers' contingent positionality in their quest to establish themselves as property-holding subjects. Measured against the rights of white male producers and managers, and even against other white female performers, as the outcome of Loïe Fuller's myriad legal struggles suggests, white women dancers held sharply delimited power, their market value as "comely" commodities taking precedence over their rights as possessive individuals. Measured against the rights of immigrant Indian dancers, as Fuller's and St. Denis's use of Nautch dancing and the outcome of St. Denis's legal imbroglio suggest, white female dancers held remarkably broad power, their status as authorial subjects and their racial entitlement to "use and enjoy" taking precedence over the (lack of) rights of non-white bodies, who were, indeed, fully open to capital. White female dancers' pursuit of copyright protection in the late nineteenth and early twentieth centuries, a time before women had won the franchise, then, must be seen at one and the same time as an act of gendered resistance against a patriarchal system and an assertion of racial privilege within a system of white dominance.

The Black Body as Object and Subject of Property

In the late 1920s, the African American comic pantomimist Johnny Hudgins (1896–1990) obtained a copyright in London on a booklet entitled *Silence*, which according to the cover, gave "full description of Johnny Hudgins own original dancing & pantomime act."[1] Printed by the Cranbourn Press (with no publication date listed) and assigned the copyright number 746, the book details Hudgins's various specialty numbers, all of which were performed in blackface. An early clause reads, "No one is allowed to impersonate me, or use any parts of said Act unless given a written consent from JOHNNY HUDGINS, and if so it must be announced on all programs or from the Stage. No infringement on my make-up or Act."

Hudgins's booklet is the only documented example of copyrighted dance by an African American that I have been able to locate from the first half of the twentieth century. Contrary to my expectations, his copyright registration does not appear to have received any special notice at the time. Although a couple of contemporaneous newspaper reports make reference to it,[2] his British copyright was not celebrated as a consequential achievement. In fact, a legal entanglement involving Hudgins several years earlier generated considerably greater excitement. In 1924, the white producer of the musical *The*

---

[1] Johnny Hudgins, *Silence*, Copyright No. 746, London, The Cranbourn Press, n.d. Jean-Claude Baker Foundation, New York City. My sincere thanks to the late Jean-Claude Baker for generously opening his collection of Hudgins material to me. Despite the absence of a publication date, the fact that the *Silence* booklet includes a quotation from a 1927 review of Hudgins in a London performance makes it likely that Hudgins obtained the copyright in 1927 or 1928. He returned to the United States in the summer of 1928.

[2] "Hudgins Protests Use of His Act by Others," *New York Amsterdam News*, August 22, 1928, Johnny Hudgins clippings collection, Jean-Claude Baker Foundation; "Johnny Hudgins Is Coming Home," *Chicago Defender*, July 28, 1928, p. 7.

Johnny Hudgins

Figure 2.1 Publicity photo of Johnny Hudgins, Emory University.

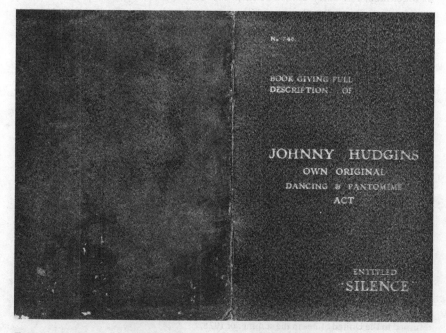

Figure 2.2 Cover of Johnny Hudgins's copyrighted booklet, *Silence*. The Jean-Claude Baker Foundation.

Chocolate Dandies sued Hudgins for violating the terms of his contract. In *Bertram C. Whitney v. Johnny Hudgins, et al.*, Whitney sought an injunction against Hudgins, claiming he was a "unique and extraordinary" performer whose services were "irreplaceable." This was reportedly the first time such a legal claim was made about an African American artist, and the black press in particular took note. In what ultimately proved a successful defense, however, Hudgins and his lawyers denied that he possessed "any unique or extraordinary ability as a dancer."[3]

On first blush, Hudgins's legal positions in these two events appear contradictory. As a defendant in the lawsuit, Hudgins maintains that his dancing services are ordinary, unoriginal, and easily replaceable. As a copyright claimant, he maintains that his pantomime routines are innovative and unique enough to warrant legal protection. Yet on closer examination, Hudgins's actions in these cases were motivated by a singular desire: to control the circulation of his choreographic material in the theatrical marketplace. In the case of the lawsuit, Hudgins sought to preserve his own ability to reproduce his routine; to do so, he asserted his rights to contract his bodily labor freely. In the case of the copyright, Hudgins sought to limit others' ability to reproduce his routine; to do so, he asserted his intellectual property rights to his embodied labor. Hudgins's seemingly inconsistent stances represent flip sides of the same coin.

But his shifting positions were more than tactical attempts to regulate the reproduction of his pantomime routines. Hudgins's legal assertions in the two cases also represent a negotiation of his body's status under a racial regime, an attempt to navigate what Eva Cherniavsky has identified as a key axis of racial division: "the difference between selling one's bodily labor and becoming a salable body in which others may traffic."[4] Looked at from this vantage point, Hudgins's legal actions were efforts to render himself less open to capital by claiming the rights of self-possession. Differently put, Hudgins's movement from defendant to copyright claimant over the course of the 1920s can be read as part of a racial project to assert himself as the subject rather than the object of property.

---

[3] *Bertram C. Whitney v. Johnny Hudgins, et al.* (Lee Shubert, Jacob J. Shubert, The Winter Garden Company, and Arthur Lyons), index no. 40459, submitted October 31, 1924, New York Supreme Court, County of New York. My ability to locate this case was made possible by the meticulous research documented in Brian Harker's "Louis Armstrong, Eccentric Dance, and the Evolution of Jazz," *Journal of the American Musicological Society* 61 (2008): 67–121. I am so grateful to Brian for his tips about tracking down primary sources on Hudgins.

[4] Eva Cherniavsky, *Incorporations: Race, Nation, and the Body Politics of Capital* (Minneapolis: University of Minnesota Press, 2006), 85.

Shifting gears from the previous chapter's discussion of early modern white female dancers who sought copyright protection for their choreography, this chapter and the subsequent one ask how African American dancers in the post-emancipation but racially stratified first decades of the twentieth century actively engaged with the discourse of intellectual property rights. Like Mohammed Ismail's lawsuit against Ruth St. Denis (discussed in Chapter 1), Hudgins's copyright claim indicates that white women were not alone in turning to the law to redress the long-standing alignment between masculine whiteness and property rights. Focusing on Hudgins's pair of legal dealings, this chapter shows how one African American performer traversed the line between objecthood and subjecthood, between the condition of the possessed commodity and that of the possessive individual. In this way, I hope to throw further light on the knotted relationship between race, property rights in the body, and personhood. How did African American performers living with what Thadious M. Davis has termed "the ideological and juridical residue of persons as property"[5] negotiate the status of their bodies in the theatrical marketplace when their bodies continued to be the things being trafficked? What was the distance for a black dancer between selling one's bodily labor and being a salable body?

In exploring Hudgins's case, I draw inspiration from Fred Moten's theorization of black performance as the resistance of the object. His 2003 book *In the Break: The Aesthetics of the Black Radical Tradition*, which riffs on and with the black musical avant-garde of the 1950s and 1960s, begins with the pronouncement that "The history of blackness is testament to the fact that objects can and do resist."[6] Moten's opening pages are a direct response to Karl Marx, who introduces the counterfactual "Could commodities themselves speak" only to underscore their lack of any intrinsic value outside a system of exchange. Where the speaking commodity is an impossibility for Marx, Moten insists on not just the possibility but "the historical reality of commodities who spoke—of laborers who were commodities before, as it were, the abstraction of labor power from their bodies and who continue to pass on this material heritage across the divide that separates slavery and 'freedom.' "[7] Moten's avowal of the commodity's powers of speech are particularly useful in interpreting the actions and utterances of a performer like Hudgins, whose legal affairs dealt head-on with questions about his exchange value and about the ownership

[5] Thadious Davis, *Games of Property: Law, Race, Gender, and Faulkner's* Go Down, Moses (Durham, NC: Duke University Press, 2003), 2.

[6] Fred Moten, *In the Break: The Aesthetics of the Black Radical Tradition* (Minneapolis: University of Minnesota Press, 2003), 1.

[7] Ibid., 6.

and reproduceability of his dancing body. Because Hudgins was a pantomimist whose onstage persona was mute, he forces us to think carefully about the different registers of speech available to and mobilized by black dancers.[8]

For Moten, the sound of black resistance "embodies the critique of value, of private property, of the sign."[9] As I detail below, however, Hudgins defended himself against his white producer by declaring his interchangeability with other black dancers, and his copyright claim rested on an assertion of private ownership of his bodily labor. What are the implications for black resistance if the commodity's speech reinforces the commodity status of the black body? In approaching Hudgins as a commodity that speaks, this chapter seeks to tease out some of the contradictions of resistance for black performers in a racially structured, capitalist marketplace—contradictions that are brought into high relief when the commodity at hand is a dancing body. In what follows, I first address African Americans' historical relationship to property rights and show how the specter of slavery permeated US copyright law in the early twentieth century. Next, I zero in on the case of *Whitney v. Hudgins*, in which Hudgins found himself in the paradoxical situation of having to devalue his worth in order to preserve his mobility. I then take up the copyright claim Hudgins made on his repertoire of pantomime acts, with particular attention to his signature "Mwa, Mwa" routine. In a theatrical economy in which whites maintained near-monopolies on the means of production, Hudgins's copyright should be regarded as a meaningful if inherently fraught attempt to counter the overdetermined commodification of his dancing body.

Slavery's Legacy: Property, Personhood, and Originality

Slavery is a necessary starting point for any discussion of property rights in the United States. From the early seventeenth century to the legal end of the slave trade in 1808, black Africans who survived the Middle Passage arrived on American shores as embodied forms of property, and until 1865, the system of chattel slavery defined life for the vast majority of African Americans. As legal scholar Cheryl Harris has written, what distinguished racial slavery from other forms of labor servitude in the early United States was "its permanency

---

[8] An early version of this chapter was presented at Northwestern University's Performance Studies Institute during the summer of 2010. Many thanks to Harvey Young for inviting me to present, and to the graduate student members of the Institute that summer, including Jasmine E. Johnson, who, if memory serves, suggested the relevance of Moten's work to my discussion of Hudgins.

[9] Moten, *In the Break*, 12.

and the total commodification attendant to the status of the slave. Slavery as a legal institution treated slaves as property that could be transferred, assigned, inherited, or posted as collateral."[10] Laws dictating that children born to slave women assume the status of their mothers rendered black female slaves a kind of hyper-property; their bodies represented both property and the capacity to multiply property.

Raced and gendered property relations thus lay at the core of the "peculiar institution." In the economy of slavery, white men were by definition the subjects of property and, because slaves were legally prohibited from owning property, enslaved black men and women were confined to being the objects of property.[11] This object status exceeded a slave's particular conditions of ownership. Saidiya Hartman points out that "the subjection of the slave to all whites defined his condition in civil society ... [and] made the enslaved an object of property to be potentially used and abused by all whites."[12] Legally required to submit to all white persons, subject to exchange between white men, slaves were also fungible—what Hartman describes as "the replaceablility and interchangeability endemic to the commodity."[13]

Although propertization is what made it possible for whites to justify the exploitation of black labor,[14] it was not without its contradictions. Dance scholar Thomas DeFrantz notes the "opposing physical demands" placed on the enslaved black body: "as commodity, it was to hold enormous labor capacity; as personal property, it was to be repressible, docile, passive."[15] Stripped

---

[10] Cheryl I. Harris, "Whiteness as Property," *Harvard Law Review* 106.8 (1993): 1720.

[11] Harris, "Whiteness as Property," 1718. In the words of Hortense Spillers, "the captive body reduces to a thing, becoming *being for* the captor." Hortense Spillers, "Mama's Baby, Papa's Maybe: An American Grammar Book," *diacritics* 17.2 (1987): 67, emphasis in original. See Dylan C. Penningroth, *The Claims of Kinfolk: African American Property and Community in the Nineteenth-Century South* (Chapel Hill: University of North Carolina Press, 2003) for a revelatory look at the informal system of property ownership that operated despite legal sanctions among African American slaves in the South.

[12] Saidiya V. Hartman, *Scenes of Subjection: Terror, Slavery, and Self-Making in Nineteenth-Century America* (New York: Oxford University Press, 1997), 24. Robin Bernstein also notes that slavery rendered "all black bodies ... inherently ownable." "Dances with Things: Material Culture and the Performance of Race," *Social Text* 27.4 (Winter 2009): 88.

[13] Hartman, *Scenes of Subjection*, 21.

[14] Harris, "Whiteness as Property," 1716.

[15] DeFrantz, "Simmering Passivity: The Black Male Body in Concert Dance," in *Moving Words: Re-writing Dance*, ed. Gay Morris (New York: Routledge, 1996), 107. See also Nell Irvin Painter's "Thinking about the Languages of Money and Race: A Response to Michael O'Malley, 'Specie and Species,'" *American Historical Review* 99.2 (April 1994), in which she notes, "Before 1865, the vast majority of African Americans were, literally, property, and they served simultaneously as an embodied currency and a labor force" (398).

of legal rights and dehumanized, yet desired for its labor potential, expected to produce and to submit, the slave-as-property was simultaneously devalued and treated as currency. As Lindon Barrett writes, "it is paradoxically the very valuelessness assigned to African American bodies that enables them to stand as the ground on which speculations of and concerning value are made. Because African Americans are positioned outside the value of the fully human, they become instruments and signs by which great value is produced and measured."[16]

African Americans' vexed relationship to value, along with the other contradictions that accompanied and undergirded the propertization of black bodies, did not end with emancipation. Rather, the implications of the "convoluted legal divide" separating persons from property in the nineteenth century "spill[ed] over" into the post-emancipation period, where they continued to shape "issues of ownership and rights to the body."[17] Property constituted "nearly a ghostly inhabitation haunting the black body" into the twentieth century and even beyond.[18]

For a dance and performance historian, the "residue" of slavery's property system is most immediately apparent in the institution of blackface minstrelsy, which overlapped with and outlived slavery and was the most popular form of entertainment in nineteenth-century America. Minstrelsy licensed white male performers to darken their faces, expropriate black performance practices, and distort them into racist caricatures. As Hartman insightfully notes, "the donning of blackface restaged the seizure and possession of the black body for the other's use and enjoyment."[19] In other words, the patterns enacted in minstrelsy—the circulation of embodied black material between white men, the objectification of "blackness" and the concomitant formation of white subjectivity, the reaping of white profit from black (cultural) labor, the prevention of African American performers from claiming ownership over

---

[16] Lindon Barrett, *Blackness and Value: Seeing Double* (New York: Cambridge University Press, 1999), 93.

[17] Davis, *Games of Property*, 2.

[18] Karla F. C. Holloway, *Legal Fictions: Constituting Race, Composing Literature* (Duke University Press Books, 2013), 18.

[19] Hartman, *Scenes of Subjection*, 31–32. Other influential scholarship on minstrelsy includes Robert Toll, *Blacking Up: The Minstrel Show in Nineteenth-Century America* (New York: Oxford University Press, 1974); Eric Lott, *Love and Theft: Blackface Minstrelsy and the American Working Class* (New York: Oxford University Press, 1993); and Brenda Dixon Gottschild, "Past Imperfect: Performance, Power, and Politics on the Minstrel Stage," in *Digging the Africanist Presence in American Performance: Dance and Other Contexts* (Westport, CT: Greenwood Press, 1996), 81–128.

their expressive practices by appearing on the minstrel stage—"cannot be extricated from the relations of chattel slavery."[20]

Inasmuch as blackface minstrelsy reproduced and extended the general property relations of slavery, it had specific repercussions for notions of originality and therefore for constructions of intellectual property. In minstrelsy, "originality" for whites meant the impersonation of "black" music, dance, and rhetorical styles. For African Americans who began performing on the minstrel stage beginning in the 1860s, "originality" was colossally fraught. Forced to apply burnt cork to their skin and to adhere to the script established by white performers, black artists performed their own imitations of white imitations. Even when African American artists found room to infuse conventional forms with their own spin—to "change the joke and slip the yoke"[21]—black performance as it emerged out of minstrelsy, and out of a set of racialized property relations that assigned whites the rights to black labor, was always already regarded as derivative. The relationship between the original and the copy in American performance is thus haunted by the legacy of slavery and its cultural corollary, minstrelsy.

The work of Stephen M. Best helps flesh out the imbrication of slavery and intellectual property in the United States from another angle. Like Moten, Hartman, and Davis, Best maintains that there is an "afterlife of slavery" and that emancipation did not mark the end of "the subjection of personhood to property."[22] Looking at the "poetics of property" in US law, Best finds direct resonances between slave law and the "expanding universe of property" in the late nineteenth century.[23] Even as jurists increasingly defined property not as relations between people and things but as a "bundle of rights" between persons, new forms of mechanical reproduction like the phonograph and the camera gave rise to new forms of intangible property like vocal style and facial expression. As a result, legal questions about the propertization of persons that were so prevalent during the antebellum period cropped up anew. "Mechanical reproduction," Best writes, "returned civil law to the problem of expropriation and the injurious commodification of personhood." Yet, even as the prospect that one could own something like another person's countenance raised the "specter of an immoral expropriation," intellectual property law found in slavery a paradigm for treating expropriation like "legitimate exchange";

---

[20] Hartman, *Scenes of Subjection*, 32.

[21] Ralph Ellison, "Change the Joke and Slip the Yoke," in *Shadow and Act* (New York: Random House, 1964).

[22] Stephen M. Best, *The Fugitive's Properties: Law and the Poetics of Possession* (Chicago: University of Chicago Press, 2004), 14, 16.

[23] Ibid., 14.

slavery offered a model for converting "property into something resembling contract."[24] Acts like the Fugitive Slave Law of 1850, Best explains, answered abolitionists' concerns about the dehumanization of chattel slavery by recasting the slave as not merely a "thing" to be owned but as one who owed a debt of labor to his master. The law thus effected a doubling—or splitting—of the figure of the runaway slave into both "pilfered property and indebted person, object of property and subject of contract."[25] This precedent paved the way for intellectual property law to treat those "fugitive" (ephemeral and intangible) forms of property that were once perceived as inalienable aspects of personhood—one's image or one's vocal style, for example—as legitimately alienable and marketable goods.[26]

Extending Best's line of argument into the twentieth century, we can also see in aspects of the 1909 Copyright Act the residue of a legal system that justified the commodification of persons. The 1909 law responded to the increasing prevalence of technology like the piano roll player and the phonograph by adding "a right of mechanical reproduction, which gave composers and lyricists the exclusive right to make the first phonographic recording or player piano roll of a work."[27] It thus enshrined the expropriation of voice from body. (The addition of photographs to the list of copyrightable works in 1865 arguably had done the same, much earlier, for the expropriation of image from body.)[28] To the extent that copyright law endorsed the alienation of bodily expression from body and the separation of owner from bodily source, it partook of some of the same logic as the Fugitive Slave Law.[29]

The 1909 Act is notable, too, for codifying the "work-for-hire" doctrine: the principle that an employer is the default "author" of a work created by his or her

---

[24] Ibid., 53.

[25] Ibid., 8–9.

[26] Ibid., 98.

[27] Saint-Amour, "Introduction: Modernism and the Lives of Copyright," in *Modernism and Copyright*, ed. Paul K. Saint-Amour (New York: Oxford University Press, 2011), 9.

[28] See Jane M. Gaines, *Contested Culture: The Image, the Voice, and the Law* (Chapel Hill: University of North Carolina Press, 1991), for more on subjecthood vis-à-vis copyright protection for photography.

[29] Significantly, much of the music that was mechanically reproduced at the turn of the twentieth century descended from blackface minstrelsy. See Lisa Gitelman, "Reading Music, Reading Records, Reading Race: Musical Copyright and the U.S. Copyright Act of 1909," *Musical Quarterly* 81.2 (Summer 1997): 265–90, for a thoughtful discussion of the 1908 case *White-Smith Music Publishing v. Apollo Co.*, which revolved around a so-called coon song and was an important precursor to the 1909 Act. Gitelman argues that the severing of the sound of (white-authored misrepresentations of) blackness from the sight of blackness was "new and uncomfortable" and "an unadmitted counterpart to the legislative debate over separating visible 'writings' from the sounds of reading" (278).

employee, entitled to the attendant rights of ownership. Although this facet of the law, which did not explicitly define a work for hire, was little commented upon at the time, it served to ratify the idea of corporate authorship. Calling the work-for-hire doctrine the "ultimate legal fiction underlying modern copyright law," legal scholar Catherine Fisk observes that it was the rise of the corporation in the late nineteenth century that "made employer control of all intellectual output of the persons in their employ more logical and more rhetorically appealing."[30] The assignment of author status to employers helped "personify" the corporation, treating a non-living entity as if it were a rights-bearing person. This amalgamation of thinghood and personhood returns us once again to Best, who finds resonances between the law's treatment of the modern corporation and of slaves: "what is true for the corporation," he writes, "had been, for all legal purposes ... also true for the slave"; both shared an uneven legal makeup as part thing, part person; part object, part subject.[31]

Decades after the official demise of slavery, its specter thus continued to haunt the legislation of property rights. As this chapter maintains, slavery's shadow equally haunted Johnny Hudgins's "speech," both performed and legal. Hudgins's proximity to slavery's "kissing cousin"[32] minstrelsy is of course evident in his use of blackface. But there are also more subtle ways in which slavery's traces bore on Hudgins's legal transactions during the 1920s. The employee/employer relationship; the laborer as debtor; the tensions between originality and imitation; the propertization of (aspects of) personhood: all were shaded by the legacy of slavery, and all were central to *Whitney v. Hudgins* and Hudgins's copyright claim. The following sections reconstruct and assess these two legal events to help illuminate the black body's post-emancipation negotiation of its simultaneous object and subject status.

The Lawsuit: Hudgins's Two Bodies

Virtually forgotten in the early twenty-first century, Johnny Hudgins was a celebrity in his day. Born in Baltimore in 1896, Hudgins began performing as a song-and-dance man on the burlesque circuit before joining Noble Sissle and Eubie Blake's all-black Broadway revue *The Chocolate Dandies* in 1924.[33]

---

[30] Catherine L. Fisk, "Authors at Work: The Origins of the Work-for-Hire Doctrine," *Yale Journal of Law & the Humanities* 15 (Winter 2003): 55, 67–68.

[31] Best, *The Fugitive's Properties*, 11–12. Best cites the legal historian Arthur W. Machen here. See Arthur W. Machen Jr., "Corporate Personality," *Harvard Law Review* 24.4 (February 1911): 253–67.

[32] Gottschild, *Digging the Africanist Presence*, 81.

[33] Mura Dehn, "Johnny Hudgins," Papers on Afro-American Social Dance, Folder 25, Dance Collection, New York Public Library for the Performing Arts (hereafter NYPL).

A successor to the song-writing team Sissle and Blake's earlier hit, *Shuffle Along* (1921), *The Chocolate Dandies* was more ambitious—it featured extravagant stage settings, including live horses running on a treadmill during a horse race scene—but ultimately less profitable, closing on Broadway after ninety-six performances.[34] During his run in the musical, Hudgins developed a series of comic pantomime acts that won him acclaim nationally and internationally. The most famous of these was his "Mwa, Mwa" routine, in which he opened and closed his mouth in silently mimicry of the "wah wah" sounds of an accompanying trumpet or cornet.[35] Branded both the successor to the celebrated blackface vaudevillian Bert Williams and "the colored Charles Chaplin," Hudgins spawned a host of imitators, among them Josephine Baker, who appeared with him in *The Chocolate Dandies*. After touring Europe for several years in the mid-1920s, Hudgins returned to the United States to star in Lew Leslie's *Blackbirds of 1928*.[36] By 1930 he was reported to be the "highest paid night club entertainer of his Race."[37] He continued to tour Europe, South America, Canada, and the United States through the 1940s. Due in no small part to his use of blackface, Hudgins fell out of favor with a later generation of performers and critics.[38] He died in 1990.[39]

[34] Allen Woll, *Black Musical Theatre from Coontown to Dreamgirls* (Baton Rouge: Louisiana State University Press, 1989), 91; Nadine George-Graves, "The Chocolate Dandies," *Encyclopedia of the Harlem Renaissance*, ed. Cary D. Wintz and Paul Finkelman (New York: Routledge, 2004), 223–24.

[35] The spelling of Hudgins's routine varied between "Mwa Mwa," "Wah Wah," and "Wow Wow." I use "Mwa, Mwa" throughout this chapter for consistency's sake and in accordance with the spelling Hudgins used in his copyright booklet. For a list of the musicians who accompanied Hudgins, as well as a fuller account of onstage collaborations between trumpetists and dancers in the 1920s, see Harker's "Louis Armstrong, Eccentric Dance, and the Evolution of Jazz."

[36] "Johnny Hudgins Is Still Going Big on Broadway," *Chicago Defender*, May 8, 1926, p. 7; Bill Egan, *Florence Mills: Harlem Jazz Queen* (Lanham, MD: Scarecrow Press, 2004), 158; "Johnny Hudgins Is Coming Home."

[37] "Johnny Hudgins Back in Night Club Revue," *Chicago Defender*, May 17, 1930, p. 10.

[38] Egan, *Florence Mills*, 158n51.

[39] In later years, Hudgins was known as Johnny "Banjo" Hudgins. By 1953, the New York *Age* remarked that "it appears that the American theatergoer looks upon pantomime as a lost art. However, Johnny keeps busy in Canada, South America and Europe, where the people really appreciate him." Alan McMillan, "New York Is My Beat," New York *Age*, August 29, 1953, Johnny Hudgins Scrapbook, Johnny Hudgins, Papers, Manuscript, Archives, and Rare Book Library, Emory University. Hudgins married the chorus girl Mildred Hudgins, who retired from show business sometime after they wed. According to Jean-Claude Baker, Hudgins was gay. It is unclear to me how public this identity was. Author interview with Jean-Claude Baker, June 18, 2008. Among the many things my study does not attend to are the intersections of sexuality and self-possession. On the possibilities of queering property, see Margaret Davies, "Queer Property, Queer Persons: Self-Ownership and Beyond," *Social Legal Studies* 8 (1999): 327-352. For a particularly good analysis of the "many ways that racial and sexual non-normativity mutually shaped each other" in cabaret spaces during the Harlem Renaissance, see Shane Vogel, *The Scene of Harlem Cabaret: Race, Sexuality, Performance* (Chicago: University of Chicago Press, 2009).

His financial success notwithstanding, the theatrical market in which Hudgins worked in the early twentieth century was a racially stratified one. With few exceptions, whites owned the means of production, even in the case of "all-black" musicals like *The Chocolate Dandies*.[40] For black performers, as Bertram Whitney's lawsuit against Hudgins illustrates, this meant the persistence of some of the racialized power relations of slavery, including racially charged debates over the value and exchangeability of black labor.

Heard before the Supreme Court, County of New York, in November 1924, *Bertram C. Whitney v. John Hudgins et al.* contended that Hudgins had committed a breach of contract by abandoning his run in the Broadway production of *The Chocolate Dandies*, which Whitney produced. As Whitney detailed in his deposition, Whitney hired Hudgins in April 1924 to fill a void in the show, then titled *In Bamville*. "After the show was out a very short time," Whitney testified,

> it became apparent that it lacked a very essential quality in a colored production—the quality of humor and comedy, and I set out to remedy this want and to procure a colored artiste who would be of Broadway calibre, that is to say, who would be good enough to appeal to the sophisticated audiences of New York City. This was a very difficult thing to do. There are not many colored actors who have sufficient ability to create comedy sufficiently original, spontaneous and pleaseing [*sic*] to a New York audience and I found it extremely arduous to obtain the services of such an artiste.[41]

For Whitney, humor was a necessary ingredient in the formula for successful black musical theater and a skill in short supply among the labor force of African American performers. Amid this supposed dearth of talent, Hudgins was an attractive choice because of the "very favorable reputation" he had garnered for himself as "a unique dancer." Hudgins's status and originality were key to—and key points of contestation within—Whitney's case.[42]

To secure Hudgins's services, Whitney bought Hudgins's release from a previous contract, at the price of $251. He also agreed to pay Hudgins a weekly salary

[40] Woll, *Black Musical Theatre*, 110–112.

[41] *Whitney, Bertram C. v. Hudgins, John et al.*, Supreme Court County of New York, Index No. 40459, 1924.

[42] Allen Woll writes that *The Chocolate Dandies* was punished at the box office for departing from the "strict limitations governing the black musical." Conversely, some black critics condemned the show for being too formulaic. See Woll, *Black Musical Theatre*, 91–92, and George-Graves, "The Chocolate Dandies," 223–24.

Figure 2.3 A photograph of publicity for *The Chocolate Dandies* (1924), included as a plaintiff's exhibit in *Whitney v. Hudgins* to highlight the notice Hudgins received. *Bertram C. Whitney v. Johnny Hudgins, et al.* index no. 40459, submitted 31 October 1924, New York Supreme Court, County of New York.

of $150 while *In Bamville* was in tryouts, and $200 a week after it opened at the Colonial Theatre on September 1, 1924. Once he joined the production, Whitney maintained, Hudgins was "an integral part of the play." In addition to being cast in the role of Joe Dolks, a horse owner, Hudgins was featured in a scene called "Dance Diversions by the New Porter," in which he performed his repertory of pantomime dance routines.[43] These acts made Hudgins "the hit of the show," according to Whitney.

Due to budget woes, *The Chocolate Dandies* performers were forced to take temporary pay cuts of 25 percent.[44] Hudgins's weekly salary declined from $150 to $112.50, until the show re-opened at the Colonial Theatre on Broadway, when he again received his contracted salary of $200 a week. In

[43] Program, *The Chocolate Dandies*, Colonial Theater, New York, September 1, 1924; submitted as evidence in *Whitney v. Hudgins*.

[44] Woll reports that *The Chocolate Dandies* had trouble paying its bills due partly to its extravagant stage settings, partly to the relatively high salaries it paid its performers, and partly to the low prices it could charge for tickets compared to white Broadway shows. *Black Musical Theatre*, 91.

mid-September, however, Hudgins announced his departure from the show, signing a contract to perform at the Club Alabam and the Winter Garden Theatre for a weekly salary of $400. Whitney's lawsuit, which named Jacob and Lee Shubert, owners of the Winter Garden Company, and Arthur Lyons, the managing director of the Club Alabam, as co-defendants, sought to enjoin Hudgins from performing for these parties. Hudgins's participation in these other attractions, Whitney insisted, was "diverting members of the public" from *The Chocolate Dandies*, placing it "in danger of being ruined." He estimated that Hudgins's departure was costing him $2,500 a week in box office receipts.

Whitney's request for an injunction hinged on the claim that Hudgins's services were irreplaceable and in his debt. Spelled out by Whitney's lawyer, Nathan Burkan, the allegations against Hudgins were as follows:

> That the defendant Hudgins is an actor, dancer, mimic and pantomime comedian of novel, special, unique and extraordinary ability; that he has an original and unique manner of performing a shuffle dance; that he performs negro [sic] dances with rare grace and ease; that he goes through the pantomime of singing a song in a most comical manner; that he is endowed with a comic stage presence and personality, and the services rendered by said Hudgins are such that no other performer could be obtained who could perform in like manner or could supply the comic effect to the plaintiff's production with the same originality and grace as the said Hudgins; therefore, said Hudgins is much sought after at the present time. Plaintiff further alleges that it was through the instrumentality of the plaintiff that said Hudgins became known and it was the exploitation of said Hudgins by plaintiff which gave him the opportunity of receiving favorable comment and making him so that he is recognized on the stage today as a high-class pantomime comedian and dancer who could be used in any musical comedy, revue or similar production. That the plaintiff has expended many thousands of dollars in advertising said Hudgins in making him known and expected that the results from such advertising would enure to the benefit of the plaintiff and not to a rival manager.

As the allegations pile up, the fluctuating location of agency is telling. In one breath, Whitney grants credit to Hudgins for his "rare grace," his "comic stage presence," and his "originality." Hudgins appears here as a fully autonomous artist. Yet in the very next breath, Whitney negates Hudgins's agency by assuming full credit for Hudgins's popularity: it is Whitney's "instrumentality" and investment that are responsible for Hudgins's rise. In line with Stephen

Best's formulation of the slave's "two bodies," Hudgins's "emancipated" body is at once subject (in his ability to render unique services that had been promised to Whitney alone) and object (in his status as valuable commodity and product of Whitney's capital investment).[45] The effect of this doubling is only to increase Whitney's claims on Hudgins.

The classification of Hudgins as "special, unique and extraordinary" was no arbitrary designation. Film and legal studies scholar Jane Gaines explains that, under US contract law, in order to secure an injunction against an entertainer, an employer had to show "that the services of the actor or actress are entirely extraordinary and unique ... [and] ... that without the services of *this* creative person, for whom no other could be substituted, he would suffer losses for which damages could not compensate him."[46] The origins of these requirements date back to the Thirteenth Amendment's ban on slavery and involuntary servitude. After emancipation, an employer could not legally force a performer to render services that had been promised. When a breach of contract occurred, the employer's only recourse, beyond seeking compensatory damages, was what Gaines calls the "negative services covenant": preventing a performer from rendering his or her services for anyone else.

The original precedent for this covenant was an 1852 English case called *Lumley v. Wagner*, in which the English Court of Equity ruled that a well-known opera singer named Johanna Wagner could not be ordered to fulfill the terms of her contract—to sing exclusively at Lumley's Theatre for a certain number of nights—but could be enjoined from singing at a rival theater for the term of the contract. According to legal scholar Lea VanderVelde, American courts did not immediately adopt *Lumley*. In the wake of the Civil War and abolition, its terms were seen as regressive in the power they granted employers to prevent employees from working. As VanderVelde writes, "When *Lumley* first appeared in the United States, the cultural repulsion to anything that even hinted of slavery led to its unequivocal rejection."[47] By the end of the nineteenth century, however, as Reconstruction reforms receded, the rule of *Lumley* "attained the status of the dominant common law rule in American courts."[48] Indeed, Hudgins's defense lawyers cited *Lumley v. Wagner* as "the leading authority" on the subject of performance contract injunctions, reminding the

---

[45] Whitney maintained that Hudgins was the highest-paid performer in the show, save for Lew Payton, one of the musical's co-authors. *Whitney v. Hudgins*.

[46] Gaines, *Contested Culture*, 153.

[47] Lea S. VanderVelde, "The Gendered Origins of the *Lumley* Doctrine: Binding Men's Consciences and Women's Fidelity," *Yale Law Journal* 101.4 (January 1992): 779.

[48] Ibid., 776. VanderVelde argues that the acceptance of *Lumley* in the United States was "due in large part to the increasing presence of women in the acting profession" and courts' willingness to see female employees as "legally subordinate to their employers" (779, 782).

court that it was Wagner's renown as an opera singer that made her irreplaceable.[49] (Their point, as I discuss below, was that Hudgins lacked such renown.) Whether *Lumley* is seen as upholding or constricting the rights of "free labor," its influence on US law cannot be disentangled from the legacy of treating persons as property.[50] Its invocation in *Whitney v. Hudgins* is evidence of how that legacy continued to affect the juridical status of black performers. Unable to compel the services of his black employee, Whitney nonetheless claimed a property-like interest in Hudgins's labor by accentuating the singularity of his bodily performance.

To support his claims that Hudgins met the criteria for an injunction, Whitney's lawyer deposed a number of theatrical figures, many of them employees in *The Chocolate Dandies*. H. P. Hill, who did publicity for the show, testified that Hudgins was

> a most unique and extraordinary dancer and comedian. His dance steps are original, graceful, and comical, and he succeeds in getting the audience to laugh at his antics. He does a song and pantomime which is very funny and his comedy is quite out of the ordinary, and is the best thing that I have seen any colored artist do since the late Bert Williams.
>
> I am quite sure that no other colored artist can approach the said Hudgins in his particular ability.

The actor and cornetist Joe Smith, who appeared in *The Chocolate Dandies* (and was one of Hudgins's accompanists for his "Mwa, Mwa" routine), described Hudgins as "an extraordinary dancer. He does not dance alike two performances in succession. He does a peculiar shuffle dance which he varies with all kinds of new steps, and he also does a very comical strut, and also performs a very original and comical song and pantomime." Al Aarons, a show business veteran, pointed to Hudgins's ability "to do a shuffling dance as no other performer can do, and ... various other dance steps that put him in a class by himself." And W. A. Hann, another actor in *The Chocolate Dandies*, characterized Hudgins as an "original and novel" dancer and comedian without equal

---

[49] *Whitney v. Hudgins.*

[50] As VanderVelde also notes, one "significant antecedent" of enticement actions, in which one party sued another for enticing an employee away from a contract, "was the multitude of cases seeking recovery of runaway slaves and indentured servants" (793). For more context on American employment relations and US employment law, see Lea VanderVelde's "An Introduction to the American Tradition of Free Labor," University of Iowa Legal Studies Research Paper, Number 09–33, June 2009, available at http://ssrn.com/abstract=1413771. Accessed February 18, 2013.

"in the colored rase [*sic*]." Such testimonials that Hudgins's dance and comedic abilities were sui generis among black performers, comparable only to the legendary blackface vaudevillian Bert Williams, who had died just two years earlier, served as Whitney's rationale for enjoining Hudgins.

However utilitarian and however detrimental to Hudgins's cause, the legal claims about Hudgins's singularity were celebrated as historic by the black press. "For the first time in theatrical annals," the *Chicago Defender* noted on December 27, 1924,

> the courts of the State of New York are being asked to consider whether the services of a Colored performer are unique, extraordinary and impossible of duplication on the stage.
>
> The performer who will thus create the best precedent to apply to the Colored Race as in originality, spontaneity and unsurpassing cleverness of shuffling feet in the various forms of dancing in which so many excel is Johnny Hudgins.[51]

For this reporter, the fact that a black performer's originality was being adjudicated at all was something of a coup.[52] The momentousness of the occasion is evidence of the extent to which black artists had been excluded from the terms of Romantic authorship. To apply the phrase "unique and extraordinary" to Hudgins in a court of law was to rebut deeply engrained beliefs that African American performers were not only derivative of whites but also fungible—indistinguishable from and interchangeable with one another. The racial parameters of the claim, the comparison of Hudgins only to other "colored actors" and Whitney's insistence that he could not employ a white actor in the all-black show, did not detract from the magnitude of the legal event.[53] From the *Defender*'s perspective, the case was precedent setting, opening the doors of originality to all African American performers who "excelled."

Hudgins was in no position to share in this celebration, at least not publicly. Instead, Hudgins's lawyers vigorously refuted Whitney's claims. Affirming that "it is an elementary proposition of law that it is incumbent upon the plaintiff to prove that the services of the defendant, Johnny Hudgins, which he seeks to restrain from rendering to others, are special, unique, and extraordinary," they found that Whitney's attempts to meet this standard fell far short. To prove this,

---

[51] "Is Johnny Hudgins, Comedian, Unique," *Chicago Defender*, December 27, 1924, p. 6.

[52] See also Ashby Deering, "Is Negro Star Unique Player—First Time in History that Colored Performer's Services Have Been Considered Extraordinary," *Morning Telegraph*, December 9, 1924, Hudgins Scrapbook, Jean-Claude Baker Foundation.

[53] *Whitney v. Hudgins.*

they turned first to the affidavits submitted on behalf of the plaintiff, contending that these were based on "general characterizations of opinions" rather than on verifiable fact. In specific, they maintained, the affidavits failed to make "any mention whatsoever … that the defendant, Johnny Hudgins, had any reputation as a unique and extraordinary performer." Submitting depositions of their own from theatrical producers, managers, and booking agents, they sought to establish

> that Johnny Hudgins never had a reputation or was a featured player;
> that he never before appeared in musical comedy or in any attraction
> on Broadway; that he was a newcomer, unknown and unheralded;
> and that he received no recognition from the general public or from
> the plaintiff; that he was not an extraordinary player; or advertised
> and exploited by the plaintiff as such.

By highlighting Hudgins's lack of professional reputation—his status as an "unknown" on Broadway—the defense sought to differentiate his case from legal precedents in which an injunction had been issued under the negative services covenant.[54] "Everyone of those cases is distinguishable from the case at bar," Hudgins's lawyers held, "because the defendants in each case were famous in their profession." Without a reputation, Hudgins possessed "no value either as a featured player or as a draw to a show."[55] And as a valueless commodity, Hudgins's absence from *The Chocolate Dandies* could hardly be the cause of substantial financial damage to Whitney.

The defense also downplayed Hudgins's worth by offering testimonials of a more subjective nature. Edgar Allen, the general manager of William Fox Vaudeville Agency, asserted that

> the professional work of said Johnny Hudgins is primarily a dance
> with shuffling steps and would be described as a slow dance specialty.
> He does slight variations in the dance, but they are neither new, novel
> or original. The singing of Johnny Hudgins is negligible and his act
> is what I would classify as a fair dance act worth about $250 a week.

[54] Precedents of successful injunctions against performers cited by the defense include *Lumley v. Wagner*, 1 DeG., M. & G., 604; *McCall v. Braham*, 16 Fed. 37, a case involving the famous actress and singer Lillian Russell; and *Philadelphia Ball Club v. Lajoie*, 202 Pa., 210, a case involving a professional baseball player. The defense also cited *Shubert Theatrical Co. v. Gallagher & Shean*, 193 N.Y. Supp, 401, as a precedent in which injunctive relief against two comedians was denied on the basis that they were not employed to perform any particular role and did not possess any special reputation at the time of their employment. *Whitney v. Hudgins*.

[55] *Whitney v. Hudgins*.

I have engaged scores of such acts at about that salary, more or less and I have found no difficulty in securing such an act or replacing such an act. Almost any good colored dancing actor can duplicate the steps, which are, as I said, not new or novel.

Likewise, the booking agent Rufus Le Maire, who had seen Hudgins's work in *The Chocolate Dandies*, opined that Hudgins "is simply a dancer of the ordinary ability, whose singing is bad, and who is in no wise unique in his work, and whose act can be produced with the same amusing results by any other colored dancer of average ability." "There is nothing especially significant in the work of said Johnny Hudgins," the booking agent Moe Schenk summed up. Directly contradicting the statements submitted by the plaintiff, Hudgins's lawyers recruited these (presumably white) theater operatives to paint him as little more than a run-of-the-mill and therefore entirely fungible black performer.

In a lengthy deposition, Hudgins himself concurred. "I am a dancer like hundreds of others among my people," he averred, "and there is nothing either unique or extraordinary in my steps. What I do, any dancer of ordinary ability can do." To back up his claims, he pointed out that he had, in fact, been "easily replaced" in the cast of *The Chocolate Dandies* by his understudy, Lee J. Randall. (This countered Bertram Whitney's contention that Randall was "not able to duplicate Hudgins' dances, nor attain his comedy effects, nor amuse the audience in the manner in which [Hudgins] is capable.") Hudgins also cited the lack of publicity he received in promotional materials for *The Chocolate Dandies*. "Neither my name nor my presence in 'The Chocolate Dandies' was ever mentioned, no less emphasized, in newspaper advertisements, electric lights, bill posters, or theatre programs, the recognized channels of publicity for the attraction of a production."[56] His name, he added, was "less conspicuous than some of the chorus girls, and in type not larger than theirs, and inconspicuously assembled with scores of other names" on the musical's theater program. Acknowledging a gendered hierarchy of onstage talent, Hudgins cites the greater type size of chorus girls' names as a measure of his lowly status. If he was as commonplace as the chorus girl, the most exchangeable of commodities, Whitney could hardly be entitled to injunctive relief against him.[57]

---

[56] *The Chocolate Dandies* featured a "star-studded cast" of performers who were much better known than Hudgins at the time of its run, including Josephine Baker, Valaida Snow, Lottie Gee, Inez Cough, and Lew Payton. George-Graves, "The Chocolate Dandies," 223.

[57] Hudgins's use of the chorus girl as a sign of fungibility is a reminder of his male privilege, and his eventual copyright on his pantomime routines stands as a stark rejection of the gendered anonymity of the chorus girl. For extremely valuable insight into the lives and careers of the African American women who made up these female choruses, see Jayna Brown, *Babylon Girls: Black Women Performers and the Shaping of the Modern* (Durham, NC: Duke University Press, 2008). That women

There was more to Hudgins's legal rebuttal, however, than these claims of unoriginality and expendability. While half of his defense consisted of downplaying his market value, the other half involved playing up his rights as the subject of contract. Hudgins's attorneys argued that it was actually Whitney who had failed to meet the terms of his employment contract with Hudgins. As detailed in a Statement of Facts memorandum, Hudgins had refused to sign the new contract that Whitney proposed in mid-July of 1924, which revised the original June 3 contract and called for a 25 percent pay cut, as well as demanding five weeks of rehearsal without pay. According to the defense, these modifications constituted a violation of the "very spirit and essence" of the original contract. Rather than accept this "bold attempt on the part of the plaintiff to use this actor-defendant for his own purposes and advantages," Hudgins considered "all negotiations off" and agreed to appear in In Bamville only on a week-to-week basis. In other words, because Whitney reneged on the terms of agreement of the original contract, Hudgins was "released from all further obligation or liability thereunder." Thus believing himself "to be a free agent to contract with whom he pleased," Hudgins accepted an engagement with the Winter Garden Company when In Bamville closed in late August. As Hudgins summarized in his deposition, "I signed the contract with the Winter Garden Company in good faith and because I believed, and still believe, that I had a right to contract for my services with whomsoever I pleased in view of the breaches committed by Mr. Whitney."

In an echo of the plaintiff's strategy, then, Hudgins's defense depended on a division of his person, a split between his objecthood and subjecthood. For both sides, Hudgins's services as a performer rendered him a commodity to be traded in the marketplace; where they disagreed was whether he was a unique and therefore valuable commodity, or an ordinary and therefore expendable one. At the same time, both sides treated Hudgins as a self-governing agent who had contracted his services willfully. For the plaintiff, this meant that he should be held responsible for breach of contract; for the defense it meant that he had the right to walk away from a breached contract. Of course, any performer who contracts his or her services might be said to hold this twofold position as rights-bearing subject and salable object. As Jane Gaines points out, the enforcement of contracts in the entertainment industry is complicated by the fact that a performer both is and is not a product.[58] Yet for Hudgins, I would argue, race and the reverberations of slavery overdetermined this duality.

campaigned so vigorously for copyright protection for choreography in the emerging field of modern dance, while the only documented example of a copyright held by an African American dancer pre-1976 belonged to a male vernacular dancer (although, as Chapter 3 addresses, there were rumors that Alberta Hunter copyrighted the Black Bottom) is an index of the gendering of dance genres.

[58] Gaines, *Contested Culture*, 153.

At its core, *Whitney v. Hudgins* involved a white employer arguing that he had been wrongfully denied the labor of a black male body and attempting to enjoin that body from performing labor for anyone else. A debate over the status of Hudgins's body in the theatrical marketplace, the lawsuit pitted two sets of rights against one another: the black performer's right to sell his bodily labor and the white producer's right to traffic in and capitalize on that labor. Made in the context of that debate, Whitney's legal allegations about Hudgins's extraordinariness stood out for belatedly acknowledging the artistry of which black subjects were capable, even as these same allegations served to amplify the exchange value of Hudgins's black body as a commodity. In the framework of the lawsuit, moreover, the more value assigned to Hudgins's body, the greater the claims of the white producer.

In the end, as indicated at the outset of this chapter, the judge decided in favor of the defense. On November 19, 1924, Judge Richard H. Mitchell denied the plaintiff's motion for a temporary injunction against Hudgins, ruling "Under the circumstances disclosed in the papers submitted on this motion, plaintiff is not entitled to an injunction pendete [*sic*] lite."[59] Because the finding came with no accompanying explanation, we can only speculate about the judge's reasoning. Was his ruling a rejection of Whitney's contention that Hudgins was "special, unique, and extraordinary"? While courts had upheld injunctions against white performers in similar cases, Hudgins had long-standing racial assumptions on his side when he claimed that he was interchangeable with other black song-and-dance men.[60] Or, was the judge's finding a vindication of Hudgins's rights to contract his labor freely in a post-emancipation era? In the absence of answers to these questions, what seems significant is that it is equally possible

---

[59] Deering, "Is Negro Star Unique Player."

[60] Recall that, in the 1892 case *Hoyt v. Fuller*, a judge upheld an injunction against Loïe Fuller on the grounds that she was "special, unique, and extraordinary"—a finding that was bolstered by her own assertions of originality in her copyright claim. In *Comstock v. Lopokowa*, 190 Fed. 599 (C.C.S.D.N.Y. 1911), a judge upheld an injunction against Russian ballerinas who, like Hudgins, had quit one show to perform in another. The judge in that case was "satisfied that the defendants are of such unusual attainments and personal characteristics and of such especial value to the complainants as to fall within the class of employes [*sic*] whose negative covenants not to enter into the employment of others may be and should be enforced in equity." And, just three years prior to Whitney's lawsuit against Hudgins, a judge for the Second Circuit Court of Appeals upheld an injunction against a pair of acrobats, Geo and Dick Rath, on the grounds that they were "unique and extraordinary." *Shubert Theatrical Co. v. Rath et al.*, No. 170 271 F. 827, 1921. For further discussion of the "unique and extraordinary services" rule and other cases in which it was invoked, see David Tannenbaum, "Enforcement of Personal Service Contracts in the Entertainment Industry," *California Law Review* 42.1 (1954): 18–27. Available at http://scholarship.law.berkeley.edu/californialawreview/vol42/iss1/3. Accessed February 5, 2013. My thanks to Menesh Patel for his assistance with this legal research.

to interpret the victory as a defeat for African Americans as it is to see it as a victory, equally possible to see in the judge's decision a validation of Hudgins's object status as of his subject status (or as a validation of both simultaneously and paradoxically). Such were the contradictions facing the object who resists in a world marked by the residue of persons as property.[61]

The Copyright: Silent Speech and Hudgins's Body in Performance

However we read the decision in *Whitney v. Hudgins*, Hudgins emerged in good shape. As music scholar Brian Harker has written, *The Chocolate Dandies* marked a crossroads in Hudgins's career, "turning him from a song-and-dance man into a pantomime artist and dramatically increasing his marketability."[62] In addition to the cultural capital he reaped from Whitney's "unique and extraordinary" claim, Hudgins doubled his salary from $200 to $400 a week by taking his pantomime act to the Club Alabam.[63] A year after the lawsuit, Hudgins was reportedly earning $650 per week.[64] Two years later, he became a sensation in Paris, earning over $2,000 per week and sparking a fad for porcelain "Wah Wah dolls" made in his image.[65] Performers on both sides of the Atlantic tried to cash in on his fame: the Lincoln Theater in Harlem held a series of "Hudgins-imitator contests," and in Europe, he earned a reputation as "The Most Imitated Comedian on the Continent."[66] Hudgins's pursuit of

[61] Whitney appealed the judge's decision. The Appellate Division of New York's Supreme Court heard the appeal on April 18, 1925. The thrust of the appeal seems to have been to deny and disqualify the statements made in the affidavits for the defendant. There is no evidence to suggest that Whitney's appeal met with any greater success. A falling out with his original lawyers, Julius Kendler and Monroe Goldstein, led Hudgins to secure new representation for the appeal. The *Chicago Defender* reported that Kendler and Goldstein sued Hudgins "on a judgment for $1034.95 awarded them for professional services rendered." Hudgins evidently failed to show up to the hearing in city court and was cited for contempt of court. *Chicago Defender*, April 11, 1925, p. 6.

[62] Harker, "Louis Armstrong, Eccentric Dance, and the Evolution of Jazz," 76.

[63] *Whitney v. Hudgins*.

[64] *Variety*, December 16, 1925, p. 48, quoted in Harker, "Louis Armstrong, Eccentric Dance, and the Evolution of Jazz," 76fn29.

[65] Harker, "Louis Armstrong, Eccentric Dance, and the Evolution of Jazz," 76; unidentified newspaper clippings, Johnny Hudgins scrapbook, Jean-Claude Baker Foundation. In 1927, Hudgins became the subject of an oil painting by the internationally renowned painter Kees Van Dongen. Titled *Johnny Hudgins, chanteur négre/Nightclub: the Singer Johnny Hudgins*, the painting depicts Hudgins in full-on minstrel mode. See an image of the painting here: http://arttattler.com/archivevandongen.html. Accessed December 5, 2014.

[66] David Hinckley, "Not Just Black and White: The Curious Case of Vaudeville Comic Johnny Hudgins," *New York Daily News*, September 3, 2000, Showtime section, p. 13; unidentified newspaper clipping, Johnny Hudgins scrapbook, Jean-Claude Baker Foundation.

copyright protection for his pantomime acts, like Loïe Fuller's before him, was unquestionably a response to these impersonations. But, coming as it did on the heels of *Whitney v. Hudgins*, his embrace of copyright law was also a rejoinder to the contorted posture into which the lawsuit forced him. If Hudgins the legal defendant was caught between objecthood and subjecthood, Hudgins the copyright claimant seemed to assert an unequivocal status as artist and self-possessive individual.

The second half of this chapter turns from the lawsuit to the copyright to probe the connections between Hudgins's act of copyright and his copyrighted act. Exploiting the fact that the record of the copyright doubles as a record of Hudgins's performance, I ask: what can attention to Hudgins's choreography, including his use of blackface, tell us about his assertions of intellectual property rights, and how should those assertions inform our reading of his choreography? As I argue, Hudgins's legal claims of ownership stood as a counterweight to multiple kinds of objectification. In addition to rebutting his prior legal stance of fungibility, Hudgins's copyright offset (even as it perhaps reproduced) the objectification enacted by his own performance as a blackface entertainer.

The primary source of evidence of Hudgins's copyright is the extant copyrighted publication itself, held by the Jean-Claude Baker Foundation in New York.[67] Titled *Silence*, the nineteen-page booklet consists primarily of blow-by-blow accounts of the entrances and exits, dance steps, and gestures that formed Hudgins's seven specialty acts: a "First Specialty"; the "Mwa, Mwa Specialty"; the "Ballroom Specialty," in which Hudgins danced with an imaginary partner; the "Oriental Specialty," which included a dance Hudgins called the "Cootie Mooch";[68] a cross-dressing "Charleston Specialty"; the "Pantomime of Ice Skating"; and the Pullman "Porter Specialty." Unlike the polyvocality of the lawsuit record, *Silence* is written in a single voice and from a single perspective: that of its author, Hudgins.

That voice emphatically sounds its originality. "Every Expression, Move, Gesture, Pedal Evolution, Manoeuvre and Shuffle," a clause preceding the description of the routine states, "is JOHNNY HUDGINS own original creation." In case this statement left any room for doubt, the book includes periodic reminders that a given specialty was Hudgins's "own original idea" or was

---

[67] Jean-Claude Baker, an unofficial adoptee of Josephine Baker, became close friends with Hudgins before Hudgins's death in 1990. Jean-Claude Baker ran the Chez Josephine restaurant in New York City before his own death in early 2015.

[68] On the interface of blackface and Orientalism, see Shannon Steen, *Racial Geometries of the Black Atlantic, Asian Pacific and American Theatre* (New York: Palgrave Macmillan, 2010), and Josephine Lee, "'And Others of His Race': Blackface and Yellowface," in *The Japan of Pure Invention: Gilbert and Sullivan's The Mikado* (Minneapolis: University of Minnesota Press, 2010), 83–120.

"originated" by him.[69] At the back of the booklet, in what could have doubled as plaintiff's evidence against Hudgins in the earlier lawsuit, are excerpts from newspaper reviews that collectively attest to his uniqueness. An "extraordinary negro comedian," trumpets the French *L'Oeuvre*[70] and "One of the most original things we have ever seen." "As unique and versatile a comic as graces the stage to-day," announces the New York *Telegraph*, while the New York *Daily Mirror* and New York *Variety* respectively declare that "He possesses a unique way and a distinct sense of originality," and that "his absolute originality places him as incomparable." (Two of these reviews predate his departure from *The Chocolate Dandies* and the November 1924 lawsuit.) Finally free to embrace reports of his uniqueness, Hudgins's copyright publication serves as an outlet for everything he had been forced to suppress while defending himself against Whitney.

These testimonials to Hudgins's originality did more than just counter his prior disavowals. In pragmatic terms, they also supported his claims of proprietorship. Under the British Copyright Act of 1911, which, in contrast to US law at the time,[71] recognized choreography and pantomime as protectable forms, copyright subsisted in every "original literary dramatic musical and artistic work" that was first published within British territory.[72] Going to the effort of documenting his entire repertoire of pantomimed specialties, finding a British publisher to print his booklet, and underscoring the originality of his stage work, Hudgins ensured that his rights as the subject of property were legally sanctioned, at least in England.[73]

[69] Hudgins, *Silence*.

[70] The program booklet attributes this quotation to the "Paris *Ceuvre*"—almost certainly a mistaken reference to the daily *L'Oeuvre* newspaper.

[71] According to the most recent *Compendium of U.S. Copyright Practices*, the Copyright Office regulations released in conjunction with the 1909 Copyright Act specified that

> Choreographic work of a dramatic character, whether the story or theme be expressed in music or action combined or by actions alone, are subject to registration in Class D. However, descriptions of dance steps and other physical gestures, including ballroom and social dances or choreographic works which do not tell a story, develop a character or emotion, or otherwise convey a dramatic concept or idea, are not subject to registration in Class D.

Registration of Claims to Copyright, 24 Fed. Reg. 4955, 4958 (1959), cited in *Compendium of U.S. Copyright Practices*, Third Edition.

[72] The British Copyright Act of 1911 deemed "dramatic work" to include "any piece for ... choreographic work or entertainment in dumb show." Copyright Act, 1911, http://www.legislation.gov.uk/ukpga/Geo5/1-2/46/introduction/enacted. Accessed June 29, 2011.

[73] As scholar Isabella Alexander points out in *Copyright Law and the Public Interest in the Nineteenth Century* (Portland, OR: Hart, 2010), Britain's 1911 Copyright Act actually moved away from granting protection only to the specific format of the "book" and toward the more abstract concept of "work," which did not necessarily require a tangible form (273–4, 289). Yet

That Hudgins's proprietary claims extended to his use of blackface makeup is worth pausing over, especially insofar as the pairing seems to index emancipation and racial subjugation in a single breath. "No infringement on my make-up or Act," his booklet proclaimed on the opening page. Two pages later, a clause clarified that his "own Original Make-up" consisted of "Face Make-up Black, using Burnt Cork." Interpolated throughout the copyright booklet are five different images of Hudgins in makeup and costume. With darkened face and brightened lips, donning a large jacket, white gloves, disheveled necktie, oversized shoes, and various "ill-used" hats, Hudgins conforms to one of the most immediately recognizable and entrenched of racialized types: the blackface minstrel, or what Henry Louis Gates Jr. describes as "Minstrel Man."[74] As was standard for minstrel performers, a sixth and final image shows him posing as "Johnny Hudgins Himself," without the blackface mask.

What to make of this declaration of intellectual property rights in an emblem of racial mimicry? On one level, Hudgins's copyright can be read as a mockery of the racialized norms that emerged out of minstrelsy: Hudgins asserts black originality in and ownership of a performance convention that for over half a century licensed white use of African American aesthetic traditions and rendered black performance always already derivative. Hudgins's copyright of blackface itself flips the script on white claims of originality in black expressive forms. On

the 1911 Act specified that unpublished works only merited protection if "the author was at the date of the making of the work a British subject or resident within such parts of His Majesty's dominions." Because, as Hudgins's booklet spells out, his pantomime acts were originated in the United States, publication appears to have been a prerequisite of copyright protection for him in England. Although at least one newspaper believed that Hudgins copyrighted his "Mwa, Mwa" routine under US law, there is no evidence in the US Copyright Office to suggest that this was true. "Johnny Hudgins Is Coming Home." British copyright law would not have protected Hudgins from infringement inside the United States. Hudgins's turn to British copyright law is significant for reasons beyond its divergence from US copyright law. Traveling beyond US borders, Hudgins established himself as part of the formation that Paul Gilroy wrote about so influentially in *The Black Atlantic: Modernity and Double Consciousness* (Cambridge, MA: Harvard University Press, 1993). This was hardly out of the ordinary for African American performers, whose lives, Jayna Brown aptly notes, were "inherently itinerant." Because these performers traversed the Atlantic on their own volition, they provide a counter-history to accounts that deny black people "any mobility, except as exported commodity." Hudgins's British copyright thus positioned him as both possessive individual and "world historical agent." *Babylon Girls*, 10, 9. Brown's book provides an important corrective to the assumption that such international travel was an exclusively male domain. See also Catherine Parsonage, *The Evolution of Jazz in Britain, 1880–1935* (Hampshire, England: Ashgate, 2005), esp. 173–83, for a historical account of the reception of black musicians in Britain in the 1920s, including expectations that they conform to minstrel-like stereotypes and opposition to their employment in stage shows.

[74] Henry Louis Gates Jr., *The Signifying Monkey: A Theory of Afro-American Literary Criticism* (New York: Oxford University Press, 1988), 108–9.

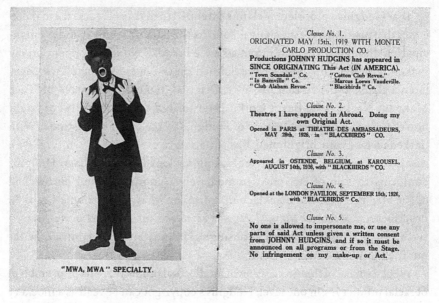

Clause No. 1.
ORIGINATED MAY 15th, 1919 WITH MONTE
CARLO PRODUCTION CO.
Productions JOHNNY HUDGINS has appeared in
SINCE ORIGINATING This Act (IN AMERICA).
"Town Scandals" Co.   "Cotton Club Revue."
"In Bamville" Co.   Marcus Loews Vaudeville.
"Club Alabam Revue."   "Blackbirds" Co.

Clause No. 2.
Theatres I have appeared in Abroad. Doing my
own Original Act.
Opened in PARIS at THEATRE DES AMBASSADEURS,
MAY 28th, 1926, in "BLACKBIRDS" CO.

Clause No. 3.
Appeared in OSTENDE, BELGIUM, at KAROUSEL,
AUGUST 14th, 1926, with "BLACKBIRDS" CO.

Clause No. 4.
Opened at the LONDON PAVILION, SEPTEMBER 15th, 1926,
with "BLACKBIRDS" Co.

Clause No. 5.
No one is allowed to impersonate me, or use any
parts of said Act unless given a written consent
from JOHNNY HUDGINS, and if so it must be
announced on all programs or from the Stage.
No infringement on my make-up or Act.

"MWA, MWA" SPECIALTY.

Figure 2.4 Photograph of Hudgins in costume for his signature "Mwa, Mwa" act. Hudgins, *Silence*, The Jean-Claude Baker Foundation.

another level, however, the copyright and the minstrel stereotype seem to be not just mirror images of one another but working at cross-purposes: while the former positions Hudgins as the rights-bearing subject of property, the latter tethers him to a history of racist objectification. Was Hudgins's reliance on the minstrel mask part of what propelled his turn to copyright law? Might we see Hudgins's legal pursuit of possessive individualism as, in some measure, a way to counteract the effects of wearing the minstrel mask, just as it counteracted the disavowals of originality necessitated by the Whitney lawsuit?

A closer look at how blackface functioned for Hudgins helps parse the relationship between his minstrel mask and his copyright claim. Interviewed in the 1960s by Russian jazz dance enthusiast Mura Dehn, Hudgins addressed the sources of his routine:

> In my dances, those steps they came to me—my first inspiration for dancing was Bert Williams. The "Blackface" I like, because it is cut out for comedy. You make your lips red and trim it. Black face is plain burned cork. I'm just a clown.[75]

[75] Dehn, "Johnny Hudgins." For more on how Hudgins narrated the development of his "Mwa, Mwa" routine, see Anthea Kraut, "Fixing Improvisation: Copyright and African American Vernacular Dancers in the Early Twentieth Century," in *The Oxford Handbook of Critical Improvisation Studies*, ed. George Lewis and Ben Piekut (New York: Oxford University Press, forthcoming).

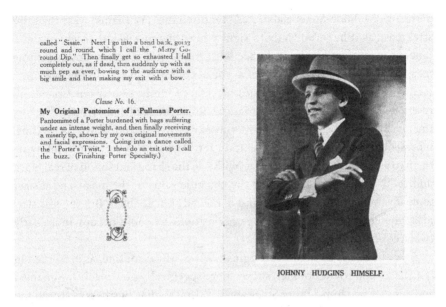

called "Sissie." Next I go into a bend back, going round and round, which I call the "Merry Go-round Dip." Then finally get so exhausted I fall completely out, as if dead, then suddenly up with as much pep as ever, bowing to the audience with a big smile and then making my exit with a bow.

Clause No. 16.

My Original Pantomime of a Pullman Porter.

Pantomime of a Porter burdened with bags suffering under an intense weight, and then finally receiving a miserly tip, shown by my own original movements and facial expressions. Going into a dance called the "Porter's Twist," I then do an exit step I call the buzz. (Finishing Porter Specialty.)

JOHNNY HUDGINS HIMSELF.

Figure 2.5 Photograph of Hudgins without blackface makeup, included in the back of *Silence*. The Jean-Claude Baker Foundation.

The syntax of statements here is both peculiar and revealing. Hudgins seems to switch gears mid-sentence, first implying that he conjured his steps out of thin air and then naming the legendary Bert Williams, to whom Hudgins was frequently compared, as his primary influence. Pivoting again, Hudgins uses Williams to segue into a discussion of blackface. Reflecting on the convention at a time when it had fallen out of favor, Hudgins tacitly justifies his use of blackface by placing himself in a lineage with Williams. His insistence that blackface was just "plain burned cork" and that he was "just a clown," meanwhile, offered up a potentially non-racialized way of understanding his stage makeup.[76]

In professing his fondness for blackface, Hudgins enters into a debate on the "various and intricate semantic or signifying possibilities" of the minstrel mask.[77] As Louis Chude-Sokei writes in his monograph on Bert Williams, the blackface mask was "what allowed [Williams] to cross [the] color line" and achieve such widespread fame. "To enter on the white stage as a black

[76] My thanks to Harvey Young for suggesting this interpretation of Hudgins's clown reference. As Eric Lott writes, the blackface minstrel tradition emerged out of "the intersection of slave culture and earlier blackface stage characters," including "the clown of English pantomime and the clown of the American circus." *Love and Theft*, 22.

[77] Louis Chude-Sokei, *The Last "Darky": Bert Williams, Black-on-Black Minstrelsy, and the African Diaspora* (Durham, NC: Duke University Press, 2006), 42.

performer," Chude-Sokei elaborates, "required that [Williams] wear the min-strel mask as if hyperbolically to signify his difference as other while simul-taneously comforting the audience with the warm, familiar, unthreatening meanings of minstrelsy."[78] Part of a "social contract" of race in the late nine-teenth and early twentieth centuries, blackface simultaneously sanctioned and restricted black performance. For dance scholar Brenda Dixon Gottschild, too, the mask signaled the egregious racism of minstrelsy and, at the same time, represented a "contradictory liberation for blacks" who donned it, allowing them to assume a persona and fill it "with *self*, the shape and sound of real black bodies."[79] Hudgins clearly prized the comedic value of the mask, and his act took advantage of what red lips and darkened skin enabled. But the minstrel mask undeniably limited the range of positions he could occupy in an early twentieth-century racial hierarchy.

Analysis of the content of Hudgins's "Mwa, Mwa" routine, as preserved in the *Silence* copyright booklet, shows more specifically how blackface enabled and constrained him. "Enter Stage with ... droll shuffle, business of stumbling over Stage, nearly falling, also Clown with audience, vamping song with an eccentric step I call 'Cutting Capers,'" the description of his most famous routine begins. Stopping suddenly, Hudgins tips his hat, smiles, and mimes a conversation with an audience member. This is quickly replaced with, in Hudgins's words, an

> expression of not recognizing them and asking them to leave [the] Theatre—by means of Pantomime and facial expressions—and just as I am about to put my hat on, it suddenly comes to me that I *do* know them and I show it by smiling back, speaking with a very broad smile, and looking very much pleased. After this ... I glide back up-stage and do a long slide to the front[,] landing right at [the] Footlights ... , then from there I go into my Pantomime song called the "Mwa, Mwa, Mwa, Mwa, Mwa, Mwa, mwa." A song in which I do not utter a word, but move my lips as if I were singing, while a muted Cornet ... gives an imitation of a human voice singing "Mwa, Mwa."

After performing a "low bow to the audience," followed by "a fast shuffle" and slide, Hudgins concludes the act by "skipping from one end of the Stage to the other" while "throwing imaginary flowers" from his hat to the audience.[80]

[78] Ibid., 35.
[79] Gottschild, *Digging the Africanist Presence*, 84–85.
[80] Hudgins, *Silence*.

Looked at from one angle, Hudgins's act consisted of a series of shuffling steps and exaggerated gestures that conform wholly to the minstrel image. "The most basic step in tap dancing," Hudgins's shuffle was also part of the "body politics of minstrelsy."[81] As dance scholar Constance Valis Hill explains, the term "shuffle" refers to "a rapid forward-and-back brushing of the foot" *and* "to the southern stereotype of the shuffling old black plantation slave, who, accused of being lazy and venal, then consciously dragged and scraped his feet noisily along the ground."[82] At a time when the "New Negro" sought to shed what Harlem Renaissance scholar Nathan Huggins describes as "the costume of the shuffling darky, the uncle and aunty, the subservient and docile retainer, the clown," Hudgins may have seemed the very embodiment of the Old Negro.[83]

But not to all. In 1924, the *Baltimore Afro-American* assured readers that "Johnny does no 'Uncle Tom' stuff, and in this respect differs from a number of blackface comedians."[84] This insistence on Hudgins's difference from the shuffling darky indicates that there was a complexity, even a level of resistance, to his act. The possibility of resistance becomes clear when we attend to the complicated racialized economy of looking and being-looked-at-ness and, concomitantly, of silence and utterance at work in Hudgins's choreography.[85]

At its core, Hudgins's performance centered around his silence—the title, recall, of his entire copyrighted work. In a visual joke, Hudgins "sings" "Mwa, Mwa" without uttering a word; lip synching to the accompanying cornet, he moves his mouth "as if" he were producing music that itself sounds "as if" it were a human voice. Hudgins's muteness in the act surely heightened its visuality. To get the joke, spectators had to "read" Hudgins's body as soundless and then sharpen their gaze on his pantomimed gestures and facial expressions.

Hudgins's minstrel mask ensured that this gaze was a racialized one. The focal point of the "Mwa, Mwa" routine, after all, was, in one critic's words, "That big red mouth, wowing without a sound, [that] always brings a laugh."[86] With painted red lips set against artificially darkened skin, Hudgins's facial movements highlighted his blackface mask, even as his blackface mask highlighted his movements. That

[81] Constance Valis Hill, *Tap Dancing America: A Cultural History* (New York: Oxford University Press, 2010), 71; Hartman, *Scenes of Subjection*, 29.

[82] Hill, *Tap Dancing America*, 71.

[83] Nathan Irvin Huggins, ed., *Voices from the Harlem Renaissance* (New York: Oxford University Press, 1995), 3.

[84] Quoted in Bill Egan, *Florence Mills: Harlem Jazz Queen* (Lanham, MD: Scarecrow Press, 2004), 158n51.

[85] On the concept of "to-be-looked-at-ness," see Laura Mulvey's classic essay, "Visual Pleasure and Narrative Cinema," *Screen* 16.3 (Autumn 1975): 6–18.

[86] *Baltimore Evening Sun* clipping, April 24, 1929, Johnny Hudgins Scrapbook, Jean-Claude Baker Foundation.

is to say, Hudgins's gestures and physical appearance reinforced one another to mark his pantomiming body as a racialized spectacle. Becoming the minstrel mask, Hudgins literally transformed himself into a non-speaking commodity.

But even as Hudgins's muteness played up his status as spectacle, it also forced attention to the expressivity and articulateness of his body. The silence created by the absence of Hudgins's voice was filled with kinesthetic utterances produced by skilled manipulations of his body. It is here that Hudgins's copyrighted account reaches its limits, for if it tells us what his movements consisted of, it offers very little by way of how he moved—what we might call the "kinesthetic materiality" of Hudgins's act.[87] For some insight there, we can turn to film footage of Hudgins performing one of his pantomime acts, which fortuitously survives in the British Pathé archives and is accessible online.[88] In a two-and-a-half minute silent clip dated 1927 and titled "Feet—Fun—and Fancy," Hudgins performs a routine containing a number of the moves described in his copyright booklet. The clip is subtitled "A silent little spasm by Johnny Hudgins of 'Black Birds' fame" and opens with an inter-title that reads, "Hush! hush! hush! Here comes the Bogey Man!" Details about the film—who made it, for what purpose, where it might have been distributed—are unknown. But, notwithstanding the racial slur and dismissive characterization of his choreography, the film provides convincing evidence of Hudgins's exceptional skill as a dancer.

Following the introductory inter-title, the first thing we see is Hudgins's gloved hand emerging from behind a curtained door. After circling his hand around, seemingly testing the waters, Hudgins slowly and hesitantly steps out. He is in blackface and wears the ill-fitting suit that his copyright booklet claims as his exclusive property. Looking around as if to see who is out there watching him, he immediately inscribes the viewer into his act. He puts on a small-brimmed straw hat, strolls forward, bows, and repeatedly tips his hat to the audience. He then waves to an imaginary spectator, appears to engage in conversation, points down at his feet, and begins a leg-swinging shuffle. This is followed by a slow-motion move Hudgins called the "Ball Bearing Pivot," in which he does a "complete pivot turn, turning very, very slowly, crossing [his] feet and not taking them off the floor while turning, whilst staying in one spot on the stage."[89] Next, he performs a succession of faster shuffling

---

[87] Here I am suggesting a parallel to the "phonic materiality" that Moten concerns himself with. *In the Break*, 1. The respective materialities of music and dance, of course, are quite different but cannot be characterized in any absolute terms.

[88] http://www.britishpathe.com/video/feet-fun-and-fancy. Accessed February 12, 2013.

[89] Most of this routine corresponds with what Hudgins describes in his copyright booklet as his "First Specialty." Hudgins, *Silence*.

moves, including a bent-kneed hip sway (à la Earl "Snakehips" Tucker), the Charleston, and a double-arm, single-leg swing. Finally, he throws imaginary flowers from his hat, skates from side to side, pivots around himself, and circles the stage while rotating his wrist in what he termed the "Snake Shuffle."[90]

Hudgins's bodily control in this footage is arresting. He is completely loose-limbed even while his pantomimed gestures are incredibly precise. Capable of moving both very slowly and very rapidly, he executes a great deal of movement, especially with his feet, while essentially staying in one place on the stage. It seems no stretch to call his corporeal facility "unique and extraordinary."

Contemporaneous reviews of Hudgins's stage act suggest that critics generally agreed. While a number of them praised the agility and litheness of Hudgins's body, proclaiming that "One has as yet not seen such a relaxation of the whole body, such a mastery over the limbs"[91] and wondering "Has this man no skeleton at all?"[92] for other critics, the most salient aspect of Hudgins's dancing was how little of it he did. "What is most striking about him," wrote a *Chicago Defender* reviewer,

> is the simplicity of the material which he is able to make effective. He neither sings nor tells any jokes nor does he work up anything with a partner.... Hudgins' great distinction lies in his economy and restraint.[93]

The *Baltimore Afro-American* likewise remarked that Hudgins "dances without dancing" and "sings ... without singing."[94]

This focus on Hudgins's economy, on what he held back in performance, calls to mind the aesthetic quality that Zora Neale Hurston identified as

---

[90] Hudgins also performed a number of these same moves in a twenty-minute silent film by French film director Jean Renoir called *Sur un air de Charleston* (or *Charleston Parade*). Made in 1926 and released in 1927, the film is set in A.D. 2028 when "years after the next war—an explorer sets forth from Central Africa into the Terra Incognita of Europa Deserta." Hudgins, in his blackface costume, plays the astronaut, an African explorer who lands in Paris in a post-Holocaust landscape only to discover the Charleston, as performed by a white woman (Renoir's wife, Catherine Hessling) playing the part of an exotic savage. She ostensibly teaches him the dance. In *The Signifying Monkey*, Henry Louis Gates Jr. reads the film as a parodic reversal of the trope of Europeans' "discovery" of Africa. Raymond Durgnat, *Jean Renoir* (Berkeley: University of California Press, 1974), 42–43. Gates, *The Signifying Monkey*, 108–10.

[91] Clipping, *Die rote Fahne*, June 17, 1928, Hudgins Scrapbook, Jean-Claude Baker Foundation (a typed translation appears alongside the original in the scrapbook).

[92] J. A. Rogers, "Johnny Hudgins Starts Home on the First Boat" *Baltimore Afro-American*, July 28, 1928, p. 9.

[93] "Johnny Hudgins Is Still Going Big on Broadway," *Chicago Defender*, May 8, 1926, p. 7.

[94] "Hudgins Terminates Paris Engagement," *Baltimore Afro-American*, April 14, 1928, p. 8.

"dynamic suggestion" in her 1934 essay "Characteristics of Negro Expression." "Every posture," she wrote,

> gives the impression that the dancer will do much more. . . . It is compelling insinuation. That is the very reason the spectator is held so rapt. He is participating in the performance himself—carrying out the suggestions of the performer.[95]

"Compelling insinuation" certainly seems an apt description of Hudgins's "Mwa, Mwa" pantomime routine, which depended on viewers to use their imaginations to fill in the negative spaces created with his body. Cast in this light, Hudgins's act emerges as much more, and much more complicated, than a one-dimensional racial spectacle, passively received by an immobile viewer. Hudgins's kinesthetic "speech" was indirect, achieved through restraint and allusion.

As much as Hurston's critical insights help explain the nature of Hudgins's prowess and appeal, her comments also return us to the power relationships inherent in the visual field of performance. While a dancer like Hudgins could hold the spectator "rapt," the spectator was left to "finish the action the performer suggest[ed]" in his or her mind's eye.[96] And it was this same eye that held the power to racialize and objectify. However much Hudgins shook up the dynamics of spectatorship as he exploited the tension between doing and not doing, his kinesthetic maneuvers took place within a visual economy of race that gave rise to comments like the following, from a German newspaper:

> [Hudgins] is a silent, a very quiet comedian, with deeply conscious and earnest, childlike eyes, black, and which shine like night at the equator. Then suddenly he begins to hear the tom-toms of his native land booming, and he begins to dance with the naïve joy and movements simply impossible to express on paper.[97]

Impossible to express, maybe, but all too easy to place decisively in a hierarchical racial schema.

The inherent proliferation of "signifying possibilities" generated by the black performer in blackface thus meant that the chances of subverting racial

---

[95] Zora Neale Hurston, "Characteristics of Negro Expression," in *The Sanctified Church* (Berkeley: Turtle Island, 1981), 55–56.

[96] Ibid., 56.

[97] Quoted in "Johnny Hudgins Is Coming Home."

stereotypes always co-existed with the likelihood of reinscribing them. Correspondingly, the prospect of asserting oneself as a self-governing subject through performance always sat in tension with the dangers of self-objectification. Such instability throws into sharp relief the appeal that copyright must have held for Hudgins. However polysemous dance is as a medium, however agile Hudgins was as a dancer, and however liberatory he found the blackface mask, embodied performance inescapably operates within a visual field and therefore within a visual economy of race that renders African Americans "other" to a privileged white norm.[98] The juridical realm of intellectual property rights provided Hudgins with another avenue in which to negotiate his subject position, one that was not overdetermined by the racializing gaze. The legal imprimatur of copyright gave Hudgins an unambiguous status as proprietor and rights-holder.

This is not to say that the complicated dynamics of blackface performance drove Hudgins's embrace of copyright. As I have suggested above, there were more proximate causes for his (re)turn to the law. The Whitney lawsuit, which forced Hudgins into a battle over the rights to his labor and required him to disavow any originality, was surely motivation for his pursuit of intellectual property rights. More immediately, Hudgins was hoping to curb the rash of copycats trying to capitalize on the popularity of his "Mwa, Mwa" routine. Irritated by "act grabbers" who, in reproducing his signature act without crediting him, threatened to transform his act into an authorless, exchangeable commodity, Hudgins used copyright to retain his authorial status and his distinctiveness in the market.[99] Nevertheless, we should not divorce Hudgins's efforts to ally himself with the power and privilege that copyright signified from the nature of his performance practice and the constrictions of race. It is important, that is, to consider the limits of what is possible through the medium of performance, and important to read an artist's expressive "utterances" in tandem with other, extra-theatrical registers of "speech."[100]

[98] On race as a visual economy, see Robyn Wiegman, "Visual Modernity," in *American Anatomies: Theorizing Race and Gender* (Durham, NC: Duke University Press, 1995), 21–42. Where Moten's *In the Break* argues persuasively for the ways that aurality and visuality interrupt and penetrate one another, I am not sure that the kinesthetic disrupts the visual in the same way that the aural might.

[99] "Hudgins Protests Use of His Act by Others." A further discussion of Hudgins's response to these imitators appears in Chapter 3.

[100] I have been playing with Moten's critique of Marx's take on the impossibility of the speaking commodity, but J. L. Austin's speech-act theory is also hovering in the background here. Distinguishing between "performative utterances," which produce "real" effect (like the legally binding "I do" of a marriage ceremony), from "constative utterances," which merely describe events, Austin deems utterances that take place on the theater stage to be "null and void." Dance and performance scholars have persuasively challenged Austin's contention that theatrical utterances lack real-world effect, and I wholeheartedly agree. My point is that both legal and theatrical

By no means, however, do I want to suggest that hegemonic racial hierarchies were easier to overturn in law than in performance. It is striking that despite an unsubstantiated report in the *Chicago Defender*, Hudgins does not appear to have pursued copyright protection in the United States.[101] Though pantomime and choreography were not yet recognized as protectable categories of intellectual property for dancers of any race, Hudgins may have felt that US law was less hospitable to a black man's performance rights than was English law.[102] For all its script-flipping, moreover, copyright law did not enable Hudgins to sidestep the hazards of objectification entirely. In fact, there is an argument to be made that copyright functioned analogously to the minstrel mask for Hudgins and yielded similar effects.

On one hand, Hudgins's assertion of intellectual property rights opened up a space between him and the thing he was portraying, much like donning blackface highlighted Hudgins's act *as* performance. In claiming rights over his repertoire of pantomime routines, Hudgins effectively announced, "I am the owner of these blackface acts, not their equivalent." It is perhaps more accurate, then, to say that Hudgins's legal claim of proprietorship was akin to the bare-faced photo he included of himself in his copyright booklet. Declaring copyright was like removing the mask, separating subject (owner) from object (thing owned).

utterances can and should be considered performative in the sense that they can effect some kind of transformation, in this case related to one's status as object or subject. J. L. Austin, *How to Do Things with Words* (Oxford: Oxford University Press, 1975). For a compelling challenge to Austin, see Jacqueline Shea Murphy, *"The People Have Never Stopped Dancing": Native American Modern Dance Histories* (Minneapolis: University of Minnesota Press, 2007), and Rebekah J. Kowal, *How to Do Things with Dance: Performing Change in Postwar America* (Middletown, CT: Wesleyan University Press, 2010).

[101] "Johnny Hudgins Is Coming Home."

[102] A separate *Defender* article gives the impression that Hudgins did threaten lawsuits against his imitators, but his British copyright would not have held weight in a US court of law. "Hudgins Says His Piece on the Present Era," *Chicago Defender*, January 17, 1931, p. 5. Peter Decherney's "Gag Orders: Comedy, Chaplin, and Copyright," in *Modernism & Copyright*, Saint-Amour, ed., recounts a successful lawsuit by the pantomimist Charlie Chaplin to halt the Mexican actor Charles Amador, who was a Chaplin imitator, from using Chaplin's image. But the decision in that case, *Chaplin v. Amador*, 269 P. 544 (Cal. Dist. Ct. App. 1928), was made on the grounds that Amador's "Charlie Aplin" films created confusion in the marketplace rather than finding that Chaplin possessed a proprietary right in his "tramp" character (151). Certainly, as did many African American performers, Hudgins encountered less overt racism on the other side of the Atlantic than in the States. Shortly after his return, he told a reporter that "There is not a thing to the thought that prejudice of any kind is seeping into that part of Europe." He also praised the "deepseated fairplay of the French" for giving "credit to whom credit is due without the slightest regard for race distinction." "Johnny Hudgins, Dog and Monkey Pay *Afro* a Visit," *Baltimore Afro-American*, October 6, 1928, p. 8.

On the other hand, in the act of creating this distance, Hudgins's copyright, like the minstrel mask, paradoxically contributed to the very objectification it sought to counter. As with the Whitney lawsuit, which figured Hudgins not only as object of property but also as subject of contract, the copyright produced both a subject of property and its object, both an author and a work. Because his work was corporeal in nature, Hudgins's body was caught up in both the subject and object sides of the equation: both "author" and "work" partook of his body. Taking fixed and tangible form in the booklet *Silence*, Hudgins's copyright claim thus re-staged the figurative splitting or doubling of his body that it seemed on the surface to counteract. The effects of copyrighting a pantomimed dance routine were not so far removed from the alienation endemic to commodification. For Hudgins the proprietor, as for Marx's alienated worker, the copyrighted act became "an object, an *external* existence ... [that] exist[ed] *outside him*, independently, as something alien to him."[103] The irony of viewing Hudgins as a commodity that speaks and of viewing that speech as an affirmation of his personhood is that his speech—whether articulated via live performance, legal affidavit, or copyright publication—at least on some level reinforced the commodity status of his dancing body.[104]

Ironic, but not surprising, given that the residue of slavery had seeped into both the theatrical and legal traditions in which Hudgins's speech materialized. If an African American dancer's assertion of possessive individualism through the mechanism of copyright was always in danger of re-enacting his own objecthood, if the idea of "possessing one's personhood" was only ever a "ghostly semblance,"[105] that should by no means diminish the significance of his effort to claim the racially wrought privileges of proprietary subjecthood. And it is precisely the contradictions of Hudgins's situation that make his case so instructive. Embracing the residual convention of blackface, labeled both the successor to Bert Williams and the black Charlie Chaplin, oscillating between labor and capital and between scarcity and surfeit, unable to

[103] Karl Marx, *Economic and Philosophical Manuscripts of 1844*, in *The Marx-Engels Reader*, ed. Robert Tucker (New York: W. W. Norton, 1978), 73.

[104] It is worth thinking here about Daphne Brooks's rubric of African American performers' "alien(ated) awareness of the self," which she identifies as a "critical theme in the work of nineteenth- and early-twentieth-century black cultural producers." Brooks's argument is that African American performers simultaneously "register[ed] the disorienting condition of social marginalization" *and* "rehearsed methods to transform the notion of ontological dislocation into resistant performance so as to become agents of their own liberation." See Daphne A. Brooks, *Bodies in Dissent: Spectacular Performances of Race and Freedom, 1850–1910* (Durham, NC: Duke University Press, 2006), 2–3. In the case of Hudgins and his copyright, I would argue, this alienation is never resolved, never converted into a fully resistant performance.

[105] Alexander G. Weheliye, *Habeas Viscus: Racializing Assemblages, Biopolitics, and Black Feminist Theories of the Human* (Durham, NC: Duke University Press, 2014), 76.

escape the shadow of black bodies as property even as he positioned himself as author and owner, Hudgins exemplifies the paradoxes of the black performer in a post-emancipation yet unfree moment and of resistance within a racially stratified, capitalist society. We may choose, therefore, to see a certain metaphoricalness and poignancy in Hudgins's literal ability to move expansively while essentially standing still.

3

"Stealing Steps" and Signature Moves

Alternative Systems of Copyright

On November 26, 1934, in the middle of the first act of the Broadway debut of the "Congo operetta" *Africana*, a well-dressed black man made his way down the center aisle and proceeded to take a swing with, depending on the account, an iron bar, a chair, or a fist at the African American orchestra leader, Donald Heywood, who was also the musical's director, composer, and author.[1] Although spectators first assumed the confrontation was part of the show, when all onstage activity came to a halt they realized that the disturbance was not scripted. The perpetrator, named Almany Dauoda Camaro, was promptly placed under arrest and led away by a patrolman, and the musical picked up where it had left off—only to close permanently two nights later after being panned by critics. Camaro later explained to police that "he had hit upon his informal entrance as the best means of registering his protest against what he termed Heywood's plagiarism."[2] Evidently having collaborated with Heywood on writing the operetta, Camaro believed he had been denied his fair share of the credit. His literally show-stopping gesture, a kind of personal injunction against Heywood, was his method of lodging his plagiarism grievance.

I first learned of the *Africana* scuffle in the course of an earlier research project when I stumbled across a newspaper clipping describing it, but the skirmish took on new meaning in the context of my research on the history and cultural politics of copyright in American dance. The fact that Johnny Hudgins remains the only documented example of an African American dancer to have successfully secured a copyright for his choreography (in England, albeit) prior to the late twentieth century is a gauge of the extent to which the copyright

---

[1] Arthur Ruhl, "'Africana,'" *New York Herald Tribune*, November 28, 1934; Stephen Rathbun, "'Africana' Opens," *New York Sun*, November 27, 1934, Harvard Theatre Collection; "Row Disrupts Premiere of Operetta," *New York Times*, November 27, 1934.

[2] "'Africana' Opens."

archives have favored the dominant. With few exceptions, the names of
non-white dancers are not present, or at least not easily detectable, in official copyright archives from the first two-thirds of the twentieth century.
The *Africana* incident becomes important, then, because Camaro chose the
medium of performance rather than a governmental office or court of law to
make his accusation of theft. Although dance was not the explicit subject of his
plagiarism grievance, his actions are a reminder that clashes over intellectual
property rights can and have played out in a corporeal, and not just a juridical,
register; the body, too, can serve as a site for the adjudication of intellectual
property claims. For those whose livelihood depended on physical expressivity, the body was arguably the most logical instrument for enacting such
claims. It follows that to write a more inclusive history of intellectual property
rights in dance, one must turn not only to the archive of copyright records
and legal actions but also to the performance archive—to the "repertoire" of
embodied practices as they have left their mark on the archive.[3]

This chapter shines light on the extra-legal means, corporeal and otherwise, used by African American tap and jazz dancers from the early twentieth century to protect bodily moves they considered their property. As in
Chapter 2, here I stress the need for law and performance to be read in tandem. But whereas that chapter underscored the ways in which the law not only
regulated performance but also provided an avenue to contest the restrictive
racial norms of performance, this one argues that performance has worked to
fill lacunas in the law. Because and despite the fact that United States copyright law has not been hospitable to black vernacular dancers, these dancers
have developed alternative systems of copyright that privilege the actions of
the body itself.[4]

The tensions between copyright law and the realm of black vernacular
dance, especially in the first decades of the twentieth century, were manifold
and can be attributed to the aesthetic codes that govern tap and jazz dance and
to a convergence of racial, class, and artistic hierarchies. Rooted in Western
Enlightenment philosophy, copyright law grants protection to "original works
of authorship fixed in a tangible medium of expression";[5] nearly every one of

---

[3] Here I refer to Diana Taylor's notion of the "*archive* of supposedly enduring materials
(i.e., texts, documents, buildings, bones), and the so-called ephemeral *repertoire* of embodied practice/knowledge (i.e., spoken language, dance, sports, ritual)." *The Archive and the
Repertoire: Performing Cultural Memory in the Americas* (Durham, NC: Duke University Press,
2003), 19.

[4] I use the term "vernacular" dance to refer to performances that occurred primarily in social
settings and on nightclub and vaudeville stages, rather than on the concert stage.

[5] http://www.copyright.gov/help/faq/faq-general.html#what. Accessed April 24, 2009.

those terms has proven troublesome when applied to black vernacular dance. To begin with, white mainstream culture has historically dismissed African American artistic forms like the blues and jazz as the product of "natural" expression rather than original authorship—as "genes, not genius," to quote dance scholar Brenda Dixon Gottschild.[6] The failure to recognize the intellect and innovation behind black expressive forms, especially those involving the body, enabled a bifurcation between individual white artistry and collective, "innate" black talent that long helped justify the denial of copyright protection to African American cultural producers. The withholding of royalties from black musicians (as in the example of Alberta Hunter below) is perhaps the most vivid example of the racialized allocation of intellectual property rights in the United States, but these inequities, as Chapter 2 established, are rooted in a history of slavery and the appropriation and misrepresentation of black culture that defined the nineteenth-century practice of blackface minstrelsy.[7]

The categorization of most African American expressive practices as "folk" culture has contributed to and exacerbated this problem.[8] As Richard Schur explains in *Parodies of Ownership: Hip-Hop Aesthetics and Intellectual Property Law*, "By construing [the creative works of marginalized people] as mere folk tales, intellectual property law has allowed dominant culture to plunder the traditions and forms of African Americans and other minority groups."[9] Because folklore is perceived "as communally produced in contrast to the law's conceptualization of the author or inventor as an individual," scholar Boatema Boateng elaborates, it is believed to belong in the "public domain."[10]

---

[6] Brenda Dixon Gottschild, *Digging the Africanist Presence in American Performance: Dance and Other Contexts* (Westport, CT: Greenwood Press, 1996), 110. Gottschild attributes this phrase to Lawrence Levine (128n24).

[7] See, for example, Norman Kelley, "Notes on the Political Economy of Black Music," in *Rhythm and Business: The Political Economy of Black Music*, ed. Norman Kelley (New York: Akashic Books, 2005), 6–23; and K. J. Greene, "Copyright, Culture & Black Music: A Legacy of Unequal Protection," *Hastings Communication & Entertainment Law Journal* 21.2 (Winter 1999): 339-392. As Greene points out, "at the time of the enactment of the first intellectual property statutes, most Blacks in America remained in slavery, unable to own any type of property" (346).

[8] See Anthea Kraut, *Choreographing the Folk: The Dance Stagings of Zora Neale Hurston* (Minneapolis: University of Minnesota Press, 2008), for a more extensive discussion of how the category of the "folk" shaped the production and reception of African American expressive culture in the 1930s.

[9] Richard L. Schur, *Parodies of Ownership: Hip-Hop Aesthetics and Intellectual Property Law* (Ann Arbor: University of Michigan Press, 2009), 164.

[10] Boatema Boateng, *The Copyright Thing Doesn't Work Here: Adinkra and Kente Cloth and Intellectual Property in Ghana* (Minneapolis: University of Minnesota Press, 2011), 11. See also Rosemary Coombe's discussion of the dichotomy between intellectual property and cultural property, which are governed by two different areas of law. Coombe explains that this bifurcated schema "reflect[s] and secure[s]" a colonialist logic that divides the realm of Art from the realm

Intellectual property laws have thus "consistently favored those white individuals who wrote down, composed, drew, or marketed the story over those African American individuals who lived or experienced it."[11]

At the same time, a number of legal scholars have argued that Western ideas of singular authorship and fixity embedded in US copyright law are genuinely incompatible with African American vernacular forms. As Kembrew McLeod writes, "The intertextual practices that characterize many aspects of African-American culture conflict with a particular way of understanding authorship and ownership that originated in Western Enlightenment and Romanticist thought."[12] Certainly, a large body of scholarship has demonstrated that black vernacular traditions are not only collectively created, orally transmitted, and improvisational, but also make regular use of "signifyin'" or intertextual techniques.[13] Consequently, the reasoning goes, they fail to conform to the very "structural elements of the copyright system—such as the requirements of tangible (written) form, and minimal standard of originality."[14]

Schur likewise sees a conflict between statutory intellectual property law and the signifyin' practices of African American culture, which, as outlined by Henry Louis Gates Jr., depend on citation and textual revision.[15] But, to

---

of culture." Citing James Clifford's mapping of an "art-culture system" that assigns different value to artistic masterpieces and cultural artifacts, Coombe describes how "authors with intellect are distinguished from cultures with property." Rosemary J. Coombe, *The Cultural Life of Intellectual Properties: Authorship, Appropriation, and the Law* (Durham, NC: Duke University Press, 1998), 243; James Clifford, "On Collecting Art and Culture," in *The Predicament of Culture: Twentieth-Century Ethnography, Literature, and Art* (Cambridge, MA: Harvard University Press, 1988), 215–51.

[11] Schur, *Parodies of Ownership*, 107.

[12] Kembrew McLeod, *Owning Culture: Authorship, Ownership, and Intellectual Property Law* (New York: Peter Lang, 2001), 71.

[13] On black vernacular aesthetics, see, for example, Houston A. Baker, *Blues, Ideology, and Afro-American Literature: A Vernacular Theory* (Chicago: University of Chicago Press, 1984); Henry Louis Gates Jr., *The Signifying Monkey: A Theory of Afro-American Literary Criticism* (New York: Oxford University Press, 1988); Richard Powell, "Art History and Black Memory: Toward a 'Blues Aesthetic,'" in *History and Memory in African-American Culture*, ed. Geneviève Fabre and Robert O'Meally (New York: Oxford University Press, 1994), 228–43; Robert O'Meally, "On Burke and the Vernacular: Ralph Ellison's Boomerang of History," in *History and Memory in African-American Culture*, 244–60; and Jacqui Malone, *Steppin' on the Blues: The Visible Rhythms of African American Dance* (Urbana: University of Illinois Press, 1996).

[14] Greene, "Copyright, Culture and Black Music," 342. See also Siva Vaidhyanathan, *Copyrights and Copywrongs: The Rise of Intellectual Property and How It Threatens Creativity* (New York: New York University Press, 2001), in which he argues that "American copyright ... clearly conflicts with the aesthetic principles of West African music and dance" (126).

[15] Gates, *The Signifying Monkey*.

the extent that signifyin' serves as a means of claiming rhetorical ownership over a cultural text by adding an original spin to it, the practice also "functions like a trademark or copyright symbol." Signifyin', in other words, amounts to what Schur terms a "clandestine or alternative property-ownership system," a means of allocating rights over creative expression that competes with official legal structures.[16]

Like Schur, I am interested in documenting practices, especially embodied practices, that functioned as extra-legal methods of claiming intellectual property rights. Like Boateng in her study of textile production and intellectual property law in Ghana, I track "systems for regulating cultural appropriation that [ran] parallel to copyright protection."[17] Yet rather than portray these alternative systems as either oppositional to or lateral with copyright law, I argue that African American vernacular dancers treated their corporeal creations in ways that occasionally converged with Western ideas of intellectual property, even as they complicated some of those same ideas. The fact that dancers' invocations of property rights often occurred outside of official legal channels, and that they were not always articulated in legal language, should not prevent us from recognizing the relevance of notions of self-possession and proprietorship to their practice. This is not to suggest that Romantic formulations of originary authorship are universally held and therefore unproblematic, nor that US copyright law has been or is the most appropriate means to protect all kinds of creative expression. Rather, in much the same vein that critical race theorist Patricia J. Williams argues that we need not discard the discourse of rights just because "the constitutional foreground of rights was shaped by whites" and "parceled out to blacks in pieces," I hope to show how the discourse of intellectual property rights, despite its limitations and its history of exclusivity, has served some African American performers seeking to assert a modicum of power over the circulation of their dances.[18]

While race is a part of the story I tell here, the examples of black vernacular dancers also offer a window onto the wide-ranging complexities involved in protecting any discrete arrangement of bodily movements. Accordingly, a secondary goal of this chapter is to re-assess the fit between copyright and dance more generally. Paramount among the various challenges dance has posed to copyright law is the problem of how what some have argued is the most fleeting of art forms might be fixed in a tangible medium of expression, especially in the years before film and video were widely accessible and before written

---

[16] Schur, *Parodies of Ownership*, 33.

[17] Boateng, *The Copyright Thing*, 3.

[18] Patricia J. Williams, *The Alchemy of Race and Rights: Diary of a Law Professor* (Cambridge, MA: Harvard University Press, 1991), 164.

notational systems like Labanotation were well known.[19] In this regard, the issue of dance's compatibility with intellectual property rights bears directly on questions about the ontology of performance. While some performance studies scholars have contended that performance's ephemerality—the fact that its very condition is its disappearance—enables it to evade capitalist regimes of ownership and commodification, others have maintained that, however fleeting, performance neither totally disappears nor operates outside of regulatory structures. Because the privileging of improvisation in African American traditions like jazz and tap dance would seem the polar opposite of copyright's privileging of fixity, the experiences of artists working in these genres provide particularly good case studies of how dance straddles the supposed divide between evanescence and durability. Asking how black vernacular dancers treated the issue of ephemerality, to what extent they considered live performance to be reproducible, and how they theorized performance-as-property, this chapter aims to further our understanding of the ontological status of performance.

To pursue its goals, this chapter relies heavily on dancers' autobiographical accounts and published oral histories, which help constitute the performance archive. Sources like Marshall and Jean Stearns's *Jazz Dance* and Rusty Frank's *Tap!*, as well as Constance Valis Hill's more recent *Tap Dancing America*, are indispensable for uncovering voices and narratives that are excluded from official copyright archives.[20] While the oral histories that fill these sources were gathered at different times and with different research agendas in mind, the information they contain remains instructive, and reading them with an eye to questions of copyright can open up new vantage points on the histories of both American dance and intellectual property law.

Toward that end, in what follows, I attend first to the disparities between the African American tradition of "stealing steps"[21] and the ideology of copyright law, exploring why on the face of it, to quote the title of Boateng's book, "the copyright thing doesn't work" in the realm of black vernacular dance. I then

[19] As the dance critic Marcia B. Siegel famously wrote in *At the Vanishing Point: A Critic Looks at Dance* (New York: Saturday Review Press, 1972): "Dance exists at a perpetual vanishing point. At the moment of its creation it is gone.... No other art is so hard to catch, so impossible to hold" (1). In the mid-twentieth century, as I discuss in Chapter 4, the question of how choreographers might meet copyright law's fixity requirement was especially pressing.

[20] Marshall and Jean Stearns, *Jazz Dance: The Story of American Vernacular Dance* (New York: Schirmer Books, 1968); Rusty E. Frank, *Tap!: The Greatest Tap Dance Stars and Their Stories, 1900–1955* (New York: Da Capo Press, 1994); Constance Valis Hill, *Tap Dancing America: A Cultural History* (New York: Oxford University Press, 2010).

[21] I take the expression, cited more fully below, from choreographer Leonard Reed. See Frank, *Tap!*, 42.

consider the codes and conventions that governed the practice of borrowing fellow performers' moves, arguing that these protocols acted like an alternative system of intellectual property rights protection. Next, I focus on what we might call rhetorical copyright, a claim of intellectual property rights unsubstantiated by the law, which I read as an attempt to combat white appropriation of black popular dance. From there, I suggest that at least some African American dancers valued the right of attribution over and above the exclusive right to copy. Finally, I reflect on how dancers' management of the ephemeral nature of their medium bears on the question of performance's ontology. Ultimately, paying heed to the ways African American jazz and tap artists limn their relationship to the movement their bodies generate and to the stories they tell about authorizing and curbing the transmission of their dances offers continued insight into the conjunctions and contradictions that have existed between constructions of intellectual property, the practice of dance, and the politics of race.[22]

"Shuck, if you could copyright a step ... nobody could lift a foot."

As this quip from Eddie Rector implies,[23] a tap dancer's ability to move depended on the fluid circulation of steps between dancers. The historical record is filled with testimonials to how vital the practice of "stealing steps" was to African American vernacular dance communities. Dancers repeatedly describe how they attended the theater for the precise purpose of taking other performers' moves: every Monday, LaVaughn Robinson went to Philadelphia's Earle Theatre to acquire moves from a tap dancer he admired; Maceo Anderson occupied the front row of Harlem's Lafayette Theatre, studiously absorbing the tap steps of the Condos Brothers; The Four Bobs "sat in a

---

[22] Throughout this chapter, I alternate between terms like "copying," "emulating," "mimicry," "stealing," and "appropriating" to describe the reproduction of one dancer's moves by another. This variation in part reflects the vacillating terminology that dancers themselves used to characterize this phenomenon. But, as was true for the dancers, these terms often carry different connotations and should not be seen as strictly interchangeable. Sometimes even the same term could take on different meanings. "Stealing" moves could denote the harmless exchange of steps; it could also mean "poaching" on another's territory. As I hope to show, the context in which the reproduction took place—particularly the relations of power between the dancers involved and the amount of capital at stake—was key to distinguishing between these significations. My intention, then, is not to avoid precision in my language but to highlight the variable ways in which the reproduction of dance could be perceived.

[23] Stearns, *Jazz Dance*, 338.

Philadelphia theater all day ... [copying] the entire performance of *Tip Tap and Toe*, including the mistakes"; "half of the audience" for a tap program at the Apollo Theatre in 1941 "consisted of tap dancers 'casing' new acts."[24] It was also common for performers on the same program to appropriate moves from one another. Tap dancer Charles "Honi" Coles reported being "astounded" at the dancing—and emulating—abilities of the female chorus dancers at Harlem's Apollo Theatre: "A dancing act could come into [the] Apollo with all original material and, when they left at the end of the week, the chorus lines would have stolen many of the outstanding things they did."[25] One of those chorus girls was Coles's wife, Marion Coles, who remembered tap dancers being "very generous" with their material: "If they had a step and you wanted to learn it, they would take it apart and show it to you. ... And if an act came in the theatre, and I'd stand in the wings ... I would pick up something from them and then take it down to rehearsal and teach it to the girls."[26] One-time chorus girl and eventual transcontinental star Josephine Baker was an equally assiduous student of her colleagues' routines. The comic pantomimist Johnny Hudgins, the subject of Chapter 2, co-starred with Baker in the 1924 musical *The Chocolate Dandies* and recalled that watching her was "like seeing [himself] in a mirror"; no matter how he changed his act, Baker managed to work up an imitation to perform publicly by the next night.[27] The tradition of stealing steps clearly flies in the face of copyright law's proscription against the unauthorized reproduction of another's original work. But if these artists' liberal copying resists the logic of US intellectual property law, so too does their practice contest the idea that live performance, because of its ephemerality, cannot be replicated. Far from disappearing, tap and jazz steps re-materialized on other bodies.

The lifting of others' steps was a matter of course in social dance and training spaces, such as the Hoofers Club, the legendary gathering place for tap dancers, located just doors down from the Lafayette Theatre. As the choreographer Leonard Reed explains,

---

[24] Frank, *Tap!*, 133, 213; Stearns, *Jazz Dance*, 272; Hill, *Tap Dancing America*, 105.

[25] Jack Schiffman, *Uptown: The Story of Harlem's Apollo Theatre* (New York: Cowles, 1971), 64–65.

[26] Heather Lyn MacDonald, dir., *Been Rich All My Life*, First Run Features, 2006. Also quoted in Jayna Brown, *Babylon Girls: Black Women Performers and the Shaping of the Modern* (Durham, NC: Duke University Press, 2008), 201.

[27] Jean-Claude Baker and Chris Chase, *Josephine: The Hungry Heart* (New York: Random House, 1993), 75. In *Remembering Josephine* (Indianapolis: Bobbs-Merrill, 1976), Stephen Papich also cites a number of male performers whom Baker imitated, including a comedy drag performer, Benny (of Bert and Benny), who performed with Bessie Smith, and Ivan Browning, a performer who collaborated with Eubie Blake.

All the dancers would hang out, and they would trade ideas. That was affectionately called "stealin' steps." Everybody did it. That's how you learned. You would do something, and you'd say to the other dancers, "You tryin' to steal it? All-right, do it!" "Let me see you do this!"[28]

Tap dancer Ralph Brown likewise recalls spending *"day* and *night"* at the Hoofers Club

> to watch the other dancers and learn—and steal. Because everybody steals—you know what I mean—to perfect their dancing. Once in a while you might get someone to show you how to do a step, but not many that would take you by the hand and carry you through it. You would just have to steal it. That's the way it went. And that's how I became a dancer.[29]

Lindy hopper Frankie Manning echoes the sentiment that stealing was a prerequisite to being a dancer. In his 2007 memoir, he points to the honing of his "observational skills" as critical to his success.[30] He also emphasizes the "trading" of steps at the Savoy Ballroom as essential to the development of the Lindy hop. "If you stop and think about it," he writes,

> how far would the dance have gone if people didn't steal from each other? Back in the early '30s, there weren't any dance schools that would even teach the Lindy because they didn't accept it as a dance. It wasn't until the latter part of the decade that Arthur Murray and other dance teachers decided that this thing was so big, they might as well put it in their schools. So the only way we could learn was by exchanging steps.
>
> If another person learned your step, they might improve on it, which happened all the time. Then when someone else did it, it could spread, and the dance could advance. Otherwise, you'd be the only one who knew that move. If we couldn't steal, I don't think Lindy hopping would have lasted as long as it has. It would have stagnated right there in one spot, but that's not what happened. I stole things from all kinds of dancers. In fact, I was the biggest crook in the Savoy. Yup. Still stealin'.[31]

[28] Frank, *Tap!*, 42.

[29] Ibid., 96–97.

[30] Frankie Manning and Cynthia R. Millman, *Frankie Manning: Ambassador of Lindy Hop* (Philadelphia: Temple University Press, 2007), 50.

[31] Ibid., 100–101.

Figure 3.1 Frankie Manning and Ann Johnson in a Lindy hop air step. Photo courtesy W. Eugene Smith © 1941, 2006 by The Heirs of the W. Eugene Smith Collection, Center for Creative Photography, University of Arizona.

Manning even attributes the invention of the "air step"—in which a Lindy hopper flips his partner over his back—to his self-described thievery; as he relates, the idea came from watching his fellow dancer and competitor Shorty Snowden perform a similar step.[32] In Manning's account, copying was the engine behind the Lindy hop's creation, dissemination, and endurance.

Imitation and innovation, it should be noted, are far from mutually exclusive here, and replication—unlike Josephine Baker's reported "mirroring" of

[32] Ibid., 96, 100.

Johnny Hudgins—is not exact. Rather, copying is accompanied by "improvements" that propel the Lindy hop forward. This mimicry with a difference was at the heart of the challenge dance, a staple of tap and jazz forms. As Constance Valis Hill has written, "In the challenge dance, you must copy an opponent's steps, only to reinvent them in your own terms. What you copy and how you copy it shape your reputation as a dancer—the how becoming the particularities of tap improvisation."[33] Even in cases when both parties did not formally agree to a challenge dance, imitation could heighten the level of performance. Singer and actress Ethel Waters describes the competitiveness between her and dancer Ethel Williams: "When Ethel Williams worked those week ends [at Edmond's Cellar, a Harlem nightclub] I'd go on first and do some of her steps as a challenge. That would make her so mad she'd get out on the floor and do those damn steps better."[34] "Stealing" thus constituted a primary mode of learning and choreographic innovation for black vernacular dancers—a far cry from copyright law's ideology of exclusive ownership.

Indeed, with its dependence on what Valis Hill terms the "dynamic and synergistic process of copying," the practice of tap dance appears to contravene directly the tenets of a market economy.[35] The steady give-and-take of dance steps among black vernacular dance communities arguably bears a closer resemblance to a gift or barter economy, in which dance material is exchanged for reasons other than profit. In genres like tap and jazz dance, the rules of the game mandated that a "stolen" step remain in circulation by being "re-gifted" in reinvented form. Transactions in these expressive traditions were thus "caught up in circuits of reciprocity" involving "chains of debt and return."[36] The apparent misfit between copyright and African American

---

[33] Constance Valis Hill, "Stepping, Stealing, Sharing, and Daring," in *Taken by Surprise: A Dance Improvisation Reader*, ed. Ann Cooper Albright and David Gere (Middletown, CT: Wesleyan University Press, 2003), 93.

[34] Ethel Waters with Charles Samuels, *His Eye Is on the Sparrow* (New York: Pyramid Books, 1951), 137.

[35] Hill, *Tap Dancing America*, 3.

[36] John Frow, "Gift and Commodity," in *Time and Commodity Culture: Essays in Cultural Theory and Postmodernity* (Oxford: Clarendon Press, 1997), 107, 124. For more on the gift economy, see also Marcel Mauss, *The Gift: The Form and Reason for Exchange in Archaic Societies*, trans. W. D. Halls (London: Routledge, 1990); and Richard Morris Titmus, *The Gift Relationship: From Human Blood to Social Policy* (London: Allen & Unwin, 1970).

vernacular dance would thus seem to be a matter not only of aesthetic but also economic principle.

"Though Shalt Not Copy Another's Steps—Exactly"

The interchange of steps in the economy of vernacular dance, however, was not invariably fluid. As Williams's reaction to Waters's preemption of her moves intimates, "borrowing" another dancer's steps was sometimes received less than warmly. Neither was it necessarily done openly. Hoofer John Bubbles, for example, developed a reputation for being "cagey" in "extracting a step from a competitor." As the Stearns report,

> Watching another dancer practicing at the Hoofers Club, Bubbles bides his time until he sees something he can use. "Oh-oh," he says, shaking his head in alarm, "you lost the back beat there—now try that step again." The dancer starts only to be stopped, again and again, until Bubbles, having learned it, announces, "You know, that reminds me of a step I used to do," and proceeds to demonstrate two or three variations on the original step. The other dancer usually feels flattered.[37]

The fact that a dancer as accomplished as Bubbles developed such furtive tactics for "extracting" steps from his peers suggests that, however commonplace, stealing was not unconditionally welcomed. Even those who proclaimed, "If you could learn it, you could do it" added the qualification that "Of course, you don't do it in the presence of the creator of the step."[38] While some dancers practiced stealing with a certain discreetness, others attempted to thwart it altogether. Putting a different spin on chorus girls' reputation for lifting material, dancer Bunny Briggs explained to Valis Hill how the men "stopped doing anything good in front of [the female dancers] ... because they would be doing their act the next day—and they were good!"[39] Briggs's comment here points to a gendered competition between female chorus lines and male performance acts. Despite the power imbalances—male tap teams garnered much greater acclaim and remuneration relative to the generally anonymous chorus girls—at least some men clearly felt threatened by the female dancers'

---

[37] Stearns, *Jazz Dance*, 214.
[38] Ralph Brown, quoted in Frank, *Tap!*, 97.
[39] Hill, *Tap Dancing America*, 109.

Figure 3.2 Hoofer John Bubbles. Photo by Maurice Chicago, 1964. Library of Congress.

appropriative tendencies. The men's determination to hold back "anything good" from their performances when the women were watching suggests that the same "double movement of circulation and restriction" that Jane Gaines identifies as central to copyright characterized the traffic in black vernacular dance.[40]

Furthermore, the custom of reproducing another's steps adhered to a set of codified regulations that prevented it from being a free-for-all. Despite her own pilfering, Ethel Waters acknowledged a "code of ethics at Edmond's

---

[40] Jane M. Gaines, *Contested Culture: The Image, the Voice, and the Law* (Chapel Hill: University of North Carolina Press, 1991), 9.

that prevented one entertainer from poaching on another's repertory."[41] The Stearns corroborate the existence of such a code:

> Protocol at the Hoofers Club fostered the invention of new steps. "Thou Shalt Not Copy Another's Steps—Exactly" was the unwritten law. You could imitate anybody inside the club, and it was taken as a compliment. But you must not do so professionally, that is in public and for pay. If and when your act appeared on the stage of the Lincoln, or even better, the Lafayette Theater in Harlem, your routine must be notably different.
>
> Once word got around that an act was booked at these theaters, other dancers lined up, and as soon as the doors opened, rushed down to the front rows. "They watched you like hawks," says Baby [Laurence], and if you used any of their pet steps, they just stood right up in the theater and told everybody about it at the top of their voices.[42]

As much as innovation in tap depended on the productive tension between mimicry and modification, when a performance occurred "in public and for pay," "stealing steps" was far from innocuous. Johnny Hudgins, too, maintained that though he did not mind imitators "using his stuff" in smaller nightclubs, "when he goes downtown that's a different question."[43] Dance steps, then, circulated in not one but two economies, one "inside the club," and one in the professional, commercial arena. As dancers moved between the two, their steps, following Arjun Appadurai, moved "in *and* out of the commodity state," and the rules for judging the appropriateness of stealing changed.[44] Indeed, Laurence's comments suggest that when exposure and money were at stake, tap dancers treated their "pet steps" as a kind of intellectual property, and theft of that property constituted blatant infringement. As was the case with *Africana*, the Hoofers Club community reacted to acts of infringement in a conspicuously corporeal manner, interrupting the performance and rowdily shaming the copycat. A similar response apparently met Lindy hoppers at the Savoy Ballroom who attempted to copy a fellow dancer's specialty. In the

[41] Waters, *His Eye Is on the Sparrow*, 125.

[42] Stearns, *Jazz Dance*, 338.

[43] "Hudgins Says His Piece on the Present Era; Finds Show Biz Rotten," *Chicago Defender*, January 17, 1931, p. 5.

[44] Arjun Appadurai, "Introduction: Commodities and the Politics of Value," in *The Social Life of Things: Commodities in Cultural Perspective*, ed. Arjun Appadurai (Cambridge: Cambridge University Press, 1986), 9, emphasis in original.

words of Leon James, they would get "whipped up, tromped in the middle of the crowd by all the others."[45]

These examples of vigilant surveillance and public castigation in response to perceived theft in commercial settings demonstrate more than the relevance of notions of intellectual property to black vernacular dancers. They also evidence an alternative system of copyright operating within these dance communities. That is, by establishing certain "specialties," jazz and tap dancers effectively registered these moves with their peers, who in turn protected their informal copyrights by collectively policing the performances they observed.[46] The fact that the policing was enacted physically—rather than, say, by sending a cease and desist letter—suggests how critical embodiment was to this system. Not only did dancers often refrain from performing "stolen" moves in front of their creator (or from performing moves in front of potential pilferers), but because the response to someone's unauthorized use of dance moves was vocal, corporeal, and immediate, the stakes of violating an informal copyright were high and immediate. The threat of getting "whipped up" and "tromped" by a group of dancers must have carried at least as urgent a force as law.

There are also indications that some tap dancers, like the legendary Bill "Bojangles" Robinson, developed unofficial ways of licensing their material. Because Robinson was notoriously protective of his choreography, particularly the "stair dance," in which he tapped up and down a staircase, other dancers didn't dare replicate his distinctive style or pet steps—except "behind his

[45] Stearns, *Jazz Dance*, 323.

[46] Sally Banes offers an analogous example from the world of ballet: she reports that New York City Ballet dancers once refused to let Jerome Robbins set another choreographer's movement on them out of respect for that choreographer's moral rights. "Homage, Plagiarism, Allusion, Comment, Quotation: Negotiating Choreographic Appropriation," in *Before, Between, and Beyond: Three Decades of Dance Writing*, ed. Andrea Harris (Madison: University of Wisconsin Press, 2007), 202. According to Peter Decherney, an informal system of protection operated in like manner among vaudeville comedians before the advent of film. Decherney writes that following a series of late nineteenth-century legal cases denying vaudeville performers copyright protection in their performances, they "began to rely on the self-policing of their industry." This included taking out ads in trade papers to shame copycats, getting theater owners to pledge not to hire copied acts, and a short-lived set of grassroots institutions that cropped up to arbitrate disputes between acts. "Gag Orders: Comedy, Chaplin, and Copyright," in *Modernism and Copyright*, ed. Paul K. Saint-Amour (New York: Oxford University Press, 2011), 136–37. Similarly, Dotan Oliar and Christopher Sprigman argue that "social norms" operate among contemporary stand-up comedians in place of intellectual property law. These norms are enforced by extra-legal sanctions that "can cause serious reputational harm to an alleged joke-thief." "There's No Free Laugh (Anymore): The Emergence of Intellectual Property Norms and the Transformation of Stand-up Comedy," *Virginia Law Review* 94.8 (December 2008): 1790–91. Many thanks to Brian Herrera for passing along this article to me.

back, when he wasn't around!"[47] It was undoubtedly risky, then, for Cholly Atkins and his partner William "Red" Porter to perform their version of the stair dance in a Buffalo theater with Robinson in attendance. Fortunately, Atkins recounts, following the performance,

> [Robinson] came up, embraced us, and did a little bit on the stairs himself. So it was with his blessing that we kept this in our act, which was an honor for us. ... Now when we took it to New York, everybody said, "Man, don't let Bill Robinson see you doing that dance." I said, "Well, he saw us in Buffalo, and he said it was okay with him." "Yeah, but you wasn't in New York! He might not want you to do it in New York!" Boy, we got a whole lot of mouth behind that, but we kept right on doing our dance.[48]

The importance of physical presence here is clear. Robinson's embodied gestures—his literal embrace of Atkins and Red and his own reiteration of the stair dance—function to authorize their use of his material, at least according to Atkins.[49] The conditions of performance were paramount as well: copying constituted a more severe threat in New York, where both the public and the pay were greater, than in smaller markets. Whereas Atkins secured Robinson's consent through corporeal means, another dancer, Fred Stone, took a different approach. He once mailed Robinson a check for $1,500 with a note that read, "In part payment for the stair dance I stole from you."[50] However unsystematic, these examples speak to the currency of the idea of permissions and royalties even in a realm where official copyright protection was absent.

Rhetorical Copyright and the "Little Ewe Lamb of Originality"

In fact, copyright was not entirely absent from the domain of African American vernacular dance in the early twentieth century, as we saw in Chapter 2 in the

---

[47] Ralph Brown, quoted in Frank, *Tap!*, 97.

[48] Cholly Atkins and Jacqui Malone, *Class Act: The Jazz Life of Choreographer Cholly Atkins* (New York: Columbia University Press, 2001), 27. During a later encounter, Robinson reportedly told Atkins, " 'I know you, boy. You and your partner did a stair dance, and you apologized to me for not getting my permission and I appreciated that. I remember you' " (43).

[49] Of course, it is also possible to read Robinson's performance of "a little bit on the stairs" as an attempt to re-claim the dance.

[50] Jim Haskins and N. R. Mitgang, *Mr. Bojangles: The Biography of Bill Robinson* (New York: William Morrow, 1988), 101.

Figure 3.3 Bill "Bojangles" Robinson in his famous Stair Dance in 1928. Photo by Vandamm Studio © Billy Rose Theatre Division, The New York Public Library for the Performing Arts.

discussion of the copyright registration Johnny Hudgins received in London. However exceptional Hudgins's case, though, his was not the only copyright claim involving black vernacular dance to circulate in the 1920s. In 1926, reports surfaced that the African American blues singer Alberta Hunter had copyrighted the Black Bottom, a dance that gained popularity on the US theatrical stage and became a national and international craze. The accuracy of those reports aside, the contention itself is noteworthy, especially because, as a social dance with no single author, the Black Bottom is precisely the kind of dance the law has consistently barred from copyright protection. A closer look at the allegation thus provides further evidence of the complicated intersection between the discourse of intellectual property rights and the circulation of black vernacular dance.

There is no consensus on the origins of the Black Bottom as either a social or stage dance. In 1919, the African American musician and songwriter Perry Bradford published a dance-song called "The Original Black Bottom Dance." He maintained that it was a version of a much earlier dance popular in Jacksonville, Florida, updated with new lyrics and a new name. Others claimed that the "Black Bottom" referred to a black section in Atlanta—or to an area of Nashville or Detroit—and still others that the dance originated along the banks of the Suwanee River, or, alternately, in the Louisiana swamps.[51] According to Marshall and Jean Stearns, African Americans had been performing variations of the Black Bottom dance in tent shows and vaudeville for years prior to Bradford's publication, and the dance may have first reached New York in Irvin C. Miller's 1924 revue *Dinah* at the Lafayette Theatre.[52] Whatever its genesis, the white dancer Ann Pennington's rendition of the Black Bottom in the 1926 version of George White's annual Broadway revue *Scandals* introduced the dance to a much broader audience, and it quickly came to rival the Charleston as the latest rage. The Black Bottom spread across the country and jumped the Atlantic, appearing on theatrical stages, in dance halls, and, in "refined" form, in ballrooms. Performed to the same syncopated music of the Charleston, the Black Bottom required moving on the off-beat and involved, as Thomas DeFrantz writes, "slapping your hips and hopping forward and back, touching the ground, and letting your backbone slide from side to side."[53]

[51] Stearns, *Jazz Dance*, 110–11; Betty Lee, *Dancing: All the Latest Steps* (Chicago: Franklin, 1926, 1927), 289. Other songs devoted to the Black Bottom followed Bradford's. In 1927, Jelly Roll Morton recorded the "Black Bottom Stomp," and in 1928, Ma Rainey recorded "Ma Rainey's Black Bottom," whose lyrics touted her skill at performing the popular dance. Sandra Lieb, *Mother of the Blues: A Study of Ma Rainey* (Amherst: University of Massachusetts Press, 1981), 142–45.

[52] Stearns, *Jazz Dance*, 110–11.

[53] Thomas F. DeFrantz, "Popular Dance of the 1920s and Early '30s: From Animal Dance Crazes to the Lindy Hop," in *Ain't Nothing Like the Real Thing: How the Apollo Theater Shaped American Entertainment*, ed. Richard Carlin and Kinshasha Holman Conwill (Washington, DC: National Museum of African American History and Culture through Smithsonian Books, 2010), 68. Hill breaks the Black Bottom down into "four simple movements, all making use of the body as an instrument to express rather than accompany the music. The first was a syncopated walk, with two slow steps and four quick ones marking the time (in this step the body is erect, the head raised, the arms in a sort of corrupted ballet fifth position) in which 'the colored people twist the wrist and move the fingers to follow the tempo,' then clap the thigh and the buttocks to follow the tempo; the second movement was a slow shuffle, wherein the foot dragged languidly around in a circle; the third movement was a side step where one leg was straight and the other bent away from the guiding foot almost in the shape of the letter C; the fourth movement was the Camel Walk with its slow and shiftless moves that turned the knees and toes definitely inward." Hill, *Tap Dancing America*, 78.

Two chronicles of American theater state that Alberta Hunter copyrighted the Black Bottom. In their history *Show Biz: From Vaude to Video*, published in 1951, *Variety* reporters Abel Green and Joe Laurie Jr. assert that Hunter was "the first woman to present the dance" and "had it copyrighted."[54] (This was the quotation included in Marshall Stearns's unpublished notes for *Jazz Dance* that caught my attention years ago and helped launch this project.) In the 1970 edition of the *New Complete Book of the American Musical Theater*, David Ewen writes that the Black Bottom was, in the opinion of some, "invented by Alberta Hunter, who copyrighted it in 1926."[55] One possible source for these texts is a 1926 newspaper article written by Lester Walton, found in a clippings file on the Black Bottom at the New York Public Library, which states: "Alberta Hunter, a well-known Negro singer of the blues, claims the distinction of having done the [Black Bottom] before the first white audience at one of the New York vaudeville houses in 1925. She says she had it copyrighted."[56] In his 1987 biography of Hunter, Frank Taylor refers to Green's and Laurie's contention about Hunter's dance copyright but does not corroborate it. Instead, Taylor explains, "Alberta was embarrassed by the suggestion that she had much to do with a dance that was heavy bump and grind. When asked to describe it, she said, 'Oh, it was just a certain, tricky kind of step.' "[57]

A search of records conducted by the Library of Congress's Copyright Office turned up no documentation of Hunter's registration of the dance.[58] It is possible that Hunter submitted the Black Bottom for copyright protection and that her claim was rejected on the grounds that the dance was not a dramatic composition. But it is also possible that Hunter's claim was only rhetorical, that telling a newspaper reporter that she had the dance copyrighted was as official as she needed the claim to be. If this was the case, and if Hunter later distanced herself from the Black Bottom, the invocation of a copyright on an African American popular

---

[54] Abel Green and Joe Laurie Jr., *Show Biz: From Vaude to Video* (New York: Permabooks, 1951), 227

[55] David Ewen, *New Complete Book of the American Musical Theater* (New York: Holt, Rinehart and Winston, 1970), 175. Oddly, Ewen's entry on George White's *Scandals* in an earlier edition of the volume contains no reference to Alberta Hunter or her purported copyright of the Black Bottom. Ewen, *Complete Book of American Musical Theater* (New York: Henry Holt, 1958). Neither volume contains a bibliography or footnotes.

[56] Lester A. Walton, "Lucky Roberts Autographs Songs for the Prince," n.s., October 17, 1926, p. 6, Black Bottom Clippings File, Dance Division, NYPL. Walton also points to an earlier source for the Black Bottom, explaining "So far as known, the first time the Black Bottom was put on at a New York theatre was in 1923, by Ethel Ridley in a colored musical comedy at the Lafayette Theatre in Harlem."

[57] Frank C. Taylor with Gerald Cook, *Alberta Hunter: A Celebration in Blues* (New York: McGraw-Hill, 1987), 74.

[58] The search was conducted by the Copyright Office in January 2006.

Figure 3.4 Blues singer (and dancer) Alberta Hunter performing in an unidentified USO show, 1940s. Photographs and Prints Division, Schomburg Center for Research in Black Culture, The New York Public Library, Astor, Lenox and Tilden Foundations.

dance just as it was capturing the fascination of the white mainstream is no less significant. The rhetoric of intellectual property rights could attempt to perform work similar to that of the law itself.

Though Hunter is known primarily as a singer and songwriter, she also headed up a vaudeville act that toured the Keith circuit for several years in the mid-1920s, performing a combination of song, dance, and comedy.[59] And if she believed she was among the first to introduce a stage version of the Black Bottom to a white audience, she had good reason to claim copyright protection. When *George White's Scandals* began its 424-performance run at the Apollo Theatre on Broadway in June 1926, its chief claim to fame was the originality of the Black Bottom dance it featured. As the display advertisement that ran in the *New York Times* announced, "The Dance Black Bottom was invented and staged by George White and the Black Bottom can be seen only at George White's Scandals."[60] An

[59] Taylor, *Alberta Hunter*, 68–86. The Keith circuit was a network of vaudeville theaters run by B. F. Keith.

[60] Display ad, *New York Times*, November 22, 1926, p. 29.

article in the *Times* reiterated and elaborated on the assertion, stating that White hoped to "make it clear that he, and he alone, was the originator of those grotesque gyrations to which the name Black Bottom has been applied."[61] Though White was a hoofer before he became a producer, there is little question that his declarations were, at best, exaggerated hype.[62]

Challenges to White's claims were immediate. In a letter to the editor written in response to the *Times* article, famed African American composer Will Marion Cook took exception to the contention that White was the creator of the Charleston and Black Bottom:

> I have the greatest respect for Mr. White, his genius as an organizer and producer of reviews; but why do an injustice to the black folk of America by taking from them the credit of creating new and characteristic dances?
>
> From "Old Jim Crow" to "Black Bottom," the negro dances came from the Cotton Belt, the levee, the Mississippi River, and are African in inspiration. The American negro, in search of outlet for emotional expression, recreates and broadens these dances. Either in their crude state, or revised form, in St. Louis, Chicago or New York the dance is discovered (?) by white theatrical producers and sold to the public as an original creation. . . .
>
> [F]or many years, the "Black Bottom" has been evolving in the South. Irvin Miller first produced the dance about three years ago in New York at Lafayette theatre. Two years ago Louis Douglass [*sic*], famous in Europe, thrilled all Paris as he and Josephine Baker "Black Bottomed" at the Champs-Elysée Theatre.
>
> Messrs. White et al. are great men and great producers. Why, with their immense flocks of dramatic and musical sheep, should they wish to reach out and grab our little ewe lamb of originality?[63]

Though couched in deferential language, Cook's indignation is plain. Accusing White of depriving "the black folk of America" rightful credit for the products of their creativity and labor, Cook implies that the "little ewe lamb" of originality is African Americans' one source of capital in a cultural marketplace dominated by "flocks" of white wealth and resources.

---

[61] "Concerning George White and His 'Scandals,'" *New York Times,* December 19, 1926, p. X4.

[62] Perry Bradford was convinced that White first saw the Black Bottom in the Harlem show *Dinah* and subsequently enlisted *Scandals*'s three white composers, Buddy de Sylva, Lew Brown, and Ray Henderson, to compose a song for it. Stearns, *Jazz Dance,* 110–11.

[63] Will Marion Cook, "'Spirituals' and 'Jazz,'" letter to the editor, *New York Times,* December 26, 1926, p. X8.

For Cook, the mis-credited authors of the Black Bottom are African Americans as a group, not Alberta Hunter. Still, her claim to have secured a copyright on the Black Bottom may have been motivated by precisely the sentiments he articulates. For Hunter, that is, copyright may have functioned largely as a "defense mechanism" against a "racist history of exploitation exclusively weighted to dominant white interests."[64] Whereas Cook counters George White's professions of originality by alerting newspaper readers to the African American progenitors of the Black Bottom, Hunter's copyright claim (even if only rumored) raises the stakes by declaring the Black Bottom a work of individual black authorship deserving of intellectual property rights.

Hunter's experience with exploitation in show business was firsthand. As a solo singer at the Dreamland Café in Chicago, Hunter attracted notice from a number of white entertainers, including Al Jolson, Sophie Tucker, and Eddie Cantor, who attended her performances, studied her style, and put it to their own use.[65] Under a racist power structure, these white performers invariably received top billing and greater remuneration than the African American performers from whom they borrowed.[66] Record executives, meanwhile, routinely cheated black talent out of royalties. Always interested in securing credit and compensation for her musical compositions, Hunter received her first copyright in 1922 for "Down Hearted Blues," her most successful song, co-authored with Lovie Austin. Yet for years, as biographer Taylor writes, "she got no royalty payments for most of the songs she recorded, much less for the songs she wrote that other people recorded."[67] Part of the problem was that the black manager of Paramount's "race" record series, Mayo Williams, regularly added names to the list of authors of Hunter's compositions, and then withheld their cut of the royalties.[68] Hunter's experiences made her vigilant. As she once told an interviewer, "I never hum a song for anybody until I have it copyrighted."[69]

---

[64] Andrew Ross, "Hip, and the Long Front of Color," in No Respect: Intellectuals & Popular Culture (New York: Routledge, 1989), 68.

[65] Taylor, Alberta Hunter, 38–39; Daphne D. Harrison, "She's Got a Mind to Ramble: Alberta Hunter," in Black Pearls: Blues Queens of the 1920s (New Brunswick, NJ: Rutgers University Press, 1988), 203–4, 210.

[66] See Brenda Dixon Gottschild, Waltzing in the Dark: African American Vaudeville and Race Politics in the Swing Era (New York: St. Martin's Press, 2000) for numerous examples of the exploitation of black performers in the white-controlled entertainment industry.

[67] Taylor, Alberta Hunter, 65.

[68] Once Hunter caught on to Williams's scheme, she arranged for artists like Ethel Waters and Fletcher Henderson to write letters to the record company avowing that they had nothing to do with songs Hunter had written. Taylor, Alberta Hunter, 65.

[69] "On Stage: After 20 Years of Silence, Alberta Hunter Sings 'Remember My Name'—and Memphis Gives Her the Key to the City," People n.d., p. 118, Alberta Hunter Clippings, Theatre Collection, NYPL.

Though Hunter fought hard to receive due credit and payment for her work, white control over the means of production made for an unequal playing field that put African American performers at a serious disadvantage. By way of comparison, as a singer in the touring production of the musical revue *How Come?*, one of her most financially successful gigs in the early 1920s, Hunter made around $125 a week. This was no paltry sum when the average annual salary for an American worker was around $1,400.[70] But by 1920, the white dancer Ann Pennington, who began her career earning $40 a week in 1916 as a Ziegfeld Follies chorus girl, was making $1,000 a week.[71] And the weekly box office receipts of George White's 1926 edition of *Scandals*, in which Pennington danced her version of the Black Bottom, topped $40,000.[72] Economic disparities aside, the productions in which Alberta Hunter appeared could hardly compete for audiences with a white-produced musical revue with white stars and a long run on Broadway. Her ability to garner recognition for her staging of the Black Bottom was thus severely compromised. Without the (rhetorical) stamp of copyright to authorize Hunter's version as an original, George White's claim to be the inventor and exclusive exhibitor of the Black Bottom was capable of steamrolling evidence to the contrary. Asserting collective authorship was not enough for the law; a work had to be individually authored to qualify as intellectual property. Even unsubstantiated, Hunter's copyright claim should thus be seen as a weapon against and check on white hegemony in the theatrical marketplace.

Approached in this light, the assertion that Hunter copyrighted the Black Bottom, a dance so frequently associated with artists like George White and Ann Pennington, may hint at an alternative interpretation of copyright: as an individual claim made partly on behalf of a disenfranchised group. As Hunter told the *Daily Worker* in 1939, "For every Negro who reaches the top in the face of all the rank discrimination in the commercial theatre … thousands of other gifted Negroes never have a chance. Their folk songs … eventually die without ever being recorded, and if they are recorded, then some song promoter gets the credit for composing them and the cash for selling them."[73] I am not suggesting

---

[70] Harrison, "She's Got a Mind to Ramble," 207. According to a survey of wages conducted in the 1920s, the average annual earnings of an American worker in 1926 were $1,473. Robert H. Zieger and Gilbert J. Gall, *American Workers, American Unions: The Twentieth Century* (Baltimore, MD: Johns Hopkins University Press, 2002), 45. Brenda Dixon Gottschild reports that the average musician who toured the black vaudeville circuit in the 1920s received a weekly salary of $35 plus a $5 meal ticket (*Waltzing in the Dark*, 93).

[71] William M. Freeman, "Ann Pennington, Dancing Star, Dies," *New York Times*, November 5, 1971, p. 46.

[72] "News and Gossip of the Rialto" *New York Times*, November 21, 1926, p. X1.

[73] Richard Randall, "Thousands Never Get a Chance, Says Gifted Alberta Hunter," *Daily Worker*, November 3, 1939, n.p., Alberta Hunter Clippings File, Theatre Collection, NYPL.

that Hunter was somehow uninterested in her own personal advancement. But given her relative commercial success, it is certainly possible that her claim on the Black Bottom was made in recognition—rather than in contradiction—of communal African American authorship of the dance.[74] The fact that reports of Hunter's copyright persisted in several channels is proof of its effectiveness as a discourse of power. At least some in the theater world believed that however collective the creation of the Black Bottom, it was deserving of copyright protection when transformed into a stage routine and that, as such, Hunter was entitled to credit.

"My Name on the Program": Rights of Attribution

Unlike a legally sanctioned copyright, of course, a rhetorical claim on the Black Bottom could not be used in a court of law to enjoin other performances of the dance. But, to continue a speculative line of inquiry, Hunter may have been interested less (if at all) in curbing the circulation of the Black Bottom than in the issue of credit. Here it is worth briefly revisiting Johnny Hudgins's copyright claim, discussed in Chapter 2, for what it reveals about the importance of attribution in the code of ethics governing the practice of stealing steps. Speaking to one newspaper about the imitators trying to cash in on his "Mwa, Mwa" act, Hudgins reportedly said, "I wouldn't mind if they would give me credit and put my name on their programs as Josephine Baker has done."[75] As he elaborated in a 1928 letter to the Chicago Defender, "Josephine Baker has been doing an impersonation of me for the past six months at the Folies Bergère, but she certainly gave me credit as she had my name on the program as big as hers."[76] That same newspaper also observed that black performers like Adelaide Hall, Putney Dandridge, and even Bill Robinson had been performing variations of Hudgins's routine. "But Hudgins has never sought to enjoin any actors from using his routine unless they fail to give him credit for it."[77]

[74] This would accord with Rosemary Coombe's reminder that the use of "the idiom of property" by indigenous peoples may be a call for "a preliminary recognition of proprietary claims—not as exclusivity of possession but as bundles of multiple rights and relationships." Coombe, Response to Michael F. Brown, "Can Culture Be Copyrighted?" Current Anthropology 39.2 (April 1998): 208.

[75] "Johnny Hudgins with 'Songless Song and Frisky Feet,'" January 12, 1928, Johnny Hudgins clippings collection, Jean-Claude Baker Collection.

[76] "Hudgins and Wife Write to Whitney," Chicago Defender, March 10, 1928, p. 7. Indeed, the playbill for the 1927 Folies Bergère program, called Un Vent de Folie, lists one number as: "HIGGINS [sic], Le Célèbre Fantaiste Noire, imité par Miss Joséphine BAKER." Harvard Theatre Collection.

[77] "Hudgins Says His Piece on the Present Era," Chicago Defender, January 17, 1931, p. 5.

Demanding neither the complete cessation of impersonations of his "Mwa, Mwa" number nor compensation for reproductions of it, Hudgins expressed a desire for nothing more than a program note indicating that an act was "An imitation of Johnny Hudgins."[78] Herein lies a key distinction from official copyright law in the United States, which by definition grants exclusive rights (for a limited time) to authors. Hudgins may have believed he was due public recognition for originating his dance number, not exclusive performance rights to that dance; he sought the cultural capital of artistic credit, not the economic capital of royalties.

A similar desire for recognition is evident in Lindy hopper Frankie Manning's discussions of choreographic authorship, despite his self-described status as a crook. More accurately, Manning evinced an ambivalence about notions of artistic credit in dance. On the one hand, he repeatedly disavowed formulations of singular origination, insisting, "At the time, you never heard anybody going around saying, 'I made up that step.' We never thought about who created this or who created that."[79] He also went to some length to dispute the depiction of stealing steps offered in *Jazz Dance*:

> In Marshall Stearns's book, Al Minns said that Lindy hoppers never stole from each other, that it wasn't allowed. I don't know why he said that, because everybody was always showing their moves to other people, and we were all copying off each other. If you didn't get steps this way, then you'd always have to make them up. There was a friendly competitiveness when we got out on the floor, but I never heard anybody say, "You shouldn't do that step because it's mine." Nobody ever thought of copyrighting their moves, making people pay them for a step, or saying, "I'm the only person who's going to do this."[80]

Yet even as he rejected ideas of exclusive ownership, his writing was tinged with regret over others' failures to acknowledge his role in creating Lindy hop air steps. When air steps took off, he explains,

> My name got kind of lost in the shuffle, and I never mentioned what I had done to anybody. Leon James and Al Minns probably didn't even know who started doing air steps, because Leon was in Europe at that time and Al hadn't joined the Lindy hoppers yet. When *Jazz Dance* came out, I read that Al said he and some other dancers had come up with air steps.

[78] "Hudgins Says His Piece."
[79] Manning and Millman, *Frankie Manning*, 88.
[80] Ibid., 100–101.

That's when I first had the thought, *Hey, wait a minute, I did that.* I confronted Al about it later, and he admitted he didn't know who had done the first one. That's because I hadn't run around saying it was me.[81]

The ambiguities here are telling. While Manning maintained that conventional notions of copyright made no sense in a form like the Lindy hop, he could not shake the singular "I" of the sentiment "I did that," nor its assertion of authorial responsibility. However dismissive of copyright per se, Manning tacitly endorsed the right to have one's creative agency acknowledged.

Together, the emphasis these dancers (at times hesitantly) place on attribution suggests a conception of intellectual property rights that more closely resembles the moral rights protection afforded under European copyright law, which grants authors the right of attribution and the right to preserve the integrity of a work.[82] As Jane Gaines notes, "French copyright law is historically based on the author's right (*le droit d'auteur*), whereas the parallel Anglo-American law is based upon the right to copy."[83] There are also similarities between these African American artists' approach and the more recent development of the Creative Commons, a licensing system that exists alongside copyright law, which allows others to "copy, distribute, display, and perform your copyrighted work—and derivative works based upon it—but only if they give credit the way you request."[84] From a certain perspective, in fact, the model of the commons seems a useful construct for theorizing the practice of stealing steps. Legal scholar Yochai Benkler describes the commons as "a particular institutional form of structuring the rights to access, use, and control resources" that is "the opposite of 'property'" in that, unlike the sole proprietor of a property system, "resources governed by commons may be used or disposed of by anyone among some (more or less well-defined) number of persons, under rules that may range from 'anything goes' to quite crisply articulated formal rules that are effectively enforced."[85] With its "If you could

---

[81] Ibid., 102, emphasis in original.

[82] As Mark Rose writes in *Authors and Owners*, "European copyright law has developed the concept of *droit moral*, the notion that along with the author's property rights there exists a separate body of personal rights, including the right to control first publication, the right to be acknowledged as the author, and the right to be assured that the integrity of the work will be preserved." *Authors and Owners: The Invention of Copyright* (Cambridge, MA: Harvard University Press, 1993), 18n3.

[83] Gaines, *Contested Culture*, 50. Gaines here cites Paul Hirst's "Introduction" to Bernard Edelman's *Ownership of the Image: Elements for a Marxist Theory of Law*, translated by Elizabeth Kingdom (London: Routledge and Kegan Paul, 1979).

[84] http://creativecommons.org/about/licenses/. Accessed March 29, 2009.

[85] Yochai Benkler, *The Wealth of Networks: How Social Production Transforms Markets and Freedom* (New Haven, CT: Yale University Press, 2006), 60–61.

learn it, you could do it" ethos, tempered by a context-specific set of rules for pilfering, we might view the African American vernacular dance community, following Boateng, who draws on Benkler, as a "restricted commons."[86] But unlike the examples of adinkra and kente cloth production, which functioned "as a kind of commons within which there is a lot of borrowing and sharing and, over time, blurring of individual authorship lines," the dancers examined here worked to *undo* the blurring of authorship lines that resulted from the steady exchange of steps.[87] This was the contradiction of black vernacular dance: ideas of individual authorship and credit existed alongside copious borrowing and sharing, and the paradigms of property and commons existed in tension with one another rather than in opposition. For at least some African American dance artists, stealing steps was acceptable only so long as the provenance of those steps continued to be publicized.

Signature Steps as Corporeal Autography

Among the structural features of copyright law that scholars have pointed to as disadvantaging African American artists is the idea-expression dichotomy. Under this doctrine, copyright law protects only the material expression of ideas, not the concepts themselves. As K. J. Greene has argued, because the doctrine treats styles as non-protectable ideas, it has effectively "penalized the most innovative artists in blues, jazz, and rock." (He cites W. C. Handy and Little Richard as examples.)[88] Jane Gaines also notes that "the creative 'work' that actors and musicians performed on [the] notated 'work' has historically been unseen by copyright law. It is as though the interpretive labour which always tends to evaporate for audiences as soon as it is apprehended has never been solid enough for copyright law to recognise."[89] But this aporia in the law has also created space for corporeal enactments of ownership. In the unprotected sphere of vernacular dance, outside the law's rigid distinctions between idea and expression, between performance style and "the work," artists were free to declare discrete steps, arrangements of steps, and ways of moving as their own.

For a number of dancers, the choreographic decision to feature specific dance moves in their repertoires was a means of staking a claim on embodied

---

[86] Boateng, *The Copyright Thing*, 36.

[87] Ibid., 57.

[88] Greene, "Copyright, Culture and Black Music," 383.

[89] Jane M. Gaines, "Bette Midler and the Piracy of Identity," in *Music and Copyright*, ed. Simon Frith (Edinburgh: Edinburgh University Press, 1993), 89.

material they considered their intellectual property. The very existence of "specialty"—or "signature"—moves intimates as much. As Lindy hopper Norma Miller tells us (in contradistinction to Manning), "Each of Whitey's dancers was unique, and we never copied each other's steps. That was taboo, dancers were known by the steps they created. . . . [Their] nicknames were taken from their steps."[90] In other words, by mastering certain steps or styles, performing them over and over again, and linking their identities to them, dancers established a proprietary relationship to these moves. So, for example, Leon James was dubbed Wiggly Legs, Stompin' Billy had his foot slapping,[91] Rubberneck Holmes moved his upper body as if it were made of rubber,[92] "Buzzin' Burton" closed his act with the Buzz, and Earl "Snake Hips" Tucker stopped shows with his infamous pelvic rolls.[93]

Josephine Baker is another case in point. A catalog of signature moves helped propel Baker from her Broadway days as a chorus girl to an international solo career: the shimmy; the classic Charleston "monkey knees," in which her hands criss-crossed her splaying knees; standing struts, in which she bent one knee at a time and swung her arms in opposition; the crow or chicken pose, in which she froze in a turned-in plié with her elbows bent and her hands pointed out; as well as eye-crossing, fingertip flexing, and the placement of her finger on the crown of her head. Baker did not invent these moves; they were all based on extant African American vernacular idioms. As Jayna Brown has written, not a few of Baker's "gestural strategies" were eccentric dancing conventions of black child performers, known as "picaninnys," which Baker made "her own."[94] That is, by executing these steps and gestures time and again in a variety of venues, Baker turned them into corporeal autographs—bodily writings of her name in and through performance.[95]

---

[90] Norma Miller and Evette Jensen, *Swingin' at the Savoy: The Memoir of a Jazz Dancer* (Philadelphia: Temple University Press, 1996), 101.

[91] Ibid.

[92] Manning and Millman, *Frankie Manning*, 115.

[93] According to the Stearns, the Buzz consisted of "long, sliding steps forward, knees bent and arms flung out alternately to the sides, with hands turned down at the wrist and fingers vibrating in imitation of a bee's wings" (*Jazz Dance*, 233). A description of Tucker's dancing can also be found in the Stearns, *Jazz Dance*, 236–37.

[94] Brown, *Babylon Girls*, 206, 251.

[95] See, for example, Michael Borshuk, "An Intelligence of the Body: Disruptive Parody through Dance in the Early Performances of Josephine Baker," in *emBODYing Liberation: The Black Body in American Dance*, ed. Dorothea Fischer-Hornung and Alison D. Goeller (Hamburg: Lit Verlag, 2001); and Terri Francis, "Embodied Fictions, Melancholy Migrations: Josephine Baker's Cinematic Celebrity," *Modern Fiction Studies* 51.4 (2005): 824–45.

Peggy Kamuf's work on "signature pieces" is germane here. As Kamuf explains, a signature is not merely a name; rather, it is "a device repeatedly associated with a subject" and a "mark of an articulation at the border between life and letters, body and language."[96] The signature, to put it another way, creates the subject as separate from but inextricably linked to her work. Just so, a signature step gives a dancer a coherent identity without becoming equal to that identity; a corporeal autograph links dancer and dance without collapsing the two. While Kamuf is concerned with written signatures and the relationship between authors and texts, her emphasis on the compulsory repeatability of the signature is instructive. Drawing upon Jacques Derrida, who has written of the "impossibility" of the signature, which must possess a "repeatable, iterable, imitable form" even as it maintains an "absolute singularity,"[97] Kamuf writes,

> The singularity of the autograph ... cannot be absolute; on the contrary, verifiability or authentication relies on its reproducibility by "the subject named." If every time you sign your name, you deliberately make a significantly different mark, if no two signature acts resemble each other, then there is no telling after you have signed whether it was indeed you who signed.[98]

The corporeal autograph, too, must be constantly re-enacted, and re-enacted in a consistently distinctive enough manner, to achieve the effect of an inscription of identity and to thereby function as an assertion of authorship.[99] And like the handwritten signature, itself an embodied act, the corporeal autograph can never be exactly identical with itself, for no two performed moves are ever precise duplicates of one another. For all its contradictions, because it is so crucial to the institution of authorship, the signature regulates questions of proprietorship and economic value. "Under the liberal regime of the marketplace," Kamuf states, "the signature designates a property owner to whom

[96] Peggy Kamuf, *Signature Pieces: On the Institution of Authorship* (Ithaca, NY: Cornell University Press, 1988), 3, 39–40.

[97] Jacques Derrida, "Signature Event Context," in *Limited Inc* (1977; Evanston, IL: Northwestern University Press, 1988), 20.

[98] Kamuf, *Signature Pieces*, ix.

[99] For a compelling argument about how gesture can function as inscription, see Sally Ann Ness, "The Inscription of Gesture: Inward Migrations in Dance," in *Migrations of Gesture*, ed. Sally Ann Ness and Carie Noland (Minneapolis: University of Minnesota Press, 2008), 1–30. Gabriele Brandstetter has also written thoughtfully about the "irresolvable ambivalence" that characterizes the operation of signing in dance. See "Transcription—Materiality—Signature. Dancing and Writing between Resistance and Excess," in *Emerging Bodies: The Performance of Worldmaking in Dance and Choreography*, ed. Gabriele Klein and Sandra Noeth (Bielefeld: Transcript-Verlag, 2011), 129.

Figure 3.5 Josephine Baker performing standing struts, one of her signature steps, wearing a stylized version of her signature banana skirt in the 1936 edition of the *Ziegfeld Follies* at the Winter Garden Theater in New York. AP Photo.

certain benefits accrue."[100] Although copyright law has refused to protect performance style, the fact that a dancer's signature steps were also commonly referred to as his or her "trademark" signals their correlation with an informal, embodied system of intellectual property rights regulation.

There are also interesting parallels between the idea of safeguarding a dance move by tying one's public persona to it and the "right of publicity," a cousin of intellectual property law.[101] According to Gaines, this right, which descended

[100] Kamuf, *Signature Pieces*, 65. See Gaines on how the face also functions as a "guarantee of property." Gaines, "Bette Middler," 94–95.

[101] I am indebted to an anonymous reviewer of an earlier iteration of this chapter for pointing out this parallel.

from the right of privacy, took shape on a state-by-state basis in the United States between the 1950s and 1970s as a way to prevent the unauthorized commercial use of a celebrity's likeness.[102] As with a celebrity's voice or visage, a dancer's distinctive steps were an extension of his or her image. And as with the "right of publicity," the concept of a protected signature step rests on an understanding of embodied personhood—one's bodily identity—as private property. In the unofficial but nonetheless codified system of tap and jazz dancers, aligning one's personhood with a particular move could serve as a declaration of proprietorship. Yet crucially, as the centrality of the celebrity to the evolution of publicity rights suggests, the better known the dancer, the greater has been his or her claim to that move.

Renown was precisely what gave force to ownership claims in this alternative system of property rights.[103] Writing about cloth production in Ghana, Boatema Boateng observes that "claims over culture are not always a function of location and origin. They also have to do with the power to make such claims 'stick' long enough that their association with specific locations appears naturalized."[104] Equally so, the ability of signature steps to serve as copyright-like claims on movement depended on more than physical skill alone; their effectiveness was also contingent on power and access.

This is made clear in the example of Bill Robinson's stair dance. Robinson claimed to have discovered the routine around 1918 when he spotted some friends in the audience of a matinee performance and, on the spur of the moment, tapped down the set of stairs flanking the stage in order to greet them, all the while continuing his dancing.[105] Yet Robinson was by no means the first to perform a stair dance. Fellow tap dancer King Rastus Brown was

---

[102] Gaines, *Contested Culture*, 142. See also J. Thomas McCarthy, *The Rights of Publicity and Privacy* (New York: Clark Boardman, 1988). In "The Right of Publicity" (*Law and Contemporary Problems* 19.2 [Spring 1954]: 203–23), Melville B. Nimmer argues for the right of publicity to be considered a property right. Although not involving the right to privacy or publicity per se, Peter Decherney argues that the 1928 case *Chaplin v. Amador* (which actually stretched across much of the 1920s) inaugurated the idea that a comic actor could possess a copyright in a character he developed—here, Charlie Chaplin's Little Tramp character. See Decherney, "Gag Orders: Comedy, Chaplin, and Copyright," 135–54.

[103] Caroline Joan S. Picart similarly argues that developing a star persona was critical to dancers' pursuit of copyright protection in their choreographic works. See *Critical Race Theory and Copyright in American Dance: Whiteness as Status Property* (New York: Palgrave Macmillan, 2013), 12.

[104] Boateng, *The Copyright Thing*, 120.

[105] Haskins and Mitgang, *Mr. Bojangles*, 99. There were other origin tales surrounding Robinson's stair dance. He told the *New York Times Magazine* that he "first dreamt that dance. I thought I was being made a lord by the King of England and he was standing at the head of a flight of stairs and I had to walk up to get my crown and I didn't like the idea of just walking up the steps before the King, so I thought I'd dance up, and the next morning when I woke up I knew I had a good idea." "Bill Robinson, 60, Taps Out the Joy of Living," *New York Times Magazine*, May 22, 1938, p. 4 +, Bill Robinson Clippings File, Jerome Robbins Dance Division, NYPL.

reportedly "loudly and insistently grieved by" Robinson's "theft" of *his* stair dance.[106] Robinson biographers Jim Haskins and N. R. Mitgang explain that

> neither man could claim to have originated the idea. Vaudeville legends abound with "firsts" in this area. Some credit Al Leach (and His Rosebuds). Then there were the Whitney Brothers, who did a musical stair dance at Hyde and Behman's Theater in 1899. A team called Mack and Williams did a single, a double, and a triple stair dance in 1915. Paul Morton and his wife, Naomi Glass, also did one as part of their act.[107]

Its multiple predecessors aside, by 1921, Robinson had made the stair dance a regular feature of his act, which evidently led to a dispute with The Four Mortons (possibly Morton, Glass, and their children) when both acts were booked on the same program at a Minneapolis theater. According to Haskins and Mitgang, F. W. Vincent, a booking agent for the Orpheum Circuit, sent Robinson a telegram asking him to refrain from performing his stair dance routine "this week" as a "personal favor." Robinson refused, appealing instead to white vaudeville star Rae Samuels to intervene on his behalf with the local theater manager. She did, and the Mortons were forced to yield. "After that," Haskins and Mitgang write, "Bill tried to secure a patent on his stair routine, and though the U.S. Patent Office in Washington, D.C., declined to accept his application, Bill rarely had to go to great lengths to protect his 'professional territory' again. Soon, he was so well identified with the stair routine that no one would dream of impinging on his territory."[108]

This 1921 confrontation was thus a critical point in Robinson's career. Although King Rastus Brown also vied with Robinson over the stair dance, the two were not equally matched in the theatrical marketplace. Brown never "crossed over" to dance before white audiences, whereas Robinson was one of the few African American dancers to perform solo on the white vaudeville

---

[106] Stearns, *Jazz Dance*, 179; Haskins and Mitgang, *Mr. Bojangles*, 99–100.

[107] Haskins and Mitgang, *Mr. Bojangles*, 100.

[108] Ibid., 100–101. A *New Yorker* profile of Robinson in 1934 told the story differently, reporting that Robinson consented to drop the stair dance from his routine "without hesitation." In this telling, it was only "when the stair dance began to be appropriated by hoofers Robinson did not even know," that he attempted to patent the dance, "like Edison's lamp or Bell's first telephone." The *New Yorker* also reported that "Bill tried to have this done, but the Patent Office at Washington, after a period of frank bewilderment, declined to accept the application." St. Clair McKelway, "Bojangles I," *New Yorker*, October 6, 1934, p. 26. Bill Robinson Clippings, Jerome Robbins Dance Division, NYPL. A November 2013 search by archivists of the Patent Office's records, which are housed in the National Archives in Kansas City, uncovered no documentation of Robinson's rejected patent application. It is possible that the application was destroyed or lost

circuit.[109] His celebrity therefore exceeded Brown's. But when pitted against the Four Mortons, a white tap dance act, Robinson needed the intercession of an influential white ally to preserve his (perceived) rights to the stair dance. The fact that it was Robinson's claim on the stair dance that eventually "stuck" thus had everything to do with "the opportunity and showmanship"—and relative advantage within a white power structure—he possessed to "make it famous."[110] If repetition was key to turning a given step into a signature one, sufficient success to secure repeat performance engagements was the necessary precondition.

(In) Imitability and (Non)Reproducibility

This is not to discount the sizable role that Robinson's talent played in his ability to make the stair dance his "own" (such a common refrain in the discourse of dance). A New York dance teacher told a reporter in 1931 that "he could teach Robinson's stair dance to any dancer, but no one could do it, or sell it, like Bill Robinson himself."[111] For dancers aiming to shore up their claims to choreography, honing a unique performance style was as critical as the repeated enactment of certain moves; signature steps, that is, required a signature style. A style that was impossible to copy was even better. Josephine Baker again serves to illustrate. Part of what allowed her to claim circulating moves as her own was the idiosyncrasy of her dancing body. Commentators, struggling for the right words to characterize her physicality, pointed frequently to the energy, eccentricity, and humor of her moving body. As one London critic wrote, "any inch of her body, an elbow-tip, or a shoulder-blade, is more sentient and expressive than most people's countenances."[112] Even in the flattened medium of film, Baker's kinetic articulateness and fluidity are unmistakable. For instance, in a dance sequence in the 1927 film *La Sirène des Tropiques*, we see Baker kicking her legs,

---

at some point; it is also possible that Robinson never actually filed the patent application. Either way, lack of recognition from the Patent Office apparently did little to deter Robinson from invoking property rights: a 1950 newspaper article about the white tap dancer Tony DeMarco, who also performed a version of the stair dance, reported that "Bill claimed patent rights on the stair thing, and Tony had to talk fast to him to retain the number and keep out of a lawsuit." Chris Wall, "Top of Heap in Taps Ranks Tony DeMarco," *Sunday Herald,* November 19, 1950, p. 8

[109] Stearns, *Jazz Dance,* 140, 184, 181.

[110] Ibid., 179.

[111] J. Francis Haney, "Analyzing Bill Robinson and His Dancing," *American Dancer,* January 1931, p. 38, Bill Robinson Clippings, Jerome Robbins Dance Division, NYPL.

[112] Hubert Griffith, "Josephine Baker at Home," *London Observer,* October 8, 1933, Harvard Theater Collection.

swinging her arms, swaying her hips, tilting her head, smiling, and rolling her eyes all at once one minute, and abruptly switching directions, dropping into a deep lunge, and bounding across the floor the next. These "high-affect juxtapositions"[113] and dynamic facial expressions contributed to the comedic tenor of her dancing—what the French critic André Rouverge described as "the genius to let the body make fun of itself."[114] Immediately recognizable but difficult to describe, Baker's dancing body exuded a zaniness and exuberance that became her personal calling card. If her moves were reproducible, her eccentric and charismatic style was much less so. Just as a blues singer like Muddy Waters possessed a "signature sound," so too could a dancer enjoy a "natural monopoly" on her performance style.[115]

In contrast to Baker, John Bubbles's steps themselves were difficult to duplicate, so much so that some came to believe (falsely) that he was left-footed. The white choreographer Nick Castle had a different explanation: "I could never steal a step from Bubbles," he remarked, adding, "he never repeats—he's the greatest *ad lib* dancer in the world."[116] Here it is the continual variation of one's steps—the converse of the signature step—that proves the most effectual protection device against theft. Like the Lindy hoppers who, according to Gottschild, "densely packed their routines with speed and step clusters to prevent others from stealing them,"[117] Bubbles danced in a way that, intentionally or not, was impossible to pin down and therefore impossible to reproduce.

In addition to differing starkly from the idea that dance moves are inherently imitable (the premise on which the custom of stealing steps rests), the idea that choreography could be made non-reproducible would seem to lend support to what some scholars have asserted is performance's ontology. The argument, most prominently articulated by Peggy Phelan, is that performance's ephemerality—the fact that its very condition is its disappearance—gives it a "distinctive oppositional edge" and enables it to "elude ... regulation and control."[118] "Performance's only life," she writes,

---

[113] Brenda Dixon Gottschild identifies "high-affect juxtaposition"—the "mood, attitude, or movement breaks" that contrast the smooth transitions of European aesthetic codes—as one of the core principles of an Africanist aesthetic. *Digging the Africanist Presence*, 14–15.

[114] Quoted in Patrick O'Connor and Bryan Hammond, *Josephine Baker* (London: Little, Brown, 1988), 42.

[115] Vaidhyanathan, *Copyrights and Copywrongs*, 123.

[116] Stearns, *Jazz Dance*, 214.

[117] Gottschild, *Waltzing in the Dark*, 74. Honi Coles likewise recalled a group of chorus girls at the Apollo Theatre—Ristin Banks, Berite Lou, and Yak Taylor—who were so good at stealing moves from male tap dancers that "most acts used to try and load their steps up to the point that they couldn't be stolen" (Schiffman, *Uptown*, 65).

[118] Peggy Phelan, *Unmarked: The Politics of Performance* (London: Routledge, 1993), 148.

is in the present. Performance cannot be saved, recorded, documented, or otherwise participate in the circulation of representations
of representations: once it does so, it becomes something other than
performance. To the degree that performance attempts to enter the
economy of reproduction it betrays and lessens the promise of its own
ontology.[119]

Not all performance scholars have accepted Phelan's argument about the
ontology of performance, nor her contention that performance operates outside
of regulatory systems. Philip Auslander, for example, casts doubt on the notion
"that any cultural discourse can actually stand outside the ideologies of capital
and reproduction that define a mediatized culture or should be expected to do
so, even to assume an oppositional stance."[120] Nevertheless, in his examination
of intellectual property law's treatment of live performance, he concedes that
copyright doctrine, like Phelan, regards live performance as subject to ownership and regulatory control only when it has been "fixed" in another, more
"tangible" medium.[121] Because "live performance cannot be copyrighted," that
is to say, Auslander maintains that "it escapes ownership, commodification, and
other processes of regulation within a reproductive capitalist economy."[122]

Yet the anecdotes of black vernacular dancers, this chapter has tried to show,
suggest otherwise. True, their choreography—considered neither fixed creations nor "original works of authorship" by the white mainstream in the early
twentieth century—existed outside the jurisdiction of US copyright law. And
true, some dancers used the ephemeral nature of their medium to their advantage, thwarting would-be thieves by avoiding recurring, isolatable moves. But
such efforts to prevent the copying of specific steps and styles call into being a
concept of property and would not make sense without it. That dancers had to
go to some length to render their routines non-reproducible suggests that the
condition of ephemerality alone was no guarantee that one's work would escape

[119] Ibid., 146.

[120] Philip Auslander, *Liveness: Performance in a Mediatized Culture* (London: Routledge,
1999), 40. In "From Playhouse to P2P Network: The History and Theory of Performance under
Copyright Law in the United States" (*Theatre Journal* 59.1 [2007] 75–95), Oliver Gerland argues
that it is a mistake to believe that "because it is ephemeral, performance is somehow the opposite
of a capitalist economy that circulates cultural objects" (94). See also Fred Moten, who presents
his book *In the Break* as in part a "respectful challenge to Peggy Phelan's ontology of performance
that is predicated on the notion of performance's operating wholly outside economies of reproduction." Moten, *In the Break: The Aesthetics of the Black Radical Tradition* (Minneapolis: University
of Minnesota Press, 2003), 258n4.

[121] Auslander, *Liveness*, 9, 112–13, 150–51.

[122] Ibid., 150–51.

circulation within a capitalist economy. The "trademarking" of certain pet steps, moreover, a concept undeniably imbricated in notions of authorship and owner-ship, depended on just the opposite—on the reproducibility of moves and styles. If, as Phelan maintains, "Performance clogs the smooth machinery of reproduc-tive representation necessary to the circulation of capital," it does not follow that performance sidesteps this machinery; dance's ephemerality may have compli-cated but did not cancel out the ideology of intellectual property.[123]

What role did race play in this ideology? If property rights are, as legal scholar Cheryl Harris has asserted and this book reaffirms, "contingent on, intertwined with, and conflated with race," how should we understand the difference race made to black vernacular dancers' approach to intellectual property rights?[124] There is no contradicting the fact that, as Eddie Rector captured in his pithy summation of the obstacles copyright would pose to lifting a foot, Western legal constructions of intellectual property were in many respects incongruous with the practice of African American tap and jazz performers in the early twenti-eth century. Innovation in these forms depended not on copyright's incentive of limited monopolies for original works but on dancers' capacity to reproduce and refine moves they borrowed from one another. But there is still the equally incontrovertible fact that some black vernacular dancers developed proprietary interests in their choreography. Is it reasonable to view the manifestation of these ownership interests as a response to the long history of white appropriation of black culture? Surely, it is too simplistic to say that the pervasiveness of white theft wholly determined concepts of private property within black vernacular dance communities. As evidenced by the examples cited above, including the show-stopping plagiarism row between Almany Camaro and Donald Heywood recounted at the opening of this chapter, intellectual property contests were not exclusively inter-racial affairs. African American tap and jazz dancers not only stole from one another but also crafted measures to prevent unlicensed copy-ing of one another. Crucially, however, the admonition not to copy another's moves "in public and for pay" should serve as a reminder that the reproduction of dance steps within black vernacular communities cannot be divorced from the larger economy in which black performance circulates. Because the com-mercial marketplace was (and remains) so heavily controlled by white produc-ers, and because white dancers had such greater access to the marketplace, the specter of white exploitation loomed constantly. In this context, we might regard the idea of intellectual property itself as a tool of power for African American vernacular dancers—a protection device that mobilizes a discourse that power

---

[123] Phelan, *Unmarked*, 148.
[124] Cheryl I. Harris, "Whiteness as Property," *Harvard Law Review* 106.8 (1993): 1714.

understands.[125] In a nation shaped by a system of racial slavery, where "the seizure and appropriation of labor" was realized "by treating Black people themselves as objects of property," African American tap and jazz dancers both flouted and found utility in the hegemonic logic of intellectual property rights.[126]

Much, of course, has changed since the first half of the twentieth century, when segregation dominated the dance world and black dancers were largely confined to forms like jazz and tap. In addition to the increased presence of African Americans in the "high art" concert dance sphere, the rise of electronic and digital technologies has transformed the circulation and reproduction of embodied arts in significant ways. Still, it is worth keeping in mind that most if not all of the dances considered here would fail to qualify for copyright protection even after the passage of the 1976 Copyright Act. As I discuss further in Chapter 4, although the Copyright Act neglected to define choreography explicitly, reports issued by the House and Senate explained that it was not necessary "to specify that 'choreographic works' do not include social dance steps and simple routines."[127] Such a proscription would surely exclude tap dance steps and jazz dances like the Lindy hop. Indeed, the most recent *Compendium of U.S. Copyright Practices*, a guide to the Copyright Office's administrative decisions, lists "swing dances" as an example of a social dance ineligible for protection."[128] The *Compendium* justifies this exclusion on the basis of social dances' participatory aim. In a much drier echo of Eddie Rector's concerns about how copyright would affect his ability to lift a foot, the *Compendium* states, "If a social dance could be considered a choreographic work ... every individual who performed that dance in public would infringe the rights of the copyright owner."[129] Certainly, the testimony of black vernacular

---

[125] See Richard Handler, "Who Owns the Past? History, Cultural Property, and the Logic of Possessive Individualism," in *The Politics of Culture*, ed. Brett Williams (Washington: Smithsonian Institution Press, 1991), 71.

[126] Harris, "Whiteness as Property," 1715, 1716.

[127] House Report No. 94-1476, US Code Congressional and Administrative News, vol. 5, 94th Congress Second Session, 1976, pp. 5666–67. An earlier Copyright Office circular did spell out that "Ballroom, social, and folk dance steps are not considered copyrightable material." See Borge Varmer, "Copyright in Choreographic Works," Study No. 28, *Studies Prepared for the Subcommittee on Patents, Trademarks, and Copyrights of the Committee on the Judiciary*, United States Senate, 86th Cong., 2d Sess. (Washington, DC: US Government Printing Office, 1961): 96.

[128] "Ballroom dances," "Folk dances," "Line dances," "Square dances," and "Break dances" are the other listed examples of social dances. The *Compendium* also identifies a "discrete routine within a variety show" as an example of an ineligible "simple routine." *Compendium of U.S. Copyright Practices*, Third Edition, US Copyright Office, Public Draft, August 19, 2014, Chapter 800, section 805, 78

[129] Ibid.

dancers verifies that jazz and tap dances depend on the kind of imitation and give-and-take that makes both problematic and impractical the idea of granting a dancer a performance monopoly on a particular step or set of steps.[130] But "social dance steps" and "simple routines," these same dancers suggest, routinely migrate from recreational public spaces to professional, for-profit public spaces, raising questions about when sequences of bodily movements that occur in both might constitute a "choreographic work." With the "copyright-ability" of dance a matter of ongoing debate, the protection devices adopted by African American vernacular performers in the first part of the twentieth century have a continued relevance precisely because copyright registration was not readily available to them. Attention to these devices forces us to confront the ways in which notions of intellectual property play out in and around practices that the law refuses to recognize.

In order to write a history of intellectual property rights for choreography that does not become a chronicle of the same celebrated white artists who already dominate extant dance historical accounts, then, we must be careful to be confined neither by the exclusionary configuration of official legal archives, nor by the exclusionary logic of US copyright law—nor by assumptions that African American vernacular culture is altogether antithetical to Western constructions of intellectual property. Expanding our archive to include the practices and discourse of dancers themselves reveals that notions of individual proprietorship, as well as economies of reproduction and racial ideologies, operate as much in performance as they do in law.

---

[130] Although acknowledging a continuum between "choreographic works" on the one hand and "social dances" and "simple routines" on the other, the *Compendium* offers the following distinctions:

> Performing a social dance is often a participatory, social experience, while the performance of a choreographic work is an expressive act that is typically intended to be performed for the enjoyment of others. Whereas social dances are generally capable of being performed by members of the public, choreographic works typically cannot.

Ibid., 78.

4

"High-brow" Meets "Low-Down"

Copyright on Broadway

In 1952, the German-born modern dancer Hanya Holm (1893–1992) successfully obtained a US copyright registration for the choreographic score of the dances she composed for the 1948 Broadway production *Kiss Me, Kate*. Although the score was registered as a dramatico-musical composition rather than a choreographic work—it would be another twenty-five years before Congress changed the law to make choreography the explicit subject of copyright protection—observers celebrated Holm's achievement as a historic first and an "epoch-making event."[1] The *Dance Observer*'s Lucy Wilder proclaimed, "Thus the battle of choreographers for legal recognition and protection passed into history. From now on, dance works are to be considered artistic property and must be protected as such."[2] In *Dance Magazine*, Nelson Lansdale wrote that the "creation of dance has at last been legally accepted in the same way, and on the same level, as creation in other fields. Protected by a copyright, the choreographer has the same rights as the author, the composer, and the playright [*sic*]."[3]

Holm was not truly the first to register a choreographic work with the US Copyright Office. As we have seen, both Loïe Fuller and Ruth St. Denis before her submitted narrative prose scores of their choreography. Throughout the 1910s and 1920s, moreover, a Russian-born dance teacher named Louis H. Chalif secured copyrights on numerous books filled with directions for

---

[1] Paul V. Beckley, "Choreography Is Copyrighted for First Time," *New York Herald Tribune*, March 14, 1952, Hanya Holm Clippings File, NYPL.

[2] Lucy Wilder, "U.S. Government Grants First Dance Copyright," *Dance Observer* 19.5 (May 1952): 69.

[3] Nelson Lansdale, "Concerning the Copyright of Dances," *Dance Magazine*, June 1952, 21.

performing hundreds of ballroom dances.[4] What made Holm's registration different was her reliance on Labanotation, a standardized system of symbols for recording human movement on paper, devised by the Austro-Hungarian choreographer and theorist Rudolf von Laban, to create her score. The fact that in the early 1940s, the Copyright Office apparently refused to grant protection to Eugene Loring's ballet choreography for *Billy the Kid* on the basis that the Labanotated method in which it was documented was "not yet recognized as a set system for recording movement" heightened the sense of momentousness surrounding Holm's copyright.[5] Following Loring's rejection, Holm's accomplishment was taken as a victory for the dance field at large. According to John Martin of the *New York Times*, the development not only gave "official recognition to the dance creator" but also demonstrated the "practicability of dance notation" and laid the ground for establishing "an available literature of dance compositions ... for future generations to study and consult."[6] Or, as he later summarized, "technological progress, property rights and the tangibility of artistic creation are all served."[7]

However much Holm's copyright win signaled the growing currency of Labanotation as a method of "fixing" movement, it is the elevation of the choreographer and the choreographic work afforded by Labanotation that most interests me here.[8] If, as Lucy Wilder maintained, "Th[e] seemingly simple procedure [of Holm submitting her Labanotated score to the Copyright Office] has changed overnight the status of choreographers and their works," what kind of conceptual re-definition of the choreographer accompanied—or precipitated—her new legal standing, and what can this tell us about shifting constructions of authorship and ownership in US dance?[9] This chapter takes up these questions by exploring some of the implications (and contradictions)

---

[4] Anatole Chujoy, "New Try Made to Copyright Choreography," *Dance News* 22.2 (February 1953): 4. Chalif s publications, such as the *Chalif Text Book of Dancing* (1914) are all listed as books in the Copyright Office's card catalog.

[5] Lansdale, "Concerning the Copyright of Dances."

[6] John Martin, "The Dance: Copyright" *New York Times,* March 30, 1952, p. X10.

[7] John Martin, "The Dance: Progress," *New York Times,* June 8, 1952, p. X2.

[8] A 1961 article in *Dance Magazine* attributed reports that Congress was considering revising the Copyright Statute to cover choreographic works explicitly to the "emergence of a feasible means of recording on paper all manner of dance movements." Barbara L. Meyer, "The Copyright Question: Some Words to the Wise," *Dance Magazine,* April 1961, 45. This chapter's focus on the elevation of the white female choreographer rather than on solutions to the problem of fixing dance is part of my overall attempt to provide a different perspective on the legal sanctioning of choreographic copyright.

[9] Wilder, "U.S. Government Grants First Dance Copyright," 69.

of bestowing property rights on a choreographer associated with the concert stage for dances enacted on Broadway.

That Holm's copyright success coincided with a turning point in the history of the Broadway musical warrants attention. In standard narratives of the genre, the 1940s and 1950s marked a "Golden Age" for the musical, a period during which, led by the music- and song-writing team of Richard Rodgers and Oscar Hammerstein, the songs, dances, and narrative elements of the musical became newly unified, or "integrated."[10] It was not any and all dance, however, that was integrated with the musical's character development and plot: while tap, jazz, and social ballroom dances were the most popular styles on Broadway in the 1920s and 1930s, ballet (or, more precisely, a modern- and jazz-influenced style of ballet) came to dominate in the 1940s. The person almost single-handedly credited for this shift is the ballet-trained Agnes de Mille (1905–1993). Although George Balanchine created a ballet for the 1936 musical *On Your Toes*, de Mille's choreography for the 1943 smash hit *Oklahoma!* is generally regarded as launching the ascendance of ballet on Broadway and the increased centrality of dance within the musical.[11]

De Mille also became one of the most vocal advocates for copyright protection for choreography. In the wake of *Oklahoma!*'s success, feeling she had been denied an adequate share of the show's royalties, de Mille began a vigorous campaign to establish intellectual property rights for choreographers: organizing her peers, writing at length on the topic, and lobbying Congress. Legislative change, of course, occurs at a sluggish pace, but de Mille's efforts undeniably helped pave the way for the eventual passage of the 1976 Copyright Act.

While there are surely many reasons that Holm and de Mille were motivated to seek copyright protection for their Broadway choreography and an assortment of reasons that their efforts gained traction with the Copyright Office and, eventually, with Congress, this chapter proposes that it is not happenstance that two of the most significant players in the crusade for choreographic copyright first sought legal recognition for work they did in the

---

[10] See Larry Stempel, *Showtime: A History of the Broadway Musical Theater* (New York: W.W. Norton, 2010), 654–55, on the origins of the nostalgic identification of a "Golden Age" for the musical. As Stempel points out, "There is no critical consensus on how long the Golden Age of the Broadway musical lasted or on precise criteria for determining of what it consisted," though "most commentators agree that it started in the early 1940s, emblematically with either *Pal Joey* ... or *Oklahoma!* ... and ended in the late 1950s or early 1960s with *West Side Story* ... or *Fiddler on the Roof*" (742). See also Dan Rebellato, "'No Theatre Guild Attraction Are We': *Kiss Me, Kate* and the Politics of the Integrated Musical," *Contemporary Theatre Review* 19.1 (2009): 61–73, on how *Oklahoma!* serves as a pivot point in standard histories of the musical.

[11] See, for example, Jane Feuer, *The Hollywood Musical*, 2nd ed. (Bloomington: Indiana University Press, 1993), 7–8.

commercial realm of Broadway rather than in the "high art" realm of concert dance. Nor, I argue, is it coincidental that their pursuit of copyright protection corresponded with the displacement of the racially marked genres of tap and jazz from the Broadway stage. Building on Rosemary Coombe's assertion that "Authorship as a social and legal institution historically originated and was shaped by encounters with others," I see the campaign for choreographic ownership at mid-century as an outgrowth of encounters between white women with established (or escalating) reputations in the worlds of ballet and modern dance and Broadway's various "others."[12] This chapter charts those encounters in an attempt to illuminate the convergence of race, class, gender, and sexuality in the development of intellectual property rights for choreography in the years leading up to the 1976 Copyright Act.

In making this case, I draw on and extend the arguments of two important works in dance and theater studies: David Savran's *Highbrow/ Lowdown: Theater, Jazz, and the Making of the New Middle Class* (2009) and Susan Manning's *Modern Dance, Negro Dance: Race in Motion* (2004). Savran's book examines the pivotal role that the musical form of jazz played in the emergence of an American art theater in the 1920s. During that decade, Savran demonstrates, more commercial forms of theater, such as vaudeville, musical comedy, and burlesque, absorbed jazz's influence, making "the boundary between jazz performance and theatrical performance ... indistinct."[13] In contrast, "theater professionals intent on the elevation of the legitimate theater were made distinctly anxious by the ubiquity of a low-class music that emerged from African Americans, eastern European Jews, and other immigrant groups."[14] It was through the efforts of this latter group to distance themselves from the cultural force of jazz that a so-called serious theater developed and that playwrights like Eugene O'Neill acquired canonical status.

Although my temporal focus in this chapter is later than Savran's, I too trace the relationships between artistic practices within a shifting cultural hierarchy, in my case the practices of ballet and jazz/tap as they interfaced with the Broadway musical. By the 1940s, of course, jazz was no longer an emergent form. Nonetheless, like a number of the playwrights that Savran examines, Hanya Holm and Agnes de Mille manifested "ambivalent and contradictory attitudes toward jazz," working alongside and at times absorbing tap and jazz dance even as they sought to distinguish themselves from the associations

---

[12] Rosemary J. Coombe, *The Cultural Life of Intellectual Properties: Authorship, Appropriation, and the Law* (Durham, NC: Duke University Press, 1998), 257.

[13] David Savran, *Highbrow/Lowdown: Theater, Jazz, and the Making of the New Middle Class* (Ann Arbor: University of Michigan Press, 2009), 4.

[14] Ibid., 4–5.

those forms continued to carry.[15] Like Savran as well, I emphasize the entanglement between "brow" level, class, and race. Citing Lawrence Levine's influential book *Highbrow/Lowbrow: The Emergence of Cultural Hierarchy in America* (on which Savran's book title riffs), Savran reminds us that the terms "highbrow" and "lowbrow" are rooted in the nineteenth-century racial science of phrenology, in which the measuring of cranial size and shape was used to justify European supremacy.[16] The term "highbrow" in particular recurs in contemporaneous accounts of Holm's and de Mille's foray into the world of the Broadway musical, where jazz dance styles once prevailed and still lingered. Understanding these women's efforts to secure intellectual property rights for choreography as the outcome of an encounter between "highbrow" and "lowbrow" at a decidedly "middlebrow" site, this chapter tries to stay attuned to the intersection of class and race, as well as gender and sexuality.[17]

Susan Manning's book, meanwhile, chronicles the fluctuating relationship between white modern dance and "Negro" dance from the 1930s to the 1960s. As she argues, these formations were "mutually constitutive categories, and their interdependent representations of blackness and whiteness shifted in tandem over time."[18] For Manning, the early 1940s marked a "crucial turning point" in which "Negro dance achieved a new authority within black and white public spheres" and "modern dance redefined its whiteness."[19] Where white

---

[15] Ibid., 173.

[16] Ibid., 47; Lawrence Levine, *Highbrow/Lowbrow: The Emergence of Cultural Hierarchy in America* (Cambridge, MA: Harvard University Press, 1988), 221–22.

[17] In his chapter on "Middlebrow Anxiety" in *A Queer Sort of Materialism: Recontextualizing American Theatre* (Ann Arbor: University of Michigan Press, 203), 3–55, Savran explains that the term "middlebrow" first arose in the 1920s and gained traction in the middle of the twentieth century (3–4). Savran positions theater as an emphatically "middlebrow" art form and argues that "the most salient characteristic of middlebrow [is] the unstable, unpredictable, and anxious relationship between art and commerce" (15, 17). Savran is also careful to stress that "social class and brow level were not (and are not) synonymous." So, for example "highbrow taste is by no means the exclusive property of the upper classes or those with the most education. It is, in fact, more often than not associated with intellectual rather than economic elites." *Highbrow/Lowdown*, 8. For an analysis of the gendered dimensions of middlebrow culture, see Janice Radway, "On the Gender of the Middlebrow Consumer and the Threat of the Culturally Fraudulent Female," *South Atlantic Quarterly* 93.4 (Fall 1994): 871–93. In *A Problem Like Maria: Gender and Sexuality in the American Musical* (Ann Arbor: University of Michigan Press, 2002), Stacy Wolf also observes that "musicals were seen as distinctively middlebrow, middle-of-the-road entertainment" (12). My thinking in this chapter is, like Savran's, indebted on a fundamental level to the theories of French social scientist Pierre Bourdieu, particularly his notion of players competing for power and capital within a field of cultural production.

[18] Susan Manning, *Modern Dance, Negro Dance: Race in Motion* (Minneapolis: University of Minnesota Press, 2004), xiv–xv.

[19] Ibid., xx, 118.

modern dancers in the 1930s claimed the privilege of representing non-white subjects, a practice Manning terms "metaphorical minstrelsy," after 1940, as African American dancers began to command a new artistic authority, white modern dancers asserted the privilege of "mythic abstraction": the right to represent the unmarked, universal body.[20]

Like Manning, I see the 1940s as a transitional period for the positioning of racialized dance genres in relation to one another. The features of this transition, however, are different when we turn our attention from the concert stage to Broadway. Rather than finding "Negro" dance and the convention of black self-representation in ascendance, we find the African American–based forms of tap and jazz dance in decline, supplanted by the "unmarked" (read: white) forms of ballet and modern dance. And, because my interest here is less in the representational conventions of particular genres than in the extra-theatrical means by which artists construct their authority, the privilege of mythic abstraction is less relevant to my argument than the ways in which whiteness consolidated itself via the assertion of intellectual property rights. Attention to dancers' pursuit of copyright therefore helps us understand race as not only a "perceptual construct," a way of reading bodies, but also as a contest over cultural and economic capital.[21]

This chapter examines some of the contours of that contest at mid-century through case studies of Holm's and de Mille's experiences on Broadway and their quest for copyright protection. Both women's choreography for the musical theater stage, I show, relied on and concealed a set of racialized power relations, as did the acclaim they received for their choreography. Ultimately, that acclaim served to elevate the figure of the white female choreographer and, as much as did the growing legitimacy of Labanotation as a means of fixing movement, cleared a path for the passage of the Copyright Act of 1976. Yet, the status afforded Holm and de Mille did not extend to all white female dance-makers on Broadway. The chapter concludes by looking at the case of Faith Dane, a(n ambiguously) white dancer who, in 1962, claimed that she originated a choreographic composition—a satiric striptease number—during her audition for the Broadway musical *Gypsy* (1959). She consequently sued the producers for royalties under common law copyright protection. The court's ruling,

---

[20] Manning devises the concept of "cross-viewing," the process by which "spectators ... catch glimpses of subjectivities from social locations that differ from their own" (ibid., xvi), to account for these shifts in the meanings that accrued to blackness and whiteness. As she argues, by the early 1940s, cross-viewing made it possible for white spectators to read the performances of diaspora staged by black choreographers, lending the latter a new authority. Crucially, for Manning, cross-viewing also occurs across axes of class, gender, and sexuality.

[21] Manning, *Modern Dance, Negro Dance*, xv.

which rejected her claim on the grounds that her performance was immoral, indicates the continued sexed and classed divisions structuring female bodies' access to white privilege.

White Female Choreographers at Mid-Century

Before turning to the particularities of Holm's, de Mille's, and Dane's ventures, it is helpful to sketch some of the transformations of the 1940s as they impacted the formations of race, class, and gender on Broadway. By the 1940s, both women and theater dance held a markedly different status from where they stood at the end of the nineteenth century, when Loïe Fuller first pursued copyright protection for her choreography. For women and dance, too, the years surrounding World War II constituted a period of flux. The passage of the Nineteenth Amendment in 1920 had given women the right to vote, "the most basic right of citizenship," though women of color, like their male counterparts, remained virtually disenfranchised. Nevertheless, in the 1940s, as historian Susan Hartmann points out, even white women "found themselves subject to numerous state and federal laws which denied them rights and opportunities available to men," including being barred from jury service in twenty-four states.[22] Wartime transformations, especially the entry of unprecedented numbers of women into the workforce, "brought the most serious attention to women's status under the law since the days of the women's suffrage campaign."[23] The pressure on women to return to traditional domestic roles at the war's conclusion signaled the limits to the gendered social change the war provoked, but the 1940s gave new energy to women's campaign for equal pay and for passage of the equal rights amendment, first proposed in the 1920s (and yet to be ratified).[24]

In 1940, dance on the theater stage also occupied a very different position in the American cultural landscape from the one it had at the turn of the twentieth century. In the 1930s, building on the efforts of the so-called early moderns like Fuller and Ruth St. Denis, an array of dancers worked to establish a "high art" concert dance tradition in the United States. Although bifurcated into the racialized genres of "modern dance" and "Negro dance," artists like Martha Graham, Helen Tamiris, Doris Humphrey, Charles Weidman, Hanya Holm, Edna Guy, Hemsley Winfield, and Katherine Dunham cobbled

---

[22] Susan M. Hartmann, *The Home Front and Beyond: American Women in the 1940s* (Boston: Twayne, 1982), 123, 127.

[23] Ibid., 123.

[24] Ibid., 23, 130, 137.

together patronage from the New School for Social Research, the Bennington Summer School of the Dance, and a leftist network of organizations to produce evening-length dance concerts that, with the support of influential critics, gave concert dance a new legitimacy.[25] By the start of World War II, as dance scholar Julia Foulkes writes, modern dance was "no longer battling for legitimacy or shocking audiences": "Acknowledged leaders gave regular performances, and training flourished in colleges, universities, and dance schools."[26] With the founding of the School of American Ballet in 1934 by impresario Lincoln Kirstein and choreographer George Balanchine, ballet, too, was gaining a secure foothold in US culture.

As it did for women, the war years brought change to the field of concert dance. While ballet was on the rise, and African American dancers were finally beginning to find an expansion in their performance opportunities, white "modern dancers struggled to maintain momentum and growth."[27] As Manning explains, leftist dance waned as the 1930s came to a close, and the discontinuation of the School of the Arts at Bennington in the early 1940s meant the disappearance of a vital venue for the training and production of modern dance.[28] Even as Martha Graham's career continued to blossom, "the careers of other choreographers who had taught at Bennington chart a narrative of crisis and change." In 1944, the dance companies led by Hanya Holm, Humphrey-Weidman, and Helen Tamiris all disbanded.[29]

With sources of patronage drying up, it is little wonder that a number of concert dancers, Hanya Holm and Agnes de Mille among them, looked to the commercial sphere of Broadway for employment in the 1940s. Even in the preceding decade, the financial challenges facing ballet and modern dancers were sizable. Writing about these challenges in *And Promenade Home*, one of many books she authored, de Mille provides a sense of how dire the economic conditions were for dancers like her:

> Very few concert dancers succeeded during the thirties. The opportunities simply did not exist. There were, for one thing, no ballet companies, and for another, the musical theater was closed to us. So I found myself with not even a checking account of my own.... I tried

[25] See Manning, *Modern Dance, Negro Dance*.

[26] Julia Foulkes, *Modern Bodies: Dance and American Modernism from Martha Graham to Alvin Ailey* (Chapel Hill: University of North Carolina Press, 2002), 158–59.

[27] Ibid.; Manning, *Modern Dance, Negro Dance*, 121.

[28] Manning, *Modern Dance, Negro Dance*, 120.

[29] Ibid., 120–21.

to subsist on what I could earn teaching dancing classes, which was less than thirty dollars a week.[30]

Although de Mille had begun to find artistic success in the early 1940s—her evening-length ballet *Rodeo*, which was commissioned by the Ballet Russe de Monte Carlo and premiered in 1942, was well received and prompted Richard Rodgers and Oscar Hammerstein to invite her to choreograph the dances for *Oklahoma!*—the concert dance world could hardly compete with the financial remuneration that Broadway offered.[31] By 1950, according to biographer Carol Easton, de Mille earned over $125,000 for her work on several Broadway musicals; by contrast, royalties from her ballets that year amounted to only $1,400.[32]

However much Broadway "subsidized Agnes's ballet habit," the migration of concert dancers like de Mille and Holm to the commercial stage intensified the sense that modern dance was in crisis.[33] Gay Morris's book on modern dance in the postwar years opens with a discussion of the anxiety created by so many "high-art" dancers' pursuit of commercial work in the 1940s. Morris quotes *Dance Observer* editor Horton Foote, who lamented in 1944 that "Every day on the Theatrical Page we read of one more well-known dancer going to Broadway or Hollywood. It has become a mammoth exodus, a giant trend."[34] Dance critic Gertrude Lippincott shared Foote's concern that commercialism would squelch modern dance's experimental bent and endanger its "position in the field."[35] In a 1946 piece, she warned modern dancers not to "lower [their] standards by becoming 'chi-chi,' Broadway-theatrical, or downright cheap."[36] For these arbiters, Broadway not only represented an unequivocal step down on the hierarchy of culture; it also threatened to undermine modern dance's

---

[30] Agnes de Mille, *And Promenade Home* (Boston: Little, Brown, 1958 [1956]), 7.

[31] As Tim Carter reveals in his exhaustive account of the inception, rehearsing, production, and reception of *Oklahoma!*, de Mille quite forcefully angled for the role of choreographer, penning a letter to the Theatre Guild producer Teresa Helburn that urged Rodgers and Hammerstein to attend a performance of *Rodeo*. Tim Carter, *Oklahoma!: The Making of an American Musical* (New Haven, CT: Yale University Press, 2007), 44–45.

[32] Carol Easton, *No Intermissions: The Life of Agnes de Mille* (New York: Da Capo Press, 1996), 321.

[33] Ibid.

[34] Horton Foote, "The Long, Long Trek," *Dance Observer* (October 1944): 98; quoted in Gay Morris, *A Game for Dancers: Performing Modernism in the Postwar Years, 1945–1960* (Middletown, CT: Wesleyan University Press, 2006), 1.

[35] Morris, *Game for Dancers*, 3.

[36] Gertrude Lippincott, "Pilgrim's Way," *Dance Observer* (August–September 1946): 85; quoted in Morris, *Game for Dancers*, 6.

hard-won stature. Concert dancers' move toward Broadway thus highlighted the tensions between cultural and economic capital.

For female choreographers, the turn toward Broadway meant negotiating another kind of tension. Well prior to the upheaval of World War II, women who pursued choreographic careers on the concert stage challenged gender norms. In the emerging field of modern dance (in contrast to the fields of classical ballet and commercial theater), women assumed leadership positions by claiming for themselves the roles of choreographer and teacher as well as dancer.[37] De Mille chalked up women's power in this arena to dance's relative marginality, deeming it "no accident that the great dance revolutionaries have been largely women."[38] "No man ever barred the way" in the field of choreography, de Mille speculated, "because no man thought highly enough of the business to keep women out, as he had done from so many august, holy, or honorable occupations."[39] In the world of Broadway, however, a patriarchal structure remained firmly in place, making female choreographers subordinate to male producers, directors, and song- and music-writing teams. This proved challenging for an outspoken woman like de Mille. As biographer Easton puts it, "Agnes fought fiercely for what she believed in, and quite often she was right. But in a business run by men, there was real antagonism toward a woman who spoke her mind."[40] Like Loïe Fuller before her, de Mille often butted heads with the men whose authority trumped her own on Broadway.[41]

The move from the concert stage to the Broadway stage, accordingly, was not a seamless one for white female choreographers. Propelled by the promise of financial reward at a time when funding for concert dance was growing more scarce, artists like de Mille and Holm sacrificed a good deal of autonomy and, at least according to some observers, jeopardized their cultural status when they took jobs on Broadway. It was precisely the destabilizing threat of this move, I am proposing, that gave force to their pursuit of choreographic property rights. Copyright for Holm and de Mille, that is, was as much about bolstering their positions in a shifting cultural landscape as it was about halting the circulation of their choreography or collecting royalties on it. To get a

[37] Linda J. Tomko, *Dancing Class: Gender, Ethnicity, and Social Divides in American Dance, 1890–1920* (Bloomington: Indiana University Press, 1999), ix–xiii.

[38] De Mille, *Dance to the Piper* (Boston: Little, Brown, 1952 [1951]), 59.

[39] De Mille, *And Promenade Home*, 219. Linda Tomko also points out the converse: that "women's achievement of predominance in dance occupations, even their ascendance as choreographers, has won subordinate status for dance" (*Dancing Class*, 217).

[40] Easton, *No Intermissions*, 241.

[41] Tim Carter, for example, describes the "famously stormy" relationship between de Mille and the *Oklahoma!* production team. *Oklahoma!*, 123.

fuller sense of that landscape, we must bear in mind that the Broadway stage onto which white female choreographers migrated was hardly an empty one.

The "Golden Age" of Dis/Integration

There is no small degree of irony in the fact that "integration" was regarded as one of the central achievements of the so-called Golden Age of the Broadway musical. As Arthur Knight points out in *Disintegrating the Musical: Black Performance and American Musical Film*, the term "integration" carries multiple meanings: it can refer to corporate efforts to "rationalize, control, and expand the production and consumption" of products in the creation of "homogenized markets"; to the civil rights project of combating legally and socially enforced racial segregation; and to a "formal quality specific to the musical," namely, "a pattern of commensurability, coherence, and appropriateness between the story or drama and the music."[42] According to Knight, this last sense of the term first appeared in a 1943 review of Rodgers and Hammerstein's *Oklahoma!* and, shortly thereafter, in a review of the musical *Carmen Jones*, also by Hammerstein.[43] Because *Oklahoma!* contains no black characters and *Carmen Jones* no white ones, Knight observes, the aesthetic and "racial-social" meanings of integration fundamentally contradict one another. Yet the contradiction was no coincidence. Rather, Knight argues, the aesthetic integration of the musical—and the concomitant pleasure that the unification of formal elements produces for the spectator—is better seen as a response to the "disorienting" aspects of the other forms of integration.[44] At a time of great upheaval for the nation at large—World War II restructured the economy and precipitated the mass internment of Japanese Americans, even as civil rights groups like the NAACP were organizing large-scale challenges to racial segregation at a national level[45]—integration in the formal sense may have helped

[42] Arthur Knight, *Disintegrating the Musical: Black Performance and American Musical Film* (Durham, NC: Duke University Press, 2002), 8, 13.

[43] Ibid., 13. The review to first use "integration," according to Knight, was Lewis Nichols, "*Oklahoma!* A Musical Hailed as Delightful," *New York Times*, April 1, 1943, p. 27. Just a month later, dance critic John Martin praised de Mille's ballet "Laurey Makes Up Her Mind" for being "so integrated with the production as a whole that it actually carries forward the plot." "The Dance: De Mille's *Oklahoma*," *New York Times*, May 9, 1943, http://query.nytimes.com/mem/archive/pdf?res=F5081EF73C54107B93CBA9178ED85F478485F9. Accessed June 12, 2013.

[44] Knight, *Disintegrating the Musical*, 15.

[45] In 1941, President Franklin D. Roosevelt issued an executive order prohibiting racial discrimination in government services and the defense industry, but it was not until 1948 that the armed forces were desegregated.

assuage (or at least cover over) the disruptions and tensions accompanying the other two modes of integration.

Oklahoma! is a case in point of how "the creation of the ultimate utopian feeling in the integrated musical relied on an explicit social-racial segregation."[46] Based on a 1931 play titled *Green Grow the Lilacs*, the 1943 musical is, on the surface, a frontier romance between cowboys and farm girls set against the backdrop of Oklahoma's transformation from territory to state in the early twentieth century. According to theater scholar Andrea Most, however, the real subject of the musical is America and the unification of community.[47] Premiering just a little over a year after the bombing of Pearl Harbor, *Oklahoma!*'s celebration of American statehood tapped into a strong nationalistic spirit and ran continuously on Broadway for five years. Crucially, Most observes, the triumphant cohesiveness that the show achieves by the time the final curtain falls requires certain sacrifices, including and especially the expulsion of outsiders. In this all-white musical, the Other is figured most dramatically through the character of Jud, the brooding hired farmhand who competes with the good-natured cowboy Curly for the affections of the farm girl Laurey.[48] (Indeed, de Mille's most famous contribution to the musical was the ten-minute "dream" ballet she created to dramatize Laurey's dilemma in choosing between Jud and Curly.) An object of fear and fascination for Laurey, Jud is associated with a primitive sexuality and savageness and, in Most's insightful analysis, is "racially characterized" as a "dark" man who cannot be assimilated into "civilized" society.[49] His death during a battle with Curly in the musical's conclusion "cleanses the community of darkness" and enables the musical to achieve its "utopian vision of love, marriage, and statehood" in a "whitewashed landscape."[50]

Jud was not *Oklahoma!*'s only sacrificial victim. For those with an investment in tap, the musical also "killed" an entire genre of dancing. Actually, as

---

[46] Knight, *Disintegrating the Musical*, 16.

[47] Andrea Most, *Making Americans: Jews and the Broadway Musical* (Cambridge, MA: Harvard University Press, 2004), 104.

[48] The other Other in the musical is the character of Ali Hakim, a Persian peddler who, Most argues, actually represents the figure of the Jew (*Making Americans*, 107–8). Unlike Jud, Ali is successfully assimilated into the Oklahoman community by the musical's end.

[49] Most, *Making Americans*, 107. Building on Most's argument, Bruce Kirle suggests that Jud embodies "several kinds of Otherness"—signifying both the African American and the Native American, as well as an outsider to middle-class values. "Reconciliation, Resolution, and the Political Role of *Oklahoma!* in American Consciousness," *Theatre Journal* 55.2 (2003): 251–74. See also Carter, *Oklahoma!*, who surveys various interpretations of the Jud character (204).

[50] Most, *Making Americans*, 111, 117. See also Kirle, "Reconciliation, Resolution" for a thoughtful read of the political ideology of *Oklahoma!*

dance scholar Jacqui Malone describes, a host of factors contributed to the decline in tap dance's popularity in the 1940s: the economic depression of the 1930s, the conversion of vaudeville theaters into movie theaters, the overexposure and sloppy presentation of tap dance, the rise of bebop and rock-and-roll and the waning of big band jazz, and the 1944 tax levied against establishments with dance floors. But, "when asked what caused the demise of tap," Malone writes, "many of the living experts point to rock and roll or Agnes de Mille."[51] The perception that de Mille and *Oklahoma!* were responsible for the death of tap, which "reigned supreme" on Broadway during the 1920s and 1930s, was pronounced.[52] In the words of African American choreographer Buddy Bradley, "Agnes de Mille did a fine job of making dance advance the plot in *Oklahoma[!]*, but she turned her back on real American dance and everybody followed her example."[53] Bradley's wry comment reveals how keenly felt the rivalry was between dance genres, both on stage and within the national imaginary. It also makes evident the extent to which "from an African American perspective the so-called integrated musical was ... manifestly *not* integrated."[54] Whereas African American choreographers like Katherine Dunham experienced the 1940s as a period of expanding opportunities and managed to find success in overturning segregation policies in theaters across the country,[55] the opposite was true for tap dancers like Bradley, who experienced the so-called Golden Age of the Broadway musical as a period of shrinking opportunities and increasing ghettoization.

There is no disputing that *Oklahoma!* set in motion ballet's colonization of Broadway in the 1940s. De Mille biographer Easton notes that "Agnes's work was so influential that forty-six of the seventy-two Broadway musicals to open during the next three and a half years would include ballets. Twenty-one would have dream sequences, many of them bad imitations of *Oklahoma!*'s."[56] De Mille herself described the newfound vogue for "the ballet look" in department stores and on the streets of New York during *Oklahoma!*'s record-breaking run on Broadway:

[51] Jacqui Malone, *Steppin' on the Blues: The Visible Rhythms of African American Dance* (Urbana: University of Illinois Press, 1996), 114. See also Constance Valis Hill's section on tap's "so-called decline" in *Tap Dancing America: A Cultural History* (New York: Oxford University Press, 2010), 168–69.

[52] Malone, *Steppin' on the Blues*, 114.

[53] Marshall and Jean Stearns, *Jazz Dance: The Story of American Vernacular Dance* (New York: Schirmer Books, 1968), 168.

[54] Knight, *Disintegrating the Musical*, 16.

[55] Manning, *Modern Dance, Negro Dance*, 125.

[56] Easton, *No Intermissions*, 208.

Capezio devised a ballet shoe for street wear and every woman with or without an instep went flat-heeled. . . . Helena Rubenstein considered a new cosmetic called "The Ballet Look" and I was taken to lunch at the Russian Tea Room and asked to describe "The Real Ballet Look." "Exhaustion," I replied, and the idea was abandoned.

The boys and girls with the true ballet look, the erect, brisk and quiet figures carrying their boxes and baskets of practice clothes, began to scuttle hatless through the 40's of Times Square during that April. They were to become a familiar figure in the next decade. Frequently, their long black woolen tights could be glimpsed under their coats as they rushed from audition to audition.

The chorus girls and the chorus boy of the past, corrupt, sly, ruthless and professionally inept, gradually disappeared. And in their place came singers and dancers, trained and self-respecting.[57]

De Mille does not directly reference tap dance here, and when asked by a reporter "if she thought the craze for ballet would mean the end of tap dancing," she responded that she hoped not "because tap dancing is part of our culture—filtered down to us through the Negroes who picked it up from the Irish immigrants who settled in the Southern mountain country."[58] Still, her paean to the ballet dancer comes at the expense of the degraded chorus dancer, who presumably traded (but, according to de Mille, did not "train") in the tap styles that formerly dominated Broadway. (Elsewhere, de Mille specified that prior to the 1940s, dance on the commercial stage was comprised of "tap, acrobatic, ballroom, or musical comedy, the last a vague term applicable to anything successfully cute.")[59] Ballet's ascendancy also assumes a corporeal dimension in de Mille's telling, with the erect, efficiently moving body of the ballet dancer—what Brenda Dixon Gottschild would call the Europeanist aesthetic—becoming increasingly prevalent in Manhattan's public spaces.[60] The converse look—the grounded, Africanist aesthetic of the tap dancer—was presumably not in fashion in the wake of *Oklahoma!*, nor could legions of tap dancers be seen scuttling to and from auditions.

Of course, *Oklahoma!* did not literally send tap dance to its grave. While the practice certainly declined in popularity and may have gone "underground" in the 1940s and 1950s, tap dance acts were not entirely eradicated from the

---

[57] De Mille, *And Promenade Home*, 36.

[58] Clipping, n.d., n.s., Agnes de Mille Clippings File, Dance Division, NYPL.

[59] De Mille, *Dance to the Piper*, 116.

[60] See Brenda Dixon Gottschild, *Digging the Africanist Presence in American Performance: Dance and Other Contexts* (Westport, CT: Greenwood Press, 1996).

Figure 4.1 Agnes de Mille rehearsing the ballet aesthetic with dancers in *Allegro* (1947). Jerome Robbins Dance Division, The New York Public Library for the Performing Arts, Astor, Lenox and Tilden Foundations.

Broadway stage.[61] Actually, tap dancing was not even absent from the 1943 production of *Oklahoma!* As Tim Carter reports in his monograph on the making of *Oklahoma!*, an audition call went out for both tap and ballet dancers, and originally, the show contained two "specialty" tap dance numbers: one performed by George Church, who played the part of Jud in the dream ballet, and one performed by a red-headed tap dancer named Eric Victor.[62] During the show's out-of-town tryout run, both numbers were cut because they failed to advance the plot, and Victor subsequently resigned (or was fired).[63] But tap dancing was not expunged

[61] Hill, *Tap Dancing America*, 169.

[62] Carter, *Oklahoma!*, 59. Carter also notes that Merce Cunningham's name appears on an early rehearsal call list for the musical (60).

[63] Max Wilk, *OK!: The Story of* Oklahoma! (New York: Grove, 1993), 138–39; letter, Agnes de Mille to *Oklahoma!* cast, Agnes de Mille Collection, Dance Division, NYPL. Wilk's book states that Victor "took a settlement of his contract and left the show" (139), while de Mille tells the cast that Victor was fired because his tap dance number was no longer needed. Carter's book bears out that Victor was fired, noting that Victor threatened legal action against the Theatre Guild, who were forced to pay him ten weeks' salary if he did not book another engagement (*Oklahoma!*, 156).

from the number "Kansas City," which was integral to the musical's plot. Showing off the new dancing learned during a visit to the metropolis, the character Will Parker explains, "That's rag-time. Seen a couple of colored fellers doin' it."[64] Played by Lee Dixon in the original production, Will performs "the two-step, tap dancing ... and occasional square dance steps" in what scholar Ann Sears calls a "potpourri of popular culture."[65] Because de Mille, by her own account, knew only four basic tap steps, she relied on the dancers to choreograph these numbers.[66] Her professed lack of knowledge notwithstanding, de Mille "used tap fairly often in her work," including in her ballet *Rodeo*, where its appearance was considered "revolutionary."[67] Even as it conquered Broadway, ballet at times shared stage space with tap dance, the practice it helped push aside.

The ballet that appeared on the musical theater stage, moreover, was not purely classical in style but, rather, a modified version that had absorbed elements of modern dance, various American folk traditions, and pedestrian gestures. De Mille was quite open about her indebtedness to folk forms, once telling a reporter that "practically everything she knows of choreography has its roots in folk-dancing forms," and that "her dancing comes naturally out of her enormous affection for and interest in folk dancing, which she calls our most legitimate racial heritage."[68] De Mille's "racial" surely denotes "national" here, but she encouraged young dancers to study both "square dances and jazz" since those forms were indigenous to the United States.[69] She also compared the process of "diversify[ing] the root impulse" of ballet to George Gerswhin's infusion of classical music with (African American) jazz influences. Placing herself in a cohort of American and British choreographers, including Anthony Tudor, Ninette de Valois, Eugene Loring, and Jerome Robbins, de Mille explained that their collective contribution consisted of "adding gestures and rhythms we had grown up with, using them seriously and without condescension for the first time."[70] This embrace of vernacular movements is evident

---

[64] Richard Rodgers and Oscar Hammerstin II, *Oklahoma!* in *Six Plays by Rodgers and Hammerstein* (New York: Modern Library, n.d.), 16; quoted in Knight, *Disintegrating the Musical*, 252n23. In the 1955 film version, the line has been changed to "seen a couple of actors doin' it." Fred Zinneman, director, *Oklahoma!* Twentieth Century-Fox, 1955.

[65] Ann Sears, "The Coming of the Musical Play: Rodgers and Hammerstein," in *The Cambridge Companion to the Musical*, ed. William A. Everett and Paul R. Laird, 2nd ed. (Cambridge: Cambridge University Press, 2008), 153.

[66] Agnes de Mille Clippings File, Dance Division, n.d., n.s., NYPL.

[67] Easton, *No Intermissions*, 210, 427, 195.

[68] "The Dancing De Mille," *Cue*, May 6, 1944, pp. 11–12, Agnes de Mille Clippings File, Dance Division, NYPL.

[69] De Mille, *To a Young Dancer: A Handbook* (Boston: Little, Brown, 1960), 62.

[70] De Mille, *Dance to the Piper*, 235.

even in *Oklahoma!*'s celebrated dream ballet, which contains not only jetés, developés, and lifts, but also pantomimed hand clapping, heel-click jumps, bow-legged galloping, hip rolls, and can-can kicks. It was the development of this "new style of American ballet closer to acting than before, closer to natural body rhythms," film scholar Jane Feuer writes, that made these choreographers' work more accessible to Broadway (and subsequently Hollywood) in the first place.[71]

Ballet's displacement of tap, then, was neither immediate nor wholesale, and when the two traditions, so often positioned as opposites, met up on the Broadway stage, the aesthetic and rhythmic distance between them had begun to close. The formally integrated but racially segregated musicals of the 1940s contained moments and spaces of overlap between genres—modern, ballet, folk, tap—that carried different raced, classed, and gendered resonances but were all competing for status as "American" dance.[72] For "high-brow" choreographers, the next section shows, the assertion of intellectual property rights helped ease the friction created by this generic intermingling. But quite a bit had to be papered over for the white female choreographer to emerge as a legally sanctioned author and owner of an "original" work on Broadway.

Hanya Holm and *Kiss Me, Kate*: Resolving the "Temptation to Be Startled"

On December 30, 1948, *Kiss Me, Kate*, the backstage musical about a group of performers in a Baltimore production of Shakespeare's *The Taming of the Shrew*, opened at the New Century Theatre on Broadway. Written by

---

[71] Feuer, *The Hollywood Musical*, 8.

[72] The term "ballet Americana," so strongly associated with de Mille, is itself a site of racial contestation. In 1999 and 2000, the dance scholar Constance Valis Hill conducted interviews with the late Katherine Dunham and asked her what she made of the claim that de Mille's *Oklahoma!* choreography was the first to fuse "American vernacular dancing, ballet, and Broadway show dancing." By 1943, when *Oklahoma!* premiered, Dunham had already begun her innovative experiments that integrated African American social dances, Afro-Caribbean ritual dances, and ballet. In response to Hill's question, Dunham conceded that she was "really annoyed" with de Mille for neglecting to mention Dunham "as a counterpart." Hill, "Collaborating with Balanchine on *Cabin in the Sky*: Interviews with Katherine Dunham," in *Kaiso!: Writings by and about Katherine Dunham*, ed. VéVé A. Clark and Sara E. Johnson (Madison: University of Wisconsin Press, 2005), 242–43. De Mille's failure to credit Dunham is part and parcel of the "invisibilization" of African American contributions to American dance that scholars like Brenda Dixon Gottschild have documented. See Gottschild, *Digging the Africanist Presence*.

Bella and Samuel Spewack, with music and lyrics by Cole Porter, the show ran for 1,077 performances, becoming "one of the outstanding successes of the American theater."[73] Hanya Holm, the musical's choreographer, was a disciple of German expressionist dancer Mary Wigman and had moved to the United States in 1931 to direct the New York branch of the Wigman School, renamed the Hanya Holm school in 1936. From 1934 to 1939, Holm also taught at the Bennington School of Dance in Vermont, the precursor to the American Dance Festival. In 1937, she premiered her celebrated dance work *Trend* and began touring the country with her own dance company. Forced by financial pressures to disband her troupe in 1944, as noted above, Holm went on to choreograph dances for several Broadway musicals in addition to *Kiss Me, Kate*, including *My Fair Lady* (1956) and *Camelot* (1960).

The choreography for the "relentlessly danced" *Kiss Me, Kate* ran the gamut of dance styles, including, as Walter Terry wrote in the *New York Herald Tribune*, "classic ballet, modern dance, jitterbugging, soft-shoe, acrobatics, court dance, folk dance and episodes which might be described as rhythmic playfulness."[74] The musical's show-within-a show framework lent itself to this variety, with the Shakespearean segments facilitating a pavane court dance, for example, and the backstage scenes calling for jazzier, more contemporary dance numbers.

This was not exactly the kind of material for which Holm was known. Her lecture-demonstrations and choreographic compositions from the 1930s and 1940s melded German expressionist and emerging American modern dance styles and were comprised of ballet-inflected lyrical movements, repetitive exercises, and methodical explorations of space. Though Holm made her Broadway debut earlier in 1948 in *Ballet Ballads*, a suite of three one-act dances to which she contributed a number called "The Eccentricities of Davey Crockett," *Kiss Me, Kate* was seen as a departure for her, and critics took note. As John Martin gushed in the *Times*, "Nobody could have stepped more gracefully into a new field than Hanya Holm has done in her transition from the concert dance to show business." The dances in *Kiss Me, Kate*, he wrote, "have retained the taste, formal integrity and the respect for the movement of the human body which belong to the concert

[73] David Ewen, *New Complete Book of the American Musical Theater* (New York: Holt, Rinehart and Winston, 1970), 277.

[74] Ethan Mordden, *Beautiful Mornin': The Broadway Musical in the 1940s* (New York: Oxford University Press, 1999), 256; Walter Terry, "Dance: Miss Holm and Her Fine '*Kiss Me, Kate*' Choreography," *New York Herald Tribune*, n.d., n.p., Hanya Holm Clippings File, Dance Division, NYPL.

Figure 4.2 Glen Tetley, Shirley Eckl, and other performers in the "Pavane" section of Hanya Holm's choreography for the original Broadway production of *Kiss Me, Kate* (1948). Eileen Darby Images, Inc. Jerome Robbins Dance Division, The New York Public Library for the Performing Arts, Astor, Lenox and Tilden Foundations.

dance, without in the least disturbing the equanimity of the paying customers." This was all the more impressive to Martin because of the choreography's frequent dalliance with "the hot and the blue and the jittery." As such, Holm's work on the musical struck him as "so remote from what she has done in the past that there is a temptation to be startled, even to feel a momentary doubt that she could have had anything to do with it." "Nowhere," he emphasized, "from the rise of the first curtain to the fall of the last, is there a characteristic Holm movement." Instead, he found proof of Holm's artistry in her capacity to make dances that were "completely of the texture of the show." Grumbling that "it is highly unorthodox to think of a Broadway musical as having style," Martin admitted that *Kiss Me, Kate* possessed two distinct styles:

> It is, on the one hand, smart, witty, intellectually fresh and charming, as when it deals with a pair of actors playing their own marital give-and-take against a background of "The Taming of the Shrew"; on the other hand, chiefly in a series of fairly irrelevant interludes, it

goes in for a style that can perhaps be described as a kind of chichi low-down.

Holm, he concluded, gave herself over to bringing out both styles "to the top of their bent."[75]

Martin's celebration of Holm is striking for its apparent paradoxes. He seems to bend over backward to applaud her for bringing her concert dance sensibility to Broadway and for simultaneously effacing herself, so much so that he briefly questions whether she choreographed the musical's dancing at all. There is no unique "stamp" of the choreographer here, no signature movements, but their absence only increases the praise for Holm.[76] For the influential critic Martin, it is the ability of the "highest-browed of modern dance creators" to produce "a set of completely un-highbrow dances" that merits such approbation.[77]

The class dimensions of Martin's appraisal are barely veiled. Though Holm hails from the "high art" realm of concert dance, she refuses to "look down her nose at the Broadway medium," as he wrote in another review. Rather, she delivers dance numbers "rich in invention and in formal design" to "paying customers" who are "not aware that they care about such things."[78] Martin's disdain for show business is palpable, and the effect of his comments is only to reify the art versus entertainment divide. We can almost see the energy he expends to re-establish the dividing lines between concert dance and commercial fare that have been clouded by Holm's move to Broadway.

The shock of Holm's engagement with the "chichi low-down" and the reliance on a hierarchy of highbrow and lowbrow also betray a racial dynamic at work in Martin's class distinctions. While, as David Savran writes, "the nineteenth-century phrenology that coined the words ["highbrow" and "lowbrow"] had long been discredited, the racist implications of these categories were less forgotten than disavowed in a society that was just beginning a long and violent process of desegregation."[79] If the racial connotations of Martin's

[75] John Martin, "The Dance: Debut," New York Times, January 30, 1949, p. X6.

[76] Unlike Martin, the Dance Observer's Nik Krevitsky found "the unmistakable Holm stamp ... very much in evidence" in Kiss Me, Kate. For him, the "dances build in a typical Holm manner" with a "simple theme develop[ing] with almost infinite variations until a brief dance interlude builds symphonically into thrilling proportions." Nik Krevitsky, "Hanya Holm's Dances in 'Kiss Me, Kate,'" Dance Observer (May 1949): 68.

[77] John Martin, "Broadway on Its Toes," New York Times, January 23, 1949, p. SM18.

[78] John Martin, "The Dance: Broadway," New York Times, January 14, 1951, p. X8.

[79] Savran, "Middlebrow Anxiety," 3.

"brow" terminology were only latent, his reference to "the hot and the blue and the jittery" was a less opaque code for the presence of African American dance styles in Holm's choreography. Noting his preference for the "elegan[t] dances of the Shakespeare scenes," Martin also admires Holm's efforts in two of the backstage numbers: "Another Op'nin', Another Show," in which Holm's "compositional skills ... give distinction to what might otherwise be just an ordinary jazz routine," and "Too Darn Hot," "one of the show's more popular but less memorable items," for which she provides "a background and a continuity."[80]

In contrast to Martin, most critics favored these two numbers, described by Holm as "intrinsically American jazz dancing."[81] "Another Op'nin'," which launched the first act, was sung by Hattie the maid, one of a handful of black parts in the almost exclusively white musical, played in the original production by Annabelle Hill. The dancing, however, featured an all-white ensemble—six men and six women—who performed in a "lyric jazz" style that was essentially an amalgamation of jazz and ballet.[82]

"Too Darn Hot," meanwhile, which opened the second act, displayed a "different style of jazziness" that was no doubt attributable to its black performers.[83] Set in a backstage alley where cast members played dice and smoked cigarettes, the number was sung by Lorenzo Fuller, who played the black valet Paul, and spotlighted what one critic termed the "lusty Harlem hoofing," and another the "torrid pavement dancing," of a pair of "Specialty Dancers": the African Americans Fred Davis and Eddie Sledge (known as Fred and Sledge), who were eventually joined by the white soloist Harold Lang.[84] Notwithstanding Martin's quibble, "Too Darn Hot" was a showstopper.

Holm's contributions to "Too Darn Hot" were limited to creating "some non-intruding but atmospherically effective jitterbug passages" for the Dancing Ensemble, who supported Fuller, Davis, Sledge, and Lang.[85] The Labanotated

---

[80] Martin, "The Dance: Debut," X6.

[81] Hanya Holm, "*Kiss Me, Kate,*" n.s., n.p., September 23, 1951, Hanya Holm Scrapbooks, Dance Division, NYPL.

[82] *Kiss Me, Kate* Labanotated score, Dance Notation Bureau Archives; Arthur Todd, "A Brace of Musicals This Season on Broadway," *Dance*, March 1949, 28–29; *Kiss Me, Kate* Dance Clippings File, Dance Division, NYPL.

[83] Ann Hutchinson Guest, "The Golden Age of the Broadway Musical: A Personal Reminiscence," *Dance Chronicle* 16.3 (1993): 363.

[84] "Theater Dance," Clipping from *PM Star,* January 4, 1949, Hanya Holm Scrapbooks, Dance Division, NYPL; Brooks Atkinson, "At the Theatre: 'Kiss Me, Kate,'" *New York Times on the web*, December 31, 1948, http://www.nytimes.com/books/98/11/29/specials/porter-kate.html. Accessed June 30, 2011.

[85] Terry, "Dance: Miss Holm."

score for "Too Darn Hot" records only this background dancing, with the following explanation:

> This is a jazz number done with three negros [sic] who sang and danced. The exact arrangement varied according to what the negros [sic] could do, it was worked out as a duet with the third taking over as soloist part of the time. None of this is recorded as it was so individual. What is recorded is what the group did in the background. If the dance were to be reconstructed the solo parts would have to be inserted which would mean fresh choreography.[86]

This parenthetical description, intended only to account for an absence in the score, is freighted with meaning. So "individual" that it could not be recorded, so variable that it required "fresh choreography" each time the musical was staged, "Too Darn Hot" epitomizes the "excisable, free-standing" nature of the specialty number.[87] As Arthur Knight writes, in its fragmentary form, the specialty number disrupts the ideal of the unified, integrated musical. And because it was often the only segment to feature African American performers in an otherwise all-white musical, as was the case with "Too Darn Hot," specialty numbers represented a means of "dis/integrating" the musical—a way for African American performers, critics, and spectators to contest the contradictory and exclusionary logic of the so-called integrated musical and to create "new forms and feelings."[88] Registering to some as "rather alien to the rest of the choreography," the jazz dance of "Too Darn Hot" interrupted both the whiteness of Kiss Me, Kate and the "integration" of its aesthetic components.[89]

Knight writes that the provenance of specialty numbers, given their tendency to "wander," is "often murky."[90] The written record of Kiss Me, Kate contributes to such murkiness by cloaking the African American dancers of "Too Darn Hot" in anonymity. Like the Labanotated score, the Kiss Me, Kate script describes the players in this scene only as "THREE NEGROES"—not to be confused with the "DANCERS," a reference to the all-white ensemble.[91]

[86] Kiss Me, Kate Labanotated Score.

[87] Knight, Disintegrating the Musical, 19.

[88] Ibid., 16–17.

[89] Todd, "A Brace of Musicals," 28–29. Kiss Me, Kate was generally regarded as a successfully integrated musical. See Rebellato, "'No Theatre Guild Attraction Are We,'" 65, 67, although he takes issue with the critical consensus on this point.

[90] Knight, Disintegrating the Musical, 19.

[91] Kiss Me Kate—Script, n.d., NYPL.

Nevertheless, the record does make clear that the specialty dancers themselves, not Holm, created the core choreography for "Too Darn Hot."

Quite a few African American dance duos rotated in and out of this slot in the late 1940s and early 1950s. Fred and Sledge performed continuously in the musical for roughly two years and were succeeded by Charles Cook and Ernest Brown while *Kiss Me, Kate* was still on Broadway (it ran until July 1951).[92] Bobby and Foster Johnson appeared in "Too Darn Hot" in the national touring ensemble, and a pair named the Wallace Brothers assumed the roles of specialty dancers for the British production.[93] In 1953, Honi Coles and Cholly Atkins performed in a summer stock production of the musical in Texas.[94] All were part of a black vernacular tradition of two-man comedy and class-act dance teams that peaked during the swing era of the 1930s and early1940s.[95] Where comedy teams typically incorporated humor and eccentric dancing into their routines and class or "flash" acts emphasized elegance and technical exactitude, both combined virtuosic, rhythmic tapping with spectacular acrobatics. In a minute-long 1950 television appearance on "The Colgate Comedy Hour," Fred and Sledge can be seen cartwheeling, sliding, dropping into the splits, and performing trenches.[96] Although Holm's ensemble performed only in the background in "Too Darn Hot," at least for the duration of this jazz number, black tap dancers appeared beside white ballet- and modern-trained dancers.

One way of reading the absence of the "Too Darn Hot" choreography from the *Kiss Me, Kate* Labanotated score is as resistive. In their evasion of documentation, that is, we might see the African American specialty dancers as skirting possession by Holm.[97] We might even read this evasion along the same lines as

---

[92] Stearns, *Jazz Dance*, 245.

[93] Hanya Holm Scrapbooks, NYPL. Bobby Johnson also evidently sang "Too Darn Hot" alongside Cook and Brown in the Boston production of the musical in 1950. *Kiss Me, Kate* Clippings File, Theatre Collection, NYPL. Program, *Kiss Me, Kate*, New Theatre Oxford, London, 1951 in *Kiss Me, Kate* Programs, Hanya Holm Collection, Dance Division, NYPL. The Wallace Brothers, Norman and Scott, performed at the Cotton Club in the 1930s, toured London and Paris, and appeared on *The Ed Sullivan Show* in 1963. Norman, who also performed with the Crackerjacks, a tumbling and tap comedy troupe, was known for his acrobatic talents. Stearns, *Jazz Dance*, 264–66; J. M. Lawrence, "Norman Wallace; Tap Dancer Who Started in Vaudeville," *Boston Globe*, September 16, 2008, p. D8.

[94] Cholly Atkins and Jacqui Malone, *Class Act: The Jazz Life of Choreographer Cholly Atkins* (New York: Columbia University Press, 2001), 97.

[95] Stearns, *Jazz Dance*, 244–45.

[96] *Colgate Comedy Hour*, NBC, November 5, 1950; producer-director Charles Friedman, Inventory Number VA 10728 T, UCLA Film & Television Archive.

[97] See Anthea Kraut, "Fixing Improvisation: Copyright and African American Vernacular Dancers in the Early Twentieth Century," in *The Oxford Handbook of Critical Improvisation*

Figure 4.3 One of the Wallace Brothers, likely Norman, performing some virtuosic choreography in a 1951 London production of *Kiss Me, Kate* as other cast members look on. Photo by Bert Hardy/Getty Images.

Knight's "dis/integration," as a rupture in the unity of the choreographic work and therefore a destabilization of the choreographer as a cohesive figure. But the recognition that Holm received as choreographer of *Kiss Me, Kate*, including her copyright victory and a New York Drama Critics' Award, poses some problems to an oppositional reading. It is hard to ignore how readily white authorship could swallow up black choreographic labor, suturing any fissures in the coherence of the choreographer-subject.

A brief detour to consider the experience of Coles and Atkins in another Broadway musical, choreographed not by Holm but by de Mille, serves to illustrate. In 1949, prior to their appearance in *Kiss Me, Kate*, the pair joined the cast of *Gentlemen Prefer Blondes*. Although they were recruited for the show, tensions were present from the onset because, as Coles relayed, "ballet dancers looked down on tap then."[98] Initially asked by the playwright

Studies, Volume 1, ed. George E. Lewis and Benjamin Piekut (New York: Oxford University Press, forthcoming) for more on that line of argument.

[98] David Hinckley, "A Honey of a Hoofer," *New York Daily News*, Sunday Magazine, August 7, 1983, p. 9.

Anita Loos to speak in Negro dialect, the pair refused and consequently sat idle for weeks.[99] Marshall and Jean Stearns describe how Coles and Atkins eventually found their way into a second-act number called "Mamie Is Mimi":

> "During rehearsals Agnes de Mille didn't know what to do with us," says Coles, "so finally Julie [*sic*] Styne, who hired us, took us aside and said, 'Look, why don't you fellows work up something, and I'll get her to look at it.'" They located arranger Benny Payne, who knew how to write for tap-dance acts, and the three of them worked out a routine. "One afternoon, Miss de Mille took time off to look at it," says Atkins. "She liked it and told us to keep it in."
>
> On went the show with the Coles-Atkins-Payne routine a hit, and Agnes de Mille listed as choreographer in the program. "Later on we had to get her permission to use our routine on Jack Haley's Ford Hour," says Coles. "She was very nice about it." In her autobiography Miss de Mille writes that the 'Mamie Is Mimi' number, along with several others, was devised 'in a single short rehearsal,' presumably by Miss de Mille. This was the standard practice.[100]

Though it would be specious to treat the cases of Coles and Atkins in *Gentlemen Prefer Blondes* and Davis and Sledge in *Kiss Me, Kate* as interchangeable, it seems safe to assume that "Too Darn Hot" was put together in a somewhat analogous way. Returning to the missing notation in the copyrighted Labanotated score, the use of the passive voice to recount how the jazz tap number evolved—"it was worked out"—assumes greater significance. This same syntactical logic, which withheld agency from the African American dancers, surely facilitated statements like those of Charles Bowden, an assistant to *Kiss Me, Kate*'s director: his recollection about the evolution of the "Too Darn Hot" number was that "Hanya seemed to choreograph it at once."[101] However much the tap dancing in "Too Darn Hot" contrasted with Holm's "brisk and lyrical ballets," it was all too easy for her cultural capital, as the "highest-browed of modern dance creators," to eclipse the labor of the African American dancers on whose creativity her choreographic success partly depended.[102]

---

[99] Hill, *Tap Dancing America*, 170.

[100] Stearns, *Jazz Dance*, 309

[101] William McBrien, *Cole Porter* (New York: Vintage, 1998), 315.

[102] Brooks Atkinson, "At the Theatre," *New York Times*, January 9, 1952, p. 24. One instance of the elision of the choreographic labor of the African American dancers is Lisa Jo Sagolla's citation

Holm's legally sanctioned status as sole choreographer of *Kiss Me, Kate* masked the labor of additional dancers as well. As others have noted, Holm characteristically relied on improvisation as a compositional method in both her classes and her choreography. Modern dancer and choreographer Alwin Nikolais, for example, recalled that "when Hanya was working on a particular subject she would frequently ask the dancers to improvise on the subject and she would spot the interesting aspects the individual dancer might come up with. Once recognizing these aspects, she would hold onto them, remake them, or develop them from that point into her choreography."[103] Holm biographer Walter Sorell emphasizes the importance of this method for choreographing solo dances in musicals, describing how "Hanya watches the particular attributes of a soloist and then tries to find a range of movement to suit that particular body."[104]

Interviews with dancers from the original *Kiss Me, Kate* production, recorded on the 1988 video *Hanya: Portrait of a Pioneer*, make clear the extent to which she imported this modern compositional technique into the Broadway milieu. Glen Tetley, who danced in and worked as Holm's assistant on *Kiss Me, Kate*, explained that "this was an unheard of way of working in the speeded-up atmosphere of a Broadway stage, and when Hanya ... set up the structure of an improvisation class, say for the first day of a show like *Kiss Me, Kate*, there were a lot of blank looks." Some, like Harold Lang, one of the musical's leads, were openly hostile to Holm's improvisational methods. A principal at the American Ballet Theatre, Lang initially protested, declaring, "I will do anything you want but you are going to have to show me. I am not going to make up steps." Eventually relenting, he "threw in a few steps of *Swan Lake*" and started to "blend what she was giving me with the techniques that I had learned in performing musical comedy and ballet."[105] Like Lang, Shirley Eckl, another lead dancer in the musical, was a renowned member of the American Ballet Theatre, so it is likely that her classical technique also left its mark on *Kiss Me, Kate*.[106] It would seem, then, that what critic John Martin identified as

of the "Too Darn Hot" tap number as an "example of Holm's inventiveness." "While adhering to the standard tap vocabulary," she writes, "Holm used sharp diagonal lines and triangular formations (two of her spatial trademarks) to develop simple tap rhythms into a dance that toyed with space and speed in a most sophisticated manner." "The Influence of Modern Dance on American Musical Theatre Choreography of the 1940s," *Dance: Current Selected Research* 2 (1990): 64.

[103] Quoted in Walter Sorell, *Hanya Holm: The Biography of an Artist* (Middletown, CT: Wesleyan University Press, 1969), 165.

[104] Ibid.

[105] *Hanya: Portrait of a Pioneer* [videorecording], produced by Nancy Mason Hauser, Dance Horizons Video, 1988.

[106] Ann Hutchinson Guest's discussion of the musical corroborates the recollections of the original cast members. "The nature of the dances in *Kate*," she writes, "allowed for specific

the musical's stylistic split between the more "elegant" Shakespearean dancing and the jazzier interludes was in part a manifestation of the different corporeal dispositions and choreographic contributions of the dancers with whom Holm worked. That is not to say that Holm was undeserving of the credit she received for the majority of the dances in *Kiss Me, Kate*, nor that her own choreographic labor was any less than that of the cast. It is to point out, rather, that the choreography that became her intellectual property did not originate solely or directly from her.[107]

If Holm's use of improvisation to generate movement seemed "out of this world" to the ballet-trained Lang, it was a compositional strategy that was far from alien to those trained in African American dance traditions.[108] Malone names improvisation as "one of the key elements in the creation of vernacular dance," and both Brenda Dixon Gottschild and Susan Leigh Foster have pointed to the Africanist influences on white modern and postmodern choreographers' turn to improvisation.[109] Though Holm's improvisational practice traced back to her training with Mary Wigman, the co-presence of European "high art" and Africanist "low art" choreographic approaches in the making of *Kiss Me, Kate* suggests how constructed the opposition between the two is. At the very least, there is irony in the fact that a white modern dance artist "made history" by winning copyright protection, thereby elevating the figure of the choreographer, using a compositional technique long embraced by African American artists, whose expressive output has so often been dismissed as custom-bound and derivative rather than experimental and innovative.

Instead of calling into question notions of the choreographer as the autonomous creator, however, Holm's working methods in the mixed-race and mixed-genre venue of Broadway seem to have had precisely the converse effect. As John Martin's comments evidence, perceptions of a stark contrast between the "high-browed" Holm and the "middle-browed" arena of musical theater served to make Holm's choreographic expertise more conspicuous, not less. I would even suggest that the elevation of Holm was a necessary byproduct of her migration to Broadway and the appearance of her choreography alongside

---

contributions to be made by the performers." "The Golden Age of the Broadway Musical," 364–65.

[107] Holm also relied on the work of dance collectors like Curt Sachs in deriving the folk choreography for *Kiss Me, Kate*. Her notes for the production contain descriptions of the Fandango and the Tarantella transcribed directly from Sachs's *World History of the Dance* (New York: W. W. Norton, 1963 [1937]). Hanya Holm Papers, NYPL.

[108] *Hanya: Portrait of a Pioneer.*

[109] Malone, *Steppin' on the Blues*, 33; Gottschild, *Digging the Africanist Presence*, 49; Susan Leigh Foster, *Dances That Describe Themselves: The Improvised Choreography of Richard Bull* (Middletown, CT: Wesleyan University Press, 2002), 24–34.

African American jazz-tap dancers, a means of re-stabilizing racial and artistic hierarchies and "reiterating the privilege of whiteness."[110] Just as critics insisted that, despite the disruption of the show-stopping African American jazz-tap number, all of the dancing in *Kiss Me, Kate* was "firmly integrated into the show to contribute to the achieving of a total theatrical impression," the allocation of so much credit to Holm served an integrative function, assimilating under the figure of the white choreographer the fragmented and differently located sources of the musical's dancing.[111] It is also possible that the distinction that Holm gained through her association with racialized forms and styles played a role in the Copyright Office's decision to award her a copyright for her *Kiss Me, Kate* choreography. In other words, it was not just Labanotation that was gaining acceptance in official halls of power but also the preeminence of the white choreographer.[112]

The need to reassert white privilege, it goes without saying, was never offered as a reason for Holm's pursuit of copyright protection, nor for the Copyright Office's willingness to grant it. The chain of events that led to Holm's 1952 copyright can be traced back to a 1950 article by *Times* critic John Martin. In a piece that year, titled "They Score a Dance as Others Do Music," he wrote about the coming of age of Labanotation as a method for recording movement. Martin credited the Dance Notation Bureau, established in 1940, with increasing the use and acceptance of Labanotation and reports that such choreographers as George Balanchine, Doris Humphrey, Martha Graham, and Holm had all commissioned the notation of their works.[113] For Martin, the tireless champion of modern dance, Labanotation promised to provide "cultural stability and continuity" for "dance as an art."[114] Among Martin's readers was Richard MacCarteney, the chief of the Reference Division of the

---

[110] See Susan Manning's argument about a photograph of Bill Robinson standing next to Martha Graham that ran in a December 1939 issues of *Dance Observer*, which prompted editors to re-assert modern dance's superiority to jazz dance. *Modern Dance, Negro Dance*, 115, 118.

[111] Terry, "Dance: Miss Holm."

[112] Legal scholar Evie Whiting notes that despite the credit contemporaneous observers gave to the growing acceptance of Labanotation for the Copyright Office's decision to grant Holm a copyright, "there may have been more subjective judgments at play ... given that other musical choreographers were not as lucky." Evie Whiting, "Square Dance: Fitting the Square Peg of Fixation into the Round Hole of Choreographic Works," *Vanderbilt Law Review* 65 (May 2012): 1271–72.

[113] The Dance Notation Bureau was an energetic advocate for choreographic copyright, printing articles about choreographers' legal rights in its newsletter, and, in 1977, hosting a conference for choreographers and lawyers to discuss the passage of the 1976 Copyright Act. See the "Copyright" folder in the Dance Notation Bureau Archives.

[114] John Martin, "They Score a Dance as Others Do Music," *New York Times*, July 2, 1950, p. 10 +.

Copyright Office, one of whose functions was to acquire copyright deposits for the Library of Congress. On July 19, 1950, MacCarteney composed a letter to Ann Hutchinson at the Dance Notation Bureau.[115] Describing himself as a "lay admirer of the dance," MacCarteney asked Hutchinson whether she had "at all considered the possibility of copyrighting the scores of new ballets as expressed by the dance notation." A Certificate of Copyright Registration, he ventured, "may be of great value," and he speculated that the copyright would protect not only the score but also the "dance itself against performance except when authorized by the proprietor of the copyright." In a return letter to MacCarteney, Hutchinson affirmed that Labanotation had proven itself a reliable method of documentation and inquired whether a special classification for choreographic works could be created. Replying in the negative, MacCarteney recommended "dramatic composition" as the most appropriate classification.[116]

MacCarteney's solicitation was likely also motivated by recent changes in the Copyright Office Regulations. According to a 1952 article by legal commentator Leon Mirell, in 1948, the same year that *Kiss Me, Kate* premiered on Broadway, the Office added "pantomimes" and "ballets" to its list of examples of work that could be registered under Class D, dramatic or dramatico-musical compositions.[117] "Prior to that time," Mirell writes, "the Regulations ... included 'dances' among its list of subjects *not* falling under the designation of 'dramatic compositions.'" Mirell attributed the change to a shift in the significations that dance carried. The fact that under the prior regulations, dances were grouped "with such things as 'animal shows, sleight-of-hand performances' and 'acrobatic or circus tricks'" as ineligible for protection suggested to Mirell "that the Copyright Office had tap, acrobatic and ballroom dances in mind." The use of the term "ballets" in the new regulations, in contrast, pointed to an association between dance and the much more reputable "classical dance theater." The ascendance of ballet and the decline of tap, in other words, did not go unnoticed in Washington, DC. The thinking may have been that ballets were more "dramatic" than their "low art" counterparts. But it is not much of a stretch to conclude that the growing legitimacy of American modern dance and ballet, the shifting landscape on Broadway, and the rising

[115] Richard S. MacCarteney to Ann Hutchinson, July 19, 1950, Dance Notation Bureau Archives.

[116] Richard S. MacCarteney to Ann Hutchinson, August 4, 1950, Hanya Holm Papers, Dance Division, NYPL.

[117] Leon I. Mirell, "Legal Protection for Choreography," *New York University Law Review* 27.5 (November 1952): 803.

status of the white choreographer prompted a re-thinking among Copyright Office officials about dance's suitability for protection.

The circumstances proved just right for Holm to capitalize on dance's new connotations. One month prior to MacCarteney's exchange with Hutchinson, Holm had hired her to notate *Kiss Me, Kate*'s dances during rehearsals for a replacement cast. (A dancer herself, Hutchinson wound up stepping in to perform in the musical when another dancer fell ill, and she reportedly learned the dances over the course of a weekend by studying her Labanotated notes.)[118] The notated score was finally completed sometime after *Kiss Me, Kate*'s London premiere in 1951, microfilmed, and on January 24, 1952, submitted to the US Copyright Office, along with a $4 application fee and a request that the score be copyrighted under Class D, as a Dramatic or Dramatico-Musical Composition.[119] On March 3, Holm received the official Certificate of Copyright Registration for "Dance Notation Score of Hanya Holm's Choreography for 'Kiss Me, Kate.'"

In Hutchinson's account, Holm employed her as a notator for the precise purpose of gaining copyright protection.[120] John Martin asserted that Holm took action because she felt that "the break had to be made sooner or later if choreographers were ever to have protection for their creations such as is available to writers and musicians."[121] Asked years later what prompted her to seek copyright protection, Holm maintained that she did it "because there was an awful lot of lifting going on."[122] As she told reporters at the time of the registration, "Some people have wonderful photographic memory. . . . The creative goods are used without proper credit and justice to the originator. They even do their own stuff and use your name on it."[123] Critics shared her concern about the problem of piracy, especially in the commercial sphere. "When Broadway musicals are released for stock," Martin spelled out, "it is not infrequent for a summer theater to engage as choreographer some member of the original dance company to restage the dances after the manner of the original production. For this, the original choreographer receives neither credit nor royalties."[124] Nelson Lansdale of *Dance Magazine* saw appropriation abroad as

---

[118] Guest, "The Golden Age of the Broadway Musical," 363–64.

[119] Sorell, *Hanya Holm*, 113–14. The check for $4 was actually posted in February. Letter to Mr. Kaminstein from Elsa Rainer, secretary to Hanya Holm, February 21, 1952, Hanya Holm Papers, NYPL.

[120] Guest, "The Golden Age of the Broadway Musical," 363.

[121] Martin, "The Dance: Copyright."

[122] *Eye on Dance: Yesterday Shapes Today: Tracing the Roots* [videorecording], Produced by ARC Videodance, Celia Ipiotis, and Jeff Bush, No. 160, 1985.

[123] Quoted in Beckley, "Choreography Is Copyrighted for First Time."

[124] Martin, "The Dance: Copyright."

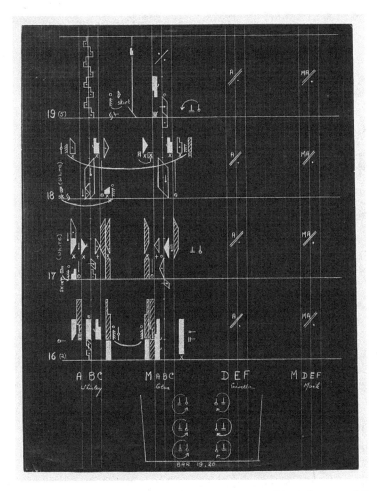

Figure 4.4 Photographic negative of the "Pavane" section of the Labanotated *Kiss Me, Kate* score. Choreographer: Hanya Holm. Notator: Ann Hutchinson Guest (1952). Courtesy of the Dance Notation Bureau. Photo courtesy of the Jerome Robbins Dance Division, The New York Public Library for the Performing Arts, Astor, Lenox and Tilden Foundations.

a more insidious threat than summer stock, citing duplications of Broadway musicals in London, Norway, Sweden, Denmark, and Australia, with neither recompense nor credit for the shows' original choreographers.[125] Holm's *Kiss Me, Kate* contract granted her sole choreographic credit in "theatre programs, billboard posters and newspaper advertisements" and gave her the option to

[125] Landsdale, "Concerning the Copyright of Dances," 41.

Figure 4.5 A story from a 1965 issue of *Dance Magazine* about Hanya Holm's 1952 copyright and images of rehearsals for a revival of *Kiss Me, Kate* based on the original Labanotated score. Holm, then in her early seventies, is pictured in the top two images along with the Dance Notation Bureau's Els Grelinger, who helped reconstruct the choreography. Photo by Harold Bergsohn. Jerome Robbins Dance Division, The New York Public Library for the Performing Arts, Astor, Lenox and Tilden Foundations.

oversee subsequent stagings by Arnold St. Subber's production team, but this was evidently insufficient to preserve her ability to capitalize on what she considered her "creative goods."[126] Having managed to hire herself out to Broadway

---

[126] Contract between Hanya Holm and Arnold St. Subber, Salem Company, September 30, 1948. The contract also provided Holm with a salary of $4,500, plus one quarter of 1 percent of

without tarnishing her reputation, Holm's success in the commercial market-place thus begat a new problem: the proliferation of her choreography in amateur and far-flung productions without a guaranteed accrual of cultural or economic capital. Like her predecessor Loïe Fuller, Holm embraced copyright as a means of securing the integrity of the choreographer (propped up as sole originator) against the threat of dispersal.

In point of fact, it is uncertain how much and what kind of legal protection Holm's registration of the Labanotated score of *Kiss Me, Kate* actually afforded. In a follow-up letter to Hutchinson, MacCarteney qualified his original enthusiasm about what a copyrighted Labanotated score would protect, admitting, "I do not know that a court of law would necessarily hold that copyrighting a dance notation score thereby resulted in the dance itself being copyrighted. The Certificate of Registration may or may not be of great value."[127] Absent an infringement lawsuit to test its validity, Holm's copyright may have held more symbolic than legal weight.

This symbolic weight, however, should not be underestimated. Reports of Holm's copyright registration rippled through the theater dance community, augmenting Holm's authority in the process. For those who championed the cause of modern and ballet as "serious" forms of artistic expression, Holm's achievement represented a proxy victory for the figure of the choreographer at large, now officially recognized as an author and owner in her own right. Yet granting the choreographer intellectual property rights necessitated suppressing the non-autonomous and non-original aspects of the creative process: its collaborations, its borrowings, and vitally, its dependence on the labor of racialized others.

"The answer is plainly in copyright and unionization": Middlebrow Anxiety and De Mille's Crusade

In the wake of Holm's successful copyright registration, other choreographers quickly followed suit. A June 1952 article in *Dance Magazine* reported that Jerome Robbins, Doris Humphrey, George Balanchine, Sophie Maslow, and

---

weekly box office grosses for tryout engagements and touring performances. It is not known how much the dancers were paid, although a later contract indicates that $2,500 of Holm's salary was deducted to pay for her assistant, Ray Harrison. Contract between St. Subber, Salem Company, and Hanya Holm, October 5, 1948, Hanya Holm Papers, NYPL.

[127] Letter from Richard S. MacCarteney to Ann Hutchinson, August 4, 1950.

Nona Schurman (a Humphrey disciple) were all in the process of Labanotating and microfilming their choreography in preparation for submission to the Copyright Office.[128] In the meantime, however, Holm's victory began to feel more hollow. In March 1952, Balanchine, who had worked briefly on Broadway in the 1930s but was then serving as the director of the newly formed New York City Ballet, attempted to register *Symphony in C*, one of his classical ballets, with the Copyright Office. He was forced to withdraw his application "when informed that it must be defined as a dramatic composition."[129] This left observers slightly baffled as to why Holm's equally abstract works (albeit put in service of *Kiss Me, Kate*'s narrative) should have qualified and not Balanchine's. Legal commentator Leon Mirell asserted that the Copyright Office's inability to read Labanotation led them mistakenly to assume that Holm's choreography possessed a storyline.[130] The fact that Schurman was asked to submit a verbal synopsis to accompany her Labanotated score of *Song from the Hebrides* lent support to the belief that the Copyright Office would only grant registrations to narrative works. Schurman's score, like Holm's, was eventually accepted for registration in May 1952, becoming "the first modern dance piece" to be successfully copyrighted.[131] Later that year, the Russian-born Nadia Chilkovsky, a modern dancer and co-founder of the leftist New Dance Group, was granted a copyright for her *Suite for Youth*.[132]

By early 1953, the question of choreography's copyrightability had only become more muddled. In January of that year, ballet choreographer Ruth Page registered an abstract work called *Beethoven Sonata* not as a dramatic composition under Class D, but as a book under Class A. Rather than notate

[128] Lansdale, "Concerning the Copyright of Dances," 21.

[129] "Choreographer Gets Copyright under New Law," *New York Herald Tribune*, January 7, 1953, p. 19. Although Nicholas Arcomano later reported that Balanchine's attempted copyright predated Holm's, the *Herald Tribune* article and other references to Balanchine's attempt in the early 1950s suggest otherwise. Balanchine was apparently more successful when he re-registered *Symphony in C* as a film in 1961. Nicholas Arcomano, "Choreography and Copyright, part one" *Dance Magazine*, April 1980, 59. John Martin, "The Dance: New Law," *New York Times*, January 11, 1953, p. X10; John Martin, "The Dance: Review," *New York Times*, December 28, 1952, p. X13; Cheryl Swack, "The Balanchine Trust: Dancing through the Steps of Two-Part Licensing," *Jeffrey S. Moorad Sports Law Journal* 6.2 (1999): 11.

[130] Leon I. Mirell, "Dance Notation and Copyright Protection for Choreography," reprinted in Dance Notation Bureau, *Dance Notation Record* (March 1952): 3, Dance Notation Bureau Archives.

[131] Newsletter of the Dance Notation Bureau, Summer 1952, Dance Notation Bureau Archives; Terese Elaine Sekora, "Dance Notation: A History of the Dance Notation Bureau, 1940–1952," MA Thesis in Dance, Graduate School of Texas Women's University, 1979, Dance Notation Bureau Archives.

[132] Dance Notation Bureau Newsletter, Fall 1952, Dance Notation Bureau Archives.

her score, that is, Page typed out detailed prose instructions for performing the choreography (as Fuller, St. Denis, and Hudgins had done before her). In Page's case, the resulting text, which she maintained had been published, comprised forty pages. Page's decision to register her work as a book, likely made in consultation with her lawyer husband, Thomas Hart Page, was a response to Public Law 575, which became effective on January 1, 1953. Passed by the eighty-second Congress, the law gave authors the exclusive right to present non-dramatic literary works (for example, reading a lecture on the radio). Page seems to have interpreted the law to be a "revolutionary development applicable generally to protect performance rights to nondramatic movements of actors and dancers in motion pictures, television, ballets, musicals, and plays."[133] This was despite the fact that Richard MacCarteney of the Copyright Office advised Page that her registration did "not mean that the Office has expressed any opinion as to whether the applicant will or will not secure protection" for her choreography against other performances under the new law.[134] Whether Page had succeeded in copyrighting her choreography or merely the written description of it remained an open question. Dance writer Anatole Chujoy, for one, deemed Page's copyright "neither revolutionary, nor a development" but held on to Holm's copyright as a "real achievement." Both Chujoy and John Martin concluded that the only resolution to the ambiguity was the revision of copyright law to expressly include choreography as a protectable category. "What the situation seems to need," Martin added, "is some kind of persistent dance lobby in Washington!"[135]

As if in answer to Martin's call, Agnes de Mille came to personify that lobby. Actually, by 1953, de Mille had already begun her mobilization efforts on behalf of choreographers' rights. While she benefited enormously from the unprecedented success of *Oklahoma!*, the terms of her contract left her with a profound sense of injustice. She recited those terms numerous times over the years: in return for her work on the musical, the Theatre Guild, who produced *Oklahoma!*, provided her with a $1,500 flat fee and an extra $500 when production costs were paid off, but no royalties. Once it was clear that the musical was a hit, she was granted an additional $50 a week, which was eventually increased to $75 after "lengthy negotiation."[136] But while *Oklahoma!* had grossed more than $7 million by the time the New York run closed in May 1948

---

[133] Telegram, Chicago Press Bureau, quoted in Chujoy, "New Try Made to Copyright Choreography," 4.

[134] Chujoy, "New Try Made to Copyright Choreography," 4.

[135] John Martin, "The Dance: New Law," *New York Times*, January 11, 1953, p. X10.

[136] De Mille, *And Promenade Home*, 34–35, 252–54; de Mille, *Dance to the Piper*, 247; Debra Cash, "Agnes de Mille's Fight for Copyright," *Houston Arts Magazine*, October 1982, 25.

(with the touring company grossing another $9 million), and while Rodgers, Hammerstein, and Lynn Riggs (on whose play the musical was based) were earning thousands each week from their share of the royalties, it took years of bitter arguments for the Guild to finally agree in 1947–48 to give de Mille a .5% percentage of the royalties.[137]

For de Mille, the answer to the inequities facing choreographers, especially those working in the commercial theater, lay "plainly in copyright and unionization."[138] In contrast to the concert arena, where it was impossible to ignore a choreographer's importance, de Mille found that it was all too easy to devalue her contributions to a Broadway musical. Claiming to have furnished twenty-six minutes' worth of stage time to *Oklahoma!* "not specified or even suggested in the original script," de Mille bristled at ranking so far below the dramatist, librettist, and lyricist.[139] "Composers and playwrights," she wrote, "are in a better position altogether" because of the protection they received under copyright law and from licensing organizations like the American Society of Composers, Authors and Publishers (ASCAP). Accordingly, she saw intellectual property rights and collective bargaining as the means by which choreographers could assert their authorial rights.[140]

De Mille's interest in unionization began as early as 1944, the year after *Oklahoma!* premiered. In May of that year, after consulting with fellow choreographers Anthony Tudor, Eugene Loring, and Jerome Robbins, she wrote to Albert B. Gins of the American Guild of Musical Artists (AGMA) with a request to speak before the Guild's board about the problems confronting choreographers.[141] "As you know," she elaborated in a June letter, "the Choreographers are guaranteed no protection ...

> As to Copy Right
> As to quality and standards of performance of their work
> As to minimum pay
> As to Royalties
> As to the expansivity of performing rights.[142]

---

[137] Carter, *Oklahoma!*, 222–25.

[138] De Mille, *And Promenade Home*, 258.

[139] See Carter, *Oklahoma!*, 127, on some of the problematic aspects of de Mille's claims about how much credit she deserved for the concepts behind the choreography in *Oklahoma!*

[140] De Mille, *And Promenade Home*, 252, 254–55, 258.

[141] De Mille to Albert B. Gins, American Guild of Musical Artists, Inc., May 15, 1944, Agnes de Mille Papers, NYPL.

[142] De Mille to Albert Gins, June 13, 1944, Agnes de Mille Papers, NYPL.

Evidently thwarted in her attempt to extend AGMA's union rights to choreographers (she later wrote that "AGMA affords me no help of any kind whatsoever in my profession"),[143] in 1945, de Mille helped organize a meeting of choreographers in New York. Canvassing fellow choreographers across the country, they uncovered "a history of exploitation" with no "attempt at recompense or rights equivalent to those enjoyed by the other arts."[144] But their efforts at reform, beginning with a plan for a standard contract that guaranteed certain rights, were frustrated by "seemingly insurmountable blocks." These included the relative smallness of their group (de Mille tallied their total number as eighty-one) and their relative poverty (they were advised that the legal and lobbying costs of amending the copyright law to include choreography would surpass $50,000).[145] In 1947, de Mille contacted the Actors Equity Association to inquire about membership for choreographers, noting "Our point of view is not represented in any group at all at the moment."[146] This request, too, was turned down.[147] In the mid-1950s, de Mille appears to have been more successful at joining AGMA,[148] but it was not until 1959, when she combined forces with directors to form the Society of Stage Directors and Choreographers, that choreographers were "at last ... formally recognized in the ranks of labor."[149]

De Mille's embrace of unions, which she saw as crucial to establishing ownership rights for choreographers, was rife with contradictions. As biographer Carol Easton notes, de Mille "equated the craft unions that represented the nonperforming side of the theater with highway robbers" and resented the fact that stagehands earned more than dancers.[150] Despite her attempts to join Actors Equity, moreover, she complained in print about "the exorbitant demands of all theatrical unions," whose stipulations on pay rates for performers made the costs of filming a three-minute dance—one of the few ways to "fix" dance in a

---

[143] De Mille to Lawrence Tibbett, American Guild of Musical Artists, n.d., Agnes de Mille Papers, NYPL.

[144] De Mille, *And Promenade Home*, 258.

[145] Ibid.

[146] De Mille to Angus Duncan, November 28, 1947, Agnes de Mille Papers, NYPL.

[147] Easton, *No Intermissions*, 388. De Mille described the decision not to join Actors Equity as mutual. *And Promenade Home*, 259.

[148] A 1957 letter addressed to "Choreographer" from DeLloyd Tibbs, Asst. Exec. Sec'y, American Guild of Musical Artists, Inc., August 28, 1957, mentions a meeting of AGMA choreographers, while a letter to "members" from Hy Faine, January 9, 1959, refers to "dancers and choreographers who are AGMA members." Agnes de Mille Papers, NYPL.

[149] De Mille, handwritten notes on Unions, Agnes de Mille Papers, NYPL; Easton, *No Intermissions*, 388.

[150] Easton, *No Intermissions*, 386.

tangible medium—ran into the thousands of dollars.[151] Though she fought for dancers' rights, de Mille "felt entitled to suspend them when she felt it necessary," by pushing dancers to work beyond the time parameters that unions set, for instance.[152] As the example of tap dancers Coles and Atkins in *Gentlemen Prefer Blondes* makes clear, as a white choreographer, de Mille was the beneficiary of a racially unequal distribution of credit, despite her self-deprecating claim to be only "a good editor."[153] Like Holm, de Mille incorporated her dancers' contributions into choreography she considered hers to own. She also blamed dancers for reproducing her Broadway choreography without permission.[154] "Dancers who have never choreographed anything in their lives," she wrote, "claim ... the ballets from *Oklahoma!, Carousel, Allegro, Brigadoon* and *Paint Your Wagon* and they take regular authorship pay and credit for staging them."[155] While she held management equally accountable for what she considered this blatant "piracy," she saw the relationship between choreographers and performers as "utterly corrupted" and described their respective interests as "not only different but in some ways divergent and hostile."[156]

De Mille, in short, alternately sided with labor and with capital, depending on the situation. This alternation, I want to suggest, is indicative of the station she occupied in the commercial theater. Even as she derived power from her position as choreographer, she remained subordinate always to the mostly male directors, producers, and composers who ranked higher on Broadway's food chain. "There is," she wrote,

> a very real rivalry between directors and choreographers for power, prestige, and percentages. Jerome Robbins and Michael Kidd have solved matters by organizing, directing, producing and choreographing their own shows. This is a heroic answer and one that is not possible for many. There could be another: simple justice.[157]

[151] De Mille, *And Promenade Home*, 168, 258.

[152] Easton, *No Intermissions*, 386.

[153] Millstein, "Agnes de Mille," *Theatre Arts*, October 1961, 14–16; Agnes de Mille Clippings File, Dance Division, n.d., n.s., NYPL.

[154] See Carter, *Oklahoma!*, 140, on how de Mille worked out the choreography for *Oklahoma!* through movement explorations with dancers in rehearsal, despite her claims of having planned it all in advance; and Easton, *No Intermissions*, 163, on how de Mille used dancer Sybil Shearer's movement in the creation of *Rodeo*.

[155] De Mille, *And Promeande Home*, 257.

[156] De Mille, handwritten notes under "Union" folder, n.d., Agnes de Mille Papers, NYPL; de Mille, *And Promenade Home*, 259. She was speaking directly about actors here, whose "interpretive" work she contrasted to the "creative" work of choreographers.

[157] De Mille, *And Promenade Home*, 259–60.

Gender was surely in part what prevented de Mille from following the "heroic" route of Robbins and Kidd. In point of fact, she did direct three shows—*Allegro* in 1947, *Out of this World* in 1950, and *Come Summer* in 1969—making her the first woman and first choreographer to direct a major musical. But de Mille felt, rightly no doubt, that she was granted less authority than a male director, and she was demoted or fired from her post as director before any of the shows opened, all of which suffered from weak books and scores and were widely deemed failures.[158] Consigned largely to a role as "just a choreographer," as she once phrased it, the intermediary position that de Mille occupied in Broadway's field of power bred a sense of marginalization and fueled her fight for "simple justice" for choreographers.[159]

De Mille's middle station in terms of capital was not altogether different from the middlebrow position of Broadway more generally.[160] It follows that she shared some of the anxiety that scholar David Savran describes as characteristic of the middlebrow. "Middlebrow cultural producers, consumers, and critics alike," Savran writes,

> are always looking over their shoulders; always fearful of encroachments from above or below; always uneasy about their own class positionality and their own tastes; always trying to negotiate between creativity and the exigencies of the marketplace, between politics and aesthetics, between an art that requires studied investment and the desire for untrammeled pleasures.[161]

I am not suggesting that de Mille was paranoid about or obsessed with her status as a result of her affiliation with the middlebrow form of the Broadway musical. But the fact that her renown was tied to her choreographic work on Broadway, which did not hold the prestige of concert dance and where there were decided limits on her power, made her status somewhat fraught. As with Holm, de Mille's crusade for copyright protection was a way of fortifying her

---

[158] Easton, *No Intermissions*, 263, 269, 299, 422. See also Robert Emmett Long, *Broadway, the Golden Years: Jerome Robbins and the Great Choreographer-Directors 1940 to the Present* (New York: Continuum International, 2001).

[159] Millstein, "Agnes de Mille," 14.

[160] For Savran, because the musical comprises an especially conspicuous mixture of high and low, it represents "the most suspect of all so-called legitimate theatrical forms" and is "the most skillful ... at arousing the critical disdain and anxiety so strongly linked to middlebrow culture" ("Middlebrow Anxiety," 26–27).

[161] Savran, "Middlebrow Anxiety," 10.

status, a way of aligning herself firmly with capital, even as she straddled a middle ground between capital and labor.

De Mille's unease about the source of her fame can be seen in her ambivalence about the suitability of the term "choreographer" for Broadway. This ambivalence is ironic given her centrality to the title's emergence in conjunction with Broadway, as a 1946 *New Yorker* profile of de Mille, titled "Choreographer," makes clear. Written by Angelica Gibbs, the article begins by noting that "Up to half a dozen years ago, the distinction between a choreographer and a dance director was—in the popular mind, at least—a fairly easy one to make." "A choreographer," Gibbs elaborates,

> was a gentleman, preferably a Russian, who devised ornamental numbers for some well-known ballerina and her company to perform at the Metropolitan. A dance director was a young man, usually reared in the buck-and-wing school, who operated only on Broadway, where his presence guaranteed that a number of young ladies would appear in the course of a musical comedy or revue, kicking their legs more or less in unison. This distinction, which was already becoming blurry toward the end of the nineteen-thirties, was wiped out almost instantaneously by the opening of "Oklahoma!" at the St. James Theatre, on the evening of March 31, 1943.[162]

There are decided classed, gendered, racial, and national undertones to Gibbs's categorizations here, although she seems to hold the upper-class, ballet-trained European choreographer (who creates only "ornamental numbers") in hardly greater esteem than the middlebrow, tap-based dance director (who generates only cookie-cutter chorus lines). Attributing the dance director's decline to ballet's infiltration of Broadway, Gibbs notes the significance of George Balanchine's 1936 ballet "Slaughter on Tenth Avenue" for *On Your Toes*—generally agreed to be the first time the title "choreographer" was used on Broadway—but points to de Mille as the one who finally took ballet out of its "niche ... as one of the esoteric arts" and found "a respectable place for it in the commercial theatre." For Gibbs, de Mille is "a choreographer in every sense of the word."

Yet de Mille herself opposed the label "choreographer" as a descriptor of her work on Broadway. In 1956, she wrote to Rodgers and Hammerstein to alert them that they had mis-credited her as "choreographer" for the show *Allegro* in their *Rodgers and Hammerstein Fact Book*, published the previous year. "I

---

[162] Angelica Gibbs, "Profiles: Choreographer," *New Yorker*, September 14, 1946, pp. 32–34 +.

have never used the word 'Choreography' in connection with a Broadway show," she explained. The billing with which she was "particularly anxious to be credited" was "Dances, musical numbers, and production staged by Agnes de Mille."[163] She made the same point in a 1961 interview with *Theatre Arts*'s Gilbert Millstein, whom she told that the term "choreographer" connoted to her the "production of a complete idea, dramatically whole and expressed through an entire dramatic presentation—costumes, scenery, lighting and so on—and running for fifteen to twenty-five minutes." "These little segments you stick into a show to illumine a moment," she maintained, "I don't consider choreography."[164] While she hastened to add that she "meant no disrespect ... either to herself or anyone else who creates dances for musical comedy," de Mille's preferred taxonomy indicates how much weight the term "choreographer," associated with integration and wholeness, bore in upholding the hierarchy between art and entertainment.

If de Mille harbored an anti-Broadway bias despite her success in that venue, a musical like *Gentlemen Prefer Blondes* (1949) was especially troubling to her. According to biographer Easton, de Mille "made no secret of her belief that the show itself was a vulgar enterprise and that, artistically, she was slumming."[165] The musical, about an American nightclub singer who travels to Paris in the 1920s, featured the jazz dance styles of that era. This setting facilitated the employment of the tap dance team of Coles and Atkins, as mentioned above. De Mille's contributions to the musical included staging versions of the Charleston, the Shimmy, and the Black Bottom—nearly twenty-five years after Alberta Hunter and George White made competing claims on that dance (see Chapter 3). While, as I have indicated, the incorporation of ballet into stage musicals did not, contrary to conventional wisdom, totally eradicate tap dance from the Broadway stage, *Gentlemen Prefer Blondes* featured African American tap dancing much more overtly than the other musicals on which de Mille worked. The fact that she found it repugnant hints at a racial underside to her anxiety about Broadway. As David Savran argues, white artists' use of jazz styles was always a "precarious operation" since "it could ... never be known in advance if the appropriation of jazz would lead to the accumulation or forfeiture of high cultural capital."[166] De Mille's particular distaste for a musical in which, as one review put it, she "abandoned her usual reliance on long ballets and specialized on fast and furious chorus routines and specialties," combined

---

[163] Agnes de Mille to Richard Rodgers and Oscar Hammerstein, October 22, 1956, Agnes de Mille Papers, NYPL.

[164] Millstein, "Agnes de Mille," 14.

[165] Easton, *No Intermissions*, 293.

[166] Savran, *Highbrow/Lowdown*, 184.

with her self-policing of the term "choreographer," are symptoms of her discomfort with the enterprise of Broadway.[167]

Activism on behalf of choreographers' rights was the antidote to de Mille's discomfort. On at least three separate occasions, she lobbied Congress for copyright reform that would recognize choreography as a protectable category in its own right. In 1959, de Mille, along with eight other members of the dance or legal professions, submitted written responses to a report commissioned by the Eighty-Sixth Congress called "Copyright in Choreographic Works."[168] Authored by Borge Varmer with the oversight of the Copyright Office, the study was designed to help guide the Committee on the Judiciary as it considered making revisions to US copyright law. Varmer's report followed two directives issued by the Copyright Office intended to clarify what kinds of choreographic works the Office would recognize as dramatic compositions: the June 18, 1959, edition of the *Federal Register*, which explained that "choreographic works of a dramatic character, whether the story or theme be expressed by music and action combined or by actions alone" were subject to registration under Class D;[169] and Circular No. 51, which stipulated that "A choreographic work is a ballet or similar theatrical work which tells a story[,] develops a character, or expresses a theme or emotion by means of specific dance movements and physical action."[170] Both documents identified "ballroom, social, and folk dance steps" as ineligible for copyright protection.[171]

---

[167] Review, *Gentlemen Prefer Blondes*, November 17, n.y., *Gentlemen Prefer Blondes* clippings file, Theater Clippings, NYPL. De Mille actually worked with African American dancers and Africanist dance forms on several occasions: on a Broadway show called *Flying Colors* (1932), which featured sixteen African American female dancers and on which de Mille was eventually replaced by Albertina Rasch; on a full-length ballet called *Black Ritual* (1940), which de Mille described as "an exotic work for Negroes using the *Creation du Monde* score of Darius Milhaud"; and on *Kwamina* (1961), a Broadway show with an interracial love story between a London-educated African doctor and the daughter of white missionaries, for which de Mille won a Tony award. See de Mille, *Dance to the Piper*, 128–29, 195–97; and Easton, *No Intermissions*, 89–90, 168–69, 381–83.

[168] Borge Varmer, "Copyright in Choreographic Works," Study No. 28, *Studies Prepared for the Subcommittee on Patents, Trademarks, and Copyrights of the Committee on the Judiciary*, United States Senate, 86th Cong., 2d Sess. (Washington, DC: US Government Printing Office, 1961): 93–116. De Mille and Hanya Holm were the only choreographers among this group of commentators. The others were legal scholars Walter J. Derenberg and John Schulman, dance critic John Martin and dance writer Anatole Chujoy, ballet impresario Lincoln Kirstein, dance educator Lucile B. Nathanson, and Frank C. Barber of the legal department of the Music Publishers' Holding Corporation, which published Labanotated scores.

[169] 24 Fed. Reg. 4955 (1959).

[170] Cited in Varmer, "Copyright in Choreographic Works," 96.

[171] Ibid. Issued by the National Archives, the Federal Register states explicitly that "descriptions of dance steps and other physical gestures, including ballroom and social dances or

Weighing in on these guidelines, Varmer's study outlines the history of case law pertaining to pantomimes and choreography, compares the United States to various other countries (most of which explicitly named choreographic works in their copyright laws), and summarizes the current state of affairs surrounding copyright protection for choreography. Concluding that choreographic works did merit copyright protection provided they "represent original creations of authorship by which a story, theme, or emotional concept is conveyed to an audience" and were "fixed in some tangible form in sufficient detail to be capable of performance therefrom," Varmer homed in on three major questions that any revision to the copyright statute would have to consider:

1. Should "choreographic works" be named specifically in the statute among the categories of copyrightable works?
2. If so, should they be named as a species of dramatic compositions or as a separate category?
3. If "choreographic works" are named in the statute, should that term be further defined? If so, how defined?[172]

These were matters of "increasing importance," Varmer noted, because "the use of choreography as a medium of public entertainment—on the stage, in motion pictures, and in television—has expanded greatly in recent years."[173]

Given de Mille's advocacy of copyright reform, she was an obvious choice for Varmer as he solicited responses to his report. (He cites de Mille's *And Promenade Home* several times in his footnotes.) There was near unanimous agreement among de Mille and her fellow commentators that choreography was a worthy subject of copyright protection; only ballet impresario Lincoln Kirstein saw "no practical advantage in attempts at protection," in large part because he believed that "there are not two choreographers to a generation whose works are of a quality to be stolen from."[174] While there was some variance of opinion over whether choreography deserved its own category and over the extent of reproductive rights for choreography, the thorniest issue by far was whether and how to define a choreographic work. It should come as no surprise that de Mille argued vehemently that choreography deserved recognition separate from drama. What is perhaps surprising is that she took issue

---

choreographic works which do not tell a story, develop a character or emotion, or otherwise convey a dramatic concept or idea, are not subject to registration in Class D" (4958).

[172] Varmer, "Copyright in Choreographic Works," 104.

[173] Ibid., 94.

[174] Ibid., 113.

with Varmer's endorsement of the idea that social dances and "ordinary 'dance routines' performed in variety shows" be excluded from protection.[175] "All inherited folk steps, classic ballet technique, basic tap devices," de Mille wrote, "are public domain. But their combination, good or bad, can be deemed to be original. It is not the province of the law to judge whether a dance, even the most trite and commercial, has creative original value."[176] Looked at from one angle, de Mille's stance here runs counter to her disparagement of Broadway and the energy she expended to uphold a hierarchy between dance genres. But when we keep in mind the use her choreography made of folk steps, ballet technique, and even basic tap devices, her assertion that "copyright must be based on the principle and not on the quality or type of performance" makes sense.[177]

In a 1961 address to the Congressional Subcommittee on Education and Labor on the subject of "Economic Conditions in the Performing Arts," de Mille returned to the theme of concert dance's superiority to Broadway. Surveying the challenges facing choreographers, including their needs for capital, time, and space, she was compelled to pronounce that "first-class training" was obtained only in "non-commercial dance companies." Although she conceded that "Broadway has been good to me," she maintained that she arrived there "with a technique and taste no business manager could shake or contaminate, although they tried."[178] Rehearsing once again her inability to collect adequate royalties on *Oklahoma!*, de Mille closed with a plea to legislators to reform copyright law. Even as she emphasized its second-rate status, Broadway thus served as her primary rationale for demanding copyright protection. This was the contradiction of de Mille's copyright crusade: she insisted that "the moment money is received for dancing, the author of the dance steps should receive a royalty"[179] even while she treated the commercial arena with disdain.

In 1970, de Mille again addressed Congress on the "State of the Arts." The occasion for the speech was Congress's consideration of funding for the National Endowment for the Arts, but during the question and answer period following her speech, de Mille mentioned that "We can't copyright dancing" and appealed to the legislators to kindly change the copyright law, something she believed was "in the works."[180] Indeed, Congress had begun the process

[175] Ibid., 100.

[176] Ibid., 110.

[177] Ibid., 111.

[178] Easton, *No Intermissions*, 388; Agnes de Mille, Typescript, Speech Made at Congressional Hearing, Agnes de Mille Papers, NYPL.

[179] Varmer, "Copyright in Choreographic Works," 111.

[180] "Agnes de Mille Speaks to Congress on the State of the Arts," *Dance Magazine*, May 1970, 85.

of re-examining the copyright law in 1955; Varmer's study on choreographic copyright was prepared as part of that re-examination. A 1961 report by the Copyright Office made preliminary recommendations for revision, and in 1964, the first revision bills were introduced to Congress. After several modifications and a six-year suspension of the process due to problems posed by the rise of cable television, the revised Copyright Act was finally passed in 1976.[181] At long last, the hard-fought battle waged by de Mille and others was won: for the first time, "pantomimes and choreographic works" were listed as their own category of copyrightable work.

Not all was settled by the 1976 Act. Most significantly, the statute declined to define "choreographic work" explicitly.[182] House and Senate reports maintained that the term was one of several with "fairly settled meanings," adding that it was not "necessary to specify that 'choreographic works' do not include social dance steps and simple routines."[183] Legal scholar Melanie Cook calls this restriction "tantamount to a legally imposed standard of artistic merit," and de Mille would surely have agreed.[184] But the taken-for-granted elitism of this exclusion should not be startling. As this chapter has tried to argue, the campaigns for choreographic copyright that played out on and around Broadway at mid-century depended fundamentally on the fortification of class- and race-based artistic hierarchies. To the extent that the migration to Broadway of white female choreographers like Holm and de Mille, known as

---

[181] William F. Patry, *Copyright Law and Practice* (Washington, DC: Bureau of National Affairs, 1994).

[182] Legal scholar Joi Michelle Lakes interprets this failure to offer a definition as evidence that Congress essentially ignored the responses of de Mille and her colleagues to Varmer's proposal. Joi Michelle Lakes, "A Pas de Deux for Choreography and Copyright," *New York University Law Review* 80 (2005): 1843.

[183] S. Rep. No. 473, 94th Cong., 1st Sess. 52 (1975) and H.R. Rep. No. 1476, 94th Cong., 2nd Sess. 53–54 (1976). See also Julie Van Camp, "Copyright of Choreographic Works," in *1994–95 Entertainment, Publishing and the Arts Handbook*, ed. Stephen F. Breimer, Robert Thorne, and John David Viera (New York: Clark, Boardman, and Callaghan, 1994), 61. In 1984, the Copyright Office issued a *Compendium of Copyright Office Practices* (known as Compendium II), which elaborated on this exclusion: "Social dance steps and simple routines are not copyrightable under the general standards of copyrightability. Thus, for example, the basic waltz step, the hustle step, and the second position of classical ballet are not copyrightable. However, this is not a restriction against the incorporation of social dance steps and simple routines, as such, in an otherwise registrable choreographic work. Social dance steps, folk dance steps, and individual ballet steps alike may be utilized as the choreographer's basic material in much the same way that words are the writer's basic material." *The Compendium of Copyright Office Practices*, Compendium II § 450.06 (1984).

[184] Melanie Cook, "Moving to a New Beat: Copyright Protection for Choreographic Works," *UCLA Law Review* 24 (1977): 1299.

"highbrow[s] with the concert approach,"[185] threatened to muddy the distinctions between the non-commercial, "high art," and implicitly white province of ballet and modern dance on the one hand, and the overtly commercial, middlebrow, and racially impure domain of Broadway on the other, the assertion of ownership rights by and for these women was a means of re-instating the privilege of the white choreographer. In contrast to the tap dancers and chorus lines who performed mere "routines," proper choreographers like Holm and de Mille composed "works of authorship" that were deserving of legal protection.

"Bumps and Grinds Involve No Property Rights":[186] Faith Dane and Lowbrow Whiteness

The hierarchy that governed Broadway choreography leading up to the 1976 Copyright Act is nowhere more explicit than in the case of Faith Dane. In 1962, Dane sued the producers of the Broadway musical *Gypsy* for $50,000, claiming infringement of the common law copyright she said she claimed to hold on a dance number performed in the show. In contrast to statutory law, copyright under common law—law based on custom and judicial precedent rather than on legislative enactments—covers unpublished "original" works upon their creation.[187] There was only one precedent involving common law copyright for dance: in the 1908 case *Savage v. Hoffman*, the creator of an unpublished opera,

---

[185] Gibbs, "Profiles: Choreographer," 40.

[186] "Faith's Bumpy Legal Travails Grind to Halt as Court Kills Suit," *New York Post*, April 8, 1963; Faith Dane Clippings, Theatre Collection, NYPL.

[187] As legal scholar Cheryl Swack explains, although the 1976 Copyright Act did away with the requirement that works be "published" to qualify for federal copyright protection, in theory, state copyright law still covers those works not fixed in a tangible medium of expression. Cheryl Swack, "The Balanchine Trust: Dancing through the Steps of Two-Part Licensing," *Jeffrey S. Moorad Sports Law Journal* 6. 2 (1999): 284–85. See also Jeffrey I. Roth, "Common Law Protection of Choreographic Works," *Performing Arts Review* 5.1–2 (1974): 75–89; Joseph Taubman, "Choreography under Copyright Revision: The Square Peg in the Round Hole Unpegged," *Performing Arts Review* 10.3 (1980): 219–56; Gary D. Ordway, "Choreography and Copyright," *Bulletin of the Copyright Society* 15 (1967): 172–89; and Leslie Erin Wallis, "The Different Art: Choreography and Copyright," *UCLA Law Review* 33 (1986): 1442–71. See Van Camp, "Copyright of Choreographic Works," for a survey of different legal commentators' views of common law protection for choreography. While some (like Taubman) view common law copyright as an ongoing, necessary source of protection for choreographers, others (like Ordway) point to the practical difficulty of proving infringement in the absence of a fixity requirement. Wallis, meanwhile, maintains that common law's variation between states makes it too unpredictable to be useful. On the history of a common law performance right in dramatic works, see

"The Merry Widow," sought an injunction against performers who staged an imitation of the dances from his opera in their vaudeville act. Although the judge in that case denied the injunction, his ruling was made on the basis that the opera's creator was not responsible for the dances performed within his show and therefore held no ownership rights in them, leaving it open whether the dances' originators would have been more successful. There was no conclusive case law, then, on whether choreographic works were eligible for copyright protection under common law.[188]

Produced by David Merrick and Leland Hayward, with music by Jule Styne, lyrics by Stephen Sondheim, and a book by Arthur Laurents, *Gypsy* ran on Broadway from May 21, 1959, to March 25, 1961. Its director and choreographer was Jerome Robbins, arguably the most successful of the so-called serious choreographers who followed de Mille onto Broadway.[189] Based on the memoirs of the 1930s striptease artist Gypsy Lee Rose, the musical told the story of an overzealous show-business mother and her two daughters, one of whom becomes a burlesque star.

Dane's background as a nightclub performer made her a natural fit for the role of Mazeppa, one of the musical's striptease dancers. For her January 1959 audition, she re-enacted a bugle number that she had developed as part of her nightclub act: accompanying herself to the bugle call "reveille," she performed a series of salutes punctuated by thrusts of her pelvis, repeatedly circled her hips, and, finally, bent over while facing upstage and blew the bugle between her legs. This movement sequence made it into *Gypsy* as part of "You Gotta Get a Gimmick," which featured the specialty acts of three different strippers and was an undisputed showstopper. As a reviewer for the *New York Mirror* put it, Dane "stops the show cold and never has 'cold' been so misused."[190]

During contract negotiations with *Gypsy's* management, Dane fought to secure compensation, as well as royalties and credit, commensurate with her choreographic contribution to the show. The negotiations resulted in a $35 a week increase to her $140 a week salary, but a production associate allegedly told her to leave the rest to the producer's "ethical judgment." When road versions of *Gypsy*—with Dane's number intact—continued to tour after the show closed on Broadway in March 1961, and Dane failed to receive any additional

Jessica Litman, "The Invention of Common Law Play Right," *Berkeley Technology Law Journal* 25 (2010): 1381–426, available at http://works.bepress.com/jessica_litman/15.

[188] Roth, "Common Law Protection"; Mirell, "Legal Protection for Choreography," 794–97.

[189] Easton, *No Intermissions*, 318.

[190] Bill Slocum, "Bumps and Bugle Stop the Show," *New York Mirror*, June 17, 1959, Faith Dane Clippings File, Theatre Collection, NYPL.

Figure 4.6 Faith Dane in her military striptease number in *Gypsy* (1959). Photo by Friedman-Abeles © The New York Public Library for the Performing Arts.

remuneration, she filed her infringement suit.[191] The suit alleged that because she was "engaged to perform a number of her own creation, which was unique and novel, produced by her labor, skill, efforts and ability," she was "entitled to common law copyright protection." In an implicit undercutting of the elevated authority of artists like Holm, de Mille, and Robbins, Dane's legal action challenged the concealment of individual dancers' contributions to a musical's

---

[191] *Dane v. M & H Company et al.*, 136 U.S.P.Q. 426, 1963; William Greaves, "Faith Dane Dances—Justice Isn't Blind," *New York Post*, December 7, 1962; Faith Dane Clippings File, Theatre Division, NYPL.

choreography. Her lawsuit asserted the rights of labor to claim credit and compensation for generating movement material, even if that material comprised, as it did in Dane's case, only thirty to forty-five seconds of the overall production.

The trial was a full-blown spectacle for court-watchers. This was largely because, as if in corroboration of performance studies scholar Philip Auslander's observation that "live performance is … essential to legal procedure," Dane's dancing body was submitted into evidence so as "to assist the court in making a judgment as to the type, form or manner of property for which plaintiff seeks appropriate relief."[192] "Sedate Manhattan Supreme Court resembled a strip joint yesterday," the New York Daily News reported.[193] Actually, the packed courtroom was treated to a double feature of dancing. In addition to screening the "You Gotta Get a Gimmick" scene from the 1962 film version of Gypsy, in which Dane appeared, she also stood up in the jury box to give a live demonstration of her bugle number, explaining that she had been forced to tone it down for the film.[194] (The film's director Mervyn LeRoy had prohibited her from blowing her bugle with her "'derriere' pointed skyward." In the film, she concludes her number instead with a deep backbend.)[195] The New York Post informed its readers that "To a man, the spectators agreed the live, Broadway version was far superior."[196]

However sensational Dane's performance, her case hinged on her ability to position her dance number as worthy of copyright protection. Claiming a uniqueness for her act in that she "portrayed a stripper without taking anything off," thus making it a "satire" of striptease, she also sought to prove that her act had a narrative dimension. Dane explained that the combination of bugle playing and provocative dancing could be interpreted to be the actions of a woman who enlisted in the military but could ultimately not repress her stripper roots.[197] Several witnesses testified in support of this reading. Clearly attuned to the importance of semantics, Dane also made a point of describing

[192] Philip Auslander, Liveness: Performance in a Mediatized Culture (London: Routledge, 1999), 113; Dane v. M & H Company et al.

[193] "Dancer Takes Court over the Bumps, Grinds," New York Daily News, December 8, 1962, n.p., Faith Dane Clippings File, Theatre Collection, NYPL.

[194] Greaves, "Faith Dane Dances"; Dane v. M & H Company et al. Kate Elswit describes a similar juxtaposition of live performance and film in a German copyright trial, Jooss v. Herzog Film GmbH, although in the case she describes, the allegation was that the film had plagiarized Kurt Jooss's choreography. Watching Weimar Dance (New York: Oxford University Press, 2014), 128–136.

[195] Dane v. M & H Company et al.

[196] Greaves, "Faith Dane Dances."

[197] Dane v. M & H Company et al.

her choreography as consisting of "forward pelvic contractions" rather than "bumps and grinds."[198] In doing so, she may have been seeking to align herself with Martha Graham, who, by the 1960s, was the country's most venerated modern dance artist and whose signature movement vocabulary included the contraction and release.

Justice Aurelio of the New York Supreme Court was not convinced. On January 23, 1963, he dismissed Dane's suit. In his written opinion, he sneered at the idea that the "the so-called 'stories'" attributed to Dane's dancing rose to the level of copyright material. Calling Dane's act "an excellent 'piece of business,'" and acknowledging her ability to perform it "in a manner which 'stopped the show,'" the judge nonetheless held that when she performed it at her audition for *Gypsy*, the producers had a right to assume it was available for their use. Justice Aurelio correspondingly determined that Dane's claims to be a choreographer lacked credibility. "The court finds," he wrote, "that plaintiff was not known in the theatrical world for her ability to create choreographic compositions and that when she performed at the audition it was her skill as an actress or dancer which she was trying to sell rather than a piece of property." Refusing to recognize Dane as a choreographer because she did not already hold that status, Justice Aurelio reduces her to the position of pure labor: because her body was essentially a commodity, subject to exchange, she could not own what her body produced. The final blow was the judge's finding that, even if Dane's act "could be characterized as a choreographic composition, it would not rise to the level of copyrightability" for these reasons:

> Where a performance contains nothing of a literary, dramatic or musical character which is calculated to elevate, cultivate, inform or improve the moral or intellectual natures of the audience, it does not tend to promote the progress of science or the useful arts. ... Thus, not everything put on the stage can be subject to copyright. While plaintiff's performance was no doubt amusing and entertaining to many, it does not fall within the purview of the statute as a production tending to promote the progress of science and useful arts.[199]

Concluding that Dane had failed to establish that her *Gypsy* performance was eligible for common law copyright protection, Justice Aurelio ruled for the defendants. Dane filed a motion to set aside this initial verdict, but it too was denied. "Bumps, grinds, pelvic contractions, and blowing the bugle," Justice

[198] Greaves, "Faith Dane Dances."
[199] *Dane v. M & H Company et al.*

Aurelio noted once and for all, "are not so unique, novel and artistic as might be developed to the status of a property right."[200]

At the heart of Justice Aurelio's sweeping dismissal of Dane's claims was the perceived immorality of her dancing. In finding that her act failed to qualify for copyright protection because it did not "promote the progress of science or the useful arts," the judge invoked the ghost of a nearly century-old case, *Martinetti v. Maguire*. In that 1867 case, tried in a California circuit court, Judge Matthew Deady denied relief for copyright infringement of a play called *The Black Crook* on the grounds that the dramatic composition was "grossly indecent, and calculated to corrupt the morals of the people" and, as such, did not qualify for copyright protection under the US Constitution. Often considered America's first musi-cal,[201] *The Black Crook* featured a dancing chorus of one hundred Parisian balleri-nas, leading Justice Heady to conclude that "The principal part and attraction of the spectacle seems to be the exhibition of women in novel dress or no dress, and in attractive attitudes or action."[202] That almost a century separates two cases that judged the exhibition of the female dancing body too morally suspect to merit copyright protection is a potent reminder of the magnitude of the obstacles that women dancers faced in gaining artistic legitimacy for their stage productions and of the precariousness of the gains they had won by 1963.[203]

Justice Aurelio's ruling is equally a reminder of the variegation within white privilege and of its complicated intersection with other axes of differ-ence. As I have argued in this chapter, Hanya Holm and Agnes de Mille stood out as highbrow choreographers on the racially hybrid, middlebrow stage of Broadway, and they leveraged this race/class privilege in their efforts to secure copyright protection for dance. Dane, in contrast, migrated to Broadway from a different location: the decidedly lowbrow, sexualized genres of nightclub dancing and burlesque.[204] Because she occupied a different rung on a classed

---

[200] "Faith's Bumpy Legal Travails Grind to Halt as Court Kills Suit," *New York Post*, April 8, 1963; Faith Dane Clippings, Theatre Collection, NYPL.

[201] For a recent reassessment of *The Black Crook*'s place in theater historiography, see Bradley Rogers, "Redressing the Black Crook: The Dancing Tableau of Melodrama," *Modern Drama* 55.4 (Winter 2012): 476–96.

[202] *Martinetti v. Maguire*, 16 F. Cas. 920 (C.C.D.Cal. 1867).

[203] Debates over the morality of sexually provocative dancing continue, although more typi-cally over questions of First Amendment rights and taxability. For a recent example of the lat-ter, see "Bump and Grind Not So Fine Art: Court," *New York Post*, October 23, 2012, http://www.nypost.com/p/news/local/bump_and_grind_not_H5t7UoDaFlb4yqK4fodyDP. Judith Lynne Hanna's *Naked Truth: Strip Clubs, Democracy, and a Christian Right Legal* (Austin: University of Texas Press, 2012) recounts her own efforts as an expert witness to defend legal attacks on exotic dance.

[204] For a history and cultural analysis of burlesque in the United States, see Robert C. Allen, *Horrible Prettiness: Burlesque and American Culture* (Chapel Hill: University of North Carolina Press, 1991).

and sexed artistic hierarchy, Dane's whiteness was not identical to Holm's and de Mille's. In fact, accounts of Dane's biography destabilize the whiteness denoted by her skin tone. Born, depending on the source, in either El Reno, Oklahoma, or Brooklyn, New York, Dane told the *New York Mirror* that she was "part Comanche."[205] True or not, Dane's performance history did not exactly align her with whiteness. Although she claimed to have danced with Holm early in her career, she also reported dancing for African American choreographer Katherine Dunham, and a *New York Times* story places her in a 1945 concert by Russian-born jazz dance aficionado Mura Dehn.[206] The *Mirror*, meanwhile, listed horse-riding in rodeos, riding a seal in a water show, and emceeing strip shows (although never stripping, she insisted) as part of Dane's "fascinating showbiz background."[207] The official Broadway program for *Gypsy* added that "Miss Dane spent last year trouping with carnivals as Little River, an Indian Princess."[208] Like Daphne Brooks, who proposes that we look to the "racial codes, the submerged metaphors indicating difference" rather than to "traces of conventional ethnographic and ethnological evidence" in reading racially ambiguous figures,[209] I want to suggest that Dane's cultural identifications—jazz dancing, exotic dancing, "playing Indian"[210]—signal her difference from the white norm.

Dane's racial identity, of course, was not on trial in *Dane v. M. & H. Co.* But Justice Aurelio did have to decide on which side of several dividing lines to place Dane: dancer or choreographer? laborer or property owner? moral or immoral? Weighing her lowbrow roots and her "bumps and grinds of monumental bluntness" against her claims of copyright, the judge refused to extend to Dane the rights of possessive individualism.[211] Instead, he upheld a more

---

[205] Slocum, "Bumps and Bugle"; Program, *Gypsy*, Broadway Theatre, New York, 1959; "Bumping Along with a Bugle," *New York Herald Tribune*, January 15, 1961, Faith Dane Clippings File, Theatre Collection, NYPL.

[206] "Bumping Along with a Bugle"; John Martin, "Dances in Jazz Form Given by Mura Dehn," *New York Times*, March 16, 1945, http://query.nytimes.com/mem/archive/pdf?res=FB0610F6 3F5B177B93C4A81788D85F418485F9. Accessed June 7, 2013. I have not uncovered any documentation of Dane's performance history with Dunham or Holm, although this lack of evidence by no means negates her claim.

[207] Slocum, "Bumps and Bugle."

[208] Program, *Gypsy*.

[209] Daphne A. Brooks, *Bodies in Dissent: Spectacular Performances of Race and Freedom, 1850–1910* (Durham, NC: Duke University Press, 2006), 143. Brooks is writing here about the nineteenth-century performer Adah Isaacs Menken. The resonances between Menken, who appeared to be nude while riding a horse in a melodrama called *Mazeppa*, and Dane, who performed a striptease without removing her clothes while playing the role of Mazeppa, are intriguing to say the least.

[210] See Philip J. Deloria, *Playing Indian* (New Haven, CT: Yale University Press, 1998).

[211] Slocum, "Bumps and Bugle."

narrow conception of who constituted a choreographer and of who therefore owned rights to the products of her labor. As was the case with Loïe Fuller some seventy years earlier, white skin alone did not automatically confer the privilege of (intellectual) property rights. Though white modern dancers had gained considerable cultural capital in the decades following Fuller's failed copyright claim, without the status of a Holm or a de Mille, Dane's efforts to assert herself as more than a sexualized commodity were, like Fuller's, thwarted by the law's limited reading of her dancing body. With the passage of the 1976 Copyright Act, Congress effectively ratified Justice Aurelio's restrictive view of choreographic copyright by enshrining the hierarchies between copyrightable compositions and uncopyrightable "social dance steps and simple routines."

Dane's migration to Broadway, then, unlike Holm's and de Mille's, did not result in the elevation of her status. And yet, for all three women, employment on the so-called Great White Way produced a shared desire for legal protection of their choreography. Although they hailed from disparate locations in the dance field, the long runs of the Broadway musicals in which their dancing appeared provided exposure for their choreography on a scale that was unprecedented for any of them. If this level of commercial success threatened to complicate Holm's and de Mille's affiliation with art rather than entertainment, it also made it impossible to ignore the fact of dance's participation in a capitalist economy of reproduction. A successful run on Broadway meant that one's choreography was reproduced eight times a week, year after year, with millions of dollars of profit at stake. For these three female dance-makers, as for those before them, the embrace of copyright was an acknowledgment of, a response to, and an attempt to control the effects of those reproductions. That the outcomes of their pursuits of copyright protection were uneven suggests how politicized and contingent the allocation of property rights remained. Because of and alongside the shifts occurring to the American dance landscape at mid-century, choreographers' pursuit of copyright protection built momentum toward legislative change and contributed to the continued stratification of dance along lines of race, class, and sex.

It is worth noting, finally, that in the same vein as Fuller before her, Dane did not let legal defeat squash her sense of proprietorship. In 2003, Dane attended a preview performance of the Broadway revival of *Gypsy*, directed by Sam Mendes. At age seventy-nine, she wore a beaded headdress, gold trench coat, and a gold fishnet tunic over a nude-colored body stocking. Asked by a *New York Times* reporter to confirm that she played the original Mazeppa, Faith—apparently having dropped her last name—responded, "Played it? It was *my act*." "My number is that show," she added, "and I made less than the animals."[212] Like de Mille, who told anyone who would listen about how little she made from her *Oklahoma!* choreography, Dane took up a rhetorical campaign for ownership rights to fill the void in legal protection—actually, rhetorical and performative. Carrying the bugle with her "all the time" (a trademark prop, if ever there was one), dressed in costume, and purportedly miffed that she was not permitted to audition for the revival production, Dane highlights the live dancing body's ability to continue taking credit for itself, even when sidelined by the law.[213]

[212] Joyce Wadler, "Boldface Names," *New York Times*, April 8, 2003, http://www.nytimes.com/2003/04/08/nyregion/boldface-names-162868.html. Accessed June 11, 2013. Emphasis in original.

[213] In the 1990s and early 2000s, Dane became a recurrent write-in candidate for mayor of Washington, DC. A 1998 article in the *Washington Post* about the independent candidates for the mayoral race describes her as a "bugle-blowing, statehood-demanding, arts-crazy Adams Morgan resident named Faith" and features a photo of her with bugle in hand. John P. Martin, "Many 'Others' Join Race for D.C. Mayor," *Washington Post*, October 2, 1998, http://www.washingtonpost.com/wp-srv/local/longterm/library/dcelections/candidates/campaign1002.htm. Accessed June 11, 2013.

5

Copyright and the Death/Life of the Choreographer

Thus far, this book has traced the efforts of an assortment of dance artists to assert intellectual property rights in their choreography prior to the passage of the 1976 Copyright Act, which first classified choreographic works as a protected subject matter. My focus has been on the ways in which dancers' positions within raced, gendered, and artistic hierarchies shaped their pursuit of copyright protection, the law's reception of those pursuits, and, by implication, the formation of choreographic copyright. This chapter shifts gears to examine the only major cases involving choreographic copyright that have gone to trial since the passage of the 1976 Act: *Horgan v. Macmillian, Inc.* (1986), in which the executor of ballet choreographer George Balanchine's estate sued the publishers of a book of photographs of Balanchine's *The Nutcracker* ballet; and *Martha Graham School and Dance Foundation, Inc., and Ronald Protas v. Martha Graham Center of Contemporary Dance, Inc.* (2002), in which Graham's heir sued the Graham Company to halt performances of Graham's work.[1] The importance of these cases to a book about the development of

---

[1] It is worth mentioning an additional, much more minor case: in December 1991, a lawsuit alleging copyright infringement and unfair competition was filed in Manhattan federal court on behalf of the deceased white musical theater choreographer Gower Champion. Champion's production team claimed that the licensing agreement for a national production of *Bye Bye Birdie* did not include Champion's original 1961 choreography. Although the parties settled out of court, *Entertainment Law & Finance* quoted the Champion team's attorney as saying that the settlement "enhances the rights of choreographers." Stan Soocher, with Richard L. Curtis and Amiana Pytel, "Bit Parts," *Entertainment Law & Finance* 8.4 (July 1992): 8. Sally Banes mentions the case, *Champion Five Inc. v. National Artists Management Co. Inc.*, 91-8503, in "Homage, Plagiarism, Allusion, Comment, Quotation: Negotiating Choreographic Appropriation," in *Before, Between, and Beyond: Three Decades of Dance Writing*, ed. Andrea Harris (Madison: University of Wisconsin Press, 2007), 210n1. I have been unable to track down any further information about the case.

choreographic copyright is twofold. First, until adjudicated in court, the passage of a law recognizing the copyrightability of choreography tells us little about the precise nature and scope of statutory protection.[2] And second, these cases allow us to ask how the claim that "All forms of property ... bear in their lineaments the traces of the struggles in which they were fabricated" plays out in the field of dance.[3] To what extent did pre-1976 efforts to assert intellectual property rights in dance affect the formulations of choreographic copyright advanced in the Balanchine and Graham cases?[4] In particular, I am interested in probing how the historical alignment between gendered whiteness and property rights shadows constructions of choreographic copyright at the end the twentieth century and the start of the twenty-first.

Unlike the examples covered in the foregoing chapters, the copyright claims examined here were made on behalf of deceased choreographers. Balanchine died in 1983, three years before *Horgan v. Macmillan* went to trial, and Graham died in 1991, eleven years before *Graham School v. Graham Center* first came before the courts. Accordingly, both cases grapple not just with whether and how to allocate ownership rights in choreography but with what happens to those rights when the choreographer is no longer living. The deaths of two of the giants of twentieth-century American dance, in other words, generate new questions about the apparatus of authorship in dance. How do Romantic conceptions of the author as genius fare once the most towering figures in the field of dance have passed? Does the literal death of the choreographer entail a corresponding theoretical death?[5] The slogan "the death of the author," associated with the French theorists Roland Barthes and Michel Foucault, generally signifies the demise of an author's significance to the meaning of a text, and the notion has been influential to the development of critical dance studies. But the literal deaths in *Horgan v. Macmillan* and *Graham School v. Graham*

---

[2] As Patricia Solan Gennerich writes in "One Moment in Time: The Second Circuit Ponders Choreographic Photography as a Copyright Infringement: *Horgan v. Macmillan, Inc.*," *Brooklyn Law Review* 53 (spring 1987), "choreographers today remain possessed of statutory protection that has delivered all that was promised, yet lacks the final test of judicial interpretation" (406). Because the parties in *Horgan v. Macmillan* settled out of court, a good deal of this uncertainty persists.

[3] Mark Rose, *Authors and Owners: The Invention of Copyright* (Cambridge, MA: Harvard University Press, 1993), 8.

[4] My gratitude to Oliver Gerland and Derek Miller and to the participants in the working session on "Intellectual Property and Performance" at the 2011 American Society for Theatre Research conference, who helped shape my thinking about these two legal cases.

[5] This line of inquiry is indebted to Jane Gallop's *The Deaths of the Author: Reading and Writing in Time* (Durham, NC: Duke University Press, 2011), which thinks through "abstract theoretical death along with the real loss of the author" (5).

Center highlight the particular complications dance poses to such theoretical constructs. Given the notorious difficulty of separating the dancer from the dance, what does the irrevocable loss of the choreographer's body mean for the figure of the author and for the afterlife of the choreographic work?

The 1976 Copyright Act provides another reason to think through choreographic copyright and the death of the author together. The act was not only a first in the recognition it extended to choreographic works; it also marked the first time that the term of copyright extended beyond the life of the author. Reflecting Thomas Jefferson's view that copyrights should not outlive their creators, the US Constitution's original copyright provision specified that protection be granted to authors and inventors "for limited times." The 1790 Copyright Act set the term of copyright at fourteen years, with the possibility of renewal for another fourteen. Over the next two centuries, Congress repeatedly extended the duration of copyright: in 1831, the term increased to forty-two years; in 1909, to fifty-six years; and in 1976, the term was set at the author's life plus fifty years. (The 1998 Sonny Bono Copyright Term Extension Act added another twenty years.)[6] This steady expansion of copyright's duration has contributed to what Ray Madoff terms "the rising power of the American dead."[7]

However coincidental, the conjunction within the 1976 Act of "postmortem copyright," seen by its critics as benefiting the dead at the expense of the living, and the granting of copyright status to choreographic works prompts a reconsideration of choreography's relationship to im/mortality.[8] Typically, of course, dance performance is more closely aligned with disappearance than with perpetuity. Indeed, in its very "liveness," dance paradoxically conjures up death. As Selby Schwartz has written,

> Dance is pressed on all sides by the concerns of bodies that are urgently moving under and against the duress of temporality. . . . This sweaty, hard-breathing, moment-by-moment experience of live time, shared by the dancers with the audience, is valuable, even beautiful; but its implications of mortality are a little terrifying.[9]

[6] Paul K. Saint-Amour, *The Copywrights: Intellectual Property and the Literary Imagination* (Ithaca, NY: Cornell University Press, 2003), 125; Ray D. Madoff, *Immortality and the Law: The Rising Power of the American Dead* (New Haven, CT: Yale University Press, 2010), 143.

[7] Madoff, *Immortality and the Law.*

[8] Saint-Amour, *Copywrights*, 124. See also Madoff, *Immortality and the Law.*

[9] Selby Wynn Schwartz, "Martha@Martha: A Séance with Richard Move," *Women & Performance: A Journal of Feminist Theory* 20.1 (2010): 62–63.

If dance itself is defined by the passage of time and haunted by the inevitability of death, the idea of postmortem copyright would seem to hold special appeal for choreographers. Coming in the wake of the 1976 Copyright Act and seen as the first tests of the law's application to choreography, the Balanchine and Graham copyright cases return us to the issue of dance's ontology (discussed in the Introduction and Chapter 3), especially its complicated temporality. My goal here is to show how copyright's own ontological and temporal concerns interface with those of dance.

The dead author is common to *Horgan v. Macmillan* and *Graham School v. Graham Center*, but the outcomes of the cases were far from identical. While the US District court in *Horgan* ruled that the book of photographs of *The Nutcracker Ballet* did not infringe on Balanchine's copyright, an appeals court judge reversed the decision on the grounds that the lower court did not apply the correct test for infringement. Although the parties subsequently settled out of court, the implication of the appeals court decision was that a set of photographs was "substantially similar" enough to Balanchine's choreography to warrant an injunction against the book's publication. The upshot was a posthumous strengthening of Balanchine's intellectual property rights. In contrast, in *Graham School v. Graham Center* a district court judge ruled that Graham was a "worker-for-hire" for the non-profit corporation that housed her company and therefore not in a position to transfer the rights in her choreography to her heir. The upshot was a retroactive diminishment of Graham's intellectual property rights. Without discounting the numerous possible reasons for the two cases' divergences, this chapter argues that approached from the standpoint of critical race and gender theory, these outcomes rearticulate the property rights of masculine whiteness and question anew white women's access to those rights. In other words, the death of the author/choreographer tested the privileges of whiteness, and the results were not even.

It is inarguable that Balanchine and Graham, both of whom occupied the upper strata of American dance, benefited from white privilege. Although Graham's early career was focused on gaining legitimacy for modern dance, and although Balanchine's initial effort to gain copyright protection for his choreography was (as mentioned in Chapter 4) rebuffed by the Copyright Office, by the time of their deaths, they held secure positions at the top of the dance field's raced/classed hierarchy. In "A Tango between Copyright and Choreography: Whiteness as Status Property in Balanchine's Ballets, Fuller's Serpentine Dance, and Graham's Modern Dances," legal scholar Caroline Joan S. Picart argues that white privilege informed not only the positionality but also the aesthetic styles of these artists.[10] Balanchine's choreography, Picart

---

[10] Caroline Joan S. Picart, "A Tango between Copyright and Choreography: Whiteness as Status Property in Balanchine's Ballets, Fuller's Serpentine Dance and Graham's Modern

maintains, exhibited a "hyper-whitened aesthetic"—a glorification of the white female ballerina and an embrace of abstract, "pure" dance movement. Graham, meanwhile, embodied an "exotic whiteness," evident in the inspiration she drew from Native American and Asian sources, inherited from her early training with Ruth St. Denis and Ted Shawn, and in her ability to "masquerade as an 'exotic' woman while remaining recognizably white."[11] I would add that Balanchine and Graham both exercised the racial privilege to "use and enjoy" and then "invisibilize" non-white movement material. As Brenda Dixon Gottschild has observed, Graham's "signature" pelvic contraction and grounded movement aesthetic owe more to African-derived dance traditions than to European ones. And as Jacqueline Shea Murphy has shown, Graham simultaneously evoked and absented American Indians in her choreography.[12] After Gottschild, moreover, it is necessary to complicate any discussion of Balanchine's "hyper-whitened aesthetic" with an acknowledgment of his absorption of a number of Africanist principles, such as angularity, high-affect juxtaposition, and an aesthetic of the cool.[13]

Picart also applies critical race theory to Balanchine's and Graham's respective copyright claims, and in a line of argument that hews closely to my own throughout this book, she sees the distinction between copyrightable private property and non-copyrightable public property as a key locus of racialization. "Crucial to the delimitation of both Balanchine's and Graham's choreographic works as intellectual property," she writes, "was their possession of whiteness as status property."[14] This delimitation, however, has a peculiar instability to it: an "original" work becomes private intellectual property when a copyright is secured (via registration with the Copyright Office, publication, or upon fixation, depending on when a work was created), but it is only when a lawsuit arises that its legitimacy is tested.[15] In *Horgan v. Macmillan* and *Graham School*

Dances," *Cardozo Journal of Law & Gender* 18 (Spring 2012): 685–725. Picart expands on this argument in her book *Critical Race Theory and Copyright in American Dance: Whiteness as Status Property* (New York: Palgrave Macmillan, 2013).

[11] Picart, "A Tango between Copyright and Choreography," 687, 699, 713, 715.

[12] Brenda Dixon Gottschild, *Digging the Africanist Presence in American Performance: Dance and Other Contexts* (Westport, CT: Greenwood Press, 1996), 49; Jacqueline Shea Murphy, *"The People Have Never Stopped Dancing": Native American Modern Dance Histories* (Minneapolis: University of Minnesota Press, 2007), 148–68.

[13] Gottschild, *Digging the Africanist Presence*, 59–79.

[14] Picart, "A Tango between Copyright and Choreography," 722.

[15] Under the 1976 Copyright Act, "Copyright protection subsists from the time the work is created in fixed form." "Copyright Basics," United States Copyright Office, page 2. Available at http://www.copyright.gov/.

v. Graham Center, that is, part of what was on trial was the legality of copyrights that had ostensibly already been secured. However privileged Balanchine and Graham were in the field of dance, the posthumous legal wrangling over the status and scope of their copyrights was also a re-adjudication of both artists' hold on whiteness-as-property.

With its focus on a pair of court cases, this chapter's methods depart somewhat from those of the preceding chapters. Rather than reconstructing the conditions surrounding dance-makers' efforts to assert intellectual property rights in their choreography, here I scrutinize two judicial rulings, read through the lenses of dance and performance theory, poststructural theory, intellectual property rights theory, and critical race and gender theory. While *Horgan v. Macmillan* and *Graham School v. Graham Center* have not suffered from a lack of attention from legal scholars, they have been little examined by dance scholars.[16] Yet the implications of these cases for the field of dance are wide-ranging, touching on everything from the ownership of choreographic legacies, to the ephemerality and reproducibility of dance, to the temporal relationships between dance and other media, to the choreographer's straddling of capital and labor. Before tackling these issues, I briefly rehearse the poststructural idea of "the death of the author" and attend to its application within dance studies. Next, I consider copyright's relationship to death, uncovering a perhaps unexpected parallel between the ontologies of postmortem copyright and of dance. I then turn to *Horgan v. Macmillan*, highlighting the conceptualizations of dance that underwrote the different conclusions reached by the district court and appeals court about the scope of Balanchine's copyright. Finally, I discuss *Graham School v. Graham Center*, spotlighting the case's chief contradiction: that granting life to Graham's choreographic works depended

---

[16] Among the many legal articles that have covered one or both of these cases are Gennerich, "One Moment in Time;" Adaline J. Hilgard, "Can Choreography and Copyright Waltz Together in the Wake of *Horgan v. Macmillan, Inc.?" U.C. Davis Law Review* 27 (Spring 1994): 757–89; Joi Michelle Lakes, "A Pas de Deux for Choreography and Copyright," *New York University Law Review* 80 (2005): 1829–61; Kathleen Abitabile and Jeannette Picerno, "Dance and the Choreographer's Dilemma: A Legal and Cultural Perspective on Copyright Protection for Choreographic Works," *Campbell Law Review* 27 (Fall 2004): 39–62; Sarah Kutner and Holly Rich, "Dirty Dancing: Attributing the Moral Right of Attribution to American Copyright Law: The Work for Hire Doctrine and the Usurping of the Ultimate Grand Dame and Founder of Modern Dance, Martha Graham," *Hofstra Labor & Employment Law Journal* 22.1 (Fall 2004): 325–51; Anne W. Braveman, "Duet of Discord: Martha Graham and Her Non-profit Battle over Work for Hire," *Loyola of Los Angeles Entertainment Law Review* 25 (2005): 471–98; Sharon Connelly, "Authorship, Ownership, and Control: Balancing the Economic and Artistic Issues Raised by the Martha Graham Copyright Case," *Fordham Intellectual Property, Media & Entertainment Law Journal* 15 (Spring 2005): 837–91; and Picart, "A Tango between Copyright and Choreography."

on reducing a figure who epitomized the authority of white modern dance to the status of a laborer.

The Deaths of the Author and Choreographer

The idea of "the death of the author," as Jane Gallop writes in her recent book *The Deaths of the Author*, is tied almost exclusively to two articles that came out in close proximity to each other: Roland Barthes's "The Death of the Author," which appeared in 1968, and Michel Foucault's "What Is an Author?" which appeared in 1969.[17] As Gallop points out, Foucault's essay actually touches only briefly on the death of the author, but his focus on the author as a function of discourse—as an "ideological figure by which one marks the manner in which we fear the proliferation of meaning"—is emblematic of poststructuralism's destabilization of authorial intent as a privileged method of interpreting a text.[18] This shift away from the primacy of the author as the producer of meaning is at the heart of Barthes's "The Death of the Author." Barthes writes, "We know now that a text is not a line of words releasing a single 'theological' meaning (the 'message' of the Author-God) but a multi-dimensional space in which a variety of writings, none of them original, blend and clash."[19] For Barthes, "To give a text an Author is to impose a limit on that text, to furnish it with a final signified, to close the writing."[20] Embracing multiplicity in place of univocality, Barthes finds that it is the reader who ultimately provides "a text's unity." His essay closes with the famous line, "the birth of the reader must be at the cost of the death of the Author."[21]

The poststructuralist notion of the author's demise gained widespread currency in the US academy in the 1980s, but, as Gallop notes, it was not uncontroversial. Feminist and critical race literary scholars in particular raised concerns about the displacement of the author at a moment when the Western and male-dominated canon was beginning to be challenged. In her 1987 article "The Race for Theory," Barbara Christian wryly observes that anti-authorial discourse "surfaced, interestingly enough, just when the literature of peoples

---

[17] Michel Foucault, "What Is an Author?" first published Paris, 1969, reprinted in *The Foucault Reader*, ed. Paul Rabinow (New York: Pantheon, 1984), 101–20; Roland Barthes, "The Death of the Author," in *Image-Music-Text*, trans. Stephen Heath (New York: Hill and Wang, 1977), 142–48.

[18] Foucault, "What Is an Author?" 119.

[19] Barthes, "The Death of the Author," 146.

[20] Ibid., 147.

[21] Ibid., 148.

of color, of black women, of Latin Americans, of Africans began to move to 'the center.'"[22] Where Foucault concluded his "What Is an Author" essay by asking "What difference does it make who is speaking?" feminist critics responded that "it matters very much who is speaking, about what, and from which particular social, historical, and political location."[23] Even so, Barthes's obituary for the author remains "the single most influential meditation on the question of authorship in modern times."[24]

This influence is apparent in dance studies as well. Susan Leigh Foster's *Reading Dancing: Bodies and Subjects in Contemporary Dance*, one of the foundational texts in the field, cites the importance of poststructuralist criticism to its survey of the conceptions of dance that govern the works of Deborah Hay, Martha Graham, George Balanchine, and Merce Cunningham.[25] Foster writes,

> One of the main premises of this book is that [Merce] Cunningham's approach to choreography points up the arbitrary nature of the relationship between dance movement, the signifier, and that to which it refers, the signified. And as a result, his work accomplishes for dance

[22] Barbara Christian, "The Race for Theory," *Cultural Critique* 6 (Spring 1987): 55.

[23] Foucault, "What Is an Author?" 120; Betsy Erkkila, "Ethnicity, Literary Theory, and the Grounds of Resistance," *American Quarterly* 47.4 (December 1995): 572. Not all feminist scholars decried the death of the author. As Nancy K. Miller remarked, "It is, after all, the Author, canonized, anthologized, and institutionalized, who excludes the less-known works of women and minority writers from the canon, and who by his authority justifies the exclusion." "Changing the Subject: Authorship, Writing, and the Reader," in *Feminist Studies/Critical Studies*, ed. Teresa de Lauretis (Bloomington: Indiana University Press, 1986), 102. See also Cheryl Walker, "Feminist Literary Criticism and the Author," *Critical Inquiry* 16.3 (Spring 1990): 551–71.

[24] Seán Burke, *The Death and Return of the Author: Criticism and Subjectivity in Barthes, Foucault, and Derrida*, 2nd ed. (Edinburgh: Edinburgh University Press, 1998), 19. Burke's text, a close reading of anti-authorial discourse in the works of Foucault, Barthes, and Jacques Derrida, argues that the author does not and cannot stay dead. In fact, as both Burke and Gallop point out, in a lesser-known publication that appeared just three years after "The Death of the Author," Barthes writes that "The pleasure of the Text also includes a friendly return of the author." Roland Barthes, *Sade, Fourier, Loyola*, trans. Richard Miller (New York: Hill and Wang, 1976), 8. Gallop's reading homes in on the term "friendly" in Barthes's statement and explores what she calls the "perverse" and potentially queer desire for the dead author in Barthes's work. See Gallop, *Deaths of the Author*, esp. 5, 38, 40. For Burke, the death of the author is an untenable concept to begin with; he calls it a "blind-spot" for Foucault, Barthes, and Derrida, "an absence they seek to create and explore, but one which is always already filled with the idea of the author." *The Death and Return of the Author*, 172.

[25] As Foster notes, her book "charts the progression from structuralist to post-structuralist theoretical positions" in its survey of four dominant choreographic conventions. Susan Leigh Foster, *Reading Dancing: Bodies and Subjects in Contemporary Dance* (Berkeley: University of California Press), 234n11.

what recent literary criticism has referred to as "the death of the author."[26]

Although this statement is located in a footnote, Foster's focus on "the codes and conventions" of a choreographic work rather than on choreographic intent "as an interpretive itinerary for the viewer" is the crux of the methodological approach she advocates in *Reading Dancing*.[27] In pointing to Cunningham's embrace of the arbitrariness of signification, furthermore, Foster emphasizes the role that artists (and not just French philosophers) have played in shifting understandings of meaning as reader/viewer-centered rather than author-centered.[28]

The impact that "the death of the author" has had on the discipline of dance studies, whether stemming from literary criticism or contemporary choreographic practices themselves, is perhaps nowhere more palpable than in Roger Copeland's 2011 essay, "The Death of the Choreographer."[29] Copeland opens by noting that the summer of 2009, during which Merce Cunningham and Pina Bausch died within a month of one another, "marked a melancholy milestone in the history of dance as an art form."[30] But he quickly shifts gears to lament the fact that "from the perspective of academic dance studies, the era that Bausch and Cunningham represented—that of 'The Great Western Individual Choreographer'—had already come and gone." Copeland cites as evidence the dearth of doctoral dissertations devoted to "dances created by 'individual' Western choreographers such as Nijinsky, Ashton, Tudor, Graham, Balanchine, Cunningham, Tharp, Morris (et al.)" and the increase of scholarly attention to "traditional, culture-specific and/or collectivist movement-forms such as salsa, flamenco, kapa haka, break dancing, capoeira, contra-dance, belly dancing, Bharata Natyam and contact improvisation."[31]

---

[26] Ibid., 242n43.

[27] Ibid.

[28] By the same token, art critic Craig Owens sees a close relationship between Barthes's "The Death of the Author" and a concern "to register the disappearance of the figure of the author" in the visual art of the 1960s, '70s, and '80s. "From Work to Frame, or, Is There Life after 'The Death of the Author'?" in *Beyond Recognition: Representation, Power, and Culture*, ed. Scott Bryson, Barbara Kruger, Lynne Tillman, and Jane Weinstock (Berkeley: University of California Press, 1994), 123. Even Barthes himself, Owens notes, traced the author's diminished significance to the late nineteenth-century Symbolist poet Stephane Mallarmé, and Owens adds Marcel Duchamp, with his "readymade" found objects, and the collaborative production practices of visual surrealists to a genealogy of the author's supposed death (125).

[29] Roger Copeland, "The Death of the Choreographer," in *Dance and Politics*, ed. Alexandra Kolb (Bern, Switzerland: Peter Lang, 2011), 39–65.

[30] Ibid., 39.

[31] Ibid.

Although he concedes that this shift is "an inevitable (and wholly welcome) consequence of globalization and its curricular corollaries: multiculturalism and cultural diversity," he maintains that it is ideologically driven by the "misguided belief that 'collectively created' works are superior (at least in some theoretically 'political' sense) to dances whose 'authorship' can be attributed to unique, Western individuals."[32] Susan Foster's scholarship comes in for particular attack by Copeland. He sees the focus in her recent writings on conceptualizing the choreographer as a worker and co-creator (rather than "inspired genius") as part of a trend of "demonizing the auteur."[33] Surely Copeland would also find fault with my own contention, published elsewhere, that the term "choreographer" has functioned historically "to authorize and exclude."[34] Indeed, in its attempt to expose the constructedness of choreographic authorship, this book is also guilty of contributing to the trend Copeland excoriates.

It should not go unremarked that all of the choreographers on Copeland's list of "Great Western Individual Choreographers" are white, and that the majority of practices that have, to his mind, replaced these individual figures are associated with black or brown dancing bodies. It would appear, then, that the racial politics of "the death of the author" in literary studies and dance studies are not equivalent. Unlike in literary studies, where some scholars worried that anti-authorial discourse would siphon attention away from the agency of long-marginalized writers, in dance studies, the destabilization of the author has had the effect of opening up the field to non-white subjects and practices previously excluded from the dance historical canon.

Yet the copyright cases of Balanchine and Graham make clear that Copeland's concern for the fate of the "The Great Western Individual Choreographer" is far from exceptional. While their literal deaths may have signaled the end of an era, the mechanism of copyright allowed their authorial rights to endure. What was implicitly on trial in their copyright lawsuits, therefore, was nothing less than the choreographer-as-genius.

Postmortem Copyright and Dance's Ontology

On first glance, the institution of copyright seems fully insulated from "the death of the author." Copyright, after all, is predicated on the idea that an originating author is entitled to the rights in the work he creates. Title 17 of

---

[32] Ibid., 39–40.

[33] Ibid., 40, 44.

[34] Anthea Kraut, *Choreographing the Folk: The Dance Stagings of Zora Neale Hurston* (Minneapolis: University of Minnesota Press, 2008), 56.

the Constitution explicitly states that "Copyright in a work protected under this title vests initially in the author or authors of the work."[35] As Mark Rose notes in *Authors and Owners*, copyright, "by endowing it with legal reality, helps to produce and affirm the very identity of the author as author."[36] The gap between copyright's sanctioning of the author and poststruturalism's rejection of the stable, unified text and the autonomous genius-author thus appears vast.[37] Yet to a great extent, it has been scholars working at the intersection of copyright studies and literary studies who, taking up Foucault's call to examine "how the author became individualized in a culture like ours," have exposed the historical constructedness of the modern author.[38] In "The Genius and the Copyright: Economic and Legal Conditions of the Emergence of the 'Author,'" for example, Martha Woodmansee traces the concept of the author to the eighteenth-century rise of a group of writers in Germany whose increasing dependence on the marketplace for their economic livelihood prompted them to re-frame writing as a site of unique originality. Such work demonstrates that the relationship between copyright and Romantic notions of individualized authorship is more complex than it looks on the surface.

To be sure, intellectual property law's definition of who can qualify as an author is technically quite capacious. Although copyright is reserved for "original works of authorship," the threshold for originality is low. As Paul Saint-Amour explains, "The 'original expression' a work must exhibit in order to win copyright is not a transcendent iconoclasm or singularity but something more modest: the absence of verbatim copying and the demonstrable presence of a modicum of creativity."[39] Viewed through the lens of these minimal requirements, copyright law's author more closely resembles a craftsperson than a genius.

Customary deployments of copyright, however, fly in the face of this modest interpretation of authorship. "Although it may have been established as a category of circumscription," Saint-Amour asserts, "original expression was consecrated by the Romantic cult of the individual genius, and that legacy of Romanticism ... has proven both durable and adaptable."[40] The reliance on the

---

[35] 17 USC § 201. See http://www.copyright.gov/title17/92chap2.html.

[36] Rose, *Authors and Owners*, 2.

[37] Ibid., 3.

[38] Foucault, "What Is an Author?" 101. Rose, Martha Woodmansee, and Paul Saint-Amour are exemplary scholars of this interdisciplinary work.

[39] Saint-Amour, *Copywrights*, 7. The defining ruling on the matter of originality is the Supreme Court case of *Feist Publications, Inc., v. Rural Telephone Service Co.*, 499 U.S. 340 (1991), which ruled that the information compiled in a telephone book did not possess sufficient creativity to merit copyright protection.

[40] Saint-Amour, *Copywrights*, 6.

term "genius" to describe Balanchine and Graham in their legal trials is a testament to the entwinement of copyright discourse and the Romantic discourse of authorship. Indeed, even those aspects of copyright law that highlight the fictiveness of authorship have done little to dislodge the idea of individual inspiration. For instance, the legal invention of corporate authorship enabled by the "work-for-hire doctrine" (discussed in Chapter 2 and explored further below) that was first enacted in the 1909 Copyright Act seems to give the lie to the model of the author as solitary genius. Yet, as legal scholar James Boyle has argued, "a striking feature of the language of romantic authorship is the way it is used to support sweeping intellectual property rights for large corporate entities."[41] To cite a recent example, many of the arguments made in favor of the 1998 Sonny Bono Copyright Term Extension Act, which lengthened the duration of copyright from fifty to seventy years after the author's death, were made in the name of individual authors, although the benefits that accrued to corporations like the Walt Disney Company as a result of the law earned it the moniker the Mickey Mouse Protection Act.[42]

If the Romantic notion of an individuated, authoring self thus remains alive and well in the arena of copyright law, the rise of posthumous copyright casts light on the relationship between copyright and authorship from another angle. Saint-Amour's discussion of the extension of copyright beyond the life of the author provides an important guide to understanding intellectual property law's treatment of death and proves useful for this book's consideration of the vexed nature of choreographic copyright. In a chapter in his 2003 book *The Copywrights*, titled "The Reign of the Dead: Hauntologies of Postmortem Copyright," Saint-Amour argues that "copyright law has no less a cultural function than to determine and police the border between the living and the dead."[43] In its steady expansion, he notes, copyright in the United States "seems to be making a bid for perpetuity, for immortality."[44] Postmortem copyright means that the dead author, "having relinquished his physical body ... [can] return in the legal body" and continue to bequeath his estate to his heirs.[45] The multiplicity of the author's bodies will become critical below, but

---

[41] James Boyle, *Shamans, Software, and Spleens: Law and the Construction of the Information Society* (Cambridge, MA, Harvard University Press 1996), xiii.

[42] Saint-Amour, *Copywrights*, 5, 122.

[43] Ibid., 124. Saint-Amour borrows from Jacques Derrida's notion of hauntology—a concept designed to create space for liminal states of being that confound binary oppositions, such as between presence and absence—to illuminate the "spectral operations" of postmortem copyright. Saint-Amour, *Copywrights*, 129–31.

[44] Ibid., 125.

[45] Ibid., 127.

for now I want to emphasize the uncanny temporality of the author's return. In Saint-Amour's words:

> In creating copyrightable works, as in making a will, I participate through the prosthesis of the law in a future I will not corporeally experience. In this respect, postmortem copyright gives authors the virtual experience of being undead before they are dead.[46]

In the wake of the 1976 Copyright Act, the first to extend copyright terms past the life of the author, copyright thus simultaneously anticipates and simulates a deferral of death.

The oddness of this temporality is compounded by the fact that, at least for the moment, copyrights do expire; the immortality they confer on authors is "strictly limited."[47] It is that very limitedness, Saint-Amour argues, that sets intellectual property apart from tangible forms of property, like real estate, which can be "privately owned, exchanged, and bequeathed indefinitely." Its temporariness also makes copyright "seem more akin to the human creator whose mortality ... it shares." In its impermanence, intellectual property "can stand in as a surrogate for its creator." "Yet paradoxically," Saint-Amour goes on to say,

> that kinship also gives rise to the desire, at least among advocates of perpetual copyright, to immortalize intangible property in the place of its mortal copyright. . . . If literary property law helps construct the boundary between ideality and materiality, mortality and immortality, it is also caught between those states, pulled in the direction of immortality because it is mortal, and toward materiality because it is ideal. [48]

As is clear from this quotation, Saint-Amour's point of reference is intellectual property rights for literary works. But his remarks about the tension between temporariness and a desire for permanence would not be out of place in a discussion of dance's ontology. While dance's evanescence has been identified as a "problem" at least since the first notation systems were devised in the eighteenth century, in the wake of dance critic Marcia Siegel's assertion in the 1970s that dance exists "at the vanishing point," and of performance theorist

---

[46] Ibid., 128.
[47] Ibid.
[48] Ibid., 129.

Peggy Phelan's argument in the 1990s that "performance's only life is in the present," it is nearly impossible for dance scholars to avoid some mention, however perfunctory, of the medium's alleged ephemerality.[49] At times celebrated as a means of circumventing economies of commodification, this transience has more often been lamented as depriving dance of a history and consigning it to a low status relative to the other arts. In fact, one way to theorize choreography has been to see it as an "apparatus of capture," a way to manage dance's evasiveness.[50] André Lepecki's contention that "the choreographic" is a field defined by the question, "How does one make dance stay around, or create an economy of perception aimed specifically at its passing away?" could be taken as evidence of the way im/mortality haunts the discipline of dance.[51]

What I am proposing is that there is a parallel between the temporal instability built into copyright—an instability brought to the fore by the inevitability of the author's death—and the temporal instability of dance. The correspondence that Saint-Amour sees between intellectual property's lack of permanence and that of the human author is shared as well by dominant conceptions of dance performance, tinged as it is with "implications of mortality."[52] The irony for dance is that copyright, with its requirement that works be "fixed in a tangible medium of expression," has represented the temporal solidity—the past and the future—which it supposedly lacks; choreographic copyright is nothing if not an "apparatus of capture." While the primary concern of the dance-makers in this book was to achieve copyright status for their work rather than to lengthen the term of copyright, the conversion of choreography into property required contending with dance's perceived intangibility. What, then, if copyright is no less "caught" between states—between materiality and immaterality, disappearance and persistence, mortality and immortality—than dance itself? Turning now to the copyright cases of

---

[49] See Susan Leigh Foster, *Choreographing Empathy: Kinesthesia in Performance* (London: Routledge, 2011), 30; Marcia B. Siegel, *At the Vanishing Point: A Critic Looks at Dance* (New York: Saturday Review Press, 1972); Peggy Phelan, *Unmarked: The Politics of Performance* (London: Routledge, 1993), 146.

[50] André Lepecki, "Choreography as Apparatus of Capture," *TDR: The Drama Review* 51.2 (Summer 2007): 119–23. Lepecki's use of the phrase "apparatus of capture" comes from Gilles Deleuze and Félix Guattari's *A Thousand Plateaus: Capitalism and Schizophrenia*, trans. Brian Massumi (London: Athlone Press, 1987), 424–73.

[51] Lepecki, "Choreography as Apparatus of Capture," 120.

[52] Schwartz, "Martha@Martha," 63.

Balanchine and Graham, we can ask what the implications of this caughtness are for the dead white choreographer.

Horgan v. Macmillan, Inc.: The Afterlife of Balanchine's Property Rights

Although born in Russia, George Balanchine (1904–1983) is synonymous with the Americanization of ballet. Trained at St. Petersburg's Imperial Ballet School, Balanchine began his choreographic career with Serge Diaghilev's Ballets Russes. In 1933, at the invitation of impresario Lincoln Kirstein, Balanchine settled in New York, where the two founded the School of American Ballet and, in 1948, the New York City Ballet. Of all the dancers covered in this book, Balanchine carried the most privilege—racial, gendered, and artistic. The ease with which Balanchine claimed American citizenship (cultural and legal) is one clear index of his white privilege.[53] As Gay Morris has written, "Between 1945 and 1955 Balanchine was transformed from a foreign interloper out of touch with American dance into the creative genius of a native American ballet."[54] He also exemplifies the privilege inherent in the term "choreographer." Reportedly the first to earn the credit "choreography by" on Broadway for his work for the 1936 production *On Your Toes*, Balanchine highlights the gendered dimensions of the term within ballet.[55] Unlike the female-dominated tradition of modern dance, where leadership roles were held by women, ballet, especially under Balanchine, adhered to a remarkably rigid gendered division of labor between male choreographers and feminized dancers. (Agnes de Mille was a notable exception.) As Carrie Gaiser Casey argues, Balanchine embodies the conventional dance history narrative in which "the male genius conceives the divine Idea of choreography, which he then externalizes through the ballerina, whose body functions purely as a vessel for his inspiration."[56] Casey's work demonstrates how the genealogy that positions Balanchine as the "father of American ballet"[57] elides the "rich heterogeneity of

[53] Balanchine officially became a US citizen in 1939. Bernard Taper, *Balanchine: A Biography* (1984; Berkeley: University of California Press, 1996), 217.

[54] Gay Morris, *A Game for Dancers: Performing Modernism in the Postwar Years, 1945–1960* (Middletown, CT: Wesleyan University Press, 2006), 44. Morris notes that "Balanchine aided the notion of his Americanness" in part by marrying Native American Maria Tallchief (61).

[55] Taper, *Balanchine*, 180. Prior to this, playbill credit lines read "Dances by …" According to Taper, the change was made at Balanchine's request.

[56] Carrie Gaiser Casey, "Ballet's Feminisms: Genealogy and Gender in Twentieth-Century American Ballet History," PhD diss., University of California, Berkeley, 2009, 9.

[57] This was the title of the 1984 PBS episodes of *Great Performances* and *Dance in America* about Balanchine. See Judy Kinberg et al., *Balanchine: The Father of American Ballet*, video (West Long Branch, NJ: Kultur, 1984).

Figure 5.1 George Balanchine in 1960. Photo courtesy of Photofest.

ballet in the early twentieth century," and, in particular, disavows "ballet's feminine popular past."[58] By the time of his death at the age of seventy-nine, the cloak of Balanchine's "genius" status obscured even his own early choreography for the commercial sphere.[59]

In its deliberation of the scope of Balanchine's postmortem choreographic rights, *Horgan v. Macmillan* put that genius status and its corollary entitlements to the test. As Julie Van Camp writes in her thorough analysis of the case, the *Horgan* decision broached a number of issues relevant to the field of dance scholarship, including the definition of "choreographic work," the test of "originality" for choreography, the legal distinction between "expression" and "idea," methods of fixation, and what constitutes infringement.[60] What interests me about the lawsuit is the way in which differing assessments by

[58] Casey, "Ballet's Feminisms," 4, 5.

[59] The George Balanchine Foundation launched the Popular Balanchine Project in 1999 as a way of rectifying this oversight of Balanchine's commercial works. http://www.balanchine.org/balanchine/03/popularbalanchine.html. Accessed July 15, 2013.

[60] Julie Van Camp, "Copyright of Choreographic Works," in *1994–95 Entertainment, Publishing and the Arts Handbook*, ed. Stephen F. Breimer, Robert Thorne, and John David Viera (New York: Clark, Boardman, and Callaghan, 1994), 59–92.

the district court and appeals court of dance's temporality and reproducibility led to different rulings on the question of choreographic infringement. In large part, as I see it, the case grappled with the temporal instability of dance and, concomitantly, with the instability of the choreographer as author and property-owner.

The legal suit arose in April 1985 when Barbara Horgan, the executrix of Balanchine's estate, learned of the impending publication by Macmillan's Atheneum imprint of a book of photographs depicting the New York City Ballet (NYCB) Company's version of *The Nutcracker*, choreographed by Balanchine in 1954 and staged annually by the NYCB at Christmas time. Designed for young readers, the book interspersed text by Ellen Switzer about the story of the Nutcracker with color photographs of scenes from the NYCB's production of the ballet, taken by Caras and Costas, the official photographers for the Company.[61] Framing the book were a title page with three black and white photographs of Balanchine directing a rehearsal of the ballet and a final section with interviews and photographs of ten Company dancers. Upon receiving galleys for the book from Lincoln Kirstein, Horgan contacted the attorney for Balanchine's estate, who in turn contacted the publishers to question their right to "create such a derivative work" "in light of the Estate's ownership of the work in question." In a subsequent series of exchanges, Horgan advised Macmillan that she was unwilling to give the requisite licenses for the book, to which Macmillan responded that they deemed it "unnecessary ... to obtain any authorization from the Ballanchine [*sic*] Estate ... since, as a legal matter, we are completely satisfied that the work in no way violates or infringes upon any proprietary rights of Mr. Balanchine or his successors-in-interest."[62] Six months later, upon the publication of the book, Horgan filed suit on behalf of the estate, seeking declaratory relief[63] and a preliminary and permanent injunction against the publication of the book. Horgan's claims of infringement were that the Switzer book violated the Balanchine estate's exclusive right to present his version of *The Nutcracker* either because the book was an unauthorized "copy" that portrayed "the essence of the Balanchine Nutcracker," or because it was "derivative" of the pre-existing choreographic work.[64]

---

[61] Ellen Switzer, *The Nutcracker, A Story and a Ballet*, photographs by Steven Caras and Costas (New York: Macmillan, 1985).

[62] *Horgan v. MacMillan, Inc.*, 789 F.2d 157 (2d. Cir. 1986) at 159.

[63] "Declaratory relief" seeks a "binding judgment from a court defining the legal relationship between parties and their rights in the matter before the court." Legal Information Institute, http://www.law.cornell.edu/wex/declaratory_judgment. Accessed July 15, 2013.

[64] *Horgan v. MacMillan, Inc.*, 789 F.2d 157 (2d. Cir. 1986) at 161.

That there was an estate to police Balanchine's property rights at all was not a given. Balanchine was famously nonchalant about the future of his choreographic works. Known to make statements like, "What's the matter with Now?" and "When I die, everything should vanish,"[65] Balanchine seemed to endorse the Siegel/Phelan view of dance as a present-tense medium. Toward the end of his life, however, he reportedly told the ballet mistress Rosemary Dunleavy, "You know, these are my ballets. In the years to come they will be rehearsed by other people. They will be danced by other people. But no matter what, they are still my ballets."[66] Running alongside his embrace of ballet's ephemerality, then, was an insistence on proprietorship—even beyond the grave. When a mild heart attack in 1978 gave Balanchine a brush with mortality, he agreed to consult a lawyer, who, according to biographer Bernard Taper, convinced Balanchine that his ballets could be considered assets. The resulting will left 113 of his ballets to fourteen different legatees, including Tanaquil Le Clercq and Karin von Aroldingen, both ballerinas, and Horgan, who had been Balanchine's personal assistant at the NYCB for twenty years.[67] For the dance world, the will represented "a historic crux." Taper writes,

> What it sought to transmit was the greatest choreographic legacy of all time, which also happened to be the essential inventory of the New York City Ballet. Never before in the history of dance, that most evanescent of the arts, had there been a successful transmission of such a body of work from one age to the next.[68]

Taper's dramatic rhetoric indicates how high the stakes of Balanchine's will were: at issue was whether, transformed into choreographic property, Balanchine's works could defy the logic of ephemerality and survive the death of the author's body. At stake too, however implicitly, was how death would affect the author's rights of ownership.

To deal with the distribution of Balanchine's choreographic rights across so many individuals, in March 1987, Horgan and von Aroldingen, on the advice of the estate's attorney, Paul H. Epstein, formed the Balanchine Trust, which administers the licensing, staging, and maintaining of the ballets. Although not all legatees chose to join, the Trust consolidated the bulk of Balanchine's

---

[65] Taper, *Balanchine*, 399; Karen Wilkin, "Remembering Balanchine," *Hudson Review* 46.4 (Winter 1994): 708.

[66] Wilkin, "Remembering Balanchine," 708.

[67] The rest of the more than four hundred works Balanchine choreographed during the course of his life had fallen out of existence. Taper, *Balanchine*, 400.

[68] Ibid.

choreographic property into a single legal entity. As such, the Trust functioned as the legal body that took the place of Balanchine's physical body, with a "corpus" consisting "of the rights attached to the ballets."[69] A key feature of this legal corpus was its ability to outlive the legatees: as Horgan told a journalist, "The trust came about because I was concerned with what would happen after I'm gone."[70] Yet, because trusts have legally imposed life spans, Horgan and von Aroldingen also founded the George Balanchine Foundation to house the rights to the ballets upon the Trust's termination.[71] A desire for immortality is thus embedded in the Trust and the Foundation, although, per the 1976 Copyright Act, the copyrights to Balanchine's ballets will eventually expire fifty years after his death, in 2033.[72] The Trust also took action to extend the reach of Balanchine's property rights by securing trademarks on Balanchine's name and the terms "Balanchine Technique" and "Balanchine Style" with the US Patent and Trademark Office and requiring that the trademark and servicemark appear on programs for performances by companies other than the NYCB.[73] According to Horgan, this added protection was a legal safeguard against misuse of the Balanchine name, as well as "a way of gaining added recognition in society at large for ballet as a serious art form."[74] Under the aegis of the Trust, Balanchine's death led to an unmistakable expansion of his property interests.[75]

The District Court Decision: "Flow" and Non-Reproducibility

Horgan's infringement suit against Macmillan was the first legal test of the Trust's power, and the decision by the District Court for the Southern District of New York placed distinct limits on that power. On November 19, 1985, after

---

[69] Cheryl Swack, "The Balanchine Trust: Dancing through the Steps of Two-Part Licensing," *Jeffrey S. Moorad Sports Law Journal* 6.2 (1999): 271.

[70] Sheryl Flatow, "The Balanchine Trust: Guardian of the Legacy," *Dance Magazine*, December 1990, 58.

[71] Ibid., 59.

[72] Marilyn Hunt, "The Balanchine and Ashton Inheritance, Part 1, The Balanchine Trust," *Dancing Times*, April 1993, 669.

[73] Hunt, "The Balanchine and Ashton Inheritance," 669; Swack, "The Balanchine Trust," 272; Taper, *Balanchine*, 410.

[74] Hunt, "The Balanchine and Ashton Inheritance," 669.

[75] In fact, some found the expansion and more rigorous policing of Balanchine's posthumous property rights at odds with the generous approach Balanchine took when he was living. Taper, *Balanchine*, 410. According to Flatow, Balanchine rarely charged fees for other companies to perform his work, and when he did, they were nominal ("The Balanchine Trust," 59–60). For more on choreographers' use of trusts, see Francis Yeoh, "The Choreographic Trust: Preserving Dance Legacies," *Dance Chronicle* 35.2 (2012): 224–49.

hearing oral arguments, Judge Richard Owen denied Horgan's request for an injunction against the publication of the book "because photographs in defendants' book did not infringe deceased's choreography, because plaintiff unduly delayed in seeking an injunction, and because defendants' book did not violate the deceased's name's right to be free of publicity."[76] Although the judge faulted Horgan for taking no action between the initial exchange of letters in the spring of 1985 and the filing of the lawsuit in October, I read his decision as an outgrowth of his circumscribed view of Balanchine's authorship and property rights.

To reach the conclusion that photographs did not infringe on Balanchine's choreographic rights, Judge Owen had to improvise a theory of dance's temporality and reproducibility. "As I see it," he wrote in his opinion,

> choreography has to do with the flow of the steps in a ballet. The still photographs in the Nutcracker book, numerous though they are, catch dancers in various attitudes at specific instants of time; they do not, nor do they intend to, take or use the underlying choreography. The staged performance could not be recreated from them.[77]

Brief as this rationale is, it coheres around an ontological understanding of choreography that simultaneously converges with and ever so slightly diverges from that of Siegel and Phelan. Like Phelan, Judge Owen sees choreography as eluding photography's economy of reproduction: while the still photographs "catch dancers" at given moments in time, they do not and can not capture the "underlying choreography." Photographs are not copies of choreography, nor can copies (reproductions) of that choreography be re-enacted from the photographs. Yet, even as he assigns a kind of non-reproducibility to choreography, Judge Owen's emphasis on choreography's "flow" is not identical, at least to my mind, to Siegel and Phelan's alignment of dance performance with an always-receding present. Instead, Judge Owen positions choreography as steadily expanding outward from "specific instants of time," as forward-moving and ongoing. "Flow," in other words, is not the same as disappearance.

Still, for Judge Owen, choreography's distinctive temporality renders it non-reproducible in other mediums, and this view helps justify a restrictive treatment of Balanchine's choreographic property. Balanchine's rights, the judge rules, do not extend beyond the medium in which he created. Choreography's evasion of any temporal fixity thus sits in tension with the

---

[76] *Horgan v. MacMillan, Inc.*, 621 F. Supp. 1169 (S.D.N.Y. 1985).
[77] Ibid., at 1170.

finiteness of Balanchine's property. Where choreography is remarkably dynamic in Judge Owen's assessment, moreover, Balanchine's authorship is rather unremarkable. Legal scholar Caroline Picart points out that the judicial opinion's opening line—"Each Christmas, the New York City Ballet features the ballet *The Nutcracker*"—renders the production "run-of-the-mill" rather than affording it the status of masterpiece.[78]

Here the photographs of Balanchine directing rehearsals of *The Nutcracker* that appear on the title page of the book in question come into play. As Julie Van Camp notes, these photographs serve to establish Balanchine's authorship of the NYCB's version of *The Nutcracker*; they visually document that the ballet originated with Balanchine, a requirement of copyright.[79] But, for Judge Owen, who considers the photographs in relation to the plaintiff's allegation that the book infringes on Balanchine's right to be free of publicity, the images do little more than convey "interesting information concerning life around us." The photographs of Balanchine, to put it another way, are more pertinent as part of the landscape of the living than they are as an emblem of the rights of the dead. This is a decidedly unsentimental and unheroic view of Balanchine. Refusing to mourn Balanchine's death as the loss of a genius, refusing to treat static photography as a copy of fluid choreography, Judge Owen also refuses to find evidence of any infringement of Balanchine's property rights.

The Appellate Court Decision: The Still Image as Choreographic Copy

Not surprisingly, Horgan appealed Judge Owen's decision, and on March 5, 1986, the three-judge panel of the US Court of Appeals for the Second Circuit heard arguments in the case. On April 28, the appellate court reversed and remanded the district court judgment. While holding that any delay on Horgan's part in filing suit against Macmillan should not bar injunctive relief, the core of the reversal was the appeals court's finding that "the district court applied the wrong legal standard for determining whether the photographs infringe the copyrighted choreography." The correct standard, the court ruled, "is not whether the original could be recreated from the allegedly infringing copy, but whether the latter is 'substantially similar' to the former."[80] In reaching this conclusion, the appeals court offered a very different reading of the

---

[78] *Horgan v. MacMillan, Inc.*, 621 F. Supp. 1169 (S.D.N.Y. 1985) at 1169; Picart, "A Tango between Copyright and Choreography," 707.

[79] Van Camp, "Copyright of Choreographic Works," 74.

[80] *Horgan v. MacMillan, Inc.*, 789 F.2d 157 (2d. Cir. 1986) at 158, 162.

relationship between choreography's ontology, the status of the author, and the borders of choreographic property.

In a much lengthier opinion (translating into seven Lexis Nexis pages compared to the district court's one), Chief Judge Wilfred Feinberg reviewed the details of the case and underscored its legal significance. Calling the question of whether still photographs can infringe choreography "novel," the court acknowledged that the recentness of "explicit federal copyright protection for choreography" made "the scope of that protection ... an uncharted area of the law." In order to review this "matter of first impression," the court began by verifying Balanchine's authority in the dance world. "It is undisputed," the court wrote, "that Balanchine was a recognized master in his field." Citing Taper's biography of Balanchine, a footnote clarified that "Balanchine has been described as a 'genius' and as 'an artist of the same magnitude as Picasso.' "[81] As Picart argues in her analysis of the case, the appellate court's description of Balanchine departed from Judge Owen's more matter-of-fact treatment of him. The rhetorical positioning of Balanchine as genius, Picart asserts, was designed "to showcase Balanchine's dominance as an artist and, therefore, to justify more stringent measures in delimiting Balanchine's choreographic works from the public domain."[82] Picart also finds meaningful the attention the court gave to the royalties that the NYCB paid first to Balanchine and then to his estate each time *The Nutcracker* was performed, and to Horgan's status as Balanchine's legatee and executor of his estate.[83] Implicitly, the court legitimates the chain of ownership connecting the author's physical body to the legal body that succeeded him in death.

Yet Judge Feinberg also leaves the door open for challenges to Balanchine's exclusive claims of authorship of *The Nutcracker*. Rehearsing the appellees' argument that "little, if anything, of Balanchine's original choreographic contribution to the New York City Ballet production of The Nutcracker is shown in the photographs," the court notes that Balanchine's version of the ballet "is based on extensive preexisting material," both the nineteenth-century author E. T. A Hoffman's folk tale "The Nutcracker and the Mouse King" and the Russian choreographer Ivanov's 1892 rendition of the ballet; each of these sources was in the public domain.[84] In fact, a potential problem for Horgan was

[81] Ibid., at 158, 160, 158.

[82] Picart, "A Tango between Copyright and Choreography," 708.

[83] Ibid., 708–9.

[84] *Horgan v. MacMillan, Inc.*, 789 F.2d 157 (2d. Cir. 1986) at 162. For a history of *Nutcracker* productions, both prior and subsequent to Balanchine's, see Jennifer Fisher, *"Nutcracker" Nation: How an Old World Ballet Became a Christmas Tradition in the New World* (New Haven, CT: Yale University Press, 2003).

that the 1981 copyright registration Balanchine obtained for *The Nutcracker* failed to specify the non-original, pre-existing portions of the choreography, a legal requirement. Lawyers for Macmillan also pointed out that the photographs in Switzer's book included non-choreographic elements, such as costumes by Karinska and sets by Rouben Ter-Arutunian, to which Balanchine held no claim. Weighing these concerns, Judge Feinberg went so far as to suggest that

> The validity of Balanchine's copyright, the amount of original Balanchine choreography (rather than Ivanov's) in the New York City Ballet production of The Nutcracker and in the photographs, and the degree to which the choreography would be distinguishable in the photographs without the costumes and sets (in which appellant claims no right) are all matters still to be determined, preferably on a fuller record including expert testimony....

The court also indicated that the appellees' claim that the NYCB Company might be considered a "joint owner with the estate of the choreography" would benefit from a fuller hearing.[85]

Notwithstanding the "considerable confusion" about the proprietary rights of Balanchine's estate,[86] the court hesitated not at all in completely reversing the lower court's finding that photographs could not infringe upon Balanchine's choreographic rights. Substituting a "substantial similarity" test for the district court's reproducibility test, the appellate court advanced a much looser standard for infringement and, correspondingly, a much broader conception of choreographic private property. While legal observers have called the substantial similarity test "amorphous and difficult to apply,"[87] the court relied on the standard, expressed by Judge Learned Hand, that the correct test for infringement was whether "the ordinary observer, unless he set out to detect the disparities, would be disposed to overlook them, and regard their aesthetic appeal as the same." To the court, the fact that photography and choreography were different mediums was insignificant; neither did the "amount of the original" in the allegedly infringing work matter. Even the acknowledgment that "recreation of the original from the infringing material is unlikely if not impossible" was deemed no defense to infringement. Instead, the court regarded the possibility that the book of photographs "portrays the essence of

[85] *Horgan v. MacMillan, Inc.*, 789 F.2d 157 (2d. Cir. 1986) at 162, 163.

[86] Ibid. at 163.

[87] Hilgard "Note: Can Choreography and Copyright Waltz Together," 774.

the Balanchine Nutcracker" as sufficient threat to Balanchine's choreographic rights.[88]

The appellate court's logic rested on a more expansive understanding of choreography's ontology than that hinted at by the district court judge. In place of Judge Owen's concise "flow of steps," Judge Feinberg turned to the definition of choreography included in the *Compendium of Copyright Office Practices* (issued in 1984)[89]:

> Choreography is the composition and arrangement of dance movements and patterns, and is usually intended to be accompanied by music. Dance is static and kinetic successions of bodily movement in certain rhythmic and spatial relationships.[90]

As Picart observes, the delineation of dance as both "static and kinetic" made room for the still poses in Switzer's book to be considered a "protected element of choreography."[91] In turn, the Court adopted a distinctive view of the temporal relationship between photography and choreography. Judge Feinberg's opinion stated that

[88] *Horgan v. MacMillan, Inc.*, 789 F.2d 157 (2d. Cir. 1986) at 162, 161.

[89] Known as *Compedium II*, this document, designed to guide the administrative decisions of Copyright Office staff, can be found here: http://copyright.gov/comp3/prior-editions.html. Accessed October 10, 2014.

[90] *Horgan v. MacMillan, Inc.*, 789 F.2d 157 (2d. Cir. 1986) at 161. Legal scholar Joi Michelle Lakes notes that "The influence of Compendium II is debatable. While it has been stated that the Copyright Office is not to decide issues of first impression, it is clear that courts turn to Compendium II when they need instruction in copyright cases." "Note: A Pas de Deux for Choreography and Copyright," 1843. A sign of the circle of influence between Copyright Office–issued Compendiums and judicial decisions, and of the weight of the *Horgan* decision, is the recently released public draft of *Compendium III*, which cites *Horgan's* citation of *Compendium II* in its definition of dance as "the static and kinetic succession[] of bodily movement in certain rhythmic and spatial relationships." See *Compendium of U.S. Copyright Practices*, Third Edition, US Copyright Office, Public Draft, August 19, 2014, Chapter 800, section 805, 70. Some legal scholars have called on the courts to turn to experts from within the field of dance to define choreography and to assess claims of infringement. For example, Abitabile and Picerno argue that the Horgan decision "shows that a judge or a court cannot be responsible for deciding how a work can or cannot be recreated. Only a trained professional (dancer, choreographer, etc.) should be able to make that determination." "Dance and the Choreographer's Dilemma," 46. See also Katie Lula, "The Pas De Deux between Dance and Law: Tossing Copyright Law into the Wings and Bringing Dance Custom Centerstage," *Chicago-Kent Journal of Intellectual Property* 5 (spring 2006): 177.

[91] Picart, "A Tango between Copyright and Choreography," 710.

the district judge took a far too limited view of the extent to which choreographic material may be conveyed in the medium of still photography. A snapshot of a single moment in a dance sequence may communicate a great deal. It may, for example, capture a gesture, the composition of dancers' bodies or the placement of dancers on the stage.

Each of these elements, the implication was, constituted a key piece of choreographic information, of which the judge found evidence in numerous photographs in Switzer's book. But he went further still, asserting, "A photograph may also convey to the viewer's imagination the moments before and after the split second recorded." By way of illustration, he pointed to a two-page photograph of the "Sugar Canes" section of *The Nutcracker*.[92] "In this photograph," he explained,

> the Sugar Canes are a foot or more off the ground, holding large hoops above their heads. One member of the ensemble is jumping through a hoop, which is held extended in front of the dancer. The dancer's legs are thrust forward, parallel to the stage and several feet off the ground. The viewer understands instinctively, based simply on the laws of gravity, that the Sugar Canes jumped up from the floor only a moment earlier, and came down shortly after the photographed moment. An ordinary observer, who had only recently seen a performance of The Nutcracker, could probably perceive even more from this photograph. The single instant thus communicates far more than a single chord of a Beethoven symphony—the analogy suggested by the district judge.

Even while referring to dance photography as a "freezing of a choreographic moment," then, the court ascribes no temporal fixity, no single tense to the image.[93] Rather, the "kinetic" is embedded in the "static," the before and after embedded in the now.

---

[92] The reference to "Sugar Canes" here is erroneous; the number the judge is describing is commonly known as the "Candy Canes." The error comes from the Switzer book, which calls out the "Sugar Canes in their striped suits." *The Nutcracker, A Story and a Ballet*, 75. The two-page photograph appears on pages 76 and 77 of the book. As Jennifer Fisher pointed out to me, the number in Balanchine's version of *The Nutcracker* involving hoops and striped costumes evolved from a Trepák or Russian dance to a jesters' dance into what is known today as Candy Canes. Email correspondence, March 9, 2015. My sincere thanks to Jennifer for generously sharing this information with me.

[93] *Horgan v. MacMillan, Inc.*, 789 F.2d 157 (2d. Cir. 1986) at 163.

Figure 5.2 New York City Ballet dancer John Clifford and other Candy Canes in a 1960s production of *The Nutcracker*, in a photo very similar to the one about which Judge Feinberg wrote in *Horgan v. Macmillan*. Photo courtesy of Photofest.

This theorization of the temporality of the dance photograph bears a striking resemblance to Mark Franko's recent discussion of Barbara Morgan's late 1930s "action photography" of Martha Graham. Writing about Morgan's emphasis on the need for the photographer to "anticipate movement," Franko endorses her view of action "as continuity in the image between a past, a present, and a future" and "equally a discontinuity or, rather, the occasion for the spectator to do the work of missing emplotment."[94] For Morgan and

[94] Mark Franko, *Martha Graham in Love and War: The Life in the Work* (New York: Oxford University Press, 2012), 38.

Franko, as for Judge Feinberg, the viewer of a photograph has the capacity to suture together the temporal gaps between the still image and the dance action. There are strong resonances here with poststructuralism's emphasis on audience-centered meaning, although the focus in these examples is less on what the photographic text signifies than on how it registers time. There are also parallels, surprising perhaps, with the lower court's view of choreography's ongoingness. If a dance photograph is both anticipatory and retrospective, the choreography it documents does not expire but resides (in perpetuity?) in the viewer's mind.

But where Judge Owen found a tension between the photograph's temporality and that of choreography, Judge Feinberg did not, and this made all the difference to the appellate court's assessment of infringement. Once any ontological gap between dance and photography is smoothed over, it becomes much less of a stretch to claim that photography constitutes a "copy" of choreography. How one approaches the question of choreography's temporality, therefore, has implications for how broad or narrow a view of choreographic property one has, and how low or high one sets the bar for infringement.[95] All of these issues, furthermore, are entangled with how one interprets the death of the author. Even while the appellate court briefly exposes holes in the narrative of Balanchine's exclusive and all-encompassing authorship of *The Nutcracker,* and even while the judicial opinion heavily weights the role of the viewer, the underscoring of Balanchine's genius and the legitimation of his estate as his surrogate give Balanchine an authorial afterlife that contributes to the court's generous view of his choreographic property.

The fact that the parties in *Horgan v. Macmillan* settled before the case could be re-heard at the district court level meant that a number of questions raised by the appellate court remained unresolved. The reasons for the settlement—whether Horgan preferred not to face further questions about the validity of Balanchine's copyright; whether Macmillan believed that the substantial similarity test proposed by Judge Feinberg fatally weakened their defense against infringement—can only be a matter of speculation. Either way, the upshot of the appellate court decision was a "resounding victory" for Balanchine's estate, which retained "absolute control of photographic

---

[95] Of course, it is also possible to find in favor of infringement without sharing Judge Feinberg's precise view of choreography. Edwina M. Watkins, for example, agrees with Judge Feinberg's instinct to find that photographs could be an infringement of a choreographic work but suggests that a violation of the public display right is the more appropriate rationale. "May I Have This Dance? Establishing a Liability Standard for Infringement of Choreographic Works," *Journal of Intellectual Property Law* 10 (Spring 2003): 437–63.

materials" of his ballets.[96] While some worried that the decision would lead to further battles between choreographers and publishers of dance books, and others that the low bar for infringement would "stifle artists' creativity," there was no outcry in the dance press over the strengthening of Balanchine's post-mortem copyright.[97] Instead, there was praise for the appellate court's ruling, deemed an "enlightened determination to accord choreography the full measure of copyright protection afforded other creative works."[98] In what was the first, albeit incomplete, judicial test of choreographic copyright following the 1976 Copyright Act, the death of the author proved no hindrance to upholding the privilege and property rights of the white male choreographer.

Graham School v. Graham Center: The Multiple Deaths of the White Female Choreographer

The outcome of the second choreographic copyright case to go to trial following the 1976 Act could hardly have been more different. The 2002 ruling in *The Martha Graham School and Dance Foundation, Inc. and Ronald A. Protas versus Martha Graham Center of Contemporary Dance, Inc. and Martha Graham School of Contemporary Dance, Inc.* awarded the copyrights to most of Martha Graham's choreography to the defendants, the Graham Center and School, rather than to Graham's heir, Ronald Protas. The decision set off a flurry of debate and discussion in the concert dance community about the ownership of choreographic works. For some, the judge's decision was cause for celebration insofar as it enabled the Graham Company to resume performing works from the Graham repertory after an imposed hiatus. But for others in the modern dance world, the basis of the court's ruling—that Graham was an employee of the non-profit corporation she set up in 1948 and therefore not in a position to bequeath the rights to her choreography to Protas—set off alarm bells. How could such an American modern dance legend *not* own her own choreography?

---

[96] Charles D. Ossola, "A Matter of Protection: Photographs, Copyright Claims Ignite Legal Battle," *Update Dance/USA* 4.3 (August 1986): 9; Picart, "A Tango between Copyright and Choreography," 713.

[97] Ronald Smothers, "Dance Copyright Case Is Reopened on Appeal," *New York Times*, April 30, 1986, http://www.nytimes.com/1986/04/30/books/dance-copyright-case-is-reopened-on-appeal.html?n=Top%2FReference%2FTimes%20Topics%2FPeople%2FB%2FBalanchine%2C%20George. Accessed July 19, 2013; Hilgard, "Can Choreography and Copyright Waltz Together," 784.

[98] Ossola, "A Matter of Protection," 10.

In examining the Graham lawsuit, I want to keep one eye on the ways it diverges from the Balanchine case. Where *Horgan v. Macmillan* suggests that the death of the author could lead to an enlargement of authorial rights, *Graham School v. Graham Center* suggests the opposite: that the death of the author could lead to a renunciation of authorial rights. Put differently, the copyright battle over Graham's choreography left Graham's legal body with much less power than the legal body representing Balanchine. This incongruence is striking given how comparable their power was in the field of dance.[99] Their shared artistic and racial privilege raises questions about whether and how gender might be a factor in the disparate consequences of their copyright cases. Why did the court reach a more expansive view of the rights of the "father" of American ballet and a more constricted view of those of the "mother" of modern dance? To be clear, I do not intend to argue that gender bias accounts for the differential treatments of Balanchine and Graham. There are too many factors at play in their respective legal trials to assign gender a causal role. But I also think it is impossible to rule out the possibility that gender played a part, however obliquely, in the two decisions' discrepant allocations of choreographic property rights. At the very least, I want to call attention to the gendered effects of the two judicial decisions, one reaffirming the privilege of a white male choreographer, the other casting a shadow over the seemingly inviolable privilege of a white female choreographer. Given the centrality of white women to the campaign to win copyright recognition for choreography, the gendered implications of the threat to Graham's intellectual property rights should not be glossed over.

Even in life, it bears noting, Graham and Balanchine adhered to different models of choreographic authorship. In contrast to the paradigm that Balanchine exemplified of the male genius choreographer inspired by female muses, Graham (1894–1991) helped forge a modern dance tradition in which white women gained legitimacy by composing and enacting their own dances.[100] Begun as "primarily a solo art form,"[101] modern dance enabled women to seize authorial control of their dancing bodies, blurring the division

---

[99] Writing about Graham, dance critic Joan Acocella remarked that "No one except George Balanchine had anything approaching her influence on twentieth-century choreography." "The Flame: The Battle over Martha Graham's Dances," *The New Yorker*, February 19 and 26, 2001, p. 181. As Picart likewise notes, "That Martha Graham rivaled Balanchine in reputational capital is not debatable." "A Tango between Copyright and Choreography," 713.

[100] Linda J. Tomko, *Dancing Class: Gender, Ethnicity, and Social Divides in American Dance, 1890–1920* (Bloomington: Indiana University Press, 1999), 32–33.

[101] Amy Koritz, *Gendering Bodies/Performing Art: Dance and Literature in Early-Twentieth-Century British Culture* (Ann Arbor: University of Michigan Press, 1995), 119.

of labor between dancer and choreographer. The consequences of this blurring were complicated. Amy Koritz has argued that a separation between author and performers is a prerequisite of elite art and that the absence of such a separation in the solo form "stymied the careers of female early modern dances in England."[102] More recently, Sally Gardner has contended that the group form was similarly problematic for the female dancer-choreographer, for "if she dances with and among her dancers she cannot actually be *seen there* as an author."[103] But if the collapsing of author and dancer impeded modern dance's early standing relative to high art, it also opened up other avenues of authorship. As I have proposed at various points throughout this book (see especially Chapter 3), dancers have embodied ways of claiming the author-function.

Compared to Balanchine's, then, Graham's hold on authorship was much more corporeal. Because she was so "fiercely attached to the act of performing live," as Selby Schwartz has written, Graham's identities as a dancer and choreographer were closely intertwined—so much so that she could state in her autobiography that "I think I really only started to choreograph so that I could have something to show off in."[104] The physical locus of Graham's authorship was amplified by the ideological conventions of modernism, which figured her choreography as "expressive" of her unique personhood.[105] Out of her self-driven choreography emerged a distinctive technique that bore the traces of her body's individualized way of moving: the "signature" Graham look consists of taught, angular movements and, especially, the contracted, or caved-in, torso. The distribution of this look across her dancers, combined with the fact that Graham's choreographic oeuvre was filled with authoritative female protagonists that she herself played—Joan of Arc in *Seraphic Dialogue*, Jocasta in *Night Journey*, for example—made Graham an author with a powerful embodied presence.[106]

The physicality of Graham's authorship, however, made mortality all the more portentous. Schwartz has written insightfully about how heavily death weighed on Graham as a result of her identification as a dancer. Her essay

---

[102] Ibid., 3.

[103] Sally Gardner, "The Dancer, the Choreographer and Modern Dance Scholarship: A Critical Reading," *Dance Research* 25.1 (2007): 40.

[104] Schwartz, "Martha@Martha," 62; Martha Graham, *Blood Memory: An Autobiography* (New York: Doubleday, 1991), 237.

[105] Mark Franko's *Dancing Modernism/Performing Politics* (Bloomington: Indiana University Press, 1995) explores various expression theories as they intersect with aesthetic modernism in dance.

[106] Indeed, Victoria Thoms posits "Graham's danced oeuvre" as "an alternative form of autobiography." "Martha Graham's Haunting Body: Autobiography at the Intersection of Writing and Dancing," *Dance Research Journal* 40.1 (Summer 2008): 4.

Figure 5.3 Martha Graham in *Night Journey* (1947). Photo courtesy of Photofest.

"Martha@Martha: A Séance with Richard Move" opens with Graham's declaration that "A dancer, more than any other human being, dies two deaths." The first death, Graham explains, is physical, occurring "when the powerfully trained body will no longer respond as you would wish."[107] Graham postponed this first death unbelievably long by performing until she was seventy-six, modifying steps to accommodate her aging body. But the knowledge of the inevitable endpoint to her dancing life haunted Graham, and once she stopped dancing, she reportedly "wished to die."[108] Schwartz characterizes Graham's first death as "not only an experience of death but also one of ghostliness, of being present in the afterlife of one's own body."[109] This ghostliness resided in a second Graham body, the non-dancing body she occupied for the thirty years between her retirement from dance and her biological death.

[107] Graham, *Blood Memory*, 238.
[108] Ibid.
[109] Schwartz, "Martha@Martha," 63.

Eleven years after that biological death began the posthumous copyright battle over Graham's choreographic works. Approached through the lens of poststructural theory, it becomes clear that Graham's first death anticipated not only her eventual literal death but other metaphorical deaths as well. The legal skirmish over Graham's choreographic property, that is, re-staged the drama of mortality that shaped her later living years. This drama played out around two additional bodies that succeeded Graham: her body of work and the legal body representing her property rights.

Graham's Legal Bodies at War

When Graham (the biological being) died at the age of ninety-six, she left behind her signature movement technique; a large body of choreographic works (she created over 180 over the course of her long life); and two institutions, the Martha Graham Center of Contemporary Dance, which housed her company of dancers and her choreographic legacy, and the Martha Graham School of Contemporary Dance, which disseminated her technique. Like Balanchine, Graham lacked any biological descendants, and her last will, executed two years before her death, designated Ron Protas as the sole beneficiary and executor of her estate. A freelance photographer fifty years younger than Graham, Protas had become Graham's confidante and companion in the last two decades of her life, in addition to taking an active role in the Center and School. What exactly Graham's estate included was less than certain. While her will specified that Protas should receive "the residue ... of all [her] property," including "any rights or interests in any dance works," Graham never registered her choreographic works with the Copyright Office during her life, reportedly because she preferred that they remain unfixed and alterable.[110] Like Balanchine, Graham embraced contradictory sentiments about what

[110] Brendan McCarthy, "Who Owns Martha Graham's Work?" *Ballet Magazine*, April 2002. http://www.ballet.co.uk/magazines/yr_02/apr02/bmc_martha_graham.htm. Accessed July 24, 2013; David Finkle, "Court Dances," *Village Voice*, November 28, 2000, http://www.villagevoice.com/2000-11-28/news/court-dances/2/. Accessed July 24, 2013. Graham's will is quoted in *Martha Graham School and Dance Foundation, Inc. v. Martha Graham Center of Contemporary Dance, Inc.*, 224 F. Supp. 2d 567, 576 (S.D.N.Y. 2002). Graham's ostensible lack of interest in copyright protection during her lifetime lends further support to the idea of corporeal autography (explored in Chapter 3). Graham's long performing life and her strong association with the central roles in her choreography, that is, may have made the legal mechanism of copyright seem less necessary. Conversely, Nicholas Arcomano noted in a 1980 article that "Martha Graham has been including a copyright notice on programs of performances of her works as is often done with musical compositions." "Choreography and Copyright, Part Two," *Dance Magazine*, May 1980, 119.

should become of her choreography after her death, claiming that "it didn't matter if her works survived her" but lobbying hard for the financing to preserve her works on film.[111]

Although Protas was advised to determine exactly what rights he had inherited, he apparently never did so. Nonetheless, for the decade following Graham's death, everyone proceeded as if Protas owned the exclusive rights to Graham's works. During that time, Protas secured trademarks on the names "Martha Graham" and "Martha Graham Technique." In 1998, he formed the Martha Graham Trust to serve as the legal repository and licensing body of the intellectual property that he claimed to own and granted licenses to the Graham Center and School. The upshot was that "No one [was] allowed to perform [Graham's] dances, or even to teach anything described as Graham technique, without Protas's permission."[112]

Protas had assumed control over the Graham Center and School upon Graham's death, but his relationship with the board of directors of these institutions grew increasingly antagonistic, and in June 2000, he was forced out as artistic director. What followed was a kind of copyright arms race between the non-profit entities vying for official proxy status for the dead choreographer. In July 2000, Protas began applying for copyright registrations for forty of Graham's choreographic works and received registration for thirty of these.[113] In January 2001, the Center applied for copyright registrations for fifteen of Graham's dances. Protas and the Center ended up with competing certificates for eight works.[114] Meanwhile, under increasing financial pressure, the Center was forced to suspend operations. At the same time, following his ouster from the Center, Protas established yet another legal entity, the Martha Graham School and Dance Foundation, and in his capacity as Graham trustee, he granted exclusive licenses to the Foundation to teach Graham technique and perform Graham works.[115] In January 2001, thanks to an influx of cash,

[111] Acocella, "The Flame," 182; Graham, *Blood Memory,* 248.

[112] Acocella, "The Flame," 182. *Martha Graham School and Dance Foundation, Inc. v. Martha Graham Center of Contemporary Dance, Inc.,* 153 F. Supp. 2d 512 (S.D.N.Y. 2001); *Martha Graham School and Dance Foundation, Inc. v. Martha Graham Center of Contemporary Dance, Inc.,* 43 Fed. Appx. 408 (2d Cir. 2002).

[113] An eventual point of dispute would be the publication status of these works. While Protas claimed they were unpublished, a requirement of copyright law at the time, the court found evidence that more than half of the works for which he received certificates of copyright had been published on film or videotape. See Abitabile and Picerno, "Dance and the Choreographer's Dilemma," 50; 224 F. Supp. 2d 567 at 581.

[114] 224 F. Supp. 2d 567 at 586–87.

[115] 153 F. Supp. 2d 512 at 518.

the Graham Center re-opened. That same month, acting in the name of the Martha Graham Dance Foundation, Protas filed suit against the Center and School for copyright infringement and sought to enjoin them from using the Martha Graham trademark, teaching the Martha Graham technique, and performing seventy of Graham's dances. He also sought a declaratory judgment establishing his sole ownership of Graham's choreography, as well as the sets and jewelry associated with the works in question.[116]

The Genius versus the Hired Hand

Protas's lawsuit resulted in two separate cases, one dealing with trademark, the other with copyright. The ensuing legal struggles lasted five years. Both cases were tried in the District Court for the Southern District of New York, under District Judge Miriam Goldman Cedarbaum. In the first trial, decided in August 2001, Judge Cedarbaum ruled that Protas could not stop the Center from using the name Martha Graham or advertising that the school taught Martha Graham technique, a decision that was upheld on appeal.[117] The second trial, the copyright case, was significantly more unwieldy, chiefly because two different copyright laws—the 1909 and the 1976 Copyright Acts—had to be applied to choreographic works that were created over a sixty-five-year span. As the Second Circuit Appeals Court noted, the title of Graham's 1947 work *Errand into the Maze* served as an apt metaphor for the task of sorting through the intellectual property issues at hand.[118] The district court decision alone fills thirty-nine single-spaced pages on Lexis Nexis.[119]

Ultimately, to summarize a tremendously intricate case, Judge Cedarbaum found Protas to be an uncredible witness and ruled overwhelmingly in favor of the Center.[120] Her decision relied heavily on the "work-for-hire" doctrine, a principle first recognized by the US Supreme Court in 1903 and codified in the 1909 Copyright Act, which assigns authorship to employers rather than to the individuals who create original work, unless a written contract specifies otherwise. More specifically, the judge held that thirty-four dances created by Graham while she was employed by the School or the Center between 1956 and 1991 were works for hire; that the Center held copyrights to twenty-seven

---

[116] 153 F. Supp. 2d 512; 224 F. Supp. 2d 567; *Martha Graham School and Dance Foundation, Inc. v. Martha Graham Center of Contemporary Dance, Inc.*, 380 F.3d 624 (2d Cir. 2004).

[117] 153 F. Supp. 2d 512; 43 Fed. Appx. 408.

[118] 380 F.3d 624 (2d Cir. 2004).

[119] 224 F. Supp. 2d 567.

[120] See Julie Van Camp, "Martha Graham's Legal Legacy," *Dance Chronicle* 30.1 (January 2007): 67–99, for a useful synopsis of the copyright case.

of these; that Graham had assigned a total of twenty-one of her earlier unpublished works to the Center; that neither party had established ownership of twenty-four additional dances, ten of which had entered the public domain; and that Protas was entitled to ownership of a mere two dances. With a few minor exceptions, the decision was upheld on appeal.[121]

The central question of the copyright case, as Judge Cedarbaum states at the outset of the opinion she issued in August 2002, was, "What property did Martha Graham, the great dancer, choreographer, and teacher, own at the time of her death in 1991?"[122] To answer this question, the judge had to weigh two competing formulations of Graham: one positioning her as a possessive individual, the other as a hired hand. At stake, in short, were what rights Graham as choreographer had to begin with and whether she was more aligned with capital or with labor.

Eager to make the case that Graham was the sole owner of her choreography, Protas and his legal team did everything they could to accentuate her artistic stature. "This action," Protas's official complaint read, "seeks to preserve inviolate the extraordinary legacy, reputation, and *oeuvre* of Martha Graham, a Twentieth Century icon[,] for her contributions to the creation and performance of the art of dance." Pointing to her generation of "an entirely new vocabulary of dance movement, drawn primarily from choreography she had created" and referring to her choreographic works as "masterpiece[s]," Protas stressed "her seminal role and unique contribution to dance," comparable to the influence "Picasso, Joyce, Stravinsky, and Freud" had on their respective fields. As an original innovator, in other words, Graham should be regarded in terms equal to those exemplars of male genius. Protas also cited the accolades that had been heaped upon Graham both during and after her life: a Medal of Freedom from President Ford, a National Medal of the Arts from President Reagan, a "knighting" from the French Legion of Honor, the label "Dancer of the Century" from *Time Magazine*.[123]

Without denying either Graham's status as a "legendary dancer and choreographer" or that Protas was Graham's legitimate heir, the defense argued that "Protas could only have inherited what Graham in fact possessed herself" and that the Graham Center and Graham School were "the true owners of all rights, title and interest in and to Graham's choreographic works."[124] This

---

[121] 224 F. Supp. 2d 567; 380 F.3d 624.

[122] 224 F. Supp. 2d 567 at 569.

[123] Amended Complaint, *Martha Graham School and Dance Foundation v. Martha Graham Center of Contemporary Dance, et al.*, No. 01 Civ. 0271 (S.D.N.Y. Jan. 26, 2001).

[124] Amended Answer and Counterclaims, *Martha Graham School and Dance Foundation v. Martha Graham Center of Contemporary Dance*, No. 01 Civ. 0271 (S.D.N.Y. Feb. 11, 2002).

argument depended on a meticulous charting of Graham's relationship to the various non-profit entities that bore her name. Graham first opened a dance school in 1930, and all parties agreed that she operated the school "as a sole proprietorship" until 1956. Beginning in the 1940s, however, primarily for tax reasons, Graham began turning to non-profit corporations to support her creative work. In 1948, she established the Martha Graham Foundation for Contemporary Dance, Inc., which was renamed the Martha Graham Center of Contemporary Dance, Inc. in 1968. In 1956, Graham sold her dance school to the newly incorporated Martha Graham School of Contemporary Dance, Inc. (The Center became an umbrella organization, housing both the School and her dance company.) In exchange for a steady salary and to "insulate herself from the legal and financial aspects of her work," Graham transferred owner-ship of all works created prior to 1956 to the School. Graham's first contract with the School was for part-time employment as a teacher and program direc-tor. In 1966, she signed a new, ten-year contract with the School as a full-time choreographer; this contract was renewed indefinitely in 1976. As the defense argued and the court concurred, Graham was thus an employee of the Center and the School from 1956 until her death in 1991.[125]

Because of that status, the court ruled, the dances that Graham created from 1956 onward were "works for hire" and, in the absence of a contract specify-ing otherwise, the property of her employer, the Center.[126] The legal standard for applying the work-for-hire doctrine is the "instance and expense" test: the doctrine applies when a work was created at the "instance and expense" of an employer.[127] Judge Cedarbaum ruled, and the appellate court agreed, that "a preponderance of credible evidence" showed that Graham's post-1956 choreo-graphic works were created at both the instance and expense of the defendants. Acknowledging that Graham "was ultimately responsible for making all final artistic decisions relating to the dances," the court nonetheless found the facts that Graham received a non-itemized salary rather than royalties for her cho-reography, that she regularly reported to the Center's board about her artistic

---

[125] 224 F. Supp. 2d (S.D.N.Y. 2002) at 639; 380 F.3d (2d Cir. N.Y., 2004) at 640.

[126] An exception was choreographic works commissioned by other parties, who would pre-sumably own the rights to the commissioned work, unless specified otherwise. Two of Graham's most famous works, *Appalachian Spring* (1944) and *Night Journey* (1947), fell into this category and, due to a failure to register copyright renewals, are now in the public domain. Van Camp, "Martha Graham's Legal Legacy," 91.

[127] The relevant case law is *Brattleboro Publishing Co. v. Winmill Publishing Corp.*, 369 F.2d (2d Cir. 1966). In the absence of any contract expressing otherwise, the presumption is that the copy-right belongs to the party at whose instance and expense the work is created. *Martha Graham Sch. & Dance Found., Inc. v. Martha Graham Ctr. of Contemporary Dance, Inc.*, 380 F.3d 624, 2004 U.S. App. LEXIS 17452 (2d Cir. N.Y., 2004).

activities, and that the "tools for Graham's choreographic works"—that is, the dancers—"were also provided by the defendants" to be sufficient proof that her dances were indeed works for hire.[128]

The instance and expense doctrine effectively required the court to deflate the romanticized view of the choreographer as solitary genius. On the matter of the Center supplying Graham with dancers, Judge Cedarbaum wrote,

> The creation of the dances was a collaborative process in which the Center's employees played an indispensable role. Janet Eilber, a principal dancer at the Dance Company, testified credibly that Graham "choreographed on" dancers employed by the Center.[129]

Rather than elevating Eilber and her colleagues to the status of co-authors, the court leveled the distinctions between Graham and dancers by casting them all as salary-earning employees. Granting that Graham possessed a "high level of skill in choreography," the language of the district court opinion throughout is remarkably workmanlike: choreography becomes Graham's "duty," carried out with her employer's "tools." Under the work-for-hire doctrine, the choreographic works whose ownership was in question were "created by Graham" but "authored" by the Center.[130]

Because it shifts the locus of authorship from the creative artist to the corporate entity, legal scholars have called the work-for-hire doctrine both "a dramatic example of the ways in which the ideology of 'authorship' has been manipulated" and the one area in which "the Copyright Act expressly recognizes the author as a legal fiction."[131] Or, as Catherine Fisk has written in a witty nod to Barthes, "The author isn't dead; he just got a job."[132] What is noteworthy about Graham's case is that the author appeared to get a job only posthumously.

It is entirely possible, even likely, as some commentators have noted, that the court's decision to assign author status to the Center rather than to Graham

---

[128] 224 F. Supp. 2d (S.D.N.Y. 2002) at 590, 362, 589. For more on the work-for-hire doctrine and its application in the Graham case, see Judith Beth Prowda, "Work for Hire, Freedom of Contract, and the 'Creative Genius' after the Martha Graham Case," *Journal of the Copyright Society of the U.S.A.* 53 (Spring–Summer 2006): 645–80.

[129] 224 F. Supp. 2d at 589.

[130] 224 F. Supp. 2d at 592; 380 F.3d at 640.

[131] Peter Jaszi, "On the Author Effect," in *The Construction of Authorship: Textual Appropriation in Law and Literature* ed. Martha Woodmansee and Peter Jaszi (Durham, NC: Duke University Press, 1994), 34; Catherine L. Fisk, "Authors at Work: The Origins of the Work-for-Hire Doctrine," *Yale Journal of Law & the Humanities* 15 (2003): 4.

[132] Fisk, "Authors at Work," 1.

was an instrumental one. A tacit but decisive influence on Judge Cedarbaum's opinion may well have been the "fundamental equitable consideration of who deserves to own these works."[133] Had he won, Protas would have deprived the company that bore Graham's name from performing her works. (This would have resulted in another kind of death of the author, as I discuss below.) The fact that the judge did not find Protas to be a credible witness—she called his testimony "evasive and inconsistent"—surely did not help his cause.[134]

But even if there were unstated pragmatic reasons for Judge Cedarbaum's ruling, and even if its immediate effect was to restore life to Graham's company and choreography, for many, what became known as "the Graham debacle"[135] represented a stunning setback for the figure of the choreographer. Calling the decision an "extremely dangerous one" for the creative world, the attorney for Ronald Protas warned:

> In essence, the court concluded that Martha Graham was nothing more than a hired hand of the foundation that had been created to serve her needs. Other choreographers should be quaking in their slippers over what this case can mean to their right to control their artistic legacy.[136]

A friend-of-the-court brief filed on appeal by a group of prominent artistic directors and institutions cautioned that the district court's ruling would have "far-reaching implications in the art world."[137] Expressing the views of many, Charles Reinhart of the American Dance Festival asserted, "There's always been the assumption in the field that the choreographer owns his or her own work and can leave that work to whomever he or she would like to."[138] This

---

[133] Sharon Connelly, "Note: Authorship, Ownership, and Control: Balancing the Economic and Artistic Issues Raised by the Martha Graham Copyright Case," *Fordham Intellectual Property, Media & Entertainment Law Journal* 15 (Spring 2005): 840.

[134] 224 F. Supp. 2d at 572.

[135] Diane Solway, "Martha Graham's Legal Legacy to Modern Choreographers," *International Herald Tribune*, January 9, 2007, http://www.nytimes.com/2007/01/09/arts/09iht-dance.4147917.html?pagewanted=all&_r=0. Accessed September 10, 2013.

[136] Quoted in Jennifer Dunning, "Graham Company Leaps Back to Life," *New York Times*, September 2, 2002; also quoted in Van Camp, "Martha Graham's Legal Legacy," 68.

[137] Quoted in Connelly, "Authorship, Ownership, and Control," 839. The Brief of Amici Curiae was filed by Charles Reinhart, co-director of the American Dance Festival; Gerald Arpino, Artistic Director of the Joffrey Ballet of Chicago; and Gordon Davidson, Artistic Director of the Center Theatre Group/Mark Taper Forum of the Los Angeles County Music Center. The Graham ruling indeed spurred a number of other modern dance choreographers to take measures to ensure the protection of their works. Dunning, "Graham Company Leaps Back to Life."

[138] Jennifer Dunning, "Dance and Profit: Who Gets It?" *New York Times*, September 20, 2003, p. B9.

assumption was especially pronounced for Graham, the grande dame of modern dance. "To think that Martha is for hire," Reinhart later added, "is like the pope saying to the devil, 'Come to dinner.'"[139] Indeed, on appeal, the court was explicitly asked to consider whether an exception to the work-for-hire doctrine should be made for "the principal employee of a corporation that was, in the Appellant's view, 'created to serve the creative endeavors of an artistic genius.'"[140] The Second Circuit Court's unanimous refusal to grant any such exception sealed Graham's demotion from genius to unpropertied laborer.[141]

The sense of foreboding in the idea of Graham as a "hired hand" strikes me as especially significant. What made the application of the work-for-hire doctrine to Graham so "ominous"[142] was that it metaphorically killed the choreographer as artistic genius. Correspondingly, it threatened to undo much of what had been gained with the passage of the 1976 Copyright Act. If the act finally enshrined the choreographer as possessive individual, the Graham decision cast renewed doubt on choreographers' entitlement to that status. What good was the legal recognition of choreographic works if choreographers were only workers for hire, blocked from reaping the benefits of that recognition?

The atmosphere of crisis around the Graham decision must also be read in relation to the legacies of racial privilege that have shaped possessive individualism and the institution of modern dance alike. As I have tried to show with the aid of critical race scholarship, both the idea of property in one's person and the tradition of modern dance were forged along axes of race and gender that extended certain rights (of ownership, of protection against commodification, of representational control) to whites, while denying them from those deemed non-white. To the extent that the decision to deny Graham property rights in her choreography ex post facto seemed to shake the very edifice of modern dance, the raced and gendered configurations of that edifice were also shaken. For contemporary choreographers who regarded the Graham case as a cautionary tale, the lesson was not only to be more vigilant in establishing property rights in their choreography; it was also that, even in the twenty-first century, dance-makers were not guaranteed the taken-for-granted privileges of masculine whiteness.

[139] Felicia R. Lee, "Graham Legacy, on the Stage Again," *New York Times*, September 29, 2004, p. E1.

[140] 380 F.3d at 628.

[141] Protas appealed the decision all the way up to the Supreme Court, which declined to review it. *Martha Graham Sch. & Dance Found., Inc. v. Martha Graham Ctr. of Contemporary Dance, Inc.*, 125 S.Ct. 2518 (May 31, 2005).

[142] Van Camp, "Martha Graham's Legal Legacy," 68.

In her analysis of the decision, Caroline Picart views the application of the work-for-hire doctrine to Graham rather skeptically, noting the implausibility, given Graham's domineering personality, that she would have signed a contract that positioned her in any kind of servile relationship with the Center. She also finds it "striking that many of the arguments that wrested control over Graham's works away from her estate to the Center could equally have applied to Balanchine's estate in its battle with the New York Ballet Company."[143] In point of fact, Taper's biography of Balanchine indicates that the New York City Ballet Company did consider challenging the Balanchine Trust's ownership of his works on the basis that his ballets were created while he was an employee of the Company. Advised of the improbability of winning such a legal argument, Company board members settled for a licensing agreement with the Trust. Unlike Graham, Balanchine initially received modest royalties for his ballets rather than a salary paid by the Company. Yet, by way of explaining the Company's decision not to pursue a corporate authorship argument, Taper writes that "A salient attribute of an employee, according to case law, is that he has a boss. But Balanchine had been answerable to no one except Terpsichore and those composers in heaven with whom he claimed to commune when choreographing."[144] This is the Romantic notion of the choreographer as genius writ large. It is hard not to conclude that Balanchine's authorial status was secure enough to withstand legal scrutiny, while Graham's was not. Or, alternatively, that re-conceptualizing the white female choreographer as a salaried worker was easier than re-defining the white male choreographer as such. For Picart, the complicating factor of gender meant that "whiteness as status property functioned refractorily" in Graham's case, giving her enough privilege to establish herself as a celebrity in life but not enough to hold on to ownership of her choreography in death.[145] Even without ascribing the disparate decisions in the Balanchine and Graham cases to any kind of bias, attending to the gendered implications of those decisions allows us to see how the gendered hierarchies that reduced Loïe Fuller to nothing more than "a comely woman ... illustrating the poetry of motion" (Chapter 1), and that excluded Faith Dane's dancing from the domain of the "useful arts" (Chapter 4) continue to haunt the institution of choreographic copyright.

---

[143] Picart, "A Tango between Copyright and Choreography," 721.
[144] Taper, *Balanchine*, 404–5.
[145] Picart, "A Tango between Copyright and Choreography," 687.

"Martha Is Dead; Long Live Martha"

Not everyone, as I have hinted, viewed the Graham decision as a mortal blow to the choreographer. For many, Judge Cedarbaum's ruling was a vindication of the Graham Company and a salvation of Graham's legacy. This is nowhere clearer than in the headline to a story by Paul Ben-Itzak announcing the legal decision in the trademark infringement case: "Martha Is Dead, Long Live Martha."[146] Modifying the ritualized proclamation "The king is dead; long live the king," Ben-Itzak invokes the theory of the "king's two bodies," famously explored in Ernst Kantorowicz's 1957 monograph by the same name.[147] Where the two bodies of the king refer to his mortal body and the immortal body politic, Ben-Itzak's headline, coming as it did ten years after Graham's literal death, less clearly indexes her physical body. Instead, he invokes the competition between the entities vying to serve as Graham's effigy, in Joseph Roach's theorization of the term as that which "fills by means of surrogation a vacancy created by the absence of an original."[148] Ben-Itzak writes:

> In rejecting non-dancer Ron Protas's claim that he and he alone owns the name "Martha Graham" and the term "Martha Graham technique," Federal District Judge Miriam Goldman Cedarbaum in one swift incision excised a cancer that had gnawed away at the body Graham for years and threatened to destroy the greatest legacy in modern dance, returning that body to the dancers in which Martha truly lives and through which she truly speaks.
>
> Cedarbaum's damning 36-page ruling vindicates the dancers who for years had to stand mutely by while Protas pretended to speak for Graham.

There are at least three "bodies" in play here: "the body Graham," Graham's choreographic work; the body of Protas, who, as Graham's legal heir, certainly had some right to serve as her proxy; and the bodies of the Graham Company

---

[146] Paul Ben-Itzak, "Flash Analysis, 8-14-2001: Martha Is Dead; Long Live Martha," http://www.danceinsider.com/f2001/f814_2.html. Accessed May 20, 2011.

[147] Ernst H. Kantorowicz, *The King's Two Bodies: A Study in Mediaeval Political Theology* (Princeton, NJ: Princeton University Press, 1957).

[148] Joseph Roach, *Cities of the Dead: Circum-Atlantic Performance* (New York: Columbia University Press, 1996), 36. Selby Schwartz's thoughtful discussion of Richard Move's drag performances of Graham, which coincided with the Graham Company's hiatus, suggests Move as another worthy surrogate for Graham. Schwartz writes, "Sometimes it seems that Move's drag version of Martha has overtaken the 'real' one, and actually filled an emptiness left by her death." "Martha@Martha," 75.

dancers, who, in Ben-Itzak's opinion, are Graham's "true" surrogates. In this contest between effigies, Judge Cedarbaum's legal decision is the deus ex machina that cures the diseased body of Graham's choreography by sanctioning the transfer of that body from Protas to dancers. Insofar as Protas represented the legal body of "Martha" in the wake of her death, that body had to die in order for "Martha" the choreographic body to live.

The court-ordered death of Protas-as-Martha (which also enacted the death of Martha as Author) mirrors the metaphorical "first death" that occurred when Graham retired from the stage. The difference here is that the living Graham experienced the succession of her choreography from her body to those of her dancers as a form of violence, whereas Ben-Itzak celebrates it as the rightful order of things. To put it another way, while Graham regarded the separation of the dancer from the dance as a painful (if inevitable) fatality, Ben-Itzak approaches the separation of the choreographer from the dance as a way of "defeating death by extending bodily existence far beyond carnal boundaries."[149] For Graham, the alienation of her choreography from her person was a portent of mortality; for Ben-Itzak, that same alienation was the prerequisite for a kind of immortality.

Among the other parties claiming victory over the ruling in the Graham case was the State of New York, which saw a public interest in ongoing access to Graham's body of work.[150] Following the federal appeals court decision to uphold the ruling of the circuit court against Protas, Elliot Spitzer, at that time New York state attorney general, issued a statement declaring that "Every New Yorker has a stake in seeing these two great cultural institutions [the Graham Center and School] continue to flourish. . . . As a result of this ruling, Martha Graham's legacy in dance will ... rightfully be preserved as a public trust." Noting that Graham had received "crucial public support for her creative enterprise" through the tax benefits of forming non-profit corporations, he added that "It is important that the public also receive the benefit of this bargain, so that her great achievements can be perpetuated by the charities she founded." Spitzer's terminology—"flourish," "preserved," "perpetuated"—suggests that the attorney general interpreted the legal decision, like Ben-Itzak, as if it had bestowed immortality on Graham's choreography. But where Ben-Itzak's rhetoric treats the dancers as the vehicles for this immortality, Spitzer sees the structural entities that bear Graham's name as the appropriate vessels for her afterlife. A clear endorsement of corporate authorship if

---

[149] Stephen Greenblatt, "Introduction: Fifty Years of *The King's Two Bodies*," *Representations* 106.1 (Spring 2009): 64.

[150] http://www.ag.ny.gov/press-release/spitzer-says-court-ruling-will-preserve-martha-graham-dance-legacy. Accessed July 31, 2013.

not in so many words, Spitzer's statement also implies that the state, by virtue of its economic investment, was a fellow employer of Graham and therefore might be considered a joint author with the Graham Center of Graham's "creative enterprise." As such, it is entitled to enjoy the fruits of Graham's labor. In this view, the choreographic property in question through multiple legal hearings belongs more to the state and "the public" that the state claims to represent than to Graham, the private individual.

The opposing sets of responses to the Graham decision, then, highlight different ideas about the site of authorship and about who stands in for Graham after her biological death. Yet, however polarized, the two sides are as important for what they share as for what they don't. For Protas and the portion of the dance community that was scandalized by the retroactive stripping of Graham's choreographic rights, as well as for those who regarded the legal ruling as granting life to Graham's choreographic legacy, Graham's literal death required confronting the inevitable separation of choreographer from choreography and the temporal fragility of both. While the two sides diverged over what was most at risk as a result of this separation and fragility—the status of the choreographer or the status of the work—they both responded in ways that attempted to smooth over the rupture of Graham's death. Relying on a conception of autonomous authorship and on the legal construct of postmortem copyright, Protas and the supporters of Graham's ownership rights asserted that her entitlement to possessive individualism extended beyond the grave. In this line of thought, the literal death of the author does not and cannot mean the metaphorical death of the author. Conversely, relying on a doctrine of multiple bodies and corporeal succession—"Martha is dead; long live Martha"—the supporters of the Graham Center re-locate the choreographer inside the work. In this line of thought, the death of the author ensures the life of the work. What we find on either side of the controversy is a desire to heal the temporal fracture of death, a desire to extend life beyond the finiteness of the mortal body, a desire to assert continuity in the face of discontinuity.

The death of the choreographer, we might therefore say, replicates, or perhaps amplifies the fraughtness intrinsic to choreographic copyright. As I have suggested at various points in this book, the assertion of intellectual property rights in dance simultaneously rests on the notion of an inalienable right to one's personhood and enacts an alienation of artist from work by turning the artist into a subject of property and the work into an object of property. At the heart of choreographic copyright, that is, lies both the inextricability and the severing of choreographer from choreography. If we see death as the ultimate split between artist and work, we can see copyright, especially postmortem copyright, as a means of conquering death and as a rehearsal for it. And if we read all of the anxiety about ephemerality in the medium of dance as code for concerns about mortality, we might approach choreographic copyright as an attempt to come to terms with—and, simultaneously, to negate—the inexorability of death. It is an undertaking no less potent and no less poignant for its impossibilities.

Read along the lines I have suggested here, the Balanchine and Graham legal trials are not only case studies of choreographic copyright but also, on some level, allegories of the various kinds of stakes involved in contests over intellectual property rights in dance. At issue in both cases was not only who should control the right to reproduce choreography but also how to reconcile the overlapping but not identical temporal dimensions of the human choreographer and the embodied work. And, although neither case was "about" race or gender, both cases implicitly evaluated the choreographer's entitlement to the historically white masculine privilege of propertied personhood. As a legal mechanism for regulating dance's circulation, we might conclude, choreographic copyright is always already haunted by its own problematic ontology and by the legacies of raced and gendered inequality out of which it was forged.

Coda

Beyoncé v. De Keersmaeker

In the fall of 2011, the African American pop star Beyoncé released a music video for her single "Countdown."[1] Singing about her steadfast love for her man, Beyoncé appears in a series of quick edits, sometimes in close-up, sometimes in split screens, sometimes in long and medium shots with a small group of backup dancers. The video, co-directed by Beyoncé and Adria Petty, is packed with references to icons of the 1950s, '60s, and '70s, including Audrey Hepburn, Andy Warhol, and Diana Ross. But, as some were quick to notice, much of the movement vocabulary—floor rolls, head swings, hands running through hair, the sliding of a shirt on and off the shoulder, casual pivot turns, the shifting of positions while seated on a chair—as well as some of the mise-en-scène and camera shots, bore a striking resemblance to two works by the Belgian choreographer Anne Teresa De Keersmaeker: *Rosas danst Rosas*, from 1983, and *Achterland*, from 1990, films of both of which are accessible online. More than one YouTube user compiled a side-by-side comparison highlighting the similarities.[2] Catching wind of the likeness, De Keersmaeker issued a statement accusing Beyoncé of plagiarism and threatened legal action against Sony, Beyoncé's music label.[3]

This was not the first time Beyoncé had been accused of stealing choreography, the most well-known example being her liberal borrowing of a Bob

---

[1] The video is available at http://www.beyonce.com/photos-videos. Accessed August 21, 2013.

[2] See, for example, http://www.youtube.com/watch?v=3HaWxhbhH4c, and http://www.youtube.com/watch?v=PDT0m514TMw. Accessed August 21, 2013.

[3] It is important to point out that plagiarism and copyright infringement are often overlapping but not interchangeable offenses. In general, plagiarism is the academic infraction of using another's work without giving credit, while infringement is the legal offense of using another's intellectual property without permission. See, among others, Richard A. Posner, *The Little Book of Plagiarism* (New York: Random House, 2007).

Figure 6.1 Screenshot of a split screen comparison of Beyoncé's "Countdown" video and a Thierry De Mey film of Anna Teresa De Keersmaeker's *Rosas danst Rosas*, uploaded to YouTube by a user on October 12, 2011.

Fosse number for her 2008 video "Single Ladies (Put a Ring on It)." The prevailing response to the revelation of "Countdown"'s debt to De Keersmaeker was to denounce Beyoncé as a copycat.[4] Seen in historical context, however, Beyoncé's unauthorized reproduction takes on a different cast. In appropriating the white avant-garde, Beyoncé reverses the racialized logic of property that has helped underwrite the development of choreographic copyright in the United States. As I have tried to show throughout this book, the legacy of an equation between whiteness and property ownership has shaped dancers' engagement with copyright in meaningful ways. From Loïe Fuller's and Ruth St. Denis's use of Nautch dance sources, to George White's claim to have invented the Black Bottom (countered by Alberta Hunter's rumored copyright of the dance), to the eclipse of African American tap dancers on Broadway by Hanya Holm and Agnes de Mille, the story of choreographic copyright has time and again demonstrated both the privilege whites hold to "use and enjoy" and take credit for movement material generated by black and brown dancers and the obstacles facing black and brown dancers who have sought to occupy the terrain of possessive individualism. Beyoncé's choreographic actions in "Countdown"—turning the white

---

[4] A Google search for "Beyoncé copycat" on August 14, 2013, turned up 263,000 results. See, among them, Erika Ramirez, "Op-Ed: When Beyoncé's Inspiration Turns into Imitation," *Billboard*, May 1, 2013, http://www.billboard.com/articles/columns/the-juice/1560092/op-ed-when-beyonces-inspiration-turns-into-imitation. Accessed August 14, 2013. For a legal perspective on the case, see Francis Yeoh, "The Copyright Implications of Beyoncé's Choreographic 'Borrowings,'" *Choreographic Practices* 4.1 (July 2013): 95–117. Yeoh views Beyoncé's alleged infringement of De Keersmaeker as evidence that (concert dance) choreographers need to be more proactive in protecting their intellectual property rights.

avant-garde into fodder for her own cultural production—flip the script that has long authorized white artists to take from non-white and "high art" to borrow from "low."[5]

The Beyoncé-De Keersmaeker incident provides a fitting coda to this book for several reasons. Most saliently, it provides a chance to ask how the history I have traced in the foregoing pages haunts contests over the circulation of choreography in the age of YouTube. How might earlier dance-makers' struggles for the rights of possessive individualism inform our understanding of what was at stake in the skirmish between Beyoncé and De Keersmaeker? How does the legacy of a correlation between gendered whiteness and property rights shadow constructions of ownership in dance in the digital age? As much as Beyoncé's "Countdown" reverses the sanctioned flow of choreographic traffic, the response to that reversal, I will argue, is evidence of the lingering effects of the racialization of choreographic copyright.

Of course, the "Countdown" episode departs from the other examples covered in this book in some key ways. Although technological mediation was by no means absent from the circulation of dance in earlier copyright cases (witness the placards of Fuller's *Serpentine Dance* and the photographs of Balanchine's *Nutcracker* ballet), there is no question that the digitization of dance has increased both its availability and concerns about its "theft." The Internet was at the very center of "Countdown"'s property dispute: it was not only the stage on which Beyoncé debuted her music video and the means by which she gained access to De Keersmaeker's choreography; it was also the vehicle through which users exposed Beyoncé's choreographic debt to De Keersmaeker and the site at which much of the resulting debate transpired. Rather than viewing the Beyoncé-De Keersmaeker incident as the inevitable byproduct of dance's digitization, however, I see it as an index of the ways the interlocking racial and artistic hierarchies in which choreographic copyright was forged continue to lurk in contemporary dance-makers' intellectual property claims.

The Beyoncé-De Keersmaeker conflict also breaks from the US frame of this book. A dispute between a Belgian choreographer and an African American pop star does not fit neatly into the nation-specific historical narrative I have heretofore traced. Though intellectual property circulates globally, copyright

---

[5] In like manner, Joseph R. Slaughter writes about the postcolonial and racial politics that inform the dividing lines between different forms of intertextuality, licensing white authors to borrow from African writers but not the reverse. "The 'problem' of plagiarism," he summarizes, "has often been a problem of the color line." "'It's Good to Be Primitive': African Allusion and the Modernist Fetish of Authenticity," in *Modernism and Copyright* ed. Paul K. Saint-Amour (New York: Oxford University Press, 2011), 278.

laws remain "national or territorial in nature."[6] But if the flow of De Keersmaeker's choreography across national borders and the transnational dimensions of her plagiarism claim exceed the geographic scope of this book, they can also help us think differently about the "national" examples covered earlier. Loïe Fuller, Ruth St. Denis, Johnny Hudgins, Hanya Holm: each of these artists criss-crossed the Atlantic, as did their choreography. In many cases, those crossings fueled their investment in proprietary rights. In this sense, the transnational scuffle over "Countdown" retroactively haunts the seemingly US-specific case studies that form the pillar of this book, just as those earlier cases haunt the choreographic and legal actions of Beyoncé and De Keersmaeker.

Beyoncé and De Keersmaeker are worth considering here, finally, because the two sit at opposing poles of the contemporary dance landscape. Corresponding to their respective associations with art versus entertainment, De Keersmaeker belongs to a postmodern tradition in which the choreographer retains her author function (despite efforts to disavow it),[7] while Beyoncé is part of a music video dance tradition in which the pop star performer rather than the (usually anonymous) choreographer stands to gain the most from danced cultural production. Precisely because of the differences in their locations, racial positions, and economies in which they circulate, the skirmish between Beyoncé and De Keersmaeker suggests the extent to which "encounters with others"[8]—and the historical legacy of past encounters—continue to shape contests over authorship and ownership in dance.

"It ain't nothing that I can't do": Inverting White Privilege

Throwback is at the heart of the three minute and thirty-three-second music video for "Countdown," a song featuring "a toothsome mix of hip-hop and dancehall and Afro-beat," which was generally seen as the most experimental track on Beyoncé's fourth solo album, titled 4.[9] The chorus is a literal

[6] See Catherine Seville, *The Internationalisation of Copyright Law: Books, Buccaneers and the Black Flag in the Nineteenth Century* (Cambridge: Cambridge University Press, 2006), 2.

[7] It is certainly the case that a number of choreographers who are classified as "postmodern" or "contemporary" have sought to distance themselves from the modernist emphasis on authorial invention (by using collective improvisation, chance procedures, and pedestrian movements, for example). But these artists continue to reap the rewards, financial and otherwise, that accrue to the figure of the author.

[8] Rosemary J. Coombe, *The Cultural Life of Intellectual Properties: Authorship, Appropriation, and the Law* (Durham, NC: Duke University Press, 1998), 257.

[9] Jody Rosen, "Beyonce Gets Intimate in First of '4' Roseland Ballroom Shows," *Rolling Stone*, August 15, 2011, http://www.rollingstone.com/music/news/beyonce-gets-intimate-in-first-of-4-roseland-ballroom-shows-20110815. Accessed August 21, 2013.

countdown—and a sample from the 1990s rhythm-and-blues (R&B) group Boyz II Men's song "Uhh Ahh"—on top of which Beyoncé sings:

> My baby is a ten
> We dressin' to the nine
> He pick me up we eight
> Make me feel so lucky seven
> He kiss me in his six
> We be makin' love in five
> Still the one I do this four
> I'm tryin' to make us three
> From that two
> He's still the one.[10]

The video plays with the idea of countdown even before we reach this chorus.[11] Fifteen seconds in, Beyoncé, wearing bangs, a black turtleneck, and cropped pants, à la Audrey Hepburn from *Funny Face* (1957), circles her arms counterclockwise like the second hand of a clock. Temporal rewind is also writ large in the video's overall retro aesthetic. Described as "a technicolor dream ride through mod and vintage cinema glories," and an "homage to '60s chic," the video has Beyoncé alternately channeling various black and white female icons—not only Hepburn and Diana Ross, but also the British model Twiggy and the French model and actress Brigitte Bardot.[12] The visual look of the video, meanwhile, alternates between black and white and color blocking.

Beyoncé's resurrections of De Keersmaeker's choreography, which constitute the most extended dance sequences in "Countdown," are further evidence of Beyoncé's "affinity for recalling the past in her videos."[13] De Keersmaeker's

[10] http://rapfix.mtv.com/2011/10/06/beyonces-confusing-countdown-lyric-revealed/. Accessed August 13, 2013.

[11] Carrie Battan, "Video: Beyoncé: "Countdown," *Pitchfork*, October 6, 2011. http://pitchfork.com/news/44223-video-beyonce-countdown/. Accessed July 13, 2013.

[12] Colleen Nika, "Beyonce Takes a Fashionable Trip through Retro Cinema in 'Countdown' Video," *Rolling Stone*, October 7, 2011, http://www.rollingstone.com/music/blogs/thread-count/beyonce-takes-a-fashionable-trip-through-retro-cinema-in-countdown-video-20111007; Contessa Gayles, "Beyonce Flaunts Baby Bump in Retro 'Countdown' Video Clip," *The Boombox*, October 3, 2011, http://theboombox.com/beyonce-countdown-video-preview/. Accessed August 13, 2013.

[13] John Mitchell, "Beyonce Flaunts Baby Bump in 'Countdown' Video," *MTV News*, Oct. 6, 2011, http://www.mtv.com/news/articles/1672134/beyonce-countdown-video.jhtml. Accessed August 13, 2013.

movement, performed first by Beyoncé's dancers, who are then joined by Beyoncé, crops up less than a minute into the video and continues intermittently through its end. That the past recalled choreographically was not the 1960s but the 1980s (and 1990) did little to disturb the video's aesthetic. In fact, until those familiar with De Keersmaeker's work called attention to the correct sources, viewers mistakenly identified the 1980s dance films *Flashdance* and *Fame* as the referents for "Countdown"'s straight-up dance segments.[14] Perhaps not surprising, given the off-the-shoulder shirts and open studio space that appear in "Countdown," this misreading reveals how far off the pop culture radar De Keersmaeker was. While critics later pronounced it "weird" for Beyoncé and De Keersmaeker to occupy the same sentence, the movement qualities of De Keersmaeker's choreography—both the expression-filled, minimalist gestures of *Rosas danst Rosas* and the dramatic falls, rolls, and rippling body isolations of *Achterland*—seemed to fit right in with "Countdown"'s retro chic femininity.[15]

What was decidedly un-retro was Beyoncé's unauthorized reproduction of that choreography, insofar as it inverted the historical pattern of acclaimed white artists taking from non-white dancers. In suggesting this line of argument, I do not mean to equate Beyoncé with the generally anonymous and uncompensated African American dancers who have so frequently served as inspiration for white choreographers. Beyoncé is hardly what we could call disenfranchised. One of the most popular recording artists of this century, in 2012 she had an estimated net worth of $350 million, and in April 2014, *Time* magazine placed her on its list of the one hundred most influential people.[16] As others have observed, much of Beyoncé's music is specifically about black female empowerment and material

[14] See Mitchell, "Beyoncé Flaunts Baby Bump," and "Beyoncé 'Countdown' Music Video Look by Look," *MTV Style*, October 6, 2011, http://style.mtv.com/2011/10/06/ beyonce-countdown-music-video-look-by-look/#more-64612. Accessed August 14, 2013.

[15] Luke Jennings, "Beyoncé v De Keersmaeker: Can You Copyright a Dance Move?" *The Guardian*, October 11, 2011, http://www.theguardian.com/stage/theatreblog/2011/ oct/11/beyonce-de-keersmaeker-dance-move?newsfeed=true. Accessed August 14, 2013. In *A Choreographer's Score: Fase, Rosas danst Rosas, Elena's Aria, Bartók*, co-written by De Keersmaeker, Bojana Cvejić refers to *Rosas danst Rosas*'s "pronounced feminine character" (Brussels: Mercartorfonds/Rosas, 2012), 85. And, in her review of *Achterland*, New York Times critic Anna Kisselgoff wrote, "Before they hurl themselves against the floor and rebound at a tilt, the women practice vamping, Betty Grable-style." "Review/Dance: Belgians Go Beyond Minimalism," *New York Times*, September 28, 1991, http://www.nytimes.com/1991/09/28/arts/ review-dance-belgians-go-beyond-minimalism.html?pagewanted=2. Accessed August 14, 2013.

[16] http://www.therichest.org/celebnetworth/celeb/singer/beyonce-net-worth/. Accessed August 29, 2012; http://time.com/collection/2014-time-100/. Accessed May 25, 2014. Beyoncé's appearance on the cover of *Time* in minimal clothing ignited a firestorm of controversy over her feminist credentials, with black feminist critic bell hooks going so far as to brand her a terrorist for disseminating an image of herself that colluded with "white supremacist capitalist patriarchy" and "the construction of herself as a slave." http://www.clutchmagonline.com/2014/05/bell-

success, or, more precisely, female empowerment *as* material success. Music critic Jody Rosen notes that "from 'Independent Women' to 'Single Ladies' to 'Run the World (Girls),' Beyoncé's anthems view female self-determination in mercenary terms."[17] In her analysis of Beyoncé's 2006 album *B-day*, scholar Daphne Brooks likewise notes a "troubling ... fixation on materialism" coursing through the album. But, in a compelling reading that juxtaposes Beyoncé's assertion of black female "socioeconomic autonomy" with black women's massive dislocation and dispossession in New Orleans in the wake of Hurricane Katrina, Brooks argues that the album's focus "on ownership and personal property" represents a provocative refutation of "the spectacular marginalization of African-American women in American sociopolitical culture."[18]

Following Brooks's lead, I also read Beyoncé's choreographic moves in "Countdown" as assertions of power and agency. Instead of being about material belongings (though she does tell us, "Yup, I buy my own, if he deserve it, buy his shit too"), however, the video evidences a different kind of possessiveness: the right to acquire movement from whatever source Beyoncé sees fit. She exercises this right by borrowing whole chunks of movement from De Keersmaeker, and in so doing, corporeally claims a privilege that has historically belonged to whites. Reversing the conventional racial dynamics of borrowing and flouting the "no trespassing" signs around "high-culture white forms," Beyoncé treats De Keersmaeker's choreographic output as if it is in the public domain and therefore free for the taking.[19]

In response to accusations of plagiarism, Beyoncé issued a statement, explaining:

> Clearly, the ballet "Rosas danst Rosas" was one of many references for my video "Countdown." It was one of the inspirations used to bring the feel and look of the song to life. I was also paying tribute to the

hooks-beyonce-terrorist-impact-young-girls/?utm_source=rss&utm_medium=rss&utm_cam paign=bell-hooks-beyonce-terrorist-impact-young-girls. Accessed May 25, 2014. Beyoncé's assertion of her prerogative to take dance material from wherever she sees fit does, on some level, collude with the logic of "white supremacist patriarchal capitalism." But, I am suggesting, it is also a re-ordering of the historic equation between male privilege, whiteness, and the property rights that are the bedrock of capitalism.

[17] http://www.rollingstone.com/music/news/beyonce-gets-intimate-in-first-of-4-roseland-ballroom-shows-20110815. Accessed August 20, 2012.

[18] Daphne A. Brooks, "'All That You Can't Leave Behind': Black Female Soul Singing and the Politics of Surrogation in the Age of Catastrophe," *Meridians: Feminism, Race, Transnationalism* 8.1 (2007): 183.

[19] Brenda Dixon Gottschild, *Digging the Africanist Presence in American Performance: Dance and Other Contexts* (Westport, CT: Greenwood Press, 1996), 28.

film, "Funny Face" with the legendary Audrey Hepburn. My biggest inspirations were the '60s, the '70s, Brigitte Bardot, Andy Warhol, Twiggy and Diana Ross.[20]

Video co-director Adria Petty likewise told MTV News that she "brought Beyoncé a number of references and we picked some out together. Most were German modern-dance references, believe it or not. But it really evolved."[21] Beyoncé reported finding *Rosas danst Rosas* "refreshing, interesting and timeless," adding, "I've always been fascinated by the way contemporary art uses different elements and references to produce something unique."[22]

The inexactitudes here are noteworthy. De Keersmaeker is a Belgian not German choreographer, and her works date from none of the decades that Beyoncé invokes. Yet I can't help but be reminded of the long history of mis-recognition of African diasporic dance—perceptions, for example, of Josephine Baker as an African dancer, and of jazz dance as the sign of a timeless primitivism. Inaccuracies aside, Beyoncé's point is that she considered De Keersmaeker not some off-limits realm of high art, but, rather, one of many sources of inspiration, just as available to her as pop culture icons like Twiggy and Diana Ross. Invoking the freedom contemporary art enjoys to "use different elements and references to produce something unique," Beyoncé implies that she possesses this same prerogative.

Again, given her phenomenal wealth and celebrity status, to advance an argument about Beyoncé's assertion of possessive individualism may seem redundant, even perverse. The perception of her power to police her own work is such that, in the wake of the "Countdown" incident, *Rosas danst Rosas* filmmaker Thierry De Mey remarked,

> If tomorrow I were to look for the music, the videos by Beyonce or any other pop or rock stars and use them in my movies without asking for their authorisation, I think Exocet missiles would fall over the Charleroi dance festival and myself.[23]

---

[20] Charlotte Higgins, "Beyoncé Pleasant but Consumerist, Says Plagiarism Row Choreographer," *The Guardian*, October 11, 2011, http://www.theguardian.com/music/2011/oct/11/beyonce-pleasant-consumerist-plagiarism-row. Accessed August 21, 2013.

[21] Jocelyn Vena, "Beyonce's 'Countdown' Video Shoot Was 'Evolving, Spontaneous,'" http://www.mtv.com/news/articles/1672200/beyonce-countdown-video-shoot.jhtml. Accessed August 29, 2012.

[22] Higgins, "Beyoncé Pleasant but Consumerist."

[23] "Beyonce plagiarism claims: copying her videos would have got me killed, says Belgian director," *The Telegraph*, http://www.telegraph.co.uk/culture/music/music-news/8823834/Beyonce-plagiarism-claims-copying-her-videos-would-have-got-me-killed-says-Belgian-director.html. Accessed August 19, 2013.

Hyperbole aside, the fact that Beyoncé's legal team sent cease-and-desist letters to websites that leaked the "Countdown" music track before its official release date leaves no ambiguity about her proprietariness.[24] What is not redundant from a historical standpoint is the choreographic form this black woman's proprietariness took.

In his recent essay "Unchecked Popularity: Neoliberal Circulations of Black Social Dance," Thomas DeFrantz critiques the ease with which African American social dances spread beyond the particular sociohistorical contexts that gave rise to them. DeFrantz explains how "Appropriation ..., the re-purposing of dance to allow its entry into diverse economic markets—reconfigures black physicalities into a place of interchangeability with any who would do the dances, and allows access without concerns of situation or material circumstance of the dancer under scrutiny."[25] What is so

---

[24] Gerrick D. Kennedy, "Beyoncé's '4' leaks online, three weeks before release," *L.A. Times* Music Blog, June 7, 2011, http://latimesblogs.latimes.com/music_blog/2011/06/beyonc%C3%A9s-4-pops-up-online-three-weeks-before-release.html. Accessed August 28, 2013. As the *Hollywood Reporter* pointed out, Beyoncé's explanation about the inspiration for "Countdown" has the whiff of a fair use defense about it. Eriq Gardner, "Why an Allegation that Beyoncé Plagiarized Is Truly Unique (Analysis), *The Hollywood Reporter*, October 13, 2011, http://www.hollywoodreporter.com/thr-esq/why-an-allegation-beyonc-plagiarized-248208. Accessed August 27, 2013. Developed over a number of years through various court decisions and codified in the 1976 Copyright Act, the fair use doctrine permits the reproduction of an original work for purposes "such as criticism, comment, news reporting, teaching, scholarship, and research," http://www.copyright.gov/fls/fl102.html. Accessed August 27, 2013. See also the Dance Heritage Coalition's "Statement of Best Practices in Fair Use of Dance-Related Materials," http://www.danceheritage.org/fairuse.html#overview. Accessed August 27, 2013. While the courts have not generally been sympathetic to fair use claims invoked on behalf of the postmodern genre of appropriation art, in 2013, the United States Court of Appeals for the Second District ruled in favor of the visual artist Richard Prince, overturning a 2011 federal court decision that found him guilty of choreographic infringement for using Patrick Cariou's photographs about Jamaican Rastafarians in a series of collages and paintings. Elton Fukumoto, "The Author Effect after the 'Death of the Author': Copyright in a Postmodern Age." *Washington Law Review* 72.3 (July 1997): 903–34. Where five of Prince's works were judged to have made only minimal alterations to the original photographs such that "they might not be considered fair use by a reasonable observer," the majority were deemed "permissible under fair use because they 'have a different character' from Mr. Cariou's work, give it a 'new expression' and employ 'new aesthetics with creative and communicative results distinct' from the work that Mr. Prince borrowed." Randy Kennedy, "Court Rules in Artist's Favor," *New York Times* April 25, 2013, http://www.nytimes.com/2013/04/26/arts/design/appeals-court-ruling-favors-richard-prince-in-copyright-case.html?_r=0. Accessed August 27, 2013. Invoking the spirit of appropriation art in her comments, Beyoncé would no doubt likewise have claimed that "Countdown" transformed the aesthetic of De Keersmaeker's work had the case wound up in court.

[25] Thomas DeFrantz, "Unchecked Popularity: Neoliberal Circulations of Black Social Dance," in *Neoliberalism and Global Theatres: Performance Permutations*, ed. Lara Nielsen and Patricia Ybarra (New York: Palgrave Macmillan, 2012), 135.

captivating about the "Countdown" video is that this is almost exactly what Beyoncé has done, but with a critical difference: she re-purposes white experimental dance, and, in the process, reconfigures the predominantly white physicalities of De Keersmaeker's dancers into a place of interchangeability with her own body and those of her dancers.[26] In a description of how the movement for *Rosas danst Rosas* came into being, De Keersmaeker stated, "We wanted everything to stay close to ourselves ... it was 'Rosas danst Rosas'—we dance ourselves. So we did what we had to do and expressed what seemed natural and close to us, and not external."[27] In other words, De Keersmaeker's original choreography was anchored in the individual personalities and corporealities of the dancers with whom she worked. Beyoncé's easy access to this choreography, made possible by the posting of film versions of *Rosas danst Rosas* and *Achterland* on YouTube, allowed her to unmoor it from those bodies without any knowledge of its underlying conditions of production.

It is easy, and not unfair, to say that Beyoncé erred in neglecting to seek permission from De Keersmaeker for using her choreography and in neglecting to give her credit before accusations of plagiarism emerged.[28] But it is also vital to grasp how her failure to do either, along with her leveling of any distinction between her pop culture and high art sources, function as a usurpation of what has typically been white privilege. Claiming the experimental artist's prerogative, Beyoncé does more than co-opt choreography in "Countdown"; she also re-scripts racialized norms of authorization, authorship, and ownership.

Neither Angered nor Honored: White Avant-Garde Anxiety

The inversion of a legacy, however, does not signify its death. Before we celebrate Beyoncé's actions as an indication that we have arrived at some mythic "post-racial" moment, before we conclude that YouTube has overturned entrenched racialized hierarchies between protectable works of authorship and the unrestricted public domain, we need to consider De Keersmaeker's

---

[26] Although Fumiyo Ikeda, one of the founding company members of De Keersmaeker's company Rosas and an original cast member in *Rosas danst Rosas*, is Japanese, the dancers who appeared in the 1997 film version of *Rosas danst Rosas*—the version to which Beyoncé had access—are all white. Ikeda does appear in the 1994 film adaptation of *Achterland*.

[27] De Keersmaeker and Cvejić, *A Choreographer's Score*, 85.

[28] In an interview with *GQ*, music video co-director Adria Petty claimed that "it was everyone's intention from the get-go" to credit De Keersmaeker and that the failure to do so was "basically an oversight." "Video Deconstruction: Director Adria Petty on Beyoncé's 'Countdown,'" *The GQ Eye*, October 10, 2011, http://www.gq.com/style/blogs/the-gq-eye/2011/10/video-deconstruction-director-adria-petty-on-beyoncs-countdown.html. Accessed August 15, 2013.

response to "Countdown." More than ambivalent, De Keersmaeker's reaction betrays a racially tinged apprehension about the circulation of choreography in the global marketplace and about the boundaries between the white avant-garde and black popular culture. Her attempts to police the reproduction of her choreography, like those of Loïe Fuller a century earlier, also demonstrate the ongoing importance of intellectual property rights as a site for dancers negotiating the dividing lines between subjecthood and objecthood, art and commodification, privilege and marginalization.

De Keersmaeker responded to "Countdown" on two fronts: legal and rhetorical. A lawyer for her company Rosas evidently contacted Sony, maintaining that the music video could not be shown without the prior approval of De Keersmaeker and De Mey.[29] Although little is known about the resulting negotiations, several factors suggest that the parties reached a settlement: first, Beyoncé released an alternate version of the video with De Keersmaeker's choreography excised; second, when the video was nominated for an MTV Video Music Award for best choreography, De Keersmaeker was listed as co-choreographer (along with Danielle Polanco, Frank Gatson Jr., and Beyoncé herself); and third, the original, un-excised "Countdown" video remains on Beyoncé's website.[30]

Meanwhile, in an interview with the radio station Studio Brussel, De Keersmaeker called Beyoncé's actions outright "stealing." "I'm not mad, but this is plagiarism," she maintained, adding that she found it "rude" that "they don't even bother about hiding it."[31] De Keersmaeker also issued the following public statement, which was posted on Studio Brussel's website:

> Like so many people, I was extremely surprised when I got a message on Facebook about the special appearance of my two choreographies—Rosas danst Rosas (1983) and Achterland (1990) in Beyoncé's new videoclip Countdown. The first question was whether I was now selling out Rosas into the commercial circuit.

[29] Claudia La Rocco, "Anne Teresa De Keersmaeker Responds to Beyoncé Video," The Performance Club blog, http://theperformanceclub.org/2011/10/anne-teresa-de-keersmaeker-responds-to-beyonce-video/. Accessed September 7, 2012.

[30] The alternate video was released in late November 2011. See "VIDEO: Beyoncé releases Alternate Version of 'Countdown,'" Pop Culture Major Blog, November 27, 2011, http://www.popculturemajor.com/2011/11/27/video-beyonce-releases-alternate-version-of-countdown/. Accessed September 7, 2012.

[31] James C McKinley Jr., "Beyoncé Accused of Plagiarism over Video," New York Times, October 10, 2011, http://artsbeat.blogs.nytimes.com/2011/10/10/beyonce-accused-of-plagiarism-over-video/. Accessed August 15, 2013.

She continued:

> People asked me if I'm angry or honored. Neither. On the one hand,
> I am glad that Rosas danst Rosas can perhaps reach a mass audience
> which such a dance performance could never achieve, despite its pop-
> ularity in the dance world since 1980s. And, Beyoncé is not the worst
> copycat, she sings and dances very well, and she has a good taste! On
> the other hand, there are protocols and consequences to such actions,
> and I can't imagine she and her team are not aware of it.
>
> To conclude, this event didn't make me angry, on the contrary,
> it made me think a few things. Like, why does it take popular cul-
> ture thirty years to recognize an experimental work of dance? A few
> months ago, I saw on Youtube a clip where schoolgirls in Flanders are
> dancing Rosas danst Rosas to the music of Like a Virgin by Madonna.
> And that was touching to see. But with global pop culture it is differ-
> ent, does this mean that thirty years is the time that it takes to recycle
> non-mainstream experimental performance? And, what does it say
> about the work of Rosas danst Rosas? In the 1980s, this was seen as
> a statement of girl power, based on assuming a feminine stance on
> sexual expression. I was often asked then if it was feminist. Now that
> I see Beyoncé dancing it, I find it pleasant but I don't see any edge to it.
> It's seductive in an entertaining consumerist way.[32]

De Keersmaeker's statement has been variously interpreted as generous
and restrained and, conversely, as scathing in its ridicule of Beyoncé.[33] What
stand out to me are the subtle contradictions it contains. Stating not once
but twice that she is not angered by Beyoncé's use of her choreography, De
Keersmaeker nonetheless betrays an anxiety about the relationship between
the avant-garde, historically aligned with elite whiteness, and "global pop culture," which we might read here as subtly coded black.[34] Even as she voices
concern about the perception that she has "sold out" her choreography to the

---

[32] http://theperformanceclub.org/2011/10/anne-teresa-de-keersmaeker-responds-to-beyonce-video/. Accessed September 7, 2012.

[33] See, for example, http://www.artinfo.com/news/story/38829/avant-garde-belgian-danc er-ridicules-beyonce-for-stealing-her-moves; and http://www.culturebot.net/2011/10/11496/ anne-teresa-de-keersmaeker-vs-beyonce/, in which Andy Horwitz describes De Keersmaeker's response as "remarkably generous in her comments, preferring to take the high road." Accessed September 7, 2012.

[34] As Thomas DeFrantz writes, "A curiosity with profound economic, social, and represen-tational consequence places African American social dances at the corporeal center of global discourses of the popular." "Unchecked Popularity," 128.

commercial circuit, she ever-so-slightly grumbles about the three decades it took for her "experimental" performance to register with the mainstream. By this logic, De Keersmaeker's choreography circulates both too much and not enough, both too slowly and too quickly.

It is worth pointing out that De Keersmaeker's works were never really out of circulation. After its 1983 debut, for example, *Rosas danst Rosas* was performed between 1985 and 1987, between 1992 and 1994, between 1995 and 1997, and revived again in 2009, 2010, and 2011.[35] In 1994, De Keersmaeker made a black and white film adaptation of *Achterland*, and in 1997, De Mey made a film version of *Rosas danst Rosas*, which aired on all of the major European television channels and toured the art house cinema circuit.[36] Both choreographic works, moreover, are listed as part of the repertory curriculum for dancers training at PARTS (Performing Arts Research & Training Studios), the international school for contemporary dance that De Keersmaeker founded in 1994.[37] This means that De Keersmaeker's choreography lives in the bodies of numerous dancers. Yet within these avant-garde afterlives, the participation of "original" bodies in the transmission of the choreography to both students and company members is considered crucial. "Repertory workshops are always taught by dancers who have been in the original creations of the pieces," the PARTS website states, and De Keersmaeker has noted how much more she can transmit to dancers when she performs in the work herself. Even so, when asked about the revival of *Rosas danst Rosas* with a fourth generation of dancers, De Keersmaeker responded that because the piece "bears the personal expression of the particular dancers I made it with, of their bodies and movements ... it is always somewhat delicate whenever we renew it."[38] In contrast to the "delicacy" of these authorized body-to-body transmissions, and in contrast to the three months that students at PARTS take to "bring the work on a level where it can be performed on professional stages,"[39] sits the transmission process by which Beyoncé presumably learned De Keersmaeker's choreography: mediated by film and video, measured in hours rather than months, and assimilated by a body more proficient in African American vernacular styles than in ballet and release technique.

---

[35] De Keersmaeker and Cvejić, *A Choreographer's Score*, 115; Roslyn Suclas, "Repetitions Build Drama with Rhythm and Gesture," *New York Times*, June 14, 2011, http://www.nytimes.com/2011/06/15/arts/dance/reviving-de-keersmaekers-rosas-danst-rosas-dance-review.html?_r=1. Accessed August 15, 2013.

[36] http://www.rosas.be/en/film/rosas-danst-rosas. Accessed August 16, 2013.

[37] http://www.parts.be/en/curriculum-training. Accessed August 16, 2013.

[38] De Keersmaeker and Cvejić, *A Choreographer's Score*, 115.

[39] Ibid.

De Keersmaeker's singling out of a group of white schoolgirls' reenactment of *Rosas danst Rosas* to a Madonna tune as "touching" should give us pause, however, for it contains the hint that De Keersmaeker's objection was not to unauthorized reenactments made possible by video per se, nor to the circulation of those reenactments online, nor to having her work sit alongside popular culture (albeit from the 1980s). The fact that the Flanders girls were not poised to profit from their video reenactment, where Beyoncé most certainly was, is of course relevant. We might deduce, then, that the problem for De Keersmaeker was becoming situated *within* "global pop culture," a situating that occurred when her choreography came to reside *within* Beyoncé's body. Although she stops short of calling "Countdown" "an egregious example of the devaluing and exploitation of contemporary performance by mainstream, commercial culture," as one blog poster did, she damns Beyoncé's commercial rendition as only superficially pleasing and denuded of any critical edge.[40] This is everything to which the avant-garde is opposed.

Beyoncé's re-embodiment of De Keersmaker's choreography thus represents a clash between different types of dance economies—the unhurried reproductive economy of the avant-garde versus the sped-up reproductive economy of popular culture—and a corresponding clash between different types of capital—cultural versus economic. This clash, I would argue, engendered a kind of crisis in status and identity for De Keersmaeker. To the extent that Beyoncé's treatment of *Rosas danst Rosas* and *Achterland* as "free" source material amounted to a seizure of what has characteristically been a white appropriative prerogative, that same treatment threatened to have the converse effect for De Keersmaeker: a tacit attenuation of white privilege. While, as De Keersmaeker notes, her choreography stands to gain greater exposure by appearing in "Countdown," this comes at the expense of becoming a "fugitive" dance object, displaced from the restricted, authorial economy of the avant-garde, stripped of any special protection against capitalist exchange.[41] For De Keersmaeker, claims of plagiarism and threats of legal action against Beyoncé served as a means of resisting the commodification of her choreography and recouping her privileged status as author and property owner.[42]

One year after the release of the "Countdown" video, De Keersmaeker and Bojana Cvejić published a book containing extensive documentation and

[40] Andy Horwitz, "Anne Teresa De Keersmaeker vs. Beyonce," Culturebot, http://www.culture-bot.org/2011/10/11496/anne-teresa-de-keersmaeker-vs-beyonce/. Accessed August 16, 2013.

[41] As André Lepecki has written, "Re-enactments transform all authored objects into fugitives in their own home." "The Body as Archive: Will to Re-enact and the Afterlives of Dances," *Dance Research Journal*, 42.2 (Winter 2010): 35.

[42] The recent collaboration between the rapper Jay-Z, who is also Beyoncé's husband, and Marina Abramović presents an interesting counterpoint to the Beyoncé-De Keersmaeker incident. In July 2013, in a clear nod to Abramović's 2010 performance of immobile endurance in *The Artist Is Present*, Jay-Z performed his song "Picasso Baby" continuously for six hours at the

discussion of four early works by De Keersmaeker. Titled *A Choreographer's Score: Fase, Rosas danst Rosas, Elena's Aria, Bartok,* the book is largely a transcription of interviews with De Keersmaeker, in which she recounts in detail the process of creating these choreographies. Alongside the text are sketches, notes, and other ephemera related to each of the choreographic works, and on four accompanying DVDs, we see and hear De Keersmaeker answering questions from Cvejić. Standing before a chalkboard, onto which she at times maps the structures and concepts that undergird her dances, occasionally demonstrating bits of movement, De Keersmaeker is very much the choreographer as author and instructor here. Although Cvejić writes in her introduction that the text is "by no means a definitive or authoritative account of the four works," she acknowledges that the book "favor[s] the authorial perspective that reverberates in the title *A Choreographer's Score.*"[43] Calling the documentation a "score" may signal De Keersmaeker's anticipation of future re-enactments, and the archiving of her dances may have stemmed from a desire to reach "a broader, more heterogeneous readership," but the book unequivocally reasserts De Keersmaeker's authorial control and returns her choreography to the more circumscribed economy of the avant-garde.[44]

Or does it?

Reproductive Bodies and the Snuggie De Keersmaeker

If the conflict between De Keersmaeker and Beyoncé was, like all choreographic copyright cases, fundamentally about control over the terms of dance's participation in a reproductive, capitalist economy, reproduction of a different

Pace Gallery in Chelsea before an audience that included a number of art world elites, Abramović among them. In the song, Jay-Z raps about his desire to possess famous art works, name-checking prominent visual artists and comparing himself to a "modern day" Picasso. While we might read his engagement with Abramović as a response to the furor over Beyoncé's unauthorized use of white avant-garde choreography, Jay-Z generally seems to rank higher on an artistic hierarchy than Beyoncé (with gender certainly a factor). In contrast to De Keersmaeker, Abramović evidently viewed Jay-Z's homage to her as an amplification of her power rather than a diminishment. She told *New York Magazine*'s Vulture.com, "It's really important that I can shift the public from the one field [i.e., pop music] to the arts, which rarely happens. So, this was really a very meaningful thing." Jamie Sharpe, "Marina Abramovic Wants the Rap Community to Google 'Performance Art,'" *Vulture*, July 30, 2013, http://www.vulture.com/2013/07/marina-abramovic-jay-z-performance-art.html. Accessed August 27, 2013. See the "performance art piece" (as opposed to "music video") for Jay-Z's "Picasso Baby," which debuted on HBO, at http://pitchfork.com/news/51506-watch-jay-zs-picasso-baby-performance-art-video-featuring-marina-abramovic-judd-apatow-and-more/. Accessed August 27, 2013.

[43] De Keersmaeker and Cvejić, *A Choreographer's Score*, 18.
[44] Ibid, 7.

sort served as a point of unity between the two dance artists. De Keersmaeker concluded her public comment about Beyoncé by noting what she called "one funny coincidence":

> Everyone told me, she is dancing and she is four months pregnant. In 1996, when De Mey's film was made, I was also pregnant with my second child. So, today, I can only wish her the same joy that my daughter brought me.

Setting aside their differences, at least momentarily, De Keersmaeker finds connection with Beyoncé over their shared identity as mothers-to-be. While De Keersmaeker's pregnancy was, to my knowledge, never spotlighted in performances of *Rosas danst Rosas* or *Achterland* as Beyoncé's round belly is in "Countdown," biological reproduction collapses the distance between pop culture and the avant-garde and provides a temporary reprieve from the contest over choreographic reproduction.

Yet even the pregnant female body, or at least its image, is not immune to the dynamics of exchange and the circulatory flows of the Internet. In July 2012, a sixteen-year-old Vietnamese-American boy named Ton Do-Nguyen posted to YouTube his own re-enactment of Beyoncé's "Countdown" video, matching the original shot for shot, including all of the editing, dancing, and pregnant belly poses. Known as the Snuggie version because Do-Nguyen wears a blue Snuggie blanket throughout, the video quickly went viral, receiving hundreds of thousands of views on YouTube. As a re-enactment, Do-Nguyen's "Countdown" is remarkable for its fidelity to the original—Beyoncé herself praised Do-Nguyen for performing it better than she had—and for the absurdity that the presence of the Snuggie gives it.[45]

Beyoncé's endorsement of Do-Nguyen's reproduction, a far cry from the legal threats with which she met the online leaking of "Countdown," echoes her response to the proliferation of choreographic imitations of the 2008 video for "Single Ladies (Put a Ring on It)." In that case, Beyoncé sponsored a video contest challenging participants to post videos of themselves that adhered to the "Single Ladies" choreography as faithfully as possible. As Harmony Bench writes, the contest functioned as a way for Beyoncé to retain oversight of the viral phenomenon and thereby preserve her "status as author."[46] Along

---

[45] http://www.beyonce.com/news/brilliant. Accessed September 12, 2012.

[46] Harmony Bench, "'Single Ladies Is Gay': Queer Performances and Mediated Masculinities on YouTube," in *Dance on Its Own Terms: Histories and Methodologies*, ed. Melanie Bales and Karen Eliot (New York: Oxford University Press, 2012), 132.

similar lines, Beyoncé posted a side-by-side video comparison of the original "Countdown" video and Do-Nguyen's version on her official website, effectively "co-signing" it.[47]

But if Do-Nguyen's reenactment did not pose a threat to Beyoncé's authorship, what did it do to De Keersmaeker's? There is an interesting parallel between the Flanders schoolgirls' reproduction of *Rosas danst Rosas* and Do-Nguyen's reproduction of "Countdown," both of which constitute what Bench calls "social dance-media," a mode of production that overlaps with but is not identical to "global pop culture."[48] One wonders whether De Keersmaeker might also find the Snuggie version of her choreography "touching." Yet, to state the obvious, unlike the Flanders girls', Do-Nguyen's referent is Beyoncé, not De Keersmaeker. As far as I can tell, no mention of De Keersmaeker appeared in the flurry of overwhelmingly favorable responses to the Snuggie "Countdown."

Do-Nguyen's reproduction of Beyoncé's video thus represents another turn of the screw for De Keersmaeker's choreography, drawing it into the viral economy of the Internet. Although, unlike the movement from Beyoncé's "Single Ladies," the choreography in "Countdown" has not been re-embodied by hundreds of thousands of dancers, the Snuggie version shows how readily one reproduction can beget another. Mediated by Beyoncé, De Keersmaeker's choreography moves across bodies and time "as if it was communally created and owned and not subject to copyright."[49] As surely as the treatment of the avant-garde, first by Beyoncé and then by Do-Nguyen, *as if* it were just another fugitive source in the public domain inverts entrenched racial and artistic hierarchies, it simultaneously generates new attempts to restore them.

For the screw continues to turn in both directions. In the summer of 2013, De Keersmaeker embarked on "Re: Rosas! The fABULEUS Rosas Remix Project," which invited the public to recreate the chair section of *Rosas danst Rosas*. In an echo of Beyoncé's "Single Ladies" video contest, and revisiting the scene of the original crime, De Keersmaeker turned to the Internet to issue the call to the public to learn the *Rosas* choreography and upload videos of themselves performing it. As the site states, "Precisely 30 years ago, dance company Rosas put itself on the map with the production *Rosas danst Rosas*.

[47] Mawuse Ziegbe, "Beyonce Co-Signs 'Snuggie' Version of Her 'Countdown' Video," *Pop Radar*, http://www.boston.com/ae/celebrity/blog/popradar/2012/07/beyonce_co-signs_snuggie_version_of_her_countdown_video.html. Accessed August 19, 2013.

[48] According to Bench, "social dance-media" circulate "in internet environments" and "elaborate upon social media's ideologies of participation while remaining in the image-based domain of dance-media." Harmony Bench, "Screendance 2.0: Social Dance-Media," *Participations: Journal of Audience & Reception Studies* 7.2 (2010), http://www.participations.org/Volume%207/Issue%202/special/bench.htm. Accessed August 19, 2013).

[49] Ibid.

This choreography has since been staged all over the world. And now it's your turn."[50] In separate videos posted on the site, De Keersmaeker and Rosas dancer Samantha van Wissen demonstrate a three-and-a-half minute (simplified) segment of the choreography, break down the movements, and discuss their structure. Unlike Beyoncé, De Keersmaeker invited participants to play with the choreography, to "make up your own *Rosas danst Rosas*." According to an article in *The Guardian*, 1,500 responded to De Keersmaeker's call, and, as of this writing, 229 filmed versions of the choreography appear on the remix site, featuring dancers of all ages from around the globe.[51]

Though no mention of Beyoncé is made on the site, it is impossible not to read the *Rosas* remix project through the lens of "Countdown"'s earlier, unauthorized recreation. Indeed, *The Guardian* framed De Keersmaeker's public invitation as a way of acting on her "acid" claim that Flanders school girls performed her choreography better than Beyoncé.[52] It is as if in unleashing *Rosas* to the public, De Keersmaeker seeks to cover over the Beyoncé episode entirely. Turning *Rosas* into "a globally communal project"[53] becomes a way of removing the taint of its dalliance with "global pop culture" and recuperating its non-commercial potential. Orchestrated as part of a commemoration of *Rosas*'s avant-garde status,[54] De Keersmaeker's decision to take the work viral is, paradoxically, equivalent in some ways to a legal claim of copyright: an attempt to regulate choreography's reproduction and to separate out the right kind of circulation from the wrong.

[50] http://www.rosasdanstrosas.be/en-home/. Accessed November 22, 2013.

[51] Judith Mackrell, "Beyoncé, De Keersmaeker, and a Dance Reinvented by Everyone," *The Guardian*, October 9, 2013, http://www.theguardian.com/stage/2013/oct/09/beyonce-de-keersmaeker-technology-dance. Accessed November 22, 2013.

[52] Ibid.

[53] Ibid.

[54] Video entries received by October 1, 2013, were exhibited as part of an installation that accompanied a revival of *Rosas danst Rosas* in Brussels from October 8 to 12. http://www.rosas-danstrosas.be/en-home/. Accessed November 22, 2013.

Appendix

A TIMELINE OF INTELLECTUAL
PROPERTY RIGHTS AND DANCE IN THE
UNITED STATES

1787—Article I, Section 8, Clause 8 of the US Constitution gives Congress the power "to promote the progress of science and useful arts, by securing for limited times to authors and inventors the exclusive right to their respective writings and discoveries."

1790—The Copyright Act of 1790 is the first copyright law enacted under the new US Constitution. The act protects the authors of books, maps, and charts for a term of fourteen years with the possibility of renewal for another fourteen years.

1831—Music is added to the list of protected works under the first general revision of copyright law. The revision also extends the initial term of copyright from fourteen to twenty-eight years.

1856—Dramatic compositions are added to the list of protected works, and performance rights are added to the list of entitlements for authors of dramatic compositions.

1865—Photographs are added to list of protected works.

1867—*Martinetti v. Maguire*, tried in California circuit court, denies copyright protection for the *Black Crook*, which featured a dancing chorus of one hundred Parisian ballerinas and is often considered America's first musical, on the grounds that it is "grossly indecent, and calculated to corrupt the morals of the people."

1868—*Daly v. Palmer*, tried in U.S. circuit court, rules that pantomime is protectable on the grounds that "movement, gesture and facial expression ... are as much a part of the dramatic composition as is the spoken language."

1870—Works of art are added to list of protected works under the second general revision of copyright law. Authors' rights are extended to protect the creation of derivative works, including translations and dramatizations.

1886—Berne Convention for the Protection of Literary and Artistic Works requires signatory nations to recognize the copyrights of authors' works from other signatory nations. The United States does not sign until 1989.

1891—Congress authorizes limited protection to foreign copyright holders from select nations. The law is primarily designed to protect US publishers from an influx of cheap, pirated books from Britain.

1892—In *Fuller v. Bemis*, tried in U.S. circuit court, the white early modern dancer Loïe Fuller sues chorus girl Minnie Bemis for performing an "unauthorized" copy of her *Serpentine Dance*. The court rules that because the dance told no story, it does not merit copyright protection.

1897—Music is protected against unauthorized public performance.

1902—In *Fuller v. Gilmore*, tried in US circuit court, Ida Fuller, a Loïe Fuller imitator, successfully sues the producers of a melodrama, claiming infringement of a patent she holds on a theatrical appliance that produces the appearance of fire on stage.

1903—Supreme Court decision in *Bleistein v. Donaldson Lithographic Co.* upholds copyright in circus posters and establishes originality as a condition of copyrightability, regardless of artistic quality.

1903—Circuit court decision in *Barnes v. Miner* denies copyright protection to stage spectacle with no dramatic content on the grounds that it is immoral.

1905—White modern dancer Ruth St. Denis (under the name Ruth Dennis) registers her first two choreographies as "plays without words" in the Library of Congress: *Egypta: An Egyptian Play in One Act* and *Radha: An East Indian Idyll; a Hindoo Play in One Act without Words*.

1908—*Savage v. Hoffman*, tried in US circuit court, rules that the manner of dance or posture is not eligible for copyright protection.

1909—Third general revision of copyright law makes publication with notice of copyright (affixing the copyright symbol) the means for establishing protection; extends the term of renewal to twenty-eight years, bringing the maximum term of protection to fifty-six years; extends copyright protection to mechanical reproductions of music; and expands authorship to include employers in the case of "works made for hire."

1909—Indian dancer Mohammed Ismail sues Ruth St. Denis in New York City Court for $2,000, asserting that he originated one of her "Oriental" dances, but eventually withdraws his action.

1912—Motion pictures are added to list of protected works (previously registered as photographs).

1910s–1930s—Louis H. Chalif, the Russian-born dance teacher and founder of the Chalif Normal School of Dancing in New York, obtains copyrights on numerous books filled with his written directions for performing hundreds of ballroom dances.

1924—In *Bertram C. Whitney v. Johnny Hudgins*, tried in New York Supreme Court, the white producer of the black musical revue *The Chocolate Dandies* seeks an injunction against African American comedic dancer Hudgins to prevent him from leaving the show, claiming he is "unique and extraordinary" and therefore irreplaceable. The *Chicago Defender* celebrates the case as the first time a "Colored performer" has been sued as "unique and extraordinary." Hudgins's ultimately successful defense requires him to claim that he is neither.

1926—Reports surface that the African American blues singer Alberta Hunter holds a copyright on the Black Bottom, a popular black vernacular dance. No evidence of such a registration exists in the Copyright Office.

1927–28—Johnny Hudgins obtains a copyright in London on a booklet detailing a series of his pantomime routines, including his famous "Mwa, Mwa" number.

1928—*Chaplin v. Amador*, tried in California district court, prohibits the Mexican actor Charles Amador, a Chaplin imitator, from using white pantomimist Charlie Chaplin's dress, costumes, and mannerisms on the grounds of unfair competition.

1942—The Copyright Office refuses to grant a registration for white ballet choreographer Eugene Loring's Labanotated score for *Billy the Kid* (1938) on the grounds that Labanotation is not yet an accepted system of recording movement.

1952—German-born modern dancer Hanya Holm secures a copyright registration for the Labanotated score of dances she choreographed for the 1948 Broadway production of *Kiss Me, Kate* under the category of "dramatico-musical" composition. The registration is widely celebrated in the white modern dance community.

1952—Russian-born ballet choreographer George Balanchine attempts to register his ballet *Symphony in C* with the Copyright Office but withdraws his application when instructed that it fails to qualify as a dramatic composition.

1952—White modern dance Nona Schurman secures a copyright registration on the Labanotated score of her choreographic work *Song from the Hebrides*, reportedly the "first modern dance piece" to be successfully copyrighted. Later that year, Russian-born Nadia Chilkovsky, a modern dancer and co-founder of the leftist New Dance Group, is granted a copyright for her score of *Suite for Youth*.

1953—The white ballet artist Ruth Page receives a copyright registration for a book containing written instructions for her abstract choreography to Beethoven's *Sonata*. No one is sure whether the copyright applies to performances of the work or to the book itself.

1959—Borge Varmer publishes "Copyright in Choreographic Works," a study commissioned by the 86th Congress to help guide the Committee on the Judiciary as it considers making revisions to copyright law. The report concludes that choreography indeed merits copyright protection but does not answer the question of whether it merits its own category.

1950s–1960s—The white ballet artist Agnes de Mille becomes a vocal advocate for choreographic copyright after reaping only limited royalties from her choreography for the hit 1943 musical *Oklahoma!*

1961—George Balanchine receives a copyright registration on a film version of *Symphony in C*.

1963—In *Dane v. M & H Company et al.*, heard in New York Supreme Court, the (ambiguously) white dancer Faith Dane sues the producers of the Broadway musical *Gypsy* for royalties, claiming common law copyright protection of the military striptease number that was used in the production. The court rejects her claim, ruling that her dance does not "promote the progress of science or the useful arts."

1972—Copyright is extended to sound recordings.

1976—Fourth major revision of copyright law adds "choreographic works" to list of protected works, extends the term of protection for works to the life of the author plus fifty years, and extends protection to unpublished works. The law takes effect on January 1, 1978.

1986—The estate of George Balanchine brings a copyright infringement suit against Macmillan publishers to halt the publication of a book containing photographs of George Balanchine's *Nutcracker* ballet. In *Horgan v. Macmillan*, the US district court denies the injunction on the grounds that the photographs don't infringe the copyrighted choreography. The US Court of Appeals for the Second Circuit reverses the decision, remanding the case to the lower court for further proceedings. The parties eventually settle out of court.

1989—The United States becomes a signatory to the Berne Convention for the Protection of Literary and Artistic Works. The Berne Convention requires the protection of authors' moral (and not just economic) rights in signatory states.

1990—The Visual Artists Rights Act grants to the authors of paintings, drawings, prints, sculptures, and still photographic images certain moral rights of attribution and integrity (i.e., the right to claim authorship and the right to prevent the distortion of the work, regardless of who owns the copyright to the work).

1991—The production company representing the white choreographer Gower Champion files a copyright infringement and unfair competition suit against the management company of a national production of *Bye Bye Birdie* on the grounds that Champion's choreography for the original 1961 musical was not included in the production's licensing agreement. *Champion Five Inc. v. National Artists Management Co. Inc.* settles out of court in 1992.

1994—The Supreme Court rules in *Campbell v. Acuff-Rose Music* that 2 Live Crew's parody of Roy Orbison's song "Pretty Woman" is fair use because the markets for the two works are different.

1998—The Sonny Bono Copyright Term Extension Act (derisively known as the Mickey Mouse Protection Act because the Walt Disney Company lobbied vociferously for it) extends the term of copyright protection to the life of the author plus seventy years after the author's death. The Digital Millennium Copyright Act brings the United States into compliance with the World Intellectual Property Organization (WIPO) Copyright Treaty and the WIPO Performances and Phonograms Treaty, extending the reach of copyright law to digital works and limiting online infringement liability for Internet service providers.

2002—In *Martha Graham School and Dance Foundation, Inc. and Ronald A. Protas v. Martha Graham Center of Contemporary Dance, Inc. and Martha Graham School of Contemporary Dance, Inc.*, a federal district court in New York awards the copyrights to most of white modern dance legend Martha Graham's choreographic works to the Graham Center rather than to Graham's heir, Ronald Protas, largely on the basis that these choreographic works were "works for hire" and therefore not hers to bequeath. Protas appealed the decision all the way up to the Supreme Court, which declined to review it.

SELECTED BIBLIOGRAPHY

Abitabile, Kathleen and Jeannette Picerno. "Dance and the Choreographer's Dilemma: A Legal and Cultural Perspective on Copyright Protection for Choreographic Works." *Campbell Law Review* 27 (Fall 2004): 39–62.

Albright, Ann Cooper. *Traces of Light: Absence and Presence in the Work of Loie Fuller.* Middletown, CT: Wesleyan University Press, 2007.

Arcomano, Nicholas. "Choreography and Copyright, Part One." *Dance Magazine* 54.4 (April 1980): 58–9.

Arcomano, Nicholas. "Choreography and Copyright, Part Two," *Dance Magazine* 54.5 (May 1980): 70 + .

Auslander, Philip. *Liveness: Performance in a Mediatized Culture.* London: Routledge, 1999.

Banes, Sally. "Homage, Plagiarism, Allusion, Comment, Quotation: Negotiating Choreographic Appropriation." In *Before, Between, and Beyond: Three Decades of Dance Writing,* ed. Andrea Harris. Madison: University of Wisconsin Press, 2007, 198–215.

Best, Stephen M. *The Fugitive's Properties: Law and the Poetics of Possession.* Chicago: University of Chicago Press, 2004.

Boateng, Boatema. *The Copyright Thing Doesn't Work Here: Adinkra and Kente Cloth and Intellectual Property in Ghana.* Minneapolis: University of Minnesota Press, 2011.

Boyle, James D. A. *Shamans, Software, and Spleens: Law and the Construction of the Information Society.* Cambridge, MA: Harvard University Press, 1996.

Brace, Laura. *The Politics of Property: Labour, Freedom and Belonging.* New York: Palgrave Macmillan, 2004.

Brooks, Daphne A. *Bodies in Dissent: Spectacular Performances of Race and Freedom, 1850–1910.* Durham, NC: Duke University Press, 2006.

Brown, Jayna. *Babylon Girls: Black Women Performers and the Shaping of the Modern.* Durham, NC: Duke University Press, 2008.

Carter, Tim. *Oklahoma!: The Making of an American Musical.* New Haven, CT: Yale University Press, 2007.

Cherniavsky, Eva. *Incorporations: Race, Nation, and the Body Politics of Capital.* Minneapolis: University of Minnesota Press, 2006.

Cook, Melanie. "Moving to a New Beat: Copyright Protection for Choreographic Works." *UCLA Law Review* 24 (1977): 1287–312.

Coombe, Rosemary J. *The Cultural Life of Intellectual Properties: Authorship, Appropriation, and the Law.* Durham, NC: Duke University Press, 1998.

Davis, Thadious. *Games of Property: Law, Race, Gender, and Faulkner's* Go Down, Moses. Durham, NC: Duke University Press, 2003.

DeFrantz, Thomas. "Unchecked Popularity: Neoliberal Circulations of Black Social Dance." In *Neoliberalism and Global Theatres: Performance Permutations*, ed. Lara Nielsen and Patricia Ybarra. New York: Palgrave Macmillan, 2012, 128–140.

Demers, Joanna. *Steal This Music: How Intellectual Property Law Affects Musical Creativity*. Athens: University of Georgia Press, 2006.

Easton, Carol. *No Intermissions: The Life of Agnes de Mille*. New York: Da Capo Press, 1996.

Foulkes, Julia. *Modern Bodies: Dance and American Modernism from Martha Graham to Alvin Ailey*. Chapel Hill: University of North Carolina Press, 2002.

Foster, Susan Leigh. *Choreographing Empathy: Kinesthesia in Performance*. London: Routledge, 2011.

Frank, Rusty E. *Tap!: The Greatest Tap Dance Stars and Their Stories, 1900–1955*. New York: Da Capo Press, 1994.

Gaines, Jane M. *Contested Culture: The Image, the Voice, and the Law*. Chapel Hill: University of North Carolina Press, 1991.

Garelick, Rhonda K. *Electric Salome: Loie Fuller's Performance of Modernism*. Princeton, NJ: Princeton University Press, 2007.

Gennerich, Patricia Solan. "One Moment in Time: The Second Circuit Ponders Choreographic Photography as a Copyright Infringement: Horgan v. Macmillan, Inc." *Brooklyn Law Review* 53 (Spring 1987): 379–407.

Gerland, Oliver. "From Playhouse to P2P Network: The History and Theory of Performance under Copyright Law in the United States," *Theatre Journal* 59.1 (2007): 75–95.

Gottschild, Brenda Dixon. *Digging the Africanist Presence in American Performance: Dance and Other Contexts*. Westport, CT: Greenwood Press, 1996.

Gottschild, Brenda Dixon. *Waltzing in the Dark: African American Vaudeville and Race Politics in the Swing Era*. New York: St. Martin's Press, 2000.

Greene, K. J. "'Copynorms,' Black Cultural Production, and the Debate over African-American Reparations." *Cardoza Arts & Entertainment Law Journal* 25.3 (2008): 1179–227.

Greene, K. J. "Copyright, Culture and Black Music: A Legacy of Unequal Protection." *Hastings Communication & Entertainment Law Journal* 21.2 (Winter 1999): 339–92.

Handler, Richard. "Who Owns the Past? History, Cultural Property, and the Logic of Possessive Individualism." In *The Politics of Culture*, ed. Brett Williams. Washington: Smithsonian Institution Press, 1991, 63–74.

Harris, Cheryl I. "Whiteness as Property," *Harvard Law Review* 106.8 (1993): 1707–93.

Hartman, Saidiya V. *Scenes of Subjection: Terror, Slavery, and Self-Making in Nineteenth-Century America*. New York: Oxford University Press, 1997.

Hilgard, Adaline. "Note: Can Choreography and Copyright Waltz Together in the Wake of Horgan v. Macmillan, Inc." *U.C. Davis Law Review* 27 (Spring 1994): 757–89.

Hill, Constance Valis. *Tap Dancing America: A Cultural History*. New York: Oxford University Press, 2010.

Hyde, Alan. *Bodies of Law*. Princeton, NJ: Princeton University Press, 1997.

Knight, Arthur. *Disintegrating the Musical: Black Performance and American Musical Film*. Durham, NC: Duke University Press, 2002.

Kraut, Anthea. *Choreographing the Folk: The Dance Stagings of Zora Neale Hurston*. Minneapolis: University of Minnesota Press, 2008.

Kraut, Anthea. "Fixing Improvisation: Copyright and African American Vernacular Dancers in the Early Twentieth Century." In *The Oxford Handbook of Critical Improvisation Studies*, Volume 1, ed. George E. Lewis and Benjamin Piekut. New York: Oxford University Press, forthcoming.

Lakes, Joi Michelle. "A Pas de Deux for Choreography and Copyright." *New York University Law Review* 80 (2005): 1829–61.

Lipsitz, George. *The Possessive Investment in Whiteness*. Philadelphia: Temple University Press, 1998.

Litman, Jessica. "The Public Domain." *Emory Law Journal* 39.4 (Fall 1990): 965–1023.

Lott, Eric. *Love and Theft: Blackface Minstrelsy and the American Working Class.* New York: Oxford University Press, 1993.

Macpherson, C. B. *The Political Theory of Possessive Individualism: Hobbes to Locke.* London: Oxford University Press, 1962

Macpherson, C. B., ed. *Property: Mainstream and Critical Positions.* Toronto: University of Toronto Press, 1978.

Manning, Susan. *Modern Dance, Negro Dance: Race in Motion.* Minneapolis: University of Minnesota Press, 2004.

McLeod, Kembrew. *Owning Culture: Authorship, Ownership, and Intellectual Property Law.* New York: Peter Lang, 2001.

Moten, Fred. *In the Break: The Aesthetics of the Black Radical Tradition.* Minneapolis: University of Minnesota Press, 2003.

Phelan, Peggy. *Unmarked: The Politics of Performance.* London: Routledge, 1993.

Picart, Caroline Joan S. *Critical Race Theory and Copyright in American Dance: Whiteness as Status Property.* New York: Palgrave Macmillan, 2013.

Picart, Caroline Joan S. "A Tango between Copyright and Choreography: Whiteness as Status Property in Balanchine's Ballets, Fuller's Serpentine Dance and Graham's Modern Dances." *Cardozo Journal of Law & Gender* 18 (Spring 2012): 685–725.

Radin, Margaret Jane. "Property and Personhood." *Stanford Law Review* 34.5 (1982): 957–1015.

Rose, Mark. *Authors and Owners: The Invention of Copyright.* Cambridge, MA: Harvard University Press, 1993.

Roth, Jeffrey I. "Common Law Protection of Choreographic Works." *Performing Arts Review* 5.1–2 (1974): 75–89.

Saint-Amour, Paul K. *The Copywrights: Intellectual Property and the Literary Imagination.* Ithaca, NY: Cornell University Press, 2003.

Saint-Amour, Paul K., ed. *Modernism and Copyright.* New York: Oxford University Press, 2011.

Savran, David. *Highbrow/Lowdown: Theater, Jazz, and the Making of the New Middle Class.* Ann Arbor: University of Michigan Press, 2009.

Schur, Richard L. *Parodies of Ownership: Hip-Hop Aesthetics and Intellectual Property Law.* Ann Arbor: University of Michigan Press, 2009.

Schwartz, Selby Wynn. "Martha@Martha: A Séance with Richard Move." *Women & Performance: A Journal of Feminist Theory* 20.1 (2010): 61–87.

Shea Murphy, Jacqueline. *"The People Have Never Stopped Dancing": Native American Modern Dance Histories.* Minneapolis: University of Minnesota Press, 2007.

Siegel, Marcia B. *At the Vanishing Point: A Critic Looks at Dance.* New York: Saturday Review Press, 1972.

Singer, Barbara A. "In Search of Adequate Protection for Choreographic Works: Legislative and Judicial Alternatives vs. The Custom of the Dance Community," *University of Miami Law Review* 38 (1984): 287–319.

Srinivasan, Priya. *Sweating Saris: Indian Dance as Transnational Labor.* Philadelphia, PA: Temple University Press, 2011.

Stearns, Marshall and Jean Stearns. *Jazz Dance: The Story of American Vernacular Dance.* New York: Schirmer Books, 1968.

Tomko, Linda J. *Dancing Class: Gender, Ethnicity, and Social Divides in American Dance, 1890–1920.* Bloomington: Indiana University Press, 1999.

Traylor, Martha M. "Choreography, Pantomime and the Copyright Revision Act of 1976." *New England Law Review* 16 (1980): 227–55.

Vaidhyanathan, Siva. *Copyrights and Copywrongs: The Rise of Intellectual Property and How It Threatens Creativity.* New York: New York University Press, 2001.

Van Camp, Julie. "Copyright of Choreographic Works." In *1994–95 Entertainment, Publishing and the Arts Handbook,* ed. Stephen F. Breimer, Robert Thorne, and John David Viera. New York: Clark, Boardman, and Callaghan, 1994, 59–92. Also available at http://www.csulb.edu/~jvancamp/copyrigh.html.

Van Camp, Julie. "Creating Works of Art from Works of Art: The Problem of Derivative Works." *Journal of Arts Management, Law & Society* 24.3 (Fall 1994): 209–22.

Van Camp, Julie. "Martha Graham's Legal Legacy." *Dance Chronicle* 30.1 (January 2007): 67–99.

Varmer, Borge. "Copyright in Choreographic Works," Study No. 28, *Studies Prepared for the Subcommittee on Patents, Trademarks, and Copyrights of the Committee on the Judiciary*, United State Senate, 86th Cong., 2d Sess. Washington, DC: US Government Printing Office, 1961.

Wallis, Leslie Erin. "The Different Art: Choreography and Copyright." *UCLA Law Review* 33 (1986): 1442–71.

Woll, Allen. *Black Musical Theatre from Coontown to Dreamgirls*. Baton Rouge: Louisiana State University Press, 1989.

Wong, Yutian. *Choreographing Asian America*. Middletown, CT: Wesleyan University Press, 2010.

Woodmansee, Martha. *The Author, Art, and the Market: Rereading the History of Aesthetics*. New York: Columbia University Press, 1994.

Woodmansee, Martha and Peter Jaszi, eds., *The Construction of Authorship: Textual Appropriation in Law and Literature*. Durham, NC: Duke University Press, 1994.

REPRINT PERMISSIONS

INDEX

2 Live Crew, 285

Aarons, Al, 106
abolitionists, 99
Academy of Music, 81–82
Achterland (1990), 263, 268, 272–273,
  275–276, 278
African Americans and dance, 4, 127, 170,
  172, 191, 271
  and Beyoncé, 263, 265, 268
  and Black Bottom, 143–145, 148–150
  and blackface, 62, 115, 123, 125, 129
  on Broadway, 185–187, 189, 191–192, 264
  choreographers, 33, 177, 216
  and concert dance, 33, 163
  and Johnny Hudgins, 5, 41, 91, 93,
    115, 127
  and improvisation, 130, 132, 191
  and intellectual property rights, 27,
    94–95, 111–112, 130, 162–163
  and labor force, 102
  on minstrel stage, 97–98
  and originality, 107,
  and right of attribution, 133, 152
  scholarship on, 29, 34n132
  and tap, 5, 119, 128, 132–133, 205
  and vernacular dance, 128–133, 137–139,
    141–143, 153–154, 161–164, 187, 275
  and white mainstream culture, 129
  on white vaudeville stage, 158
Africana (1934), 127–128, 140
Agamaben, Giorgio, 13
Aladdin's Wonderful Lamp (1887), 60
Albright, Ann Cooper, 74
Allan, Maud, 61

Allegro (1943), 179, 202–204
Allen, Edgar, 108
Amador, Charles, 124n102, 283
Amberg's Theater, 75
American ballet, 181
  and George Balanchine, 233, 247
American Ballet Theatre, 190
American dance, 5, 181
  and George Balanchine, 222–223
  and copyright, 127, 132, 217, 220
  and Agnes de Mille, 177
  and Martha Graham, 222
  and Nautch dancing, 61
  and racial stratification of, 29, 33
American Dance Festival, 182, 256
American Guild of Musical Artists
  (AGMA), 200–201
American Society of Composers, Authors
  and Publishers (ASCAP), 200
Anderson, Maceo, 133
Apollo (1928), 3
  See also Balanchine, George
Apollo Theatre (Harlem), 134, 146,
  160n117
Appadurai, Arjun, 22, 140
Aronson, Rudolph, 51, 53–55, 63, 75
Art Nouveau movement, 50
Ashton, Frederick, 227
Asian Americans and dance, 29
  and Mohammed Ismail, 88
Atkins, Cholly, 142, 187–189, 202, 205
Aunt Jemima, 48
Aurelio, Thomas, 214–217
Auslander, Philip, 36, 161, 213
Austin, Lovie, 148